*I*NSIDE
*P*RIME *T*IME

*T*odd Gitlin

University of California Press
Berkeley • Los Angeles • London

To Ruth

University of California Press
Berkeley and Los Angeles, California

University of California Press, Ltd.
London, England

First University of California Press Paperback, 2000

First published 1983 by
Pantheon Books, a division of Random House Inc., New York

Paperback edition first published in 1985 by Pantheon Books
and simultaneously in Canada by Random House of Canada Limited,
Toronto.

Revised edition published in 1994
by Routledge
11 New Fetter Lane, London EC4P 4EE

Library of Congress Cataloging-in-Publication Data
Gitlin, Todd
    Inside prime time / Todd Gitlin.
        p.   cm.
    Originally published: Rev. ed. New York : Pantheon Books, 1994
    Includes bibliographical references (p.   ) and index.
    ISBN 0-520-21785-3 (alk. paper)
    1. Television broadcasting—United States.   2. Television
programs—United States.   3. Television programs—Rating—United
States.   I. Title.
PN1992.3.U5G57 2000
384.55'4'0973—dc21   99-35654
                                                                CIP

C O N T E N T S

INTRODUCTION

At century's turn, writing about television tends to betray one of two tendencies: the sentimental and the breathless. Whether academic or popular, the commentaries tend to read alike. In the sentimental mode, TV is savored as an artifact of antiquity, quaint as childhood itself, redolent with the bygone virtues of a sappy but innocent old world. The writing done in this vein is not easily distinguished from fandom. Or, more commonly, scholars scramble to keep up with the rhapsodists of new technology, who view television as the mother of still greater, faster-moving, more plenteous and convenient media forms. Here, the gee-whiz tone matches the wishful invocations of the broadcasting networks, who are driven by fear of competitors as much as by clarity about the televisual future, and wildly spinning off cable networks and Internet auxiliaries in the manner of hit series that used to spawn new programs for secondary characters. Onrushing media technologies are likened to natural engulfments—floods and tidal waves—which, on the model of the Internet, are apparently destined to drench the world with a faster-moving profusion of images and "information." Each wave, it seems, is prologue to the next, each, in endless succession, foreordained to leave a deposit of bounty that will make the informational future more fertile.

In analysis, as in technology, there is no way around television, there are only ways through it. The media future, whatever its exact shape, will surely make a central place for the organized mass diffusion of images and sounds. Print was not erased by radio, or radio by TV, or networks (at least not yet) by the much-touted "convergence" of broadcasting with cable channels and Internet bells and whistles.[1] Come what may, some brave new cornucopia will go on daily pouring its disappointing bounty into the household. High definition, video-on-demand, DVDs: all the novelties ride on a recognizable ground of cultural and technological fact. This, in a word, is television as we have known it, meaning both the technology and the cultural forms.[2] Auguries of technological wonders-to-come speed the pulses of headline writers and venture capitalists alike, but for all the convergence under way, or touted, some televisual things don't change. Television, the entertainment machine, with its comedies and dramas, its sports rituals and passing epiphanies, its sonorous tones and giggles, its chat shows and earnest harangues, has

---

1 The concept of "convergence" at the networks is discussed in Randall Rothenberg, "Go Ahead, Kill Your Television. NBC Is Ready," *Wired*, December 1998, pp. 204ff.
2 I refer to Raymond Williams' seminal *Television: Technology and Cultural Form* (New York: Schocken, 1975).

long since become normal, the ground zero of life and imagination, and its variants are variations on known themes and formulas. That programs should be regular (usually weekly), that their purpose should be to entertain, that they should look compatible with advertising, that they should aim to maximize audiences within their chosen niches—these assumptions prevail throughout TV's myriad colorations. In the course of three generations, the stream of images, stories, and sounds has become a fixture of the home, considered at least as fundamental as electric lights, indoor plumbing, and telephones, seductive and banal, ever-changing and ever the same, each successive wave of innovations just novel enough to flatter their recipients into thinking that they have been gifted this season, this year, this generation with something special.

As new technologies dazzle the press and the buying populace with every passing season, the conventional wisdom is that everything in television has changed, changed utterly. This is one of those half-truths whose half-falsehood should not be overlooked. With minor modifications, many of the "traditional" forms persist. Even Steven Johnson, one of the more articulate heralds of web-savviness and media self-awareness, acknowledged in his 1997 book *Interface Culture* how much of television has stood fast in recent decades: "Even if you factor in the lesbian plot twist, the basic structure of an *Ellen* episode looks a lot like an average *Taxi* from 1981, while a few nights with *The Honeymooners* makes *Roseanne*—herself considered something of a pathbreaker—look like a poor relation living shamelessly off the family name. . . . Television storytelling—as a medium—has made only modest advances over the past twenty years, which is why *Melrose Place* looks so much like *Dynasty*. . . ."[3]

As always in the history of technology, newcomers to the parade declare that their novelty is a sign that they are not only different but superior. The half-true part of their claim does require attention. The sheer number of televisual goodies a click of the finger away cannot be doubted, and the wired, digital, World-Wide-Webbed future promises more of the same. With 66 percent of American households hooked up to cable systems, an additional 6 percent wired to satellite dishes, and 89 percent possessed of at least one videocassette recorder, it would seem self-evident that the experience of television at century's end differs from what prevailed when only the three giants, ABC, CBS, and NBC, commanded the attention of their viewers. In 1998, the average American home received 46.6 channels.[4] With the proliferation of TV sets (34 percent of households have two, another 40 percent have three or more), in-

---

3 Steven Johnson, *Interface Culture* (San Francisco: HarperEdge, 1997), pp. 27–28.
4 *TV Dimensions '98* (New York: Media Dynamics, Inc., 1998), pp. 21, 122, 165; *Television Business International Yearbook 1997* (London: 21st Century Business Publications, 1998), p. 128.

dividuals, not families, choose their programs.[5] Television choices, once bemusedly considered the "least objectionable programming" (see p. 61), is now tailored to the individual, not the family group. Meanwhile, households are also smaller than ever before, with the average household having shrunk from 3.35 persons in 1960 to 2.65 persons in 1995, and households consisting of but a solitary person jumping from 13 percent in 1960 to 25 percent in 1995.[6] In short, more and more individuals rule their little roosts, to electronic accompaniment. No one in the family need settle for second least objectionable. Conflicts among taste need no longer be held "all in the family," but are played out on a different principle: different strokes for different demographics. The result is a culture of segments.

Accordingly, viewers have deserted the no-longer-so-Big Three in droves, and the end—even a plateau—is nowhere in sight. Even the broadcast networks number six at this writing, counting Fox, Time Warner's WB, and Viacom-Paramount's UPN. Networks are tempted to (in the current jargon) "narrowcast," especially to the young, with brash comedies like *The Simpsons* and the latest wave of serials devised (once again!) by Aaron Spelling, *Beverly Hills 90210, Melrose Place,* and their ilk, all encouraging the sense that real life is lived in a tribal subsociety of agemates, and that the only authorities worth heeding are to be found within the crowd and not among its elders. Most conspicuously, the new technologies and the relentless force of competition have worked to the advantage of younger, leaner, more specialized companies, sometimes the properties of conglomerates, that target specific markets: teenagers, middle-aged women, children, African Americans, fundamentalist Christians, Spanish-speakers, sports fans, cooks, news devotees, chat devotees, household do-it-yourselfers and so on. If television is still a hearth of national culture, it is a hearth in fragments—or rather, a mall.

With the three-network share of the evening audience down from a high of 92 percent in 1976 to the shady side of 50 percent in 1997, the popular as well as the trade press are peppered with headlines like this one from the Sunday *New York Times* of November 22, 1998: "Shrinking Network TV Audiences Set Off Alarm and Reassessment."[7] The reporter, Bill Carter, suggested that the declining audience for four out of the six networks might stem from the fact that they were self-consciously aiming for younger audiences, and that there simply were not enough of these higher-spending desirables to go around. The search for younger viewers is not altogether new, of course; chapter 10 of this book records

---

5 Nielsen statistics as reported by Monica Collins, "Clickers: The Big Schmooze in the Big Easy," *Boston Herald,* February 8, 1998, p. 5.
6 Calculated from U. S. census data, on-line at http://www.census.gov/population /socdemo/hh-fam/htabHH-4.txt.
7 Bill Carter, *New York Times,* November 22, 1998, p. A1.

an earlier episode in the incessant hunt to satisfy not only advertisers but the networks' own desire to appear "cutting-edge," "hot," worthy of "buzz." But the rush for the mother lode of all advertising dollars has grown far more intense in the last three decades. Once the networks relinquish the goal of attracting viewers of all ages—a goal never easy to attain in any event—they are vying for fractions of a limited niche. In hot pursuit of eyeballs, they yank failed series with alacrity, hire new executives from cable channels, and experiment with low-cost, down-market formats. No wonder networks consider a show a hit if it draws a 15 share, 15 percent of the audience—roughly half of what they were looking for in 1981—especially if they are young.[8]

Try what they will, ABC, CBS, and NBC are no longer the cash machines of earlier decades, when losing money was hard for broadcasters to do. So vigorous was advertiser demand for eyeballs that the worst that could be said about a failed show is that it made less money than another show might have made. Even the gigantic transfers of network ownership that took place in the mid-1980s proceeded on the assumption that business could still be practiced as usual, if with a cost-trim here and a synergy there. When the old titans faded—William S. Paley at CBS and Leonard Goldenson at ABC—these empires of glitz, so fat and smug during their flush years, were lumbering, thick-thinking prey for Wall Street hunting expeditions. During 1985 and 1986, ABC was acquired by Capital Cities, a television and radio chain; CBS by the billionaire Tisch brothers, who had made their money in hotels, theaters, oil tankers, and clever stock deals; NBC and the rest of its parent RCA by the even more gigantic General Electric combine. Then, in 1994, Rupert Murdoch's Fox—via an intermediary company—lured away 12 major urban affiliate stations, instantly boosting his access to major markets and further destabilizing the No-Longer-So-Big Three.

Network managers, having no better idea than their predecessors how to crank out hits, resorted to every corporation's prime pseudo-solution to decaying competitiveness: cost-cutting. Amenities like corporate dining rooms were trimmed. Bureaucratic layers were pruned—including censorship departments, whose diminishment, not coincidentally, brought about a boom in profanity and female flesh. Vice-presidencies, abundant during the period I was writing about, became scarcer. The networks decided to order fewer complete pilots and relied instead on vastly cheaper tapes of selected scenes.[9] By 1998 early retirement buyouts were all the rage at NBC, and employees were not completely astounded when a memo hit their desks declaring "There will be a moratorium on the purchase of all office supplies." And crueler still: "There

---

8 Carter, p. A24.
9 Bill Carter, "Networks Tuning Out Pilots As a Way to Develop Shows," *New York Times,* January 20, 1992, p. 6.

will be no departmental/divisional Holiday parties with the exception of children-related events." And: "All employee luncheons (retirement, new job) require prior approval." Orders of bottled water were canceled.[10]

What had made the networks into cash machines in the pre-cable decades was a combination of two things: low costs and limited choice. Limited choice was a function of primitive technology. Cable changed the terrain; so, in less heralded fashion, did the spread of that consequential little gadget, the remote control device, which humble clickers are found in 93 percent of American households at this writing, undermining the viewer inertia that is a network's strong suit. Low costs were a function mainly of the fact that in the largest and most lucrative markets, the networks each owned cash-cow over-the-air stations, the so-called O & O's. For this bounty of publicly-held airwaves they paid the public treasury not the thinnest dime. Advertiser revenues were theirs to keep. This tidy arrangement was the product not of free enterprise but of political power exercised over decades, lubricated by campaign contributions, secured by the best Congress that lobbyists could buy and via the unquestioning silence of the press. The broadcasters had the power to define broadcasting, and to keep any potential rivals intensely hypothetical. Even public television, instituted during the administration of Lyndon Johnson, was crippled from the start by a tangled federal power-dividing scheme and a fiscal impoverishment that kept it, to put it mildly, auxiliary.

There were limits to the networks' power, of course. One significant limit was written into government regulations keeping the networks, for the most part, from owning the shows they aired. The networks leased the shows, paying the suppliers—studios and independent production companies—license fees for the right to air them, but under the so-called financial syndication or "fin-syn" rules, the networks were shut out of the riches that accrued when the shows went into syndication. For their part, the suppliers argued that they were entitled to the lion's share of the proceeds because the prime risk was theirs; after all, in order to supply the shows to the networks, they had to go into debt, the license fees paid by the networks always amounting to less than the cost of the shows. For years, the networks fought for the right to rescind the fin-syn rules, and failed. The distributors aspired to be owners, and the owners naturally resented the threat. For years, as New York collided with Hollywood, Hollywood prevailed. During Ronald Reagan's presidency, Hollywood enjoyed special advantages.

But in 1990, the networks, less fat and rich by the year, finally prevailed; the fin-syn rules were rescinded, and the networks were now per-

---

10 Todd Gitlin, "In the Parched Peacock Era, TV Networks Slide Into Sleaze," *New York Observer*, December 7, 1998, p. 5.

mitted to sell their shows into syndication. The schedules began to fill up with network-owned shows, including newsmagazines, which were especially cheap to produce. (When a single episode of *E. R.* could cost NBC $13 million, a nightly *Dateline* hour costing $400,000 was a dandy investment.) Just between 1989 and 1993, network-owned shows boomed from 12 percent to 27 percent of the entire schedule.[11] One result was the decline of independent suppliers. In 1998, the only one left standing was Carsey-Werner Productions, wildly successful entrepreneurs of *The Cosby Show, Roseanne,* and *Third Rock from the Sun,* among other hits. When in 1998 I asked company co-founder Marcie Carsey how her business had changed in the last decade, she said immediately, "It's not as much fun as it used to be," and jumped to the subject of the fin-syn rules: "The emphasis at the networks has changed from getting the best ratings you can to getting the best ratings you can with a show you own."[12] No longer so much fun, even for a company blessed with three sitcoms on the air at once! Obeying the grow-or-die imperative, an independent producer now aspires to compete with networks. At the time I spoke with Carsey, her company was entering into a partnership to produce a women's cable channel to be coupled with Internet access.

Broadcast networks today are like networks a generation ago because they adhere to a single unswerving imperative: create, within the demographic target, the largest possible audience. That style of thought remains fixed. Numbers count. Or rather, *only* numbers count. From maximizing all eyeballs to maximizing eyeballs with particular characteristics—this is the big change. So in the era of narrowcasting, the unchanging network quest generates somewhat different results than before. In the course of the 1980s, the networks' search for winning styles carried them somewhat beyond the formulas that prevailed when *Inside Prime Time* was researched and written. For one thing, fashions changed. Enter the gauzy religious aura. Enter "alternative life-styles" with *Murphy Brown* and *Ellen* incensing the fundamentalist right. Enter, too, new looks. Hipness found a place: contemporary music, visual cleverness, fast cuts imported from MTV and commercials.[13] Self-deconstructing styles variously found their ways into the saucy *Simpsons,* into *Moonlighting's* direct address to the spectator (prefigured by the comic George Burns in the 1950s), *Max Headroom's* high-tech futurism, the trans-realist weirdness of *Twin Peaks* and *Wild Palms. Miami Vice* was as earnest as *Max Headroom* was dystopian and *Twin Peaks* campy, but they had in common their auteurist aspirations, visual ambitions, and minia-

11 John Thornton Caldwell, *Televisuality: Style, Crisis, and Authority in American Television* (New Brunswick, N. J.: Rutgers University Press, 1995), p. 294.
12 Interview, Marcie Carsey, October 31, 1998.
13 On MTV, commercials, and *Miami Vice,* see my "'We Build Excitement,'" in Todd Gitlin, ed., *Watching Television* (New York: Pantheon, 1987), pp. 136–140, 150–54.

turist avant-gardism. Visual play was one way to compete with cable, after all. Computerized frame-accurate editing, digital video graphics, collage: the film school repertory, bulging with technology, came to television along with deadpan post-modernism. It was all very well for David Lynch to say, "Television is to communication what the chainsaw is to logging,"[14] but Lynch's buttoned-down disdain was fully compatible with the cult-favorite drollery of *Twin Peaks*. The trademark Steven Bochco techniques that first showed up in *Hill Street Blues* found their way into other Bochco enterprises—disastrously in *Cop Rock*, successfully in *N. Y. P. D. Blue*—and in shaky, hand-held derivatives. In the late 1980s and 1990s, some of Hollywood's more accomplished directors found places on the networks: Barry Levinson with his series, *Homicide: Life on the Street*, Quentin Tarantino as a guest director on *E. R.*

At the same time, with cable channels drawing off a significant share of the more educated viewers, the over-the-air channels scrambled to hold onto cableless viewers who were disproportionately less educated. Led by Rupert Murdoch's Fox, the networks went downmarket with "reality" entertainments like *America's Funniest Home Videos*, an amateur-hour genre that led, in turn to the likes of Fox's *When Good Pets Go Bad* and *World's Scariest Police Chases*, until in 1998 NBC was preparing to order 13 episodes of a new series to be called *World's Scariest Home Videos*, from the producer of *When Good Pets Go Bad*. Where this trend might go is anyone's guess.

There is, then, in the end, the thud of anticlimax in the dwindling of the broadcast networks and the rise of "niche programming." There still is virtually no place in American television, commercial or public, for a serious writer or director to make a career—although one has high hopes for David Chase, whose deliciously scurrilous HBO series *The Sopranos* displayed an uncommon craft and intelligence during its first season. Indeed, since television styles have come to set the standard for pace and cleverness, there is next to no place for a serious writer in Hollywood movies, either. Feature films, increasingly, are either TV shows stretched on the rack or blockbusters aiming to give an audience precisely what it can't get on the home screen: gore, pornography, dirty words, big-screen effects, fancy sound, or all of the above.

Still, there is no sign that the viewing public laments the passing of bygone days. Why should it? On the face of it, the provision of a larger number of channels cannot be worse than their absence. Even if one shares the viewpoint of the perceptive media critic, Bruce Springsteen ("Fifty-seven Channels and Nothing On"), seven channels with nothing on would not seem preferable. Now there are more channels than ever, so the logic of competition leads to a proliferation of common denominators. Yet this does not mean that the broadcast networks are losers.

---

14 Quoted in Caldwell, p. 3.

They have lost many battles, but in the war for culture, or what passes for such, they win by losing. Their principles, or lack of same, are what prevail—so much so that the basic procedures, the values, the premises described in this book outlast the individuals whose paths are traced here, outlast even their organizations, and shape the alternatives in their snug niches. The names change, the domestic audience shrinks, but the analysis of the network industry that follows remains—in its main features, its principles, its logic—unfortunately valid.

So the twilight of network television is also its triumph—the triumph of its form of thought. This does not, thankfully, mean its absolute monopoly over culture. Individuals continue to take refuge from the blue glow. As those on the margins are sucked triumphantly into the shifting center of a spongy culture, new margins always take shape. But these margins are shaped by the center, too, even by their obsession with it and their rebellion against it. So decade after decade, what is unpredictable in television does not stay unpredictable for long. The industry evolves and still remains largely predictable. The repercussions flow everywhere. The culture as a whole has become unimaginable without endless television, including its pleasures and commonplaces, its comforts and transparent fictions, its pushbutton glamour, its anesthesia, even its irritations. Generation after generation takes this television for granted as its cultural birthright, even when they regard it as wasteful, silly, or worse. Simply by being *there,* being *available,* being *on,* as electrifying as it is and no more so, as glamorous as it is and no more so, the home entertainment machine has become indispensable to commerce, to politics, to the course of events and the texture of life—so much so as to raise, and probably answer, the question of whether there would be an American culture without it.

To understand how the machine works, the thinking that made television what it is and secured its place, remains the objective of *Inside Prime Time,* a book I wish were strictly of historical interest but is, alas, in my judgment, as germane today as when it was first published.

Todd Gitlin
New York City
December 1998

P R O L O G U E

The spring of 1982 was a cruel time for American newspapers. The *New York Daily News* was on rocky ground, the *Washington Star* failed, and CBS pulled the plug on what was arguably the best newspaper in the United States, the *Los Angeles Tribune*. The *Trib* was a fiction, of course, but far more than real papers that camouflage their methods in myths of objectivity, the *Trib* told the inside story of how, week after week, Lou Grant, Billie Newman, Joe Rossi, Charlie Hume, Mrs. Pynchon, et al. went about gathering the big and little news of our time—and against the cruelest competition of all, the fluff and flutter of prime-time TV.

When CBS yanked *Lou Grant* from its 1982–83 schedule, it shut down an enterprise that for five years had discoursed amiably, seriously, influentially—if at times sonorously and formulaically—about unemployment, dogfighting, cattle poisoning, illegal aliens, chemical dumping, blacklisting, and even the start of a nuclear war. The network terminated the longest-running character then on television: crusty, honorable, slow-moving Lou Grant, the fellow who had transferred in 1977 from local TV *(The Mary Tyler Moore Show)* to the more serious business of newspapering. Television buffs will recall that the *Mary* show went off the air with a bang when new management set out to jack up low ratings by firing virtually the entire news staff. Life does imitate a television script.

What doesn't quite match a television script—except, perhaps, the occasional *Lou Grant* episode—is that the star of the show was television's most conspicuous political activist, Ed Asner. So Hollywood automatically wondered if the cancellation amounted to punishment —blacklisting, in effect—especially after it came out that one *Lou Grant* advertiser, Kimberly-Clark, had terminated its spots to steer clear of Asner's politics. Had Asner gone too far? CBS held firm to the claim that, since ratings were falling, the cancellation was strictly business as usual. But television, like any business, keeps apprised of its customers' moods. Its primary customers are the advertisers whose business is to rent the eyeballs of the audience. And advertisers are panicky folk, especially at a moment when the Moral Majority and other right-wingers were beating the drums, and the ghost of *Red Channels* had not been so long dispelled. It turned out that at least one other *Lou Grant* advertiser, Vidal Sassoon, Inc., was also stampeded by the anti-Asner hubbub to go crying to CBS.

The *Lou Grant* case dredged up the question of the part politics

3

plays in the networks' deliberations. This book will show that it is not even an easy question to formulate clearly, let alone to answer. Business as usual is itself a kind of politics, so to differentiate between business and political motives is always difficult. Whatever the mix in this case, CBS's decision quickly reverberated throughout the industry. Producers, writers, and actors, always edgy, had something new to be edgy about: How far could they go? Asner was instantly at least graylisted. Moreover, during the first seven days of May 1982, CBS canceled not only *Lou Grant* but *WKRP in Cincinnati*, its only entertainments in which writers were not allergic to the notion that the political climate impinges upon everyday drama.

Soon after the cancellation, I spoke with two CBS executives who had attended the scheduling meetings in New York where *Lou Grant* was dumped. Both flatly denied that Asner's politics came in for mention, let alone discussion. But often a central issue is so firmly planted in everyone's mind it need not be mentioned. Nixon and his co-conspirators, for example, didn't bother to carry on in the Oval Office about the evils of Communism. Certainly no one at CBS could have forgotten that Ed Asner had become a political lightning rod. Arnold Becker, CBS's vice-president for National Television Research, told me: "Ed Asner was perceived as a pain in the ass." There was his visible support of the Screen Actors Guild when its members struck in the summer of 1980. And just after he was elected president of SAG in the fall of 1981, a Guild committee recommended that its annual award go to former SAG president Ronald Reagan. The SAG board of directors, acting within its normal mandate, said no, because of Reagan's demolition of the Professional Air Traffic Controllers Organization. The vote was 54–11, and Asner didn't vote. But never mind; Asner, said Becker, was perceived as "outspoken on all issues."

Indeed he was. A year earlier, Asner had described his style as "wielding a cudgel," which he contrasted with Lou Grant's "more elegant and more effective" style of "dealing in a soft fashion with current-day crises." "Up-and-down passions," he called his political engagements, not exactly the language of a man his opponents call self-righteous. That, however, was before he made the national evening news on February 15, 1982, with a Washington press conference on behalf of Medical Aid for El Salvador. Asner and several other actors presented a representative of the Salvadoran guerrilla front with a check for $25,000. Contrary to later right-wing attacks and liberal mutterings, the check was intended for medical aid to regions of El Salvador where the ruling junta did not include healing as part of its government service; the spending was to be supervised by a Mexican doctor; and it was not Asner's personal gift, but rather money raised through a direct-mail campaign. Former SAG president Charlton Heston denounced Asner on procedural grounds: "He can do anything he wants to with his money, as far as I'm concerned. He can give it to the Soviet Union to pacify Afghanistan if he wants to. But he has an overriding responsibility to separate his own acts from those positions of the Guild." No matter that Asner was not introduced as the Guild president; no matter that he said he was speaking only for himself. President Ronald Reagan declared that he was "very disturbed," because in his own Hollywood days—the days of the blacklist he always maintained didn't exist—"the Guild had a solid rule that it did not engage in politics."

No one on the right had seemed alarmed when Asner and SAG supported Poland's Solidarity. Now the right wing went wild. On March 1, just before *Lou Grant* came on, John Amos, chief executive officer of the American Family Corporation, which owns five stations in Missouri, Alabama, Georgia, and Iowa, read an editorial denouncing Asner for becoming "the self-appointed secretary of state of America," and decrying "the liberal left" for equating El Salvador and Vietnam. "Vietnam was on the other side of the world, while El Salvador is just two steps away from being next door to us. If El Salvador falls to the Communists, next comes Guatemala and then Mexico. We have a 1,300-mile open border with Mexico. The Rio Grande River is not an ocean; in fact, half the year it's a dry riverbed anyone can walk or drive a tank across."

On March 10, Joseph Solomon, president of Vidal Sassoon, Inc., wrote to CBS board chairman William S. Paley:

> Please find attached to this letter copies of letters we have received from viewers who have taken exception with Ed Asner using his position for political purposes. As the sponsor of the Ed Asner show we are indeed concerned. We, by sponsoring the show, did not wish to embroil ourselves in a political controversy.
>
> We do not feel that we should be pressured into withdrawing our sponsorship, but on the other hand, we do not wish to have our products suffer because of an unfortunate association with a political issue. Please advise us how this matter should be handled. We are very concerned about our company image and the image of our products, and we therefore look to you for a solution to this unfortunate situation.

By early June, the total number of letters Sassoon had received protesting its participation in *Lou Grant* was thirteen. CBS president Thomas H. Wyman responded on April 5: "CBS cannot set standards of acceptability of a performer based on his or her personal, political or religious convictions. . . . Mr. Asner stated unequivocally at his recent press conference that in expressing his views on El Salvador, he was speaking as a private citizen and in no other capacity."

Also early in March, a *Lou Grant* fan named Margot Bollock wrote to Kimberly-Clark, manufacturer of Kleenex and Kotex, to tell them she was switching *to* their products in appreciation of Asner's politics. On March 15, Kimberly-Clark replied: "Thank you for writing to us about your objections to Ed Asner's recent statement on El Salvador. We appreciate the opportunity to tell you that we have discontinued all advertising on the *Lou Grant* television program."

On March 19, Jerry Falwell sent out a mailing likening Asner to the right's darling of treason, Jane Fonda, and soliciting money to run newspaper ads asking readers to choose between Reagan and Asner. The advertisement that ran in the *Los Angeles Times* of April 30, adorned by a hammer and sickle and a map showing El Salvador dwarfing the United States, asked: "Are we supposed to stand idly by and allow Hollywood radicals to dictate America's foreign policy?"

Finally, on April 22, Congressman John LeBoutillier (R-N.Y.), the author of *Harvard Hates America*, sent out a mailing in behalf of something called the Council of Inter-American Security, calling for a boycott of eight *Lou Grant* sponsors (not including Kimberly-Clark or Vidal Sassoon). Names and addresses were thoughtfully supplied, along with a preaddressed, prewritten postcard to William S. Paley.

We do not know how much of this right-wing reaction got back to the CBS brass, or how seriously they took it. Normally the networks hate to bow to a single offended sponsor, since that would be an admission that their power could be infringed upon. After hearing from Margot Bollock, Asner called James Rosenfield, executive vice-president of the CBS Broadcast Group, who had defended *Lou Grant* years before when an episode on a nursing home scandal incurred the wrath of the American Health Care Association and led General Foods to yank its spots from the rerun. This time, Asner recalls, "he was low-key, sounding as if he was very tired of dealing with all the static about *Lou Grant*, or me." However, Rosenfield did say that the Kimberly-Clark spots would be resold with ease to another company.

Spots sell in two phases. In "up front" buying each spring, advertisers purchase spots on the next season's shows. Later in the year they purchase the remaining spots, buying access to specific demographic groups. Since such buys are normally allocated by the networks' computers, the companies may be only dimly aware of exactly which shows their spots will fall in. Indeed, the *Lou Grant* show customarily sold at a premium, for its prestige value. When the advertisers' screening services flag an episode as troublesome, last-minute substitution is normal—particularly since the fundamentalist right began attacking the networks for their "obscenity."

Lou Grant producers and writers were apprehensive, and had even talked about making Lou more conservative the next season, shifting the burden of enlightenment even further toward Billie and Rossi. They had good reason to be edgy. It seems clear now that CBS was watching both Asner and *Grant* closely. As early as February 24, syndicated *Chicago Sun-Times* TV columnist Gary Deeb floated what sounded very much like a network trial balloon, reporting that ratings were down almost 10 percent thus far that season, "and if CBS officials are searching for a reason, they probably won't have to look any further than Ed Asner's continuing flirtation with politics. . . . Many CBS executives are getting tired of Asner's crusading, particularly with the viewership for *Lou Grant* suffering damage as a result of the star's oft-stated political views." Deeb did not pause to note that other of CBS's shows were slipping about the same amount in the ratings. Indeed, by May, what with competition from both independents and cable, total network ratings were down by 7 percent compared with the previous May; and CBS's by 9 percent.

As the decisive first week of May loomed, rumors circulated among the *Lou Grant* staff that the show would be dumped. Between the November 2 season debut and February 8, *Lou Grant* averaged a Nielsen rating of 17.5 (17.5 percent of Nielsen's total sample of households tuned in) and an audience share of 28.3 (28.3 percent of all sets on during that time slot were tuned in to *Lou Grant*). Although the numbers had slipped slightly from 1980–81, this was still a respectable showing, given the competition of ABC's *Monday Night Football* and the decline in network shares across the board. But from February 15 (just after Asner's Washington press conference) through May 3, *Lou Grant* ratings slid to an average of 14.0, for an average share of 23.8.

This slippage was duly noted at CBS Entertainment headquarters in Los Angeles. Indeed, top programming executives had mused about dropping the show a year earlier, although its 1980–81 share had been identical to its 1979–80 share, and it had actually ranked higher (twenty-eighth as against thirty-third) for the season. Most of them wanted to "clean house" by dumping "marginal" shows, including the sitcom *The Two of Us* and *WKRP in Cincinnati*. There are distinct advantages to bringing a new show onto the schedule rather than retaining an old one. As Arnold Becker points out, the sales department can sometimes sell an unknown product better than a known product of marginal economic worth. In addition, there are what Becker calls "internal political considerations." Development executives are more likely to improve their relative standing by scheduling a new show than by rolling over a show in which they had no hand. "There's also a very real advantage that if you happen to get a hit you can keep it for many years."

One West Coast CBS programming executive, who spoke to me on condition he not be identified, said, "We thought, Paley's probably going to force us to keep *Lou Grant*." It was, after all, a prestige show, and the network liked to have at least one or two on the schedule to deflect criticism and to impress the impressionable critics. Paley, who married into the Social Register and was president of the Museum of Modern Art, is known to have a taste for the higher things; Ethel Winant, a former casting executive at CBS, speaks of "Mr. Paley's attacks of culture." Although Paley was known for participating in scheduling meetings as an interlocutor, not a dictator, the company was still, as more than one executive put it, "Mr. Paley's candy store."

On Monday, May 3, 1982, *Lou Grant* aired "Unthinkable," the first realistic-style television-series episode ever to dramatize the possibility of nuclear war. Some thought it fact-clogged, stiff, preachy; others thought it powerful, plausible, terrifying. For whatever reasons, "Unthinkable" drew the lowest numbers in the five-year history of *Lou Grant:* a 10.9 rating, 19 share. It was "thrashed," in the words of *Lou Grant* co-creator and executive consultant Allan Burns, by a rerun of *TV's Censored Bloopers,* which scored a 37 share. (Strikingly, though, *Lou Grant*'s share did not decline in the course of the hour. There was normal post–10:00 P.M. attrition as people went to bed, but the viewers who tuned in didn't switch channels to get away.) That 19 share, in Arnold Becker's words, "did not help."

The scheduling meetings took place directly thereafter. Paley went down the schedule and asked why each show should be renewed. "No one could arouse that much enthusiasm for *Lou Grant*," reports the same West Coast programming executive. "It was very preachy and self-congratulatory. 'Why should we keep it on?' Paley kept asking. We kept falling back on the fact that it was well made, well acted, well written most of the time. It had won lots of awards. But it had gotten dull. . . . Finally Paley said, 'If you have so little enthusiasm, why are you pushing it?' We figured, let's put a new show on. After a show's been on this number of years, you can predict it won't regain its audience.'"

"I think it's fair to say," adds Arnold Becker, "that the best we could expect would be another marginal year. No one thought there was any chance of turning it around." No one bothered to argue that the entire CBS Monday-night schedule was down from the previous year; *House Calls, Lou Grant*'s lead-in, was down by more points than *Lou Grant,* and *M*A*S*H, House Calls*'s lead-in, was down by almost as much. *Lou Grant* had actually gained relative to its lead-in —the sort of calculation that often weighs heavily with programmers.

No matter, says the West Coast programmer. "*Lou Grant* had peaked in popularity." The schedulers did talk about the idea of ordering thirteen shows, a half-season's worth. "That was seen as an oblique way of canceling. We'd see how the first three did. If ratings were bad, we'd cut the order to seven. It would have been more cowardly, or diplomatic, depending on your point of view. Critics would have congratulated us for trying. But as Sartre would say, it would have been bad faith."

Instead, CBS settled on *Cagney and Lacey,* a series about two female police officers, as a replacement. In three outings that spring, it had ranked below *Lou Grant.* Its ratings soared only during the one week it was moved to Sunday night, in the popular *Trapper John, M.D.* time period. "It was a hunch," says the same programmer. "We felt the concept was sufficiently appealing that with proper stories it would work. It's not scientific; it's intuitive. Next season it could get a 15 share and we'll look like dummies."*

In the end, CBS liked *Cagney and Lacey* well enough to renew it over *Lou Grant,* but was sufficiently dissatisfied to press for major changes. "Testing said that the women were too harsh, not feminine enough, too aggressive," commented Arnold Becker. "The world perceived them as too masculine." As a result, the blunt actress Meg Foster was replaced by the blond, more comic, more "feminine" Sharon Gless.**

No one knows why *Lou Grant*'s ratings slipped significantly from February 15 on. Most network executives tend to believe that a country in the throes of depression wants escapist entertainment above all. That is why the 1982–83 schedules sported three variations of the *Raiders of the Lost Ark* formula. Allan Burns was inclined to agree: "If I had a pilot that had a lot to do with content, I'd be concerned right now." He thinks that some part of the audience turned off *Lou Grant* because of Asner's identification with left-wing causes. Asner, however, felt that the ratings slump was simply "a fluke"; for by the end of May, *Lou Grant* reruns had bounced back to shares in the high 20s. Perhaps, though, this was partly because the Nielsen audience wanted its last looks at the show. The numbers don't speak for themselves.

All that can be said for sure is that a single rating-point difference, sustained over the course of an entire year, could be worth $50

---

*In fact, *Cagney and Lacey* finished its first season on Monday nights with an average audience share of 24—lower than *Lou Grant*'s.

**Barney Rosenzweig, the executive producer who replaced Meg Foster, is the same man who, in a complex series of maneuvers, lost a series on ABC the previous year for failing to bend sufficiently to the network's will. (See Chapter 6.) On getting his show renewed, Rosenzweig hired none other than April Smith, the *Lou Grant* story editor who had written, among many other episodes, "Unthinkable."

million or more at 1981 advertising rates; so when a show is marginal
and the numbers ambiguous, it's easy for actual and anticipated
advertiser pressure to make the difference. Had it not been for
Asner's conspicuous politics, the show's prestige would probably
have compensated for the drop in ratings, and it might well have
been renewed.

I asked NBC chairman Grant Tinker for his reaction. "I was very
surprised. I would have kept it [had I been at CBS], because it was
worthwhile. It was a flagship show." NBC, however, after some ago-
nizing, decided not to take *Lou Grant.* "We made a judgment that
it was a little tired." In any case NBC, which had picked up *Taxi* after
ABC canceled it the same month, didn't want to get a reputation as
the network that buys rejected goods. Did Tinker think there was
anything involved at CBS besides the usual numbers game? "I don't
know. Were there to be, I would guess you and I would never know.
It would be such an inner-sanctum matter."

Soon thereafter, the columnist Gary Deeb, who had sarcastically
dismissed Asner's claim that CBS was trying to dampen controversy
among its actors, reported that the network had censored two skits
making fun of Ronald and Nancy Reagan and was generally letting
producers, writers, and performers know that "politically sensitive
material" was not welcome. It was hard not to wonder about the
influence of William Paley's Republicanism; about the importance
President Reagan was known to attach to the politics of his erstwhile
union and political stomping ground; about the weight a network
might place on good relations with the executive branch in Washington, especially at a time when many regulatory and deregulatory
decisions were being considered that would affect network profit
statements for decades to come.

But even if the *Lou Grant* decision amounted to no more than
business as usual, the word was out in Hollywood that the networks
were buying fewer TV series and movies charged with potential
controversy. Producers thinking about politically charged themes
would now only be further discouraged. Whatever the complexity of
CBS's motives, the cancellation would be read as a warning to performers and others to guard their tongues. Quickly a chill settled
over the Hollywood palms. Even actors who signed pro-Asner advertisements in the trade papers refrained from joining the anticancella-
tion picket lines organized by the American Civil Liberties Union of
Southern California outside CBS headquarters. More ominously, just
days after the cancellation, when the writer of a new series pilot
proposed Asner for a regular role, the production company, one of
the majors, flatly rejected him because he was "a liability." Before
the El Salvador press conference, Asner had been deluged each
month with scores of inquiries into his availability for TV movies and

feature films. Afterward—admittedly in an economically depressed industry—the inquiries dried to a trickle.

As we talked in Asner's office on the CBS lot in the San Fernando Valley, one of the crew dropped in to say hello and good-bye. When he left, a somber Asner said, "That hurts. Since this happened, it's always been in the back of my mind that maybe there was a last chance to save the show. But no, that's childish." Both the sentiment and the hope for eleventh-hour reversal were very much in keeping with the spirit of *Lou Grant*, which was the first television series to defy formula on occasion by refusing to tie up loose plot ends. Issues emerged that the *Trib* could not set right. The shadowy story of the cancellation of a TV series would have been right up the *Trib*'s alley.

The fate of *Lou Grant* was not typical, both the show and Ed Asner being unusual. Normally there is not even the suggestion of overt political concern at the networks; and normally advertisers do not intervene so directly in network affairs. Their interests form the context that decision-makers take for granted. In effect, they leave it to the networks to choose programs that are calculated to suit their needs for showcases, although recent threats of consumer boycotts (see Chapter 12) have heightened corporate sensitivity to the slightest hint of controversy.

And yet the story of *Lou Grant* serves as an overture to the themes that run through this book: power, politics, and the nature of the decision-making process governing prime-time network television. To the extent that CBS executives were indifferent to anything about *Lou Grant* but its marginality in the ratings, that indifference exhibits the normal network mentality. Short-sighted guesses of future ratings are the alpha and omega shaping the shows that take up the prime time of Americans, the twenty-two hours a week (eight o'clock to eleven o'clock each night, with an extra hour on Sunday) when, at any given moment, one-third of all Americans are staring into the blue light. What is the logic or illogic of network decision-making? What attention do network executives really pay to ratings and program tests, and what discretion remains to them once all the numbers are counted and deployed? How do they read public moods and political swings? Why do they imitate themselves? What difference, if any, does it make who occupies the executive suites, or the studios and production offices where the shows are concocted, or the agencies that screen them? Exactly how is this industry dominated by a small world of executives, suppliers, producers, and agents spinning through revolving doors, and how does it happen that decisions made strictly for business in the land of business contain elements of—o, forbidden word!—ideology? What is the genesis of TV's images of men and women, blacks and whites, families and workplaces, authority and rebellion? Finally, now that the three networks are losing a growing part of their steady audience to independent stations, cable television, satellite networks, and soon possibly direct satellite broadcasting and other new technologies, what will prime-time television as a whole and the networks in particular look like in the future?

I started this book with a question—or rather a curiosity—about how much a show's commercial success depended on its "fit" with social trends abroad in the land. I also started with the notion that what sometimes gives commercial television its weird vitality, perhaps even its profitability, is its ability to borrow, transform—and deform—the energy of social and psychological conflict. Sometimes network television seemed to succeed in packaging images that drew on unresolved tensions in the society. Cramming these tensions into the domesticated frame of the sitcom and the action-adventure, television whether "realist" or "escapist" clearly bore some relation to the real world, even if only the real world of popular desire and fear. Obviously *All in the Family* traded on the electric current that ran between real-life Archie Bunkers and Mike Stivics of the early seventies. Obviously *M*A*S*H* capitalized on antiwar feeling. These shows demonstrated that television could be popular not by ducking reality but by doing something else to it: not reproducing it exactly, but squeezing some version of some truth into the conventions of an already established form. But *Charlie's Angels* also seemed to exploit a range of these tensions, trading on feminism, male and female backlash, and the new image of the working woman all at once. High-culture disdain, including my own, while deploring television for its stereotypes and stupidity, had nothing to say about which stereotypes would prevail at which times, and how and why.

In the seventies, network television became a contested zone without anyone knowing what effect it actually had on politics, on family life, on the image of self and other. The only given was that everybody but the networks themselves had no doubt that the effects were there. Ethnic groups began to lobby for a change in their image on television; so did women, homosexuals, big business, unions, and fundamentalist Christians, among many others. Some on the paranoid left saw network entertainment as a conspiracy to purvey capitalist values, while some on the right saw *Dallas* as a plot to undermine the patriarchal Christian family. The networks went on insisting that they simply gave people the entertainment they wanted, without facing up to the fact that people will often cease to want what they can't get even if they succeed in imagining it in the first place. Television was the national billboard, and whether you looked at news or entertainment, its space was scarce and important.

I looked at a lot of television entertainment in the fall of 1980, trying to think more or less systematically about its treatment of social issues. I started from the premise that in any society images have meaning and are not arbitrary. People do not have to watch a television show; however limited their choices, they still choose—that is, network entertainment did seem to track some version of social reality. But whose? It began to dawn on me that I could not hope to understand why network television was what it was unless I understood who put the images on the small screen and for what reasons.

So that fall and winter I began interviewing network executives, producers, writers, agents, actors, and anyone else who would talk to me about what shaped TV's images of the wider world. Among other things, I wanted to see whether the industry "knew" what "it" was doing when it came up with these images. Within a few weeks of darting around Los Angeles, I realized that I could not hope to understand the ways producers and networks decided how to treat social issues unless I understood the ways they decided how to treat everything else. For there was no sign of a special decision-making process for "social issues," whatever those were. So, to ask the specific question, I would have to ask the more general one. The book ends up asking both, and it became possible for me to ask both because I also discovered that industry people would talk to me far more freely than I had expected.

I had started cold, with a University of California, Berkeley, letterhead and the names of a few friends of friends and onetime colleagues of colleagues. One name led to another. For whatever reasons, people talked almost entirely on the record. I went to an ABC vice-president's office in Century City just after five on a Friday afternoon, and took my leave five hours later. Some producers were good enough to let me hang around on the set for weeks on end; to read successive versions of scripts and watch them change; to keep me apprised of new projects; to let me pester them unmercifully for latest developments. I was also lucky to be in Los Angeles during much of the writers' strike, when writers and producers and some executives had an unaccustomed amount of time on their hands. From January through July 1981, some 200 industry people were decent enough to let me interview them about why they do what they do. Only half a dozen refused outright to speak to me, all of them high-level. At first I relied mostly on written notes, but after my first three weeks, as I became more confident and realized hardly anyone in this high-tech world seemed to feel inhibited by machines, I asked for and received permission to tape-record almost everything. Only one low-level executive ever asked me not to take notes, and that was because she feared for her job.

Of course the television business is a talker's business. It could thrive without books sooner than without telephones. Deals are consummated on the phone before the lawyers take over and draw up the "deal memo." Selling takes place at breakfast or lunch in Beverly Hills, and executives can move up because they are known for "giving good meeting." So getting people to talk was not the problem I had anticipated; the problem was to evaluate millions of words. There is always a risk, of course, in trying to reconstruct and understand events after the fact, especially in a town devoted to the fine art of salesmanship, but when in doubt I tried to triangulate among different accounts of the same meetings and decisions; and when they still didn't agree I tried to make sense of discrepancies, on the principle that discrepancies, evasions, and blind spots are themselves clues. Confronted with interviewers, we are all special pleaders. But many special pleadings add up to an industry's view of itself, which is the central evidence I offer—though not uncritically—for an analysis of what the industry does and why.

Much of this book is what the anthropologist Clifford Geertz calls "thick description." I want to convey not only how and why I think the networks do what they do, but a sense of the ambiance and texture of the industry's life-as-it-is-lived. For this reason I recount a number of stories at some length, and often in the words of the people telling them. Anecdote is the style of industry speech, dialogue its body, and narrative its structure. If Hollywood, as one wag has it, is the land where those who can't, do, it is also the place where those who can and can't alike, *tell*. It is a place where many of the practitioners are brighter and more engaging than their products, and the story of the making of the show more revealing than the show itself. I think these stories, once scrutinized and interrogated, are the royal road to the industry's workings. Meeting these people and liking almost all of them led me to marvel at the way the American entertainment industry keeps real intelligence on a short leash.

In a nutshell, then—which is precisely where an argument is protected from the complications of digestion—the argument of this book hangs on the problem of uncertainty and the industry's attempts to overcome it. Uncertainty is the permanent condition of show business, as of much of the entire business system. As soon as capital pays its lip service to risk (for which profit is its just reward), it gets busy trying to minimize it. "The marketplace," the intended recipient of the product, is an abstraction and an imperfect guide. It cannot tell the anxious executive what to do. Therefore, the TV industry, like others, tries to develop ways to control both supply and demand—supply in order to smooth its workings, demand so that it remains of a sort the networks are set up to satisfy.

Part I is about the more or less rational calculations the networks make in pursuit of the maximum audience—program testing, audience ratings, demographic and schedule calculations, and self-imitation. This is followed by an account of a promising series, *American*

Dream, in the making, showing how the network system kept it short-lived. Part II argues that, all the calculations aside, the networks rely on a small, revolving world of major suppliers and agents. Then we see networks and producers at work in the making of television "docudrama" movies and examine the way they process political controversy. Part III looks at the everyday and extraordinary ways in which network decisions about prime-time series are affected by politics: national political trends (both well and badly understood), the crusade of the fundamentalist right, and the normal political weight of advertisers. In light of all this, the longest chapter in this book traces the history of *Hill Street Blues,* asking how this exceptional show got on the air and stayed there, and what its success (and limits) might signify. The Epilogue explores the emerging world of cable TV and concludes that competition by itself won't fundamentally relax the grip of the network style on American popular culture, for the problem of American television is the problem of American culture and society as a whole.

Many serious people pride themselves on a contemptuous ignorance of television entertainment, accompanied by a sneaking fascination with its raw cultural power and a horror of its effects on public sensibility. At least half the time I have been one of these people. When I decided to write a book about the networks, more than a few of my friends and colleagues gave me funny looks. Loss of standards? No standards in the first place? More than once I felt appalled at what I beheld, and amazed that I was there beholding it. Well, I also confess to having enjoyed the rascality and the ironies of the work. Hollywood people talk about doing a movie "for fun." Talking to the industrializers of fun can also be fun, a welcome relief from academic predictability and high-mindedness. Astonishingly, real people in real offices get paid large salaries to decide whether characters will be allowed to say "son of a bitch," or what color *The Munsters* should be.

More than once it seemed to me that to take this all seriously, even critically, misses the point, or dignifies the industry's claims to public service. The very products are throwaways. Beverly Hills is so clean, says Woody Allen in *Annie Hall,* because "they don't throw their garbage away, they turn it into television shows." In Los Angeles, many industry people get the joke and live it at the same time. The very texture of company business in the company town of Los Angeles is so much a caricature of its own aura that the outsider doesn't know whether to take the joke seriously—as the insiders have to— or to proclaim that the industry's seriousness is its grandest joke. In moments of vertigo I've reminded myself that an industry that devotes hundreds of millions of dollars to the production of junk food for the mind, whose products take up more of this civilization's waking hours than any pursuit besides work, cries out to be taken seriously.

At least as far back as the Middle Ages, popular culture has existed for the public's pleasure, passion, distraction, and occasional enlightenment. I want to analyze and criticize network television not in the name of some Puritanical ideal of Instructive Art, but because, for the most part, this entertainment barely entertains. "I think what is probably the biggest sin of the medium as it exists is that so little sticks to your ribs, that so much effort and technology goes into— what? It's like human elimination. It's just waste," said Grant Tinker a few months before he took up offices in NBC's headquarters, the RCA Building on Manhattan's Avenue of the Americas. On the Rockefeller Plaza side of that building Zeus points his compasses at the slogan WISDOM AND KNOWLEDGE SHALL BE THE STABILITY OF THY TIME. How the possible instruments of pleasure and enlightenment became the tools of stupefaction is one of the revealing tales of our time.

1

NOTHING SUCCEEDS LIKE SUCCESS

C H A P T E R 1

The Problem of Knowing

Everywhere we see signs of perplexity about why television has become what it is. Popular culture even treats us to devil theories to explain network decisions that seem otherwise unfathomable. A *TV Guide* cover story proclaims that Hollywood producers bribe network executives with cocaine to get shows on the air. Then the media chortle about ABC's brief employment of a psychic as a programming consultant. The desire to find a method in network madness runs strong, even if the answers are often simplistic and farfetched. Part of the fascination is that Hollywood radiates a cultural power eerily beyond human scale or comprehension. It is the fountainhead of what immortality our culture affords. The very look of the place —spectacular picture palaces, little clumps of corporate towers rising out of nowhere—was shaped to suit the myth; so is the look of so many industry people, with their face-lifts and their shirts unbuttoned to the navel. It is not for nothing that Hollywood's prize adjective is "fabulous." Even the very word "Hollywood" once evoked a fantasy of Nature. In this collective second nature of ours, the seedbed of national myth still sprawls in sundrenched opulence, unpolluted by real-world smog. No wonder the religious metaphors come rushing in. The blacklisted writer Alvah Bessie entitled his memoir *Inquisition in Eden.* The spectacle of innocence corrupted

19

is necessarily a large theme in a culture founded with a title to divine Providence despite much evidence to the contrary.

But the underside of the myth is corruption, failure, treachery. L.A.'s look seems prefabricated to suit that side of the myth, too: the otherworldly brilliant blue jacaranda trees blooming in lush spring light, under a canopy of suffocating smog the color of cardboard; the verdant expanse of the hills dotted with tacky mansions in styles— one mansion, one style—chosen by major and minor moguls whose very style was stylelessness. Hollywood's glamor has always been tainted by a popular suspicion that the cultural powers-that-be are men of low appetites and malignant influence. If intellectuals and know-nothings can share nothing else, they can share the belief that the Garden is run by serpents, that Eden is a suburb of Sodom and Gomorrah. (In the Bible Belt, the emphasis is on the fact that Hollywood, like Eden and Sodom and Gomorrah, is controlled by Jews.) Hollywood folklore, enshrined in best-selling memoirs, thrives on tales of the great and the innocent—from F. Scott Fitzgerald to Marilyn Monroe and Ingrid Bergman—who poured out of the provinces only to lose their virtue. Good men break like reeds; good girls go bad; the wise, like Faulkner and Garbo, get out while the getting is good. Where innocence and money meet, there is the stuff not only of dreams but of betrayals—even self-betrayals. Every Jesus his own Judas. In popular imagination, Hollywood is not only part Eden and part Sodom, but part Golgotha.

In this lush landscape of myth, scandal, and rumor, the workings of prime-time TV remain mysterious. In a way, popular confusion mirrors the networks' own uncertainty about what might actually succeed. Inside the industry as well as outside, theories abound, most as farfetched as any about cocaine or psychics. If they are so farfetched, though, it's because the workings of the system are so opaque, even to insiders, the decisions apparently so arbitrary, the errors so abundant and visible, the products seemingly so inexplicable.

If knowledgeable people have to resort to voodoo predictions and improbable conspiracy theories to make sense of the enterprise, then how does a prime-time show actually get on the air? As I repeated this naïve question, I sometimes heard a cut-and-dried answer. Each network contains an entertainment division, within which there are development departments for drama, comedy, and movies for television. They plant ideas for shows with producers, or with the major suppliers—studios and production companies—who hire the right producers and writers for the project; and they take ideas—"pitches" —directly from writers and producers. If they think the characters, the relationships, the premises will resonate with a mass audience, they underwrite a script. If they like the script, the heads of the network entertainment division give the go-ahead to shoot a pilot. Of some three thousand ideas floated each year, about a hundred will go to script, of which perhaps twenty-five will go to pilot. These are cast, shot, and tested, and then, each spring, the entertainment-division executives, with other top network executives, meet in marathon session to look at the pilots and put together the new schedule. At each network, five or ten new shows will get on the air; in the fall of 1981, for example, the three networks placed a total of twenty new series on their schedules. At each network, one or two shows will stay on long enough to be renewed for a second season. Each filtration step, in other words, screens by a factor of five, or ten, or thirty. My task, then, was to try to understand the principles, the unwritten rules and values that govern the filters.

This is, of course, a very schematic way of describing any organization's selection process. As I began to brood over the patterns, if indeed there were any, I was struck by a different response I kept getting in interviews with network executives, producers, writers, and others in and around the industry. Often I began an interview by saying that I was trying to understand how decisions got made about what to put on the air. There was one initial response that I heard so frequently it amused me at first, and later I came to expect it. It was usually said with a smile. "If you figure it out, please let me know"; or "I've been in this business X years, and I don't understand it." Grant Tinker said it: He had been an advertising-agency executive, then an executive at NBC, the husband of a star, the head of a major production company, and subsequently chairman of the board of NBC, and here he was telling me he didn't know how the business worked. Brandon Stoddard, who was in charge of ABC's movies for TV, said it. David Rintels, who wrote *Fear on Trial, Gideon's Trumpet,* and many other shows, said, "I hope you can explain it to me."

Now, lower-level managers tended toward schematic answers about orderly processes: This, this, and this happens; then So-and-so decides such-and-such, taking into account factors X, Y, and Z. Possibly these less experienced people believed that the network organization chart was an accurate description of reality; possibly, too, they were at pains to make sure that what an interloping writer heard was the party line. Younger, brasher executives were belligerent and defensive. "If I didn't know what I was doing," one told me, "they wouldn't be paying me all the money they're paying me." But the more powerful the executives, the more prestigious or experienced the television writers, the more likely it was that they would tell me there was no pattern to television planning.

It was not the first time I had heard such answers. When I was interviewing reporters and TV news producers for an earlier book, I heard similar affirmations of innocence and puzzlement. But at

least at the higher command levels of news I often heard language
that laid claim to clarity, firm-sounding phrases referring to "objective coverage" of "newsworthy events," "news judgments" about
events that were "interesting" and "important." In the world of
television entertainment, by contrast, the higher I got, the more
likely I was to hear important people half-joke that they couldn't
explain how their business operated.

The joke, if it was a joke, was disarming, and this was possibly one
of its functions, a gesture of concealment, a way of protecting power
from prying eyes. Yet it is also the characteristic defense of professionals to deny that there is method in their decision-making. This
might seem to violate the conventional wisdom that a professional is
a person whose training imparts knowledge that the professional
systematically applies to the solution of problems; but the apparent
violation dissolves when we realize that the professional's deeper
claim to privileged status—deeper than any general knowledge—is
prowess, or wisdom, or "feel," a personal quality gained from experience and grafted onto the principles and practices of the profession,
a mystery that permits him or her to make right judgments under
difficult practical circumstances.

Still, there is an important difference between the doctor's or lawyer's claim that artistry overlays the science of his or her work, and
the network executive's profession of ignorance; for real doubt exists
about what it is a TV executive *knows*. This uncertainty is linked with
a more general uncertainty about how to proceed in a business that
offers so little firm grounding in ethics, aesthetics, or rationality. It's
as if every day the executive contemplates his smooth secretaries, his
tasteful sofas, his telephone extensions scattered about the room, the
plants that bloom in his office of perpetual spring. He absorbs the
imposing view from his corner window; "takes a meeting" with
subordinates; watches the phone messages pile up, pleased that he
is more called upon than he needs to call; sees the scripts and cassettes arrive; knows that shows are being produced, getting on the
air, getting numbers if not praise or praise if not numbers—and then
tells himself that he must know something, even if he is not quite sure
what it is he knows.

Scott Siegler, who when I interviewed him was CBS vice-president
for drama development (later head of comedy there, and later still
a development executive at Warner Brothers), speaks of an executive
pragmatism that interweaves precedent and intuition: "Because it's
a mass audience—it's an unimaginably large audience—the audience
tastes are so diffused and so general that you've got to be guessing.
You can work off precedents about what's worked on television before. You can work off whatever smattering of sociological information you gleaned from whatever sources. You can let your personal

judgments enter into it to some extent. . . . [You can ask whether] this is something that people in Georgia or Nebraska will appreciate because they'll be able to translate it into their understanding. But you never really know. And there are so many variables in programming that even when you've reached a pretty general consensus about a genre not working or a kind of attitude not working, you can never quite be sure that that rule applies." So many factors bear, imponderably, on a show's prospects: casting, "look," "feel," time slot, lead-in, competition, the network's demographics. These complications, Siegler says, are "what makes the whole thing very precise and very empirical, and at the same time totally absurd and unpredictable."

To manage the flux of possibilities, the networks breed notions about live or dead genres, doomed formats, cycles that come and go. For instance, one axiom network executives now hear, says Scott Siegler, is that "single-woman leads don't work on hour-long dramatic television. Or science fiction doesn't work on television. Or black leading men don't work on television, in the hour form. Or the variety genre is dead. There are countless axioms that you hear in programming, and I think the one thing that you begin to learn is that all those axioms really represent are precedents that have been set, but not necessarily rules that work."

Network lore is momentary. Sooner or later exceptions are the rule. For all the talk about trends, says CBS old hand Herman Keld, "I've never met anyone who knew what was going to happen two seconds from now." The axioms, in short, are flimsy, flexible, *ad hoc.* This is exactly what makes them useful as a common currency of network talk. Network executives distrust them and rely on them at the same time. They are, among other things, polite ways of telling a writer, "No thanks." Writers and producers watch their ideas get rejected in the name of axioms, but never know when the old ones might get exploded by exceptions and new ones dropped into their place. The writer David Rintels is reminded of the lore at the boarding school he went to: "There are no rules until they're broken."

In the end, TV executives are left with themselves, with their irreducible power over the airwaves. The audience's time, the commodity executives sell to advertisers, is also their enemy. The hours tick off; the schedule has to be filled. Sooner or later they have to decide what no precise formulas can decide for them. There is no articulated agreement about standards. Conventions there are aplenty, but they are matters of habit more than belief. They do not rest on firm values; they are not deeply rooted in a cultural tradition. The conventions persist, in short, by being applied, and the executive's job is precisely to keep them alive by calling up precedents. To do this, executives learn to heed the institutional voice. If they possess any distinct taste, aside from a relish for show-business glitter, they have to dispel or subdue it. To keep taste and market judgment separate is "professional."

"When your taste matters, you're finished in television," says Paul Klein, the flamboyant former programming chief at NBC. Gerald Jaffe, NBC's vice-president for research projects, stresses that television is after all only another business. "Most people do not put on television what they personally like any more than executives in Detroit make cars that they personally like, any more than movie moguls make movies they personally like." Stu Sheslow, the wise-cracking vice-president for dramatic development at NBC, a former toy-company executive, delighted in a Bruce Springsteen cassette he clicked on at the end of our interview. "Rock's what's happening," he chortled, "but put it on television and it'd get an eight share." Jonathan Axelrod, vice-president at ABC before he moved through the industry revolving door to Columbia Pictures' television division, said he sometimes developed shows he had no personal interest in seeing, but anytime he liked a show he also thought it would draw a mass audience. In effect he saw himself as an instrument of the popular will, or had transformed himself into that. This fusion is accomplished with more or less ease by different executives, but accomplish it they all must.

A taste for the slick, the sentimental, and the melodramatic is normal in America; what is illuminating is the transition to it. Stu Sheslow's friend and CBS counterpart Scott Siegler represented an outer limit of taste in television's small world. In his early thirties and looking younger, he studded his conversation with quotations from Wordsworth and other luminaries. He once won a poetry award, started on a doctorate with Marshall McLuhan, worked on antiwar and prisoners'-rights documentaries, won an Emmy for a documentary on Appalachian snake-handlers. He went to L.A. to learn about movies and make some money, won a fellowship for directing at the American Film Institute, and worked in low-budget features like many would-be filmmakers looking for the main chance—until he needed more money and landed a job at NBC's Current Drama department, where future executives are groomed. "I was approving stories, looking at dailies, working on publicity and promotion," he recalls. "I feel my personal tastes are different from the public's. The first couple of shows I was assigned to, I read scripts and I said, 'I can't believe this.' It was all abysmal. I went to Brandon Tartikoff, who was head of West Coast programming. He said, 'You're not doing feature films anymore, you're doing TV.' I said to myself, 'I don't want to be a highbrow anymore.' "

Network executives often say that their problem is simple. Their tradition, in a sense, is the search for steady profits. They want, above all, to put on the air shows best calculated to accumulate maximum reliable audiences. Maximum audiences attract maximum dollars for advertisers, and advertiser dollars are, after all, the network's objective. (Network executives recite the point so predictably, so confidently, they sound like vulgar Marxists.) Quality and explicit ideology count for very little. But to desire profits is one thing, to procure them something else. The networks' problem is how to keep accumulating those profitable audiences, to keep people coming back, to ensure that they will be a receptive audience rather than a self-determining public. In a word, the network's problem is how to get people to rely on the networks. And the solution is not obvious. All sales organizations face a certain risk, for their targets may not want the commodities being offered. As biological creatures, no one needs toothpaste, let alone Crest; automobiles, let alone Pontiacs; movies, let alone *Star Wars;* television, let alone *Dallas.* That is why all modern corporations must develop strategies to shape and mobilize effective demand. To put it this way is to realize that the networks' task is not accomplished simply by avowing the goal of profit. They are still thrown back on a problem of knowledge.

How to know which shows will work? This necessary and elusive knowledge wells up in a context: In an economy devoted to selling, programs must be aids to selling; they must be compatible with the main contours of American popular culture; and they must suit the television set, a home appliance. Nature does not decree the future tastes of the American people. Information does not arrive naked and unambiguous; the facts, the numbers, never speak for themselves. Network knowledge is learned, debated, interpreted within a world view, a more or less systematic style of thought. The networks are like other large enterprises. There is a common ethos and a defining spirit, a command structure that systematically rewards and punishes for mastering the system's rules, that imposes its own style of thought on its recruits. In the television networks, as in the other centers of what Hans Magnus Enzensberger has called "the consciousness industry," part of this style of thought is the denial of it: the insistence that each executive asserts individual taste, judgment, and sense. In journalism, in academia, in advertising, the implication is always: If there is no uniform system, then I, this unique human, am central. My power, my perks, my income, the deference talented and glamorous people pay me, are all justified. This stance is especially strong in a go-go cultural industry like TV that depends on irregular, unreliable commercial assessments of what the traffic will bear.

Over and over again, when I asked executives which factors weighed most heavily in putting shows on the air, keeping them there, shaping their content, I heard a standardized list. At the top, the appeal of actors and characters. The reliability of producers, the track records of writers. Then the mysteries: whether a concept was "special," "different," "unique," even (wonder of wonders) "very unique"; whether a show had "chemistry"; whether it "clicked"; whether "it all came together." Such terms cannot be pinned down, and that is precisely their utility. They preserve the sense that executives, with their unique talents and experience, are necessary.

In the interstices of the same interviews, I often heard another theme: This show was bought because X loved it, that one got dumped because Y hated it. It is, after all, a subjective business, as virtually every executive grants. Part of what happens in the command centers of the television industry is that network executives satisfy each other, and themselves, that their subjectivity is the right kind.

Each layer in the hierarchy has the power to say no—to a proposal for a show, a script, a pilot. Only the top layer, the programmers who meet every year to revise the schedule, have the authority to say yes. This helps make Hollywood, in the words of the writer-producer Richard Levinson, "the land of the slow no." The suppliers keep busy cranking out scripts that will not get produced and making pilots that will never go to series. In this buyer's market, the sellers stay tense but ever eager, ever on tap, ever ready to translate a network notion into a potential gold mine. The slow no, combined with the lure of the possible yes, keeps the sellers organized and primed, producing an oversupply of potential shows. Before anything else, producing television entertainment is the business of satisfying executives who have to satisfy other executives—all with opinions about the opinions of a mass market. There are a lot of opinions at issue: a minefield of them.

Corporations typically evolve from entrepreneurship to bureaucracy. Defenders of this presumably iron law say that in principle what is lost in the founders' brilliance and sharpness of purpose is more than compensated for by a gain in knowledge. Hence, the multiplication of bureaucratic layers and the growth of scientific management have proceeded hand in hand. Like other giant marketing combines, the networks have come to rely on hard knowledge: the data that come from program testing, the performance of precedents, social research on popular moods, and most of all, once a show gets on the air, its performance as measured by the Nielsen ratings. In defensive and belligerent moods, executives claim the warrant of science. Yet most of them also acknowledge the limits of their data. They know that, for all their calculations, most new shows will fail to rate high enough to last into a second season. Knowing the limits, paradoxically, makes them feel knowing. Science has not triumphed. Instinct still counts for something in this unpredictable business. The premium stays on imponderables: an air of knowing-ness, or some ineffable quality of the person—like Fred Silverman's famous "gut"—that enables him to divine a show's chances.

There is a premium on this sort of knowingness in an industry whose business it is to cater to diffuse desires. What exactly will people "want to watch"? The movie mogul Samuel Goldwyn once pointed out that, after all, nothing could stop people from not going to the movies. And however habit-forming television is, nothing can stop a sufficiently decisive viewer from changing channels, even turning off the set. The problem, then, is how to paralyze the will of that potentially decisive viewer; or, to put it more positively, how to keep him or her sufficiently satisfied. Though there are scientific trappings to the testing process, most network "knowledge" is of the improvised, seat-of-the-pants variety.

For one thing, the networks fall back on certain traditional genres and styles that predate giant corporations, broadcasting, and the culture of consumer capitalism in general. What these do share with modern TV culture is the search for immediate effects. The variety format, for example, descends from popular vaudeville and club acts. The once thriving though now defunct western descends from the popular dime novels of the middle and late nineteenth century, which in turn continued the earlier convention of the American myth of the hunter-hero. The police drama descends from another nineteenth-century genre, the crime-solving puzzles of Edgar Allan Poe. Melodrama, with its inflated sentiments and simplified moral-ism on an ordinary human scale, is rooted in the very beginnings of the Anglo-European novel in the late eighteenth century, and con-tinues one of the major Western theatrical traditions. Alexis de Tocqueville would have no trouble recognizing most of the conven-tions of American television today from his survey of our popular literature, theater, and oratory a century and a half ago. "Democratic nations," he wrote in the 1830s, "cultivate the arts that serve to render life easy in preference to those whose object is to adorn it. . . . [T]he democratic principle not only tends to direct the human mind to the useful arts, but it induces the artisan to produce with great rapidity many imperfect commodities, and the consumer to content himself with these commodities. . . . [These works] substitute the representation of motion and sensation for that of sentiment and thought. . . . Style will frequently be fantastic, incorrect, overbur-dened, and loose, almost always vehement and bold. Authors will aim at rapidity of execution more than at perfection of detail. . . . There will be more wit than erudition, more imagination than profundity; and literary performances will bear marks of an untutored and rude vigor of thought, frequently of great variety and singular fecundity. The object of authors will be to astonish rather than to please, and to stir the passions more than to charm the taste."

American culture has been devoted to convenience and quick results from the start. Ironically, the victory of American-style entertainment not only at home but abroad stems from the Puritan origins of American culture. A culture founded in defiance of ornament became the crucible of show business. The key was the American passion for utility. Tocqueville already observed that Americans' "strictly Puritanical origin, their exclusively commercial habits, even the country they inhabit, which seems to divert their minds from the pursuit of science, literature, and the arts, the proximity of Europe, which allows them to neglect these pursuits without relapsing into barbarism, a thousand special causes . . . have singularly concurred to fix the mind of the American upon purely practical objects."

The entertainment tradition sprang up everywhere the populace found occasion to celebrate its release from the burdens and repressions of everyday life. But in America the taste for brisk and efficient pleasures swept through the culture with particular vigor. The open space of the market, and the absence of countertradition, made it particularly easy for cultural commodities to flourish, satisfying certain desires while generating new ones that would require new commodities. Cultural commodities, like most others, became supermarket goods. (It should not be surprising that in network lingo one standard superlative for a show is "the greatest thing since sliced bread.") Organized play becomes a rationale, a prop, a compensation, even a mirror for organized work. But in this protracted process, America only leads a larger modern tendency. Practical, processed culture everywhere aims to create easy pleasures. It is *show* business. It pays most attention to the prospects for applause, least to the internal proportions of form.

Writing before the onset of television, Hermann Broch argued that all kitsch—all synthetic, imitative cultural trash—is precisely the product of this straining for predictable effect. Impatience leads to the use of prefabricated expressions, simplemindedness, and imitations of all sorts. For Broch, the root problem was Romanticism: "Romanticism," he argued, "without being kitsch itself, is the mother of kitsch"; it led to a straining after beauty and presumably pure sentiment. Romanticism was a revolt against Enlightenment skepticism and capitalist rationality, but it was processed into a quest for practical effect. In the dime novel, the Gothic, or the sentimental romance, the writer's goal is simply tears, thrills, and laughs. Practical Romanticism is our tradition, which is why the characteristic flaw of our popular culture is sentimentality.

On this foundation the mass-cultural corporations of the twentieth century have reared their assembly lines and their fortunes. Competition among this handful has only solidified a culture already predisposed toward blunt effects. When in the 1950s television became a living-room habit, the networks could take for granted that their total audience would go on growing; if any show in a given genre was an uncertain prospect, the market would sit still for the network's next choice. Oligopolistic pressure drove the three networks (and their occasional rivals) to compete, largely, for the same vast audience within the same landscape of cultural reference points. Only their means varied. America, unlike the European capitalist democracies, lacked even a cultural reservation, an institutional home (like the BBC or a national theater) for a segment of popular culture empowered to owe allegiance to standards beyond the marketplace. Whenever, in America, educational purposes have been proposed to be as legitimate as entertainment, private capital has mobilized to beat the alternatives back.

Network executives have come to breathe these conditions with utter assurance. They take the entertainment conventions for granted without knowing their histories well; their knowledge is a shallow, aphoristic lore, including a ready-made outline of the requirements of popular entertainment: Heroes should be agreeable, villains clear, "jeopardy" definite, outcomes pleasing, story lines simple, climaxes frequent, jokes flagrant.

If most genres and formulas are rooted in tradition, some are more recent; for background assumptions are one thing and here-and-now television quite another. Executives know that genres become exhausted, as did the western, or seem unsuited to the small screen, like science fiction. New genres spring up, like the situation comedy, descendant of radio, which in turn drew on vaudeville sketches. Sitcoms, with their incessant skein of personal problems in a family-like setting, seem peculiarly tailored to the small screen, to its living-room locations, and to advertisers' desire for captive audiences whose commercials must be studded, like gems, in suitable settings.

But genres and traditions do not decide to buy new programs; executives do. If we think of popular taste as a liquid brew of conventional expectations, themes, and desires, held in suspension, then we may think of actual television programs as solid precipitates that suppliers and executives adapt and shape. (The suppliers—producers and studios—store old materials and devise new ones, but their resources are decisively limited by their sense of what the networks are buying.) What does this audience "want," they ask? The mass audience may be, say, at once alarmed about crime and admiring of stylish folk who violate the law with impunity. Executives may decide to cater to the former with a show about a high-speed, high-powered tactical police unit, or to the latter with a comedy about good ole boys who break the driving laws in the course of catching real crooks despite the incompetence and corruption of the local police. Both formulas have gotten on the air in recent years. The first, *Strike Force,* was a one-season failure; the second, *The Dukes of Hazzard,* a multiyear hit. The point is that both choices were defensible, indeed defended, with arguments about public sentiment. Other possible themes were also held in suspension, but didn't precipitate out because the executives didn't take a chance on them.

Once these precipitates form, a mass audience recognizes some of them as conforming to the contours of their desires. In that sense, only after the fact, the executives are half entitled to say that they are "giving people what they want." Another large mass of viewers might have wanted something else, but this particular mass is satisfied to want, or at least to tolerate, what they are getting, from among the possibilities that slipped out of suspension. Some shows become hits, and hits further solidify the conventions of the medium —for as long as they remain hits, and then a while longer. Through this sequence of development, selection, airing, and restricted audience "choice," conventions and conventional wisdom become enshrined. The genres that matter are television genres; the precedents adduced are largely television's own. The result is that popular television has formed its own history—though not in conditions entirely of its own making. While music, magazines, books, fashions, and radio, with their multiple distribution channels and relatively low production costs per unit, can become the fetishes, pleasures, and identity badges of specific publics and subcultures, high-cost television with its vast profits automatically caters to a hypothetical least common denominator—or dips below it. It is a cultural center without vitality, constantly changing in order to keep its purpose constant, pervading the national cultural space as has no other medium in the history of popular culture. Its style becomes ritualized because executives keep it that way and at the same time because its public expects television to look the way thirty years of commercial history have made it. Television pervades, usurps, lords it over the national cultural space. And therefore, increasingly, the tradition television belongs to is itself.

CHAPTER 2

Predicting the Unpredictable

"I'm not interested in culture. I'm not interested in pro-social values. I have only one interest. That's whether people watch the program. That's my definition of good, that's my definition of bad," says Arnold Becker, CBS's puckish vice-president for television research. If there is a network logic, its task must be to implement Becker's principle in the face of the uncertainty that dominates both the producing and receiving ends of business. At the programming end, there is a glut of products and decision-making is hectic, so much so that executives warned me the very term was too streamlined, implied too orderly a process. At the consumption end, the great majority of new shows will disappoint the network's commercial expectations; they'll run one season or less, then be plucked off the air. For however passive, deadened, habit-formed the hypothetical audience may be, the fact remains that they do not have to turn the dial to a certain spot at a certain hour on a certain evening.

This pyramid of uncertainty produces a paradox: The networks place a premium on rationality, searching for seemingly systematic, impersonal, reliable ways to predict success and failure. Like any industry that seeks to tap and shape the vagaries of public taste and tolerance, to mitigate uncertainty they institutionalize their quest. Like the marketers of Zest soap, Kent III cigarettes, and Rice-a-Roni

—indeed the thirteen-hundred-odd new consumer products American business introduces each year—they test their new lines of goods
before the investment goes too far.

There is a big difference, though. Manufacturers of soap can try out
a new brand in a test market with minimal capital investment. But
the networks have only a single national market whose medium,
time, is irreplaceable. Moreover, it will cost the network as much to
underwrite a series that thirty people watch as one that thirty million
watch. In 1982, hour-long episodes cost upward of $650,000, and
pilots can run more than twice as much. These are not investments
lightly undertaken. Therefore, the networks have created artificial
test markets in hothouse settings where audience reactions can be
cheaply reduced to numerical measures that they hope might predict the eventual ratings.

Numbers to predict numbers: This is the logic of rationalization.
Audiences accustomed to a certain style of television assess new
products in the old light. The conventions themselves are taken for
granted. That this system may be self-fulfilling does not bother its
advocates, since their job is to minimize risks. The old movie studios
also used audience surveys—still use them, in fact, to tune up a final
cut—but the networks have been far more systematic in deploying
the techniques of quantitative social science to try to predict the
unpredictable. It was indeed a social scientist turned network executive, Dr. Frank Stanton, who in his earliest years at CBS introduced
the first machinery for measuring audience reactions to radio: the
Stanton-Lazarsfeld Program Analyzer, still the basis of CBS's in-house
television testing system. The other networks contract their tests to an
outside company. To grasp and evaluate the logic of testing, we should
inspect their procedures one at a time. The networks' claim to have
transcended the whims of intuition rests heavily on these rituals.
Since CBS is the pioneer, and has gone to the greatest lengths to justify
its tests, the CBS system deserves the closest scrutiny.

CBS

Walk through Farmers Market in Los Angeles or Rockefeller Center
in New York in the early spring and you are likely to see a cheerful
youth passing out tickets for a free screening of a television program
at nearby CBS headquarters. The point is to net tourists, deemed a
more representative national sample than everyday Angelenos or
New Yorkers. But anyone except bag ladies and drunks can get
tickets.

Willing subjects are ushered into a screening room where they are
seated around a conference table. A taped introductory lecture says

that you now have a chance to talk back to the television set; producers want to know what you think. Each seat is equipped with two buttons. You hold the green in your right hand; if you like what you see, you press it. In your left hand, the red is to be pressed if you don't want to see more. If you are indifferent, you press neither.

A series pilot—or an episode in a series being fixed—is shown on a TV monitor while behind-the-scenes equipment records the responses. At the end, questionnaires are passed out: Did you like characters A and B? Did you like the setting? If this show were programmed against the X show, would you watch X or the show just seen? CBS asks open-ended questions as well, but the research department is less concerned with them. CBS recruits groups of willing subjects until they have reached a prearranged quota: eighty to one hundred respondents per pilot. Unbeknownst to the recruits, not all responses will be counted, only those needed to fill the requisite demographic categories of age and education.

Every pilot is tested, and some 80 percent of all series sell through pilots. (The remainder get on the air through special commitments to producers, actors, or production companies.) Similar tests are used to tinker with shows already on the schedule or to fix the new and failing. After a few years of its run, for example, the producers of M*A*S*H tried to convince CBS to drop the show's laugh track, which they thought distracting. Testing showed that the same show scored higher with the track than without it, so the track stayed.*

The methods that can wield such influence are standard market-research techniques: electric signals from buttons; questionnaires; sometimes focus groups, discussions meant to unearth feelings and attitudes about a show. (Focus groups are said to be a superior way to tap the opinions of people with grade-school educations, whose questionnaire answers are rudimentary.) The results from all three methods are then summarized by three staff members, two in New York, one in Los Angeles; their distillations, adorned with selected quotations, are passed on to a junior executive in charge of testing in Los Angeles (in 1981, Bob Brilliant), who in turn writes a report to be passed on to Arnold Becker, who in turn passes it on, without much change, to the top programming executives and the heads of the relevant development divisions.

CBS research people are fully cognizant that their sample is too small for statistically significant results. They plead the press of time. So many pilots arrive within a few weeks, needing to be tested in a

---

*In British syndication, though, M*A*S*H plays on the BBC without the laugh track. Americans more than the British seem to require social cues to confirm what is comical.

hurry for the spring scheduling meeting. More than one pilot a day
has to be tested; hence, there is no time to gather larger samples.
Frank Stanton acknowledges, "It's awfully difficult, in the hurly-
burly and pressures of production, to introduce much in the way of
statistical controls and evaluations. Sure enough it can be done after
the fact, but then you're so busy getting on with the next program
that you don't go back and do it."

"I know my sample isn't so great," the genial Arnold Becker told
me. "I know I get a sample of visitors to big cities, L.A. and New York.
But because I use a quota system, I get the right representation of
age and education. Those are the most important things." The demographic quotas were never updated, he said, though the population
has grown older and more educated, but Becker was unfazed: "I
don't care. The system has worked, so why change it?"

CBS research people claim that their pilot testing system is "85
percent accurate," by which they mean something very specific.
Each spring the pilots are tested, then grouped into Below Average,
Average, and Above Average. Then, the following spring, all CBS
series on the air are grouped according to Nielsen audience ratings
—also classified Below Average, Average, and Above Average. CBS
research claims that shows that test Average and Above Average,
and then get on the air, will rank Average or Above Average more
than 85 percent of the time, while shows that test Below Average and
still get on the air will rank Below Average more than 85 percent of
the time.* Using these definitions, here are CBS's figures for the years
1957–80 taken together:

Accuracy of Test 1957–1980	Average and Above-Average Test Scores	Below-Average Test Scores	Total
Correct call	81 (80%)	176 (91%)	257 (87%)
Incorrect call	20 (20%)	17 (9%)	37 (13%)
Total	101	193	294

Source: CBS National Television Research, April 1981

*To make the numbers large enough to talk about, CBS has grouped its figures for
Average and Above Average into a single category. Only about one show a year tests
Above Average.

In other words, of the 101 shows that tested Average and Above Average during these twenty-three years and then got on the air, 81, or 80 percent, ranked Average and Above Average among CBS shows that season, while of the 193 shows that tested Below Average and got on the air anyway, a full 176, or 91 percent, rated Below Average as predicted.

If it be wondered why almost twice as many shows testing Below Average than shows that tested Average or better got on the air— more than eight per season—the answer is that there were simply not enough high-testing shows to add to the schedule to replace shows seen as fading or kaput. "We expect them to fail," Becker says, "There are good business reasons, perhaps, for them getting on the air. Like you don't want to admit that you know they're no good. . . . You've got a show with a twenty-seven–share audience [i.e., about average] that's been on the air. And everybody knows it got a twenty-seven–share audience. They would rather take a chance on a new-comer, even though the odds are that the newcomer's going to do less than a twenty-seven share. So that's part of it. Part of it is the feeling that . . . maybe they'll get lucky this time. And part of it is just the antipathy toward the research: 'Who the hell are they to tell me it's no good, when I know it's good, and my friend likes it and my wife likes it?' "

Research executives enthusiastically defend their record, then, but acknowledge one major flaw in the testing system: Embarrassingly, a major hit once nearly slipped through their fingers. That case in point, *All in the Family,* is cited by virtually every producer who loathes program testing. Becker explains that pioneering shows defy the expectations of test audiences, and therefore test badly. Raw data always have to be interpreted. Knowing this, the testing reports sometimes weasel.

All in the Family tested Below Average. The 1970 CBS report on the *All in the Family* pilot was shrewd enough to hedge its predic-tion of failure with a recognition of one possible flaw in the test. The test subjects are onstage, after all, and they know it. They inhabit a social situation in which they may well wish to appear more enlight-ened—or what they think the testers will construe as more enlight-ened—than they are. Since the flaw is a more general one—research executives call it "social bias" and are always on the lookout for it— I quote the key paragraph of the CBS report on *All in the Family* in full:

As you know, the level of past program analysis predictions is 84%. We have noticed a pattern of similarity among those pro-grams for which we predict failure which then succeed on the air. We believe that many viewers were ashamed to admit, in the test situation, to enjoying certain programs and their characters. We think that when a person's real attitudes conflict with what he believes to be socially proper and desirable, he may express only the latter opinion. Because the main character in *Those Were the Days* [the original title] expressed views which are not socially desirable, viewers might feel required to criticize him, even if deep down they identify with him. It is for this reason that we are somewhat less sure of our prediction for this program than is usually the case, and caution you that although we think it unlikely, this program may be a worthwhile entry.

It happened that *All in the Family* got on the air because CBS president Robert D. Wood was taken with its potential for tapping the youth and urban market. Otherwise, we would not know or care how badly it originally tested. (Nor, of course, do we know what other potential hits never had the chance to refute their low test scores.) But a conspicuous error like *All in the Family* damages testing's authority. Research's prestige suffers when the network comes close to losing the sales of a potential smash, even if on balance testing actually does the sort of job of predicting that the networks want. Moreover, when researchers argue that tests are accurate, the fact that 20 percent of new shows get on the air without pilots also tends to drop from sight. Even testing's most fervent proponents discreetly acknowledge that testing is chancy. "This thing is not a scientific test. This is more an art form than a science," says Becker.

Such "realism" justifies the myriad little acts of interpretation that take place in the reporting of test results. Mitch Tuchman, who wrote the L.A. reports revised by Bob Brilliant on their way to Arnold Becker, told me that Brilliant's memos usually argued for clear-cut victims and villains, and he thought Brilliant sometimes looked for material to bear out his hunches about a show's weakness. Intuition can't be expelled from the decision-making process, even from the part of it that seems most firmly objective. "The judgment of the person who's head of testing really plays a major role," says Arnold Becker. Hunches, idiosyncratic choices, and conventions operate all the way up and down the network line.

ABC AND PREVIEW HOUSE

Everyone has heard of Preview House, which fairly begs for wisecracks if it does not already seem to be parodying itself. ABC contracts the bulk of its testing, as NBC once did, to this enterprise located, with mythic aptness, on Sunset Boulevard, though on neither its celebrated high-rent Strip nor its Beverly Hills mansion row. The original Preview House was founded in 1960 by Columbia Pictures, whose president Harry Cohn once boasted, "When I'm alone in a projection room I have a foolproof device for judging whether a picture is good or bad. If my fanny squirms, it's bad. If my fanny doesn't squirm, it's good." But the television age seemed to demand a more reliable barometer of the public taste, and Columbia's research arm quickly began to take on outside clients, including MGM and ABC. In 1972 the entire operation went independent, and the privately owned company Audience Studies Incorporated, or ASI, now operates not only the Preview House theater but market-research facilities around the world. ASI's major business is the testing of commercials, but it handles the bulk of ABC and NBC program tests: ABC's through Preview House, NBC's over unused cable channels.

Preview House follows CBS's program-testing principles, but instead of a conference room with TV monitors it operates a 400-seat theater with a full-size theatrical screen. Each seat comes equipped with a five-position switch: Very Dull, Dull, Fair, Good, and Very Good. ASI, like CBS, distributes some tickets on the streets—in shopping malls, at the Universal Studios tour, and in other places frequented by tourists. Unlike CBS, it also contacts prospective subjects by phone. The company knows that its test audiences are probably biased toward the lower- to lower-middle classes, people more interested in television, more likely to be lured by an evening of free entertainment, and less likely to be repelled by Preview House's dingy neighborhood. Therefore, ASI makes special efforts to attract viewers from the middle- and upper-middle-class precincts of the West Side of Los Angeles, especially males thirty-five and over, regarded as the hardest to lure out of the house at night.

Preview House questionnaires are far more intricate than CBS's, probing not only demographic facts but a variety of consumption habits and personal characteristics. (For example: "Do you consider yourself to be . . . a) a heavy perspirer, b) a medium perspirer, c) a light perspirer.") Subjects have been notified that they will be seeing television programs, and do not yet know that much if not most of their evening's entertainment will consist of commercials. Again, unbeknownst to the audience, the testers screen their population; only 150 out of 400 subjects—chosen to represent the total viewing population by age and sex—will have their responses pooled.

In order to adjust the raw data for a given night's audience, ASI from the beginning has used a single standard to gauge its "temperature." This is the famous cartoon *Mr. Magoo Goes Skiing*; ASI possesses vast repositories of data on audience responses to *Mr. Magoo Goes Skiing*, and can thus calibrate the evening's audience, hot or cold, against the average. Once calibrated, the collective judgment will be aligned on a scale of 1 to 1,000 and traced out on a fever chart of taste resembling a cardiogram. In a week's time, network executives and producers, if they wish (they usually don't), can look at the chart and tell precisely when in the show the audience signaled its aggregated peaks and valleys of sentiment. Then there are more questionnaires: Did you like the show? Do you want to see it as a series? Would you watch it against this and that competition? In the course of the evening there will also be mock shopping expeditions to test new products and their packages.

Preview House is a setup for easy criticism. For one thing, the sample is skewed toward the lower-middle classes and away from both the more and the less educated. At least on the night I attended, blacks and Hispanics were noticeably underrepresented. Second, the subjects are watching in the knowledge that their twists of the dial will be scrutinized. They are not simply viewers but judges, and they know they are judges. Conceivably they laud shows they think they ought to be lauding. Third, the order in which a show is screened may affect the results. In the course of several hours the Preview House audience is often exposed to a series of commercials and old pilots, not to mention at least one new pilot during pilot season; by late in the evening a weary audience may be hard to thrill. Fourth, because Preview House is a large theater, the subjects may be overinfluenced by the rest of the audience, a kind of audible chorus. Comedy might be particularly hard to rate: Since laughter is infectious, comedies at Preview House might bring out not simply what people find funny, but what they think other people find funny.

Industry scuttlebutt has it that small children, dogs, and easy gags send the needles soaring.* Sexual innuendo sends them plummeting —"social bias" again—although the same double entendres that test dismally may rate just fine on the air when the format is right, as in ABC's long-running hit *Three's Company.* Shows seen as "heartwarming" may rate high, like ABC's *Breaking Away,* and yet the series may not hold up. The mass audience doesn't usually want to have its collective heart warmed week after week.

By now the networks have accumulated much lore about the shortcomings of their tests. Programming executives like the comfort of hard numbers, but some research execs know that the evidence is soft, and downplay the actual test data. "My background is statistics and methodology," says Ellen Franklin, who was in charge of interpreting ABC's tests in 1981. "I don't want to apply what I know from

---

*Richard M. Levine reports: "The original pilot of *Happy Days* . . . contained eight jokes and sight gags in the main title alone, all deliberately put there by the studio to start the needle off at a high level."

statistics and methodology to that sample in Preview House, because it's nothing. It's four hundred bodies, that's all it is. I don't want to start with any kind of assumptions about generalizing to the population." By the time the numbers have been broken down to sub-categories in the search for explanations of this rise or that fall, they slip beneath the threshold of statistical significance. So Franklin says, "I really play down the quantitative aspects of the data." During her two years of reporting to programming execs in L.A. she paid more attention to the rough contours of the ASI curves; a jagged curve, for example, signifies an audience paying too much attention to particular gags, and thus a show whose essential situation and characters would probably fail to appeal week after week. "The network judges the show based on involvement with the characters, because that's what makes a hit show." For Franklin, the important thing was the open-ended questions. "You learn how to read their comments. You learn how to read, for example, that when they say, 'I didn't like the set, the room was ugly,' what it means is, 'I wasn't involved enough in the characters. I spent my time staring at the set.'"

ABC, like CBS, researches every marketable attribute of a show: pilots,* continuations, concepts, stars, titles. They test episodes of on-air series; Ellen Franklin calls it "diagnostic upkeep work." A show, in other words, is a machine whose parts wear out. Its use lies entirely in its marketability; why not let testing diagnose the faulty elements? In early 1981, for example, the sitcom *Bosom Buddies* tested very high for gags, but episodes tested low when the heroes —two men living in a women's residence hotel—dressed in drag; so ABC pushed the producers to hold down the drag and play up the men's up-against-the-world-together friendliness. In the same spirit ABC used Preview House to cast new Angels for Charlie, and to replace Suzanne Somers when she left *Three's Company* in a contract dispute. ABC also uses its own national telephone surveys to tune up sputtering series. How did viewers feel about Laverne and Shirley, about their move to California, their jobs? Should Laverne get married? (No.) Should Mork and Mindy get married? (Yes.) And how would the audience feel about their having a child? (Okay.) About Mork giving birth? (Okay.) About the return to the planet Ork? (Okay.) None of the changes that followed saved the series. ABC originally ordered a serial under the name *Oil*, but a phone-survey title test rated *Dynasty* higher.** Moreover, once a year, just

---

*In the spring of 1980, ABC tested twenty-one pilots in twenty days at Preview House. In their rush to judgment, the networks may test even rough cuts.
**Oil* was last of eight titles, and *Dynasty* only third to last. *Mile High* ranked highest, but the producers rejected it. The show belonged to Aaron Spelling, who normally paid close attention to ASI research, yet had the clout to brush it aside.

after the schedule is announced, ABC research executives meet with willing suppliers—Spelling/Goldberg, Garry Marshall, and Paramount Studios, among others—to convey the benefits of their research.

Ellen Franklin hadn't quantified ASI's success rate with pilots, although she had no doubt that "a poorly testing show is almost always a flop." No apologist for ASI, she thought the system would work better, in its own terms, if Preview House were located in the suburbs, or in Las Vegas, or anywhere else that a better cross-section of tourists congregates. But even as it is, she thought the system worked well enough, fast enough, inexpensively enough to justify its use.* Wasn't a test result in need of interpretation, with a statistically insignificant sample, better than no test result at all?

NBC AND CABLE TESTING

Since the early seventies NBC, too, has contracted its tests to ASI, but in recent years has left Preview House behind and bought a different methodology. For NBC, ASI rents unused cable channels in areas highly saturated by cable and in which, therefore, cable subscribers should be representative of the economic class level of the entire community. The night before, ASI staff call about 125 cable subscribers in four parts of the country, "more or less at random," according to NBC research vice-president Al Ordover, to tell them that a new show is going to air, unadvertised, at a certain time. Just after the show, a phone interviewer calls to ask how these people liked the show; how they liked the major characters; whether they found them "believable," "intelligent," etc.; whether they would watch the show if it were broadcast against specified competition. The results are broken down by sex, age, and income.** NBC holds that viewing conditions during the cable test closely resemble actual viewing conditions, and therefore that cable testing results are more reliable than the results garnered at Preview House. ABC's Ellen Franklin acknowledges this advantage, but points out that NBC's viewers could walk away from their sets in the middle of the shows and still answer the questions.

---

*In 1978, according to Richard M. Levine, the network paid a mere $2,000 to test each pilot.

**Ordover said the income figures aren't referred to during scheduling meetings, but might be used later to help sell a show to particular advertisers, or to help decide on renewal. NBC, lowest in the ratings, likes to emphasize the "quality"—i.e., income—of its smaller numbers.

These are small differences. The common spirit of program testing pervades all three networks, even if they pursue the same ends by rival means. Distinctive techniques help them satisfy their need to feel like distinctive enterprises.

CONCEPT TESTING

Before undertaking major investments, the networks will also test the concepts of both TV-movie and series ideas. Of course, if top management wants to make a movie, they don't even bother testing the concept. They will have tested it, in effect, by liking it. Conversely, development executives often don't bother testing concepts they don't believe can work in the first place. The executive is still the gatekeeper of first and last resort. But if intuition falters and no self-evident star rises above the horizon, or if development executives disagree among themselves, the research departments go into action.

Again, the methodologies vary slightly, but the essential approach is the same at all three networks. ABC uses thirty- to fifty-word paragraphs describing a potential movie, and shows them to passersby at shopping centers. The idea is to simulate what Ellen Franklin, like other executives, calls "the one-sentence description in *TV Guide.*" Franklin thinks it obvious that concept testing is skewed against the controversial. "I got a call a couple of months ago: 'We want to do a movie about the two homosexual boys who sued their high school who wouldn't let them go together to the high-school prom. We want to test that and see if there's any appeal for that as a movie.' I said, 'Don't test that. A concept test is never going to be able to tell you whether or not that movie is going to make it. There's no way you're going to be able to write that concept. The word *gay*, the word *homosexual*, flags it. People won't even read beyond that word.' There's no way to test that concept because the appeal in that movie is going to be in the stars and the execution. On the other hand, if you want to see a movie about the inside stories of the people who were involved in the MGM Grand fire, that's a perfect concept movie. "

Programming executives are not helpless in the face of such research. If top executives want to make a movie, they know how to write concept tests to get affirmative results. And strong concept tests are still no guarantee that a movie will get made. Ever since NBC's *King* in 1978 rated much lower on the air than it concept-tested, the idea of "social bias" has worked against any TV-movie concept deemed too high-toned—the theory being that test subjects want to see themselves, and be seen, as the kind of people who would watch a miniseries about Martin Luther King. Even at a time when executives think public interest is shifting away from political engagement and toward escape, Ellen Franklin told me the highest-testing concept ABC tried out between 1979 and 1981 was based on the story of Don Bolles, the Arizona reporter killed because of his investigative reporting of the rackets. (The second highest-testing concept was the story of the early years of Frank Sinatra.) Management dropped the Bolles project nevertheless.

CBS, which has normally relied on the paragraph-survey method, too, for several years beginning in 1977 contracted with a London-based company called TAPE Ltd., an organization that, in the words of research executive Philip Luttinger, "has developed a relationship between the elements of a made-for-TV movie and the audience that the movie is able to attract when it's on the air." Extrapolating from the elements that made up high-rated and low-rated movies since the mid-sixties, TAPE assigned number values to the main elements: characterizations, genre, locale, stars, humor, sex, violence, etc.—and, to CBS's subsequent embarrassment, the ethnicity of the heroes. Leaked to the press, the TAPE formula concluded that scores were "reduced if any of the central characters are other than white American," although black Americans were preferable to Englishmen and Australians. World War II was an auspicious setting, a desert island an auspicious locale, and "someone with a superior intellect who can outwit somebody without even soiling his hands" a negative factor. A TAPE sales representative told the *Los Angeles Times* that ratings proved that if the network wanted to reach "a mass audience, then they need to take into consideration the fact that the mass audience is a white audience . . . and prefers to see a white person in that central rôle." CBS's Philip Luttinger told me that a high TAPE score predicted a 10 to 15 percent larger audience than a low score. No matter. The bad publicity outweighed TAPE's predictive value. With a leak imminent, the top management of the CBS Broadcast Group canceled the TAPE contract forthwith in 1982.

TALE OF A TOOL

Testing, with the rest of research, has a mixed reputation at the networks, but on the whole, as operations have become rationalized and bureaucratic, the star of research has risen. Although testing has a less savory reputation than Nielsen ratings, research in general has garnered considerable prestige, and people who specialize in gathering and evaluating the numbers have climbed high in the hierarchies. Top executives may sniff at testing, but they keep their numbers at hand.

Most prominently, Frank Stanton rose from research to twenty-five years as president—number-two man—of the vast operations of CBS, Inc. Stanton's career established that research could be converted to executive power. All by himself Stanton embodied the postwar legitimacy, indeed the necessity, of facts-and-figures research in the culture industry. In CBS programming, Harvey Shephard rose from manager (the lowest-ranking junior executive in any network division) of Audience Measurement to head of prime-time programming, number-two man in the Entertainment division. At ABC, Fred Pierce, president of ABC Television, rose from the position of research analyst. Paul Klein moved from research at the BBD&O ad agency to research head at NBC, thence to the top programming job at the network from 1976 to 1979, when he was dislodged by Fred Silverman, himself a devotee of the numbers. Marvin Antonowsky also went from research to programming at NBC, then to a top position at Columbia Pictures.

These executives were able to convert the hard currency of numbers into a reputation for the right decisions, or at least the right way of going about decisions. Top research executives participate in the annual programming meetings, where they have a chance to shine. They *know* something. Now, alongside the old instinct for showmanship, there flourishes a new flair for numbers—not only a preoccupation with numbers themselves, but a sense of which numbers to count, when and how to deploy them, how far to trust them, how to match them up against other numbers. A flair for numbers became the new intuition.

So the language of numbers has become the language of first and last resort, the prime language in which the networks carry out their business. Yet testing often comes in for high-level scorn. Despite research executive Phil Luttinger's claim to the contrary, Steve Mills, the CBS vice-president for movies, maintained that movies that had concept-tested low via TAPE did just as well on the air as movies that had concept-tested high. "Research is a very imprecise instrument," he said, "and it should be used as a tool and a guide and not a be-all and end-all." As for CBS research's claim of 85 percent reliability in series testing, Mills snorted. The hit series *Hawaii Five-O* concept-tested "so badly they didn't make the pilot," he maintained. "If forty series go on the air and you predict failure for all forty, you're going to be seventy-five to eighty-five percent accurate."

Bob Wood, the bluff former CBS president who put *All in the Family* on the air despite bad tests, told me he had always looked at test results but never paid them much heed: "I read the reports, but I figured they should get a certain weight of importance of five percent of your thinking, or six percent, or something like that. I always felt that if you rely too heavily on testing, you were substitut-ing [for] your own intuition, your own instincts, your own experi-ence. I have more confidence in my own points of view about what broadcasting should do than people who are brought in off the streets, who come from other fields." Ellen Franklin said that when she arrived at ABC's West Coast headquarters, "research was not held in terribly high regard here, and a lot of my job has been politicking and soft-pedaling some of the stuff to get it to be looked at a little bit more favorably." "We give [testing] some credence," says Bud Grant, president of CBS Entertainment. "We don't really give it a tremendous amount."

Again and again, network executives say that testing is "a tool"; "a valuable index," according to Tom Werner, then in charge of prime-time programming at ABC, "which should take a back seat to in-stincts." The executives know that the results are imprecise, the samples limited, the scores manipulable, the counterexamples im-portant, the conclusions hedged. In particular, they know that a series can't be judged by its pilot, although the pilot is the only evidence they have in hand. That is why the research reports empha-size the "structural elements"—characters, relationships, settings, suitability for a long-running series.* In the end, even the testing people are forced back to modest claims. "Most programs fail," Bob Brilliant grants. "It's a matter of increasing the odds."

The tool has its uses. When it confirms what some executives al-ready think, the test amounts to an argument with a special aura, conferring the gloss of facts and figures on hunches and guesses. As Harold Wilensky points out about executives in general, "They throw in their 'research' staff ritualistically, much as a tribal leader, embark-ing on a war, calls on the shaman for supporting incantation." There-fore, the test results seem to matter most when opinion is divided. If all or almost all the top CBS executives think a show should or should not go on, says longtime programming vice-president Her-man Keld, then a dissenting test wouldn't weigh against the consen-sus.

ABC Entertainment president Tony Thomopoulos says he would use tests to check his own reactions, to sway his own opinion, in a sense. He is "a little jaded about Preview House," because producers

---

*Arnold Becker says that in 1980–81 only one high-testing pilot engendered a low-rating show. This was *Enos*, a *Dukes of Hazzard* spin-off. Genially acknowledging that his reasoning was strictly post hoc, Becker argues that the pilot wasn't representative: "In the *Enos* pilot, he was a Gomer Pyle kind of character. He was sweet and innocent, and the reason he succeeded was because of his sheer goodness. That's not how he's appearing on the screen."

know how to jazz up the audience dial-twisting with an exciting opening scene. If he thought a pilot was good, and it tested low, he would have it retested at Preview House, or better still, check it against another company's test. (To double-check, ABC might air a pilot and follow it with a national telephone survey.)

Barbara Corday, for three years ABC's head of comedy development, goes further. "I have never seen a case where testing has substantially changed anybody's mind. I think when it goes along with the general thinking, it's terrific. If it is sort of like the general thinking, we discuss it. If it is really away from the general thinking, people tend to make up a lot of excuses. They had the wrong kind of audience that night. How many kids were there in the audience that night? How many people over fifty? Did you ask them the right questions? Were they grumpy? Did they see something else before? Were they sitting there for a long time? Did they have to wait out in the rain to get in? I think testing is one of ten things that feed into a decision, and that's really all it is." On the other hand, if no one feels strongly enough about a movie—and with CBS making fifty or sixty new movies a season it is hard even to keep track of them all—testing sometimes becomes influential by default. Programming executives might approve movie ideas despite low TAPE scores if they felt "passionate" about them, according to a CBS researcher, but "in the majority of cases, no one felt passionate about a concept either way."

Tests have one more use. They lubricate the abrasive relations between networks and their suppliers. Network executives find it convenient to tell producers that their shows aren't being picked up because of low test scores, thereby deflecting some of the suppliers' anger onto the hapless research department. Like CIA intelligence officers, in a similar structural position, research executives feel that being scapegoated is part of their job description. Valued but scorned, cited but patronized, their ambiguous position represents the culture industry's uneasy attempt to accommodate its industrial reality.

In the perpetual struggle between the networks and the creative community, testing's preeminent use may be to confirm the rightness of network power. For all the limits of the test as an exercise in statistical reliability, it generates veritable facts, real numbers, the only ones at anyone's hand. The numbers give executives the warrant of hard, "objective" "fact" with which to argue for changes in a show. When the numbers speak through the mouths of the executives who deploy them, they give the network's voice a rational sound. So the tests are inadvertently useful to the network whether or not they predict commercial success. They secrete the aura of reason, the organization's main ideological defense against the merely egocentric instincts of the people who write and produce the shows. One network research executive put it to me this way: "The networks say, 'We have a broad interest in what goes out on the air.' The producers say, 'We're the creative ones. We're the ones who have the creativity.' Creativity, what's that? Hitler had creativity. He created gas chambers." Organizational rationality has to discipline creativity, for creativity unchecked can destroy.

By
the Numbers

If program tests are automatically soft, audience ratings might appear hard. Network corridors and production lots hum with talk of last week's, even last night's numbers. Research executives spend hours on the phone with programmers, relaying the numbers that will become the talk of today's lunches: *ratings,* expressed as a percentage of all the television households in the country, and *shares,* expressed as a percentage of all the households that are watching television during one particular period. Numbers are industry gold and executives are the managers waiting for up-to-the-minute reports from their mines. The common obsession is: Which network is number one for the week, the month, the year? Who's up, who's down? One's chances for promotion might hang on the ratings for programs one has developed or defended. In the back of the network's collective mind, everyone knows that company profits hang on the numbers, which become the basis for advertising rates.

Each year the numbers have seemed to come in faster, glory and ignominy becoming virtually instantaneous. By 1973, as the networks grew more competitive and the technology of audience measurement more sophisticated, it became possible to measure major market results overnight, through special samples run by the A. C.

Nielsen Company in New York, Chicago, Los Angeles, San Francisco, and, since 1982, Philadelphia and Detroit. Now executives like to say, as CBS's Steve Mills puts it, "We get a daily report card. This is one of the few businesses in the world I know where a guy comes to work every morning and looks to see how he did the day before."

Veterans gaze back fondly at the good old days when ratings weren't much mentioned unless a show did abysmally. "Occasionally we got a really disastrously low rating on *Playhouse 90,* like a seven share," the longtime CBS and NBC executive Ethel Winant remembers, "and someone would mention it to us. But it wasn't like a call from someone saying, 'My God, it's a disaster!' It was just an interesting statistical thing." When Nielsen started its Television Index in 1950, delivery of the national audience ratings took six weeks. In 1961, delivery improved to sixteen days; in 1967, nine days; in 1973, a week. "It used to be a couple of weeks before you knew you were a failure," Winant recalls. "And so it didn't matter anymore. You were on to something else. Now everybody talks about the ratings. Competition has made us crazy."

Competition and measurement technique accelerated in tandem. Indeed, the "overnights" were the fruit of a technology Nielsen would probably not have developed had competition-crazed networks not created a market for it. By 1976, when ABC first overtook CBS as the top-rated network, competition had revved to a whine, and the greater the competition, the more public attention was paid to it. By the late seventies, major newspapers were listing the week's top-rated shows, stock market analysts and major investors as well as fans were paying heed, and all this attention was cycling back to the networks in the form of still more intense competition. The drive to keep up with the latest numbers became so intense that abstention seemed odd, requiring explanation. One day, when I asked Grant Tinker, as newly appointed NBC chairman, about the ratings of a controversial movie broadcast the night before, he said, "I try not to keep up with the overnights. People in my company are amazed that I don't give a rat's ass about the overnights."

While Tinker may have disdained the fetish of immediate numerical gratification, he could scarcely afford indifference to the overall ratings. I asked him how close to the front of his consciousness he kept the price of RCA stock. "Very close," he said. He could not permit his idealism about quality "to get in front of the viability, the profitability, of the business. That is my primary mandate, to make sure NBC is healthy." The difference between the more and less enlightened top executives is that the more enlightened try to build schedules for longer-term strength, for next year or the year after that, while the others concentrate on next week and next month and claim that the farsighted have no choice, since the next week looks so dismal for them. Short-term or long-term, network purpose rests on the ratings.

Then how good are the ratings? Most producers and writers are skeptical or downright hostile. Many blacks and Hispanics in the industry believe that the Nielsen sample underrepresents minorities because Nielsen employees are loath to tread into the ghettoes. Devotees of "quality" think it overrepresents heavy TV watchers, the proverbial beer guzzlers who wander in and out of the living room, easily satisfied with fluff. Moreover, they argue, Nielsen doesn't measure anyone's satisfaction, but only the raw numbers of households and eyeballs. Indisputably, Nielsen's sample is small. In May 1982, 1,260 households were hooked up to Audimeter boxes recording the stations tuned to, with 1,121 reporting on the average day.* Common sense, innocent of the theory of statistical sampling, finds it hard to believe that so few households can represent the entire television-viewing population of the United States; each Nielsen household "represents" almost 70,000 actual households!

There is no way to explore these suspicions without a certain amount of statistical inquiry, but I shall try to keep it short and sweet. Intuition notwithstanding, the sample-size issue is a red herring. If the sample had been drawn perfectly at random from the national population, it would have been large enough so that the standard error on a rating of 20 would have been 1.2; that is, if a show were actually watched in 20 percent of the nation's households, the odds are 68 percent that the Nielsen rating would fall between 18.8 and 21.2, and 95 percent that it would fall between 17.6 and 22.4. The sample sizes and standard errors fall in the same range as national Gallup and Harris surveys. Network research executives point out that the Nielsen household figures are more rigorous, less a function of interpretation, since they measure an unambiguous fact (television set switched on to a certain channel) rather than a response to a potentially loaded question about attitudes or voting intentions.

If Nielsen has an important flaw, it would have to lie not in the size of the sample but in its representativeness. The Nielsen Company selects its initial sample randomly according to accepted statistical practice. The problem is that not everyone chosen for the sample agrees to install the Nielsen Audimeter devices. Congressional hearings in 1963 brought out the fact that fewer than half of the desig-

---

*The sample runs higher in the winter months. For purposes of demographic breakdown, Nielsen also maintains a separate diary sample in which selected households record who is watching which programs. In May 1982 this sample ran to 2,563 households, of which 1,828 reported on the average day. Late that year, Nielsen announced plans to enlarge its Audimeter sample to provide statistically significant numbers for less-watched cable and satellite channels.

nated Nielsen sample cooperated. Goaded by congressional scrutiny, Nielsen raised its payments to cooperating households and pushed its staff to solicit more aggressively. By 1966, the cooperation rate had risen to about 75 percent. But although an industry-wide committee urged Nielsen to push on to an 80 percent cooperation rate, the rate proceeded—as in all other statistical surveys during this age of public suspicion—to slump. By 1979, the Nielsen cooperation rate had sagged to 70 percent; in 1980, to 67 percent. The question is, are people who refuse to sign on different from people who do sign on in a way that affects the patterns of their viewing?

Such questions concern the industry, partly because advertisers rely on the credibility of the Nielsen sample, and partly because sloppy statistics make for bad public relations. The 1963 congressional hearings were brought about by some scandalously sloppy methods. In their wake, therefore, the three networks and the National Association of Broadcasters established a joint research group on the ratings, the Committee on Nationwide Television Audience Measurements, or CONTAM. The big problem was how to tell what non-cooperators were doing, since by definition these were the people who refused to allow the Nielsen boxes into their homes. CONTAM decided, reasonably enough, to inquire by telephone. Since Nielsen numbers of cooperators and noncooperators were too small to produce statistically significant results, the 1964 CONTAM study turned to a much larger but similarly selected and solicited population, the 200,000 households picked by the American Research Bureau (ARB) for its November 1963 "sweep." (These large samples, gathered three months each year, give the networks and local stations the circulation figures from which to set new advertising rates.) ARB supplied the phone numbers of some 175,000, of whom more than half, 94,000, were dialed. By the time unreliable interviews were weeded out, 84,302 were available; about one-third were with people who had cooperated with ARB, while the rest had originally refused to keep TV-watching diaries.

The results of this and later studies showed, as critics had charged, that cooperators did indeed watch somewhat more television than noncooperators. The cooperators were also younger, better educated, and lived in larger families. More to the point, their tastes ran, if anything, toward the more ambitious programs. Of forty-two programs checked, five ran at least 20 percent higher in the cooperators' ratings than in the total group. Among them were *East Side, West Side* and *That Was the Week That Was.* (Seven ran lower in the cooperators' ratings, only three of them by as much as 5 percent: *Rawhide, Breaking Point,* and *The Price Is Right,* the last hardly a case of an intelligent show undercounted in the ratings.) But the rankings of shows most popular among cooperators were barely different from rankings in the total sample. Of the ten ranked highest by the cooperators, nine also ranked highest in the total sample; and the same ratio held for the lowest-ranked. In other words, the major difference between the two groups was that the cooperators were disproportionately inclined toward the two most irreverent, politically liberal, and convention-subverting programs on the air: *East Side, West Side,* in which George C. Scott played a social worker trying, and failing, to solve the social problems of the ghetto (later in the series the Scott character concluded that social problems required political solutions, and joined the staff of a reform congressman); and *TW3,* a topical satire softened from its English origin but still genially acerbic. Assuming Nielsen noncooperators were like people who refused to keep ARB diaries—and there was no reason not to—the Nielsen ratings were then skewed toward programs favored by the young and better-educated.

Are there then other factors tending to undermine the representativeness of the Nielsen sample? Between them, critics and CONTAM have considered several more conceivable sources of bias: (1) Before 1964, Nielsen excluded the 4 percent of households in the Mountain Time Zone; this was rapidly remedied, although periodically some western stations argue they are still undercounted.* (2) It is conceivable that Nielsen Audimeter signals and ARB diary entries are inaccurate, or could be misread or misinterpreted. (3) Possibly some Nielsen households keep their sets turned on even when not viewing —to vote, in effect, for their favorite shows. (4) As they age, the households also grow less representative of the population, and they differ in the important respect of knowing, after all, that they are Nielsen households. The 1963 hearings revealed that some Nielsen households had been kept in the sample for a dozen years. Beginning in 1966, however, Nielsen responded to criticism by instituting a 20 percent annual turnover in the household sample, and 33 percent in its personal diaries, but even this rate could lock in certain tastes longer than they deserve. (5) Through 1963, the congressional investigators found, Nielsen violated some of its own strictures in choosing counties to sample, and some Neilsen fieldmen departed from acceptable survey practice in choosing households to substitute for noncooperators. (6) Nielsen counts only viewers in houses and apartments. In 1970, 2.9 percent of the population at any given time were living in institutions, military barracks, dormitories, boardinghouses,

---

*Nielsen still excludes Alaska and Hawaii, which air mainland shows late, but these states include only 0.6 percent of the U.S. population.

hotels, and motels. (7) It has also been charged that the Nielsen sample is not properly weighted for demographic factors including age and, most controversially, race.

Random errors cannot, of course, be ruled out. But with the exception of the race and age issues, it is not clear in what systematic direction, if at all, these factors in the aggregate would bias the Nielsen numbers for particular shows. What counts in decision-making, after all, are not absolute Nielsen numbers but their relative positions. To investigate the possible effects of all these confounding factors, CONTAM in 1964 matched Nielsen Audimeter ratings against ARB diary figures, and found they corresponded remarkably well; nineteen of the twenty highest-rated Nielsen shows were also among the ARB top twenty. More to the point, in 1969 and 1970 CONTAM checked Nielsen figures with sophisticated telephone surveys. The telephone and Nielsen figures matched within 1 or 2 percent, well within the limits of sampling error. There remains the logical possibility that Nielsen and ARB share a systematic bias with telephone surveys. People could be systematically lying, for example, about what they watch. Yet there is no particular reason to believe all three populations would be inclined to lie in the same fashion.

If cooperator bias tilts the Nielsen and ARB samples toward the younger and more educated, and the poor also have fewer phones, are the preferences of blacks, Hispanics, older people, and the poor being systematically undercounted? Advertisers might not mind if this were the case; these people are not big buyers anyway. We do know that blacks and Hispanics are drastically underrepresented in filling out the diaries that record the members of the household (as opposed to total households) who view for Nielsen and ARB. According to one study, only 15 to 20 percent of Hispanics mailed back viewing diaries in English or Spanish, compared with 55 percent of the general population. Blacks and Hispanics might also be underincluded in the Nielsen household survey, for two reasons. The first is that Nielsen draws its samples from census data. If the Census Bureau still undercounts the housing units of the poor, as minority groups have charged in the past, then the Nielsen sample, too, would be, as former NBC executive Paul Klein says, "upslanted." The second reason is that, in most surveys, the less educated are less likely to cooperate even if asked and the less educated are still disproportionately black and Hispanic. On the other hand, it is conceivable that since the cooperator studies of the early sixties, the less educated have become more willing to sign on as Nielsen households, whether for pride, money, or the desire to affect the ratings. Feeling some heat from critics, Nielsen began to offer black families $2 a month, twice the regular payment.

Although they still do not disclose the ethnic composition of their samples, Nielsen and ARB also began to change their system for choosing samples and weighting results. As advertisers grew more interested in demographic breakdowns in the seventies, and the networks followed suit, the rating companies set out to produce more precise counts of the audience in general, not just the number of households. It remains true, though, that counts of viewers, which depend on the tenacity, literacy, and veracity of diary-keepers, will always remain less reliable than the automatic, electronically scored Nielsen Audimeter signals.

Plainly the Nielsen system has had its shortcomings, but in the end there are strong pressures to keep it honest. For one thing, advertisers want to get their money's worth, and therefore want a count that is at least internally consistent. If it is in the interest of the networks to overcount their audience—or at least the wealthiest eighteen- to forty-nine-year-old segment that spends the most money—it is assuredly not in their interest to lose credibility with advertisers who pay the networks' way.

In any event, network executives are satisfied that the Nielsens are accurate and reliable; their research executives assure them that it's so. "I think it's among the finest research that is done in the social sciences," Arnold Becker says. "And to the degree that they are somewhat imprecise, in terms of the actual precise number of millions, they are not imprecise in terms of ranking what is most popular to least popular. And that's all that matters." In other words, it remains possible that factors yet undiscovered affect the accuracy of Nielsen numbers as measures of total audience size, but unlikely that such hypothetical factors would affect their use in measuring relative ratings.

Still, in the tumult of everyday figuring and judging, network executives, even research specialists, often commit the standard occupational error of unwarranted precision. When Nielsen publishes its figures every two weeks, it reminds subscribers of the standard errors, but executives functionally forget what they were taught in elementary statistics: that all survey statistics are valid only within predictable margins of error. For example, the 1981–82 series rankings showed *Dynasty* in twentieth place with a 20.4 season rating and *Hill Street Blues* in twenty-ninth place with 18.6. But statistically there was a 10 percent chance the two shows actually drew the same size audience. Once managers agree to accept a measure, they act as if it is precise. They "know" there are standard errors—but what a nuisance it would be to act on that knowledge. And so the number system has an impetus of its own. In the heat of scheduling meetings, researchers don't remind the assembled executives that the numbers are imprecise. Over the long haul, the numbers are "good enough," and the long haul is what statistics are good for. Executives compose schedules, not shows. But shows are renewed or canceled one at a time, and in the short run, so the cancellation of a show like *Lou Grant* may hang on a collective forgetting that its ratings figures are, in fact, imprecise.

Then, too, the intensity and significance of viewing are beyond Nielsen's ken. The numbers measure only sample sets tuned in, not necessarily shows watched, let alone grasped, remembered, loved, learned from, deeply anticipated, or mildly tolerated. The John and Mary Markle Foundation is attempting to work up a system for getting "qualitative ratings," measurements of the intensity of "the viewing experience." The networks are only mildly interested. After all, the current system works toward its intended purpose. Whatever Nielsen measures, it measures consistently. The ratings are like the Gross National Product, Paul Klein once said. They measure something connected with audience size, but exactly what is irrelevant, for they measure the same thing in the same way week after week, year to year, and therefore the relative differences and shifts over time should be taken seriously. The numbers are a currency for transactions. Given their commitments to gross efficiency in time and dollars, what else are networks and advertising companies to use?

The top network executives pride themselves on intuition, experience, and seasoning, on their instinct for the popular; but at each annual scheduling meeting the top research executives are always included among the five to ten people who buy, renew, and drop shows. They are there to be on tap, not on top, advising on the demographics of audiences and the consistency of evening-long blocs; but their voices are strong. They may differ with programmers on tactics and the weight of factors, but many programmers are former researchers and they are marketers all. The limits of numbers are clear: They always have to be interpreted, and of course they measure only the past, not the future. But absent a clear standard of taste or a strong sense of traditional form, absent any clear aesthetic or moral values in the mass market or in the executive suites, the numbers have the great virtue of being there, looking radiantly exact.

Audience measurement looms larger in network tactics, too, as the three-network competition grows more intense and the networks seemingly less adept at reading the public mind. The increasing sophistication of the technology for gathering and distributing the numbers matches the frenzy of short-term thinking that arose in the seventies, when scheduling became a year-round affair. As the numbers came in faster and faster, the networks began to dump failing series within a month or two, or to take them off the air for a major retooling of tone, or cast, or (as in the case of *Cagney and Lacey*) both. As the psychologist and television-effects researcher Percy Tannenbaum says, you resort to a shotgun when your aim is bad. Gone were the days when a show was ordered in thirty-nine episodes for the year. With rising costs and rising competition, the number sank to twenty-six, then twenty-two, even to thirteen. By 1980, the networks were ordering iffy new shows only four or six episodes at a time. Two or three bad weeks and the show could be banished forever. Producers gaze back nostalgically to the days when unusual shows like *All in the Family, The Mary Tyler Moore Show, M*A*S*H,* and *Lou Grant* started out slowly but got a chance to build their audience, taking off only late in the season, or even, in the case of *Lou Grant,* during summer reruns. Reliance on numbers, which once promised stability of judgment, plays a part in producing frenetic change. As on Broadway and in the bookstores, a combination of profit pressure, fierce competition, and rising costs gives new goods less and less time to prove themselves. All the more pressure on the medium to cater quickly, unambiguously, to whatever component of audience taste seems to rise to the surface at a given moment and holds out the possibility of being measured simply. But the haste to make investments pay off quickly is no better for art, even for entertainment, than it is for wine.

C H A P T E R 4

Making Schedules

If prime-time TV seems senseless, that may be because we view it through the prism of old-fashioned standards. We may expect loveliness of language, expressive acting, shadings of performance, and intimations of depths rumbling beneath the surface. We import ideals of craft and quality from ages of artisanship, even from the teleplays of the fifties. And indeed craft and quality do survive, at least as ideals, among Hollywood's craftsmen and -women. The networks, though, have a prior objective. Although executives may not be allergic to what they deem quality, the networks as a whole aim to create not purposeful or coherent or true or beautiful shows, but audiences. Any other purpose is subordinated to the larger design of keeping a sufficient number of people tuned in. That is, after all, what advertisers pay for. That is why the shows so often look concocted, forced, to critics trained to spot internal niceties. The sophistication goes not so much into shows as into calculations about audience "flow" and composition.

The networks are not only seeking aggregate eyeballs, they also aim to reach and hold particular target audiences—since inertia keeps many viewers tuned to the same network for hours on end unless they are driven away. Different histories, first of all, have furnished each network a different core of relatively reliable viewers.

As a whole, CBS's audience is disproportionately older and more rural because CBS signed up more affiliates first and has always had relatively more affiliates in the smaller markets. ABC countered younger and more urban, for it was the third network to emerge, and therefore, at least until recently, has had fewer affiliates in the small markets (many of which had only one or two stations before cable came along) and proportionately more in big cities. Having started that way, ABC reasoned that older viewers were creatures of habit, harder to woo from CBS and NBC, whereas the younger viewers would be easier to attract and keep, even as children and adolescents.* They proved right and stayed younger. NBC, in its dog years, can count on little, having even lost some affiliates to the more successful networks. With less market to take for granted, less "flow" from show to show on a given evening, NBC has to attract its audience from program to program. This leaves it, in the eyes of competitors, hopelessly floundering; or, in the hopeful words of NBC Entertainment president Brandon Tartikoff, "the most experimental of the three," aiming to "urbanize" its audience and lower its age.

So audience differences originated in CBS's small-town monopoly; CBS programmed to suit and ABC countered, which in turn solidified some expectations about what a CBS- or ABC-style show was —not in the whole audience, of course, but in enough of it to make a difference. "The three networks are department stores," says the bronzed, thirty-one-year-old Tartikoff, all California informality. "I'll go to Korvette's for a vacuum cleaner; I wouldn't think to go to them for a suit. I wouldn't go to Saks for a vacuum cleaner."

"We always look for programming that appeals to everybody," says CBS's avuncular programmer Herman Keld, "but that kind of program doesn't exist, really." So the networks tend to program for their core audiences. "Whenever we would put on programs that are what we might call the ABC-type programs," says Keld, "the more sophisticated, slick, big-city-type programs like *Three's Company, Charlie's Angels, Vega$, Hart to Hart,* we're not too successful." *Paper Chase* was a show that failed on CBS, Keld argues, because it was aiming for ABC-type demographics. ABC did well with teenage shows like *Happy Days, Laverne and Shirley, Mork and Mindy;* but at NBC, Tartikoff told me early in 1981, "the last real bubblegum show we did was *Brothers and Sisters,* " a failed 1979 *Animal House* copy. At NBC such demographic reasoning is ad hoc and transitory, like so much

---

*There is evidence to support this ABC reasoning. According to a Nielsen study, adults over forty-nine are more likely to prefer long-running programs than are younger viewers.

network lore; a year later, NBC was running the teen-conscious *Fame*.

Not only do the networks set their sights on slightly different masses, but scheduling and even development take into account the shifting demographics of time-slots. The evening starts with an audience that averages about 17 percent children under twelve, with some 23 percent adults over fifty-five. By the ten-to-eleven time period, children are only 6.5 percent of the audience, and adults over fifty-five are now 26 percent. (The percentage of teenagers falls only slightly, from 10.6 percent to 8.3 percent.) Accordingly, the networks develop shows tailor-made for particular slots: *Happy Days, The Greatest American Hero, Mork and Mindy, Little House on the Prairie* were predestined to be eight-o'clock shows; *Lou Grant, Dynasty,* and *Strike Force,* ten-o'clock shows. At the last minute, a show might fail to sell because the network doesn't have the "right" slot open for it. Demographics likewise dictate different thresholds for censorship; *Hill Street Blues* can get away with language at ten that NBC would never permit in the child-laden eight-o'clock spot.

Precise demographic calculation became appealing to advertisers and the networks in the late sixties. Advertisers wanted to be sure they were buying their money's worth of women eighteen to forty-nine, or teenagers, or whatever their target of choice happened to be. For all the sophistication in data-gathering, though, CBS's Arnold Becker, for one, thinks sales departments have come to exaggerate the importance of audience composition. Suppose, for the sake of argument, CBS and ABC each has an audience of ten, he says; CBS with four young and six old, ABC six young and four old.* ABC goes to advertisers and argues that ABC is 50 percent better because it has six of the desirable young against CBS's four. But actually 80 percent of their viewers (four young and four old) are demographically the same. If advertisers and agencies also exaggerate the difference, to make themselves look more scientific, they are mistaken, too, because they fail to take into account the number of products they can sell to young and old. Suppose further, then, that the young buy twice as many units of Product X as do the old. Then CBS can sell one unit to each of its six old, and two to each of its four young, for a total of fourteen, while ABC can sell one unit to each of its four old and two units to each of its six young, for a total of sixteen. This makes ABC's spots not 50 percent more valuable than CBS's, but only 14 percent more.

---

*This is a much greater difference than actually obtains. Becker also points out that for buying purposes the key distinction is between large and small families; but "young" and "old" are industry shorthand.

Moreover, Becker doubts whether hit programs can even be targeted so specifically to age. He puts it this way: "I have a nice group of highly skilled professional people sitting over there, whose job is to make successful programs. And I say to them, 'Fellas, go out and make me a successful. I want big numbers.' And they knock themselves out, and most of the time they fail. Now I say to them, 'Fellas, I got a new assignment for you. I want a hit program, big numbers, but I've got a little extra twist. Nothing much. I want it to be peculiarly popular with young people.' That's cruel and unusual punishment. The poor bastards don't know how to make a good show; how are you supposed to make a show that's good *and* particularly good with young? So I would just as soon they did their best to make the most popular programs they're able to make and not worry their little old heads with whether it's going to be skewed a little bit younger or a little bit older. Let ABC do that. In the meantime, I'll beat them most of the time."

ABC and CBS do reason demographically when they develop shows, and in both cases the sales department, which has to sell spots for top dollar, may have its say. During the scheduling meetings, when the top programmers know they want to "pick up" a show, they often ask the sales department's advice about where on the schedule to put it. Of course, this could easily slide over into a question of whether to put it anywhere, since there are only so many slots available. In their anxiety, ABC and NBC development go farther. At times they consult with the sales department before scheduling meetings. What did sales think of the pilot? Did they laugh? Did they cry? That way, they arm themselves with marketability arguments that might prevail. Stu Sheslow, NBC's vice-president for drama, said that *Buck Rogers in the 25th Century* got onto the 1979 schedule, for example, because sales had sounded out certain advertisers, screened the pilot, and won their enthusiasm. Demographic arguments, like others, will be deployed by those who stand to benefit from them, and ignored or fudged otherwise. Since development executives move up by getting shows they've developed onto the schedule, they make all the arguments about demography, time-slots, network suitability, lead-in, competition, and advertiser zeal they can muster.

In all these calculations and ad hoc arguments, one demographic constant stands out. Since at least the early seventies, the over–sixty-five audience (sometimes even the over–fifty-five) has ranked least desirable. From the moment CBS shifted its programming strategy in 1969–70, as we shall see in Chapter 10, eighteen to forty-nine has been the premium group. The reason is simple: As Herman Keld puts it, "that's where your money is." Advertisers would pay less for access to older people, who had less money to dispose of. By the early eighties, however, the population had aged significantly. In 1979–80, about one-third of the average prime-time audience was fifty or over. Accordingly, the prime target—at least at CBS, which started with the largest share of older viewers—shifted to twenty-five to fifty-four, even twenty-five to sixty-four. As a bloc, these people now have, and spend, more money than they did ten years before. Advertisers have shifted their interests accordingly, although their computations tend to lag a few years behind reality. "For years," says one top CBS sales executive, "the beer people marketed to eighteen to thirty-four men. In recent years, those targets have changed to eighteen to forty-nine. Many food processors, like Kraft, Quaker Oats, General Mills, who used to go for eighteen to forty-nine, some years ago changed to twenty-five to fifty-four." Whatever the vicissitudes of network strategy, programmers keep at least one eye cocked in the direction of the advertisers who bankroll the whole enterprise.

Aggregate numbers, and the breakdown of those numbers, are what count, not the fate of any particular show. Moreover, the networks' grand designs shape the careers of the shows they've paid to develop in another important way. Producers produce programs, and development executives advocate them, but the top executives as a group compose schedules. Scheduling meetings dwell not only on the demographics expected but on problems of "flow": Would an eight-o'clock audience of given demographics stay tuned to show X at eight-thirty, given the competition? Many executives have also come to believe in what is called "counterprogramming"—say, running a show watched disproportionately by men (*Hill Street Blues*) against a show that appeals more to women (*Fantasy Island*). Such scheduling is no longer an annual affair, but a year-long process of rearrangement, like a frantic, continuous round of interior redecoration. "I don't get gray hairs about competition from cable," says Brandon Tartikoff. "I don't own NBC. I might even be supplying some day. I get gray hairs about what movie am I going to have at eight-thirty?"

There are dissidents who think the game is not worth the candle. CBS Research's Arnold Becker, for example, makes a strong case that the preoccupation with flow is irrational from the network's point of view. He calls schedule-juggling "playing with yourself." "I have two shows," Becker argues, "A and B, and inherently they are of equal strength. I can cause A to have a good rating by putting it in a proper time period, and B a poor rating by putting it in an improper time period. If I switch those two around, B will do well and A will do poorly. The theory then follows that if I put everything in its optimum time period I would get optimum ratings. And a lot of time, energy, is spent on trying to figure out that optimum time period. . . . I think we have pretty well documented that there isn't an optimum schedule, that to the degree that you cause A to be high you cause B to be lower. I hate to tell you how many thousands of dollars I have paid college professors to run things through computers to try to figure out what this optimum was likely to be, or at least to give us some clues about how we should think about this. The conclusion really was, either it doesn't make any difference what you do, or we don't know how to do it."* The simplest precept of scheduling is that "lead-in," the show immediately preceding, makes a big difference to a show's ratings. But Becker makes so bold as to add, "One is hard pressed to document that lead-out [the show following], if you will, is less effective than lead-in. But everybody believes it. Even I believe it. But it's yet to be proven."

Becker is in the minority. Scheduling theories seem to impose a rational grid on decision-making. They amount to official lore; they are what network executives know. Becker and other skeptics find themselves banging their heads against a brick wall. Not only don't programming executives believe his argument, Becker complains, "it's ridiculed as absolute nonsense. Since I've moved out to Los Angeles, I don't say this anymore. I don't enjoy being hated." Programmers aren't interested in the evidence "because they can always name the one case that worked." But he thinks there are other reasons why rational argument is overlooked: "Once you have the programs, my philosophy is a very negative one, because it suggests that there is nothing you can do. There is nothing you can do but make better shows. But people like to believe that since they cannot make better shows, or they don't have better shows available to them this particular Wednesday afternoon, and they need them desperately, because they may get fired next week, that they have to do something, so they move them around and pray. It gives the feeling of doing something. It gives the feeling of movement. You don't have this feeling that you're sitting back and idly accepting your fate."

There are even a few executives and ex-executives, like Paul Klein and Deanne Barkley (formerly in charge of TV movies at both NBC and ABC), who go so far as to argue that viewers do not care much just which shows are plunked in front of them as long as they are, as Klein memorably said once, "the least objectionable programming." Klein observed that every day at the same time the number of TV sets tuned in held remarkably constant. If people simply sit in attendance, why develop so many scripts? Why make pilots and go through the rigmarole of scheduling and rescheduling? After minimal attention to demographics—you don't want to program a kids' show at

---

*What Becker called "the best experiment we've done" entailed comparing the average ratings of all shows whose times were changed at midseason to the average ratings for all new shows. The conclusion was, "We weren't better off after we had made the changes than before. Some went up, some went down."

10:00 P.M., for example—"you could choose them at random," Deanne Barkley says, "but don't you see, how does Fred Silverman justify his existence, or any of those people who are there? I maintain you could run a network with ten people. All these people justify their existence by making decisions, pretending to make decisions as to what's on."

As it is, the "science" and "art" of program development and scheduling do only a few things for certain. They bid up the market value of the executives themselves. They reinforce the networks' claim to be efficient servants of the popular will. Most important, they buttress network TV's position as the most efficient medium for advertisers. The numbers are both the wherewithal and the trappings of cost-effectiveness. Regardless of flaws, the presumed rationality of audience measurement and scheduling lore works just well enough to satisfy advertisers that they are getting their money's worth. That is all it really has to accomplish.

When the ratings are assembled for each week, the first-place network (usually CBS) rejoices and claims vindication for its judgments; the runner-up (usually ABC) can wax optimistic about its prospects; and the third (usually NBC) can comfort itself that it has taken some chances, or is building strength for the long run, or has stronger demographics. In any case, all three will go on competing on the common ground of ratings points. No one will pay them to do anything else.

Even by the network logic of maximum ratings, failures far outnumber successes. Of the total of sixty-two new shows introduced in the fall of 1980 and 1981, for example, only twenty did well enough to get renewed for a second year. But this bad commercial record—which television shares with the commercial theater, movies, and book publishing—is almost beside the point. In any system regulated by measures of quantity, winners require plenty of losers. As long as advertisers are content that network television gives them the most efficient access to the national market, then television's commercial failures are not too high a price for the networks to pay.

C H A P T E R 5

The Triumph of the Synthetic: Spinoffs, Copies, Recombinant Culture

Safety first is the network rule. There seems safety in numbers: in test results for new and revamped shows, in extrapolations from previous ratings in the case of returning shows. But in the end, the numbers don't suffice to make decisions. To build certainty, the "science" of numbers has to be joined to the "art" of hunches—consisting mostly of noting previous hits. The safest, easiest formula is that nothing succeeds like success. Hits are so rare that executives think a blatant imitation stands a good chance of getting bigger numbers than a show that stands on its own. Executives like to say they are constantly looking for something new, but their intuition tells them to hunt up prepackaged trends and then recognize the new as a variant of the old. This hedging of bets also supplies them with ready-made alibis in the frequent case of failure. Then, too, as long as the authentically and commercially new hasn't shown up, something has to be found to fill the airwaves; for time unfilled is time unsold. So why not exploit a currency already in circulation, one backed by the cachet of impressive numbers? Of course, at a certain point these gatekeepers will recognize that the market for a given formula has been stretched too far. It becomes oversaturated for cop shows, "jiggle," "fantasy," and the formula collapses. But that danger lies in the distant future, months, even years away. In the here and now, what rules is the severe pressure to show short-term results. The logic of maximizing the quick payoff has produced that very Hollywood hybrid, the recombinant form, which assumes that selected features of recent hits can be spliced together to make a eugenic success. If *M*A*S*H* and *Holiday on Ice* are both winners, why not army surgeons on skates? In this world without deep tradition, "why not?" is the recurrent question. The result is the absurd industrialization of mannerism, which is the industry's characteristic style.

SPINOFFS

I asked Sy Amlen, vice-president of ABC Entertainment in New York, what was the central element of a series that determined whether it would get picked up as a potential success. With twenty-five years in research, Amlen is respected as an old pro, one of a handful of men who personify continuity in the business. Softly, but with absolute assurance, he said, "The most important thing in a show is character."

William S. Paley, Mr. Continuity himself, once wrote, "I believe the most important and virtually unfailing indication of a good program—over and above basic good writing, direction, casting, costumes, and sets—is likable, intriguing characters who capture the imagination, interest, or concern of the audience." Again and again, when I asked executives why a show had failed, I was told, "People didn't like the characters." Then came little theories about what exactly they didn't like. NBC's Gerald Jaffe said about the failed working-class series *Skag,* for example, "Anyone with a family all of whom are ugly people inside will do badly. Good people should be overcoming adversity."

The first thing network executives wonder about a new show is whether viewers will "invite" the characters back into their proverbial living rooms week after week. "The key to series television is longevity," said Tony Thomopoulos, president of ABC Entertainment. "When you look at a series's potential, you look at the character development and the longevity of those characters: Now you can deal with those characters week after week after week." These characters exist for the audience only as actors present them, which is a large reason why an idea pitched may sound so much better than the pilot looks. These actors-as-characters have to seem like reliable repeaters, since they are prospective members of the family.

Viewers strike up mysterious, quasi-personal relations with these flickering icons: squealing for Fonzie, swooning for Farrah Fawcett (or her bathing suits), loathing—and loving to loathe—J.R. Ewing, or for that matter trusting Dan Rather or Mike Wallace. Monday night may have "belonged" to Lou Grant the way it used to "belong" to the regular poker crowd or the next-door neighbors or the folks at the Kiwanis Club. We may even talk back to these characters, complain about their marriages, decry their lapses from their usual conduct. What they have in common is that they are regulars.

But there is no technological imperative behind long-running series. Limited runs of six or thirteen episodes are common in Europe.* Historians of popular culture might argue that ample precedent exists for American TV series in the eighteenth- and nineteenth-century novels that appeared regularly in newspaper and magazine installments. But the question then remains, why aren't regular characters the staples of popular culture everywhere and at all times? Are Americans more needy of familiar figures than the English, who have royalty as their continuing quasi-family? Theories that begin from audience demand always run afoul of the fact that popular taste is not born but made.

We are on surer ground when we inspect the supply side. All modern organizations aspire to order, regularity, routine, which make for efficiency and control. The networks have proved no different; but on top of this general tendency, television inherited its forms from radio. The first American radio programs, in the early twenties, were not narrative at all but one-of-a-kind musical performances. Then came dramatic series, weekly anthologies like *Great Moments in Drama* and *Biblical Dramas.* But a new precedent was set by the hit syndicated series *Amos 'n' Andy,* which played on NBC five days a week beginning in 1928. The show was all the rage, so talked about —all the way to Calvin Coolidge's White House—that regular series, constellations of fixed stars, became axiomatic. Like the film industry, whose star system arose only after 1914, radio took a while to discover that established stars were efficient draws in a consumer society. Once the discovery was made, though, advertisers joined the networks in solidifying it. Commercials and series had an affinity. In time, advertisers learned that regular characters meant reliable audiences; if characters were popular, sponsors could borrow some of that popularity.

Within a few years, television recapitulated the history of radio. In the so-called Golden Years of the late forties and early fifties, the TV networks offered mostly variety shows, anthology drama, music, and sports—all live, most of it produced in New York. But, by the late

---

*So are episodes of uneven lengths—fifty-eight or seventy-two minutes. In this regard, though, America is indeed driven toward uniformity by technical obstacles. With hundreds of far-flung affiliates, the networks would find it virtually impossible to synchronize their transmissions if they went out at irregular intervals.

fifties, episodic series were considerably more popular than other forms. In 1958–59, nine of the ten most popular shows were episodic series featuring regular characters.*

The shift to episodes came with the shift from live performance to film and tape. *I Love Lucy* demonstrated that successful filmed episodic series were gold mines. The film studios belatedly recognized that television wasn't going to blow over, and switched to producing TV series. The networks now understood they could reach for greater profits (not to mention control) if they regularized production through film suppliers. The result was the shift of production to Hollywood and the decline of live drama. Live broadcasts dwindled from 80 percent of all network programs in 1953 to 33 percent in 1960, with the remainder split between film and videotape.** The industry came to believe that variety shows fail, anthology series fail, and an excess of movies is catastrophic.*** In series, each episode is a billboard advertising the next.

The advertisers' interest in reliable characters was more than matched by the suppliers, who quickly realized that the real money was in syndication. Production costs began to climb exponentially, exceeding the license fees the networks paid for the right to broadcast the shows. But costs could be more than matched by the promise of syndication, potentially stretching to the end of recorded time. In a sense, every series developed was an investment in the chance of syndication, although only one in forty series on the air lasts long enough to be syndicated. If a show did well its first time around, and if it could last several seasons on the network—the magic number was considered to be four or five years, or roughly a hundred episodes—then it was worth a fortune to syndicators, who usually trimmed a few minutes from the original shows so that more commercials could be inserted, and sold the package back to local stations, or even the network itself, for daily broadcast in the morning, afternoon, or late at night. Plainly, the route to syndication was in characters who became little household gods. All the more motive for suppliers to concoct characters who promised to wear well. Per-

---

*The tenth, *I've Got a Secret*, was really an episode series of its own: a mystery game show in which a regular cast encountered an adversary-of-the-week.

**As late as 1963, *Naked City*, one of the last shows to be shot in New York, made a considerable critical success and a decent enough showing in the ratings—though it never landed among a season's top twenty-five shows—with a format in which the regular cops faded into the background while the foreground belonged to each week's new character in the grip of the city. This figure-ground reversal was unusual, and in the squeeze of growing competition there have not been many attempts to repeat it.

***In 1976, Paul Klein at NBC decided that audiences were outgrowing series; he reserved two hours a night, four nights running, for miniseries and specials. Knowledgeable industry hands attribute NBC's precipitous decline to that decision.

haps most of all, the networks care which actor is going to realize the character. Only as flesh and blood, as an actor, does the character exist for an audience. That is why the networks insist on playing a major part in casting. There is a perpetual tug of war between networks and producers over who gets the last word in casting. In these skirmishes, the networks always have the upper hand: The contracts may guarantee the producers "creative control," but the networks don't have to air the show, and the producers know who is putting up the money. In recent years many producers have been dismayed that the networks have not only usurped the casting of leads but have insisted that whole committees sit in on the casting of minor parts. "I think we should be involved in casting, it's our money," says NBC's genial number-two programming executive, Perry Lafferty. He adds, "The key to every television program's success—and this will get a lot of people mad, but it's true—is casting," Lafferty insists. "It's who plays the lead. I can't tell you any plots from *The Rockford Files*. I used to love it. I love James Garner. I loved Telly Savalas's Kojak. That's what the audience goes for. They go for the performer. They don't remember the plots; you can't write that good over a period of time. So it comes down to who do you put in there."

If the single most important factor in series success is the appeal of its major characters, then it is logical to launch a show with characters whose appeal is pretested. If acquaintanceship is ready-made, so much the better. When secondary characters are "spun off" from current series to stand on their own, presumably they have already accumulated their followings on the road. Indeed, because actor/character magnetism is so mysterious, success may be transferable even when the spun-off character and the tenor of the show change considerably from the original. One case in point is *Lou Grant*, rendered serious when he moved from the comic *Mary Tyler Moore Show*. An even stranger case is *Trapper John, M.D.* This flatly written melodrama featuring a one-time *M*A*S*H* character bore not the slightest tonal resemblance to its progenitor; yet with different producers it rated high on the CBS schedule for several seasons in a row.

Such spinoffs spring from the industry logic of putting capital to maximum use. The impulse might start with the network, the supplying company, the producer, or the actor (or even the actor's agent or business manager). Spinoffs were all the rage in the seventies and early eighties. *The Jeffersons, Maude,* and *Gloria* sprang from *All in the Family; Rhoda, Phyllis,* and *Lou Grant* from *Mary Tyler Moore; Laverne and Shirley* and *Joanie Loves Chachi* from *Happy Days; Sheriff Lobo* from *B.J. and the Bear; Facts of Life* from *Diff'rent Strokes; Enos* from *The Dukes of Hazzard; Knots Landing* from *Dallas; Flo* from *Alice; Benson* from *Soap;* and in a brief third-generation flash, *Checking In* from *The Jeffersons.*

This triumph of the synthetic grew into self-caricature under the successive reigns of Fred Silverman at all three networks. Silverman was head of programming at CBS in 1970–75, president of the ABC Entertainment division in 1975–78, and president of the entire National Broadcasting Company in 1978–81; his unparalleled reign over a decade demonstrates how the networks, in effect, fused in the heat of competition. Spinoffs not only seemed good bets for success, but they gave Silverman, the son of a TV repairman, a chance to exercise his craft: to plunge his own hands into a series, to rework the elements and deploy them to network advantage. As he spun with growing intensity, he also spun with declining finesse. At NBC, in his last season, Silverman tried out five different proposed spinoffs on series episodes. None made it to the air as series.

A number of other spinoffs failed over the years: *Phyllis, Flo, Lobo, Checking In, Enos,* to name only five. Evidently acquaintanceship with character did not transfer automatically. Commercial success required the right context for the right characters.* On the other hand, *The Jeffersons* has lasted nine seasons, at this writing, finishing in the top twenty-five for four of them. *Laverne and Shirley* ranked number one for two years running. *Rhoda, Knots Landing, Facts of Life, Benson,* and *Lou Grant* were at least modest enough successes to run more than one season.

This raises the question of how reliable spinoffs really are. I could not, however, find any network research executive who had bothered to calculate their success rate as against the normal run of shows. "You don't need research for that," said Gerald Jaffe, vice-president for research projects at NBC, humoring me for asking a naïve question. It seemed obvious that spinoffs do better than the average show. So runs the conventional wisdom, which is not always wrong.**

Spinoffs are lucrative not only to networks but to suppliers; indeed, the financial rewards are so great that they routinely overwhelm such aesthetic qualms as may exist. Whoever holds the "created by" credit for a series shares title to its characters, and therefore can

---

*And at the right moment. NBC's *Bret Maverick* (1981–82) brought back the star of a bygone decade in his old role, but couldn't recapture the offhand, self-consciously spoofing charm of the original now that the western form being spoofed was no longer current. It was as if James Garner had come back to the screen telling Eisenhower jokes.

**In the seventies, Hollywood made a counterpart discovery, too: Sequels are to movies as spinoffs are to TV series. Faced with rising costs and declining movie attendance except among teenagers, the studios minimized risk by proliferating *Superman, Smokey and the Bandit, Star Trek, Star Wars, Halloween, Friday the 13th, Grease* . . . almost always to considerable payoff, although rarely as much as the original.

collect a royalty of $25,000 or more per episode, whoever writes and produces the show. Moreover, any writer who devises a character is entitled to a minimum of $657 per half-hour episode, or $1,248 per hour, for each episode in which the character ever appears, no matter who writes it; for an hour-long show the payment would amount to over $27,000 over a short season. The "created by" credit is like the patent on an invention. That is why there are often heated battles over who holds title; adjudicating such matters is a central function of the Writers Guild of America.

Spinoffs are not altogether unprecedented in the history of drama and story-telling, yet television has stretched self-imitation far beyond the limits of previous forms. When Sophocles continued Creon from *Antigone* into *Oedipus the King,* he was not "spinning off Creon"; he was giving body to deep myth and carrying it to completion. Each tragedy was autonomous. When Shakespeare bore Falstaff from the two parts of *Henry IV* into *The Merry Wives of Windsor,* he may have been mindful of Falstaff's popularity, but *The Merry Wives* had a life of its own. When Balzac threaded Rastignac and Vautrin through many volumes of his *Comédie Humaine,* and Trollope did likewise in his *Barsetshire Chronicle,* they almost certainly had commercial motives, but they were not going through the motions of contriving a new situation to keep a character alive. They were populating an entire microcosm with characters who already could be said to exist, prolonging the lives of those already living. By contrast, most spinoffs are like wealthy heirs, living off capital accumulated by the forefathers.

COPIES

If a spinoff exploits success by transferring a character, a copy exploits it by reproducing a formula. Copies are legion. As Brian Winston has aptly written, a goodly number of pilots "are to creativity what Xeroxing is to writing."

But what exactly is a copy? When I asked NBC's Gerald Jaffe about the success rates of imitation shows, he said matter-of-factly, "Everything's an imitation. You can't sort them out. Everything's an imitation of something else." And it is true that in television it is not easy to say what exactly qualifies as a copy, what is a distillation from common trendy materials, and what is simply a normal variation on run-of-the-mill themes.

Only an innocent is shocked by the dryness of the tone in which the immensely successful producer Aaron Spelling says, "There are only seven original plots; you try to do them with style and moderation." In businesslike recognition of this perhaps sad but inevitable truth, the industry speaks with a single jaded voice. NBC's Brandon Tartikoff, for example, said cavalierly about three new CBS shows, "*Magnum* is *Rockford* with another guy in a moustache; *Ladies' Man* is *WKRP* sideways; *Midland Heights* is a ripoff of *Dallas.*" He was talking about the competition, but his tone by no means signaled that these were venial sins. A year later, since *Magnum* was the only new hit of the bunch, it was *Magnum* that was getting cloned by other strapping, half-whimsical "hunks." With imitation so taken for granted, sometimes not even "ripoff" is a term of great opprobrium.

Of course, the entire history of art is rife with imitation. When art was one aspect of ritual, it even aspired to repetition, which hoped to approximate the transcendent. In medieval Europe, the church, crown, and nobility, who sheltered art and hired artists, were devoted principally to conserving traditions. Only as the Middle Ages waned did artists move beyond refinements of technique to search after personal style. Much later, with romanticism, the artist's calling shifted definitively from the refining to the smashing of idols. The desire to break molds now became a philosophical position. William Blake expressed the new attitude strikingly when he belittled the very formulas of rational cognition: "Man by his reasoning power can only compare and judge of what he has already perceived." From this it was only a step to Walt Whitman's call to the open road, Baudelaire's invitation to the voyage, and Pound's supreme modernist ultimatum, "Make it new."

Still, romanticism turned out Janus-faced. Romanticism invoked novelty, inviting artist and reader alike to press beyond the known; but at the same time it proclaimed that nothing was so important as the expression of true feeling. Straining for effect, romanticism invited the artist to repeat prefabricated conventions whose effects on the audience had already been demonstrated.* Romanticism encouraged not only avant-garde forays into the unknown, but academic art's repetition of the altogether known. From the formal rules of academic art to the formulas of popular culture is not so great a leap. Barbara Cartland romance novels, Agatha Christie detective stories, Marvel Comics, and *Dukes of Hazzard* episodes are all of a piece with genre paintings and the general run of sonatas and sonnets. On the premise that people want to repeat a pleasurable experience, to

---

*This argument follows Hermann Broch, "Notes on the Problem of Kitsch." But one should not exaggerate the shift from art-as-self-contained-artifact to art-as-stimulus-to-audience. T. W. Adorno usefully reminds us: "It would be romanticizing to assume that formerly art was entirely pure, that the creative artist thought only in terms of the inner consistency of the artifact and not also of its effect upon the spectators. Theatrical art, in particular, cannot be separated from audience reaction."

make it familiar, the present-day culture industry has erected an apparatus for the mass production of self-imitating artifacts.

On TV, this impulse to imitate also becomes quality control, precisely to check the individualistic excesses of episode writers. Writers are hired by the job, to write "a *Dukes of Hazzard*," "a *M*A*S*H*." Once it was even commonplace for series to provide these journeymen with a "bible," which specified all the salient features of the format. Now, producers, story editors, and staff writers ensure the uniformity of the product. Accordingly, episode writing is entry-level work, the lowest-status and poorest-paid in television's writing hierarchy. (By the terms of the 1981 Writers Guild contract, the 1983–84 minimum payment for a thirty-minute prime-time script is $6,406; for story and script together, $8,933. The comparable figures for sixty minutes are $8,642 and $13,136. Pilots pay a minimum of 150 percent of the applicable episode figures, and in practice pay considerably more.) Episode writers are usually modest and often embarrassed about their labors. "You don't have to have a talent to write for television," says one veteran comedy episode writer. "I thought it was writing, but it's not. It's a craft. It's like a tailor. You want cuffs? You've got cuffs." As a television product moves through the factories of the production companies and the networks, the singular elements are trimmed back, the corners knocked off. Even "novelty" is stereotyped, because only certain forms of novelty are considered salable. Talk of "innovation" is relative in the extreme.

So one must distinguish between the normal imitativeness of art and the industrialized excess that is television's sincerest form of fawning on itself. Throughout the mass-market culture industries—books, magazines, pop music, movies—imitation runs rampant, but in television the process was raised to self-parody by the economics of competition among the three networks. In the mid-seventies, ABC finally elbowed into serious competition with CBS by scoring with teenage shows and the new "jiggle" genre, or what the industry casually and cynically called "T & A," for "tits and ass." A new go-go competition was spawned by the coupling of greed and fear. After ABC's smash *Charlie's Angels* did so well in 1976–77 that frequently more than half the total audience tuned in, imitation became feverish as the other networks rushed in. Within the year, for example, the writer just quoted was hired to rewrite at least three pilots that were variations of *Charlie's Angels*—nubile, adventure-seeking women platonically working for (or symbolically, under) dapper men. At CBS, Mr. Paley was said to have asked his programmers, "Where are *our* beautiful girls?"

At the time, the networks were somewhat at a loss. They had been riding high with cop shows, but pressure groups led by the PTA had prevailed upon some advertisers to cut back their purchase of televised violence. Fleshly display seemed a plausible substitute for fleshly destruction. Brandon Tartikoff, then vice-president of NBC's West Coast programming, had a practical explanation for the new trend: "All of television boils down to excisable elements that you can put in twenty-second promos. If you can't have Starsky pull a gun and fire it fifty times a day on promos, sex becomes your next best handle." It was also the easiest element for executives to notice and copy.

What could be more surface than skin? By the spring of 1978, the networks had commissioned dozens of T&A scripts and pilots with titles, in case the point was obscure, like *The Beach Girls, California Girls, Pom Pom Girls, Roller Girls, The Cheerleaders, California Co-eds, The El Paso Pussycats,* and *Legs.* Only three got on the air: ABC's *The Feather and Father Gang,* about a gorgeous lawyer working with her ex-con father; CBS's *Flying High,* with three stewardesses; and CBS's *The American Girls,* with two TV reporters. Like *Charlie's Angels,* the American Girls worked for a male boss on a long leash. In the pilot, the "girls" were captured by white slavers in Phoenix. Like most pornography, the show contained only enough melodrama to show off the abundant jiggling. (As journalist Richard M. Levine wrote, their "biggest scoops are their necklines.") The producer couldn't reproduce the Angels' tone and the show got unplugged after six episodes. *Flying High,* meanwhile, was the brainchild of an executive producer who cast three voluptuous actresses from top New York modeling agencies. They had done commercials, but none had ever acted a script. Since the Angels formula was read as what one former executive called "three broads, one blonde," one of the stewardesses was obligingly dyed blonde. *Flying High* went down in flames within four months.

These transparent thefts were unavailing partly because *Charlie's Angels* had the gloss of coming first, but partly because the copies were only surface-deep. They copied the elements but not the aura. And the aura was everything. The great critic Walter Benjamin thought art was losing its aura in an age of photographic reproduction, but he did not live long enough to see that trash could acquire its own aura by virtue of finding its formula first. Overnight the Angels became "originals." The formula proved alluring enough to withstand a series of cast changes, although no one ever duplicated Farrah Fawcett's pinup mystique.

Indeed, the *Charlie's Angels* formula was a bit more complicated than generally recognized. The copies failed to sufficiently fathom the Angels' attraction to women, who made up the majority of the Angels' audience. I have heard women say that they were attracted by the Angels' glamorous and frequently changed fashions, and by the spunk they displayed as they played at their Southern California "life-style." Men could tune in to ogle women's bodies; women could tune in to study what those men wanted. Moreover, without having set out to do so, producer Aaron Spelling appealed at once to elements of the new feminism and its conservative opposition. The Angels were skilled working women and sex objects at the same time. Barney Rosenzweig, who produced part of the first season, and whose "consciousness was being raised" by reading Molly Haskell's book on women in the movies, *From Reverence to Rape*, and by going out with a feminist writer, says he persuaded Spelling that the majority of the audience would be "young girls" who were going to take the Angels as role models. The Angels "must be terrific and bright and nonsexist," he said. He wanted to stop the blatantly sexist dialogue, as in one case where a man who had bought a hot dog from an Angel said, "This dog's cold," and she replied, "You should taste the buns," "You should see my buns," or words to that effect, Rosenzweig recalls. Later, after he left the show, the sexist cracks came back.

Throughout the run, the Angels got in and out of jeopardy while relying on Charlie, their unseen detective boss, to bail them out. It was probably no small part of the show's appeal to men that Charlie was heard but never seen. Male authority was invisible, and the "girls" kept free of romance. Charlie's ambassador on the scene was the sexless Bosley, eunuch to Charlie's harem. In the male viewer's fantasy, he could *be* Charlie, ever supervising, ever needed, ever returned-to monopolist of Angels. Spelling had kept Charlie off-screen as a gimmick, but it proved to be a charmed gimmick with psychological point.* The imitation Angels reported to their male bosses on-screen, and lacked the Angels' delicate balance of spunk and subservience.

The commercial problem with copies is that the numbers garnered by an "original" rarely certify an entire trend. Whatever consolation the precedents provide anxious executives, the crude elements of formula are more easily observed and recycled than the singular. The truth is that when it comes to imitations, the networks lack an internal thermostat. Typically, the T&A craze ran out of control until the oversaturated audience finally tuned its channel selectors elsewhere. Then, as the trend was waning, the fundamentalist right administered the *coup de grace* with its protests against "skin," "im-

---

*After the fact, one top network executive acknowledged the show's social function when he said in all seriousness, "A series like *Charlie's Angels* performs a very important and valuable public service. No only does it show women how to look beautiful and lead very exciting lives, but they still take their orders from a man." Rarely do executives theorize about social reasons for a smash hit; there is a virtual taboo against analyzing a golden goose to death. This makes the occasional exception all the more interesting.

plied sexual intercourse," and "sexual innuendo."

By 1982, necklines were up and no new jiggle was being bought. But such boom-and-bust cycles can take years to run their course, while vast sums of money and vast energies go into the copying process along the way. As long as the boom mood prevails, shows that don't fit the mold are starting with higher than normal odds against them. But complaints about executive tastelessness are somewhat beside the point. As long as commercial success is the transcendent goal in the TV market structure, competitors are always likely to copy each other's successes, reasoning that successful Product A is a litmus test that has succeeded in registering a popular desire. Moreover, imitators are always easier to find and hire than are innovators. The same logic leads to TV versions of successful movies, whether serious adaptations (*M*A*S*H*), domestications (*Alice* as a comic version of Martin Scorsese's *Alice Doesn't Live Here Any More*), or capitalizations on a hot genre (*Tales of the Gold Monkey* as a derivative of *Raiders of the Lost Ark*). Executives do not seem to know what to do instead, and don't want to be left out of a good bet. Sooner or later, the mass audience, having gone along with the fad, grows weary, bored, resentful—in its odd way, discriminating. It takes its revenge.

The cultural marketer's problem is how to know which were the magical elements in the original success. What, precisely, is to be extrapolated? The quest for borrowed glory promises security, but it is easy to guess wrong by guessing simple. In 1981, for example, Fred Silverman was by no means the only industry theorist to behold the vast ratings success of CBS's *The Dukes of Hazzard*, which regularly pulled down a 40 share, and conclude that what made it popular was the spectacle of cars crashing, cars sailing through the air, especially the successful chase that at the end of each episode proved the prowess of the show's good ole boys in time for them to gloat over the ineptitude of the hapless sheriff. But despite the show's hayseed reputation—Hollywood writers considered it synonymous with "shit-kicker," the lowest of low-life products—the show was more complex than the chase. An odd family of good-ole-boy brothers, their buxom Daisy Mae cousin (actually named Daisy, to make her archetypal origin clear), and their wise uncle, each week rose up against the wicked, white-suited Boss Hogg, a mean-spirited penny pincher who owned the bank as well as the restaurant where Daisy worked, and seemed to have the sheriff in his back pocket. Each week the town was invaded by bad-guy outsiders, the sheriff proved incompetent, and the good ole boys saved the day after a chase in their custom car, the "General Lee," with its car horn that tooted "Dixie."

The producers thought that the car and the chase were what many men tuned in for—and the show did draw an unusually high proportion of male viewers, though still, like most of television, a female majority. The writer Gy Waldron "always said that General Lee is the most critical character in the show," says Phil Mandelker, *Dukes*'s first producer. "He was right, and so we gave it a personality." But it is a reasonable starting premise that no show draws its viewers all for the same reason. The producers and the network responsible for the original always attribute success to the magic, the "chemistry," of concept, casting, and "execution," and they may be right. But plausibly, too, an element in *Dukes*'s success was its ideology: its fusion of populism, good-ole-boy fraternity, and adolescent high-jinks in behalf of law and order. Phil Mandelker thought as much. "On one level, I saw *Smokey and the Bandit* [a hit movie starring Burt Reynolds] and related very strongly to it, and felt that, wait a minute, there's something really terrific going on here. I felt [*Dukes*] was Robin Hood and Little John in Sherwood Forest. I felt that all of us have a sense that we're in Sherwood Forest today, in which the law no longer seems to work. I took that to its most extreme position, to find the comedy of it, a core of very honest people trying to do good in the middle of Sherwood Forest."*

But when NBC set out to parse the success of *The Dukes of Hazzard*, they came out with buddies and technology. And so, owing a series commitment to Johnny Carson's company, the network ordered from Carson a pilot called *The Stockers*, starring Pittsburgh Steeler quarterback Terry Bradshaw as one of a pair of southern stock-car racers. The show rated badly, and sank quickly. More clones end up in speedy demise than network executives like to think. Television audiences spot a copy when it is hurled right between their eyes. Clones beg for comparison and usually suffer by it. But they are easy to conceive, they do not stretch the imagination, and they keep the assembly line moving.

RECOMBINANTS

If clones are the lowest forms of imitation, recombinants of elements from proven successes are the most interesting. Much of what passes for creativity in Hollywood is additive. In 1981, Fred Silverman's

---

*Mandelker's version of Robin Hood wasn't robbing the rich to help the poor, though. His was the middle-class lament that things don't work: "Part of the trees in the forest that are surrounding us is that we assume a system of justice works, and it doesn't seem to work. We assume that if you pay a man to do a job for you, the job will be done and he will stand by it. And that doesn't work, because the man doesn't need our work. If you call the plumber, he doesn't really need your work," except during economic depression.

NBC made the movie *The Harlem Globetrotters on Gilligan's Island* and the series *The Brady Brides,* based on an earlier hit, *The Brady Bunch.* Once again, Silverman was carrying recombination to his characteristic point of self-parody. "Freddie's in some kind of time warp, and he just keeps groping into the hat for shows that were hits," as the *Hill Street Blues* writer/producer Michael Kozoll put it. But Silverman's vulgarity lay only in excess: He spliced a bit too frantically, imitated one or two decades back too far.

For in normal network doings, not only are many of the products deliberately recombinant, so is industry jargon. Grant Tinker, who had earned his reputation as a high-taste TV proprietor, still told me about a project in the works at MTM that, "just to be quick about it" —and quick is the way projects are bought and sold—he called *Hill Street in the Hospital.* (In 1982, NBC bought it under the title *St. Elsewhere.*) An ad agency referred to CBS's series *Falcon Crest* as "a taste of *The Good Earth* and a dash of *Dallas* in the middle of a California vineyard." Producer Garry Marshall told writer Sally Bedell that he conceived of *Happy Days* as "a look back, a humorous *Waltons.* In my head I was doing Norman Rockwell and *Huckleberry Finn* and *Tom Sawyer.*" "I have never been in a TV development meeting," says Michael Kozoll, "where someone does not use that language and ask, 'What's it like?'"

What is good enough shorthand for shows also applies to characters. One old writing hand, Richard Powell (no relation to the actor), was writing a pilot for NBC about a man in his late sixties who had suffered a stroke and maintained "an acerbic relationship" with a black woman therapist. "We constantly fight," Powell said, "because they will say things to you like, 'Well, we want the man to be more like Archie Bunker, and we want the woman to be more like Maude,' and they want a kid in there who'll be like the kid in *Diff'rent Strokes.*"

This was Silverman product, too. As it happens, Silverman's network reigns were the periods of maximum competition for booming advertiser dollars, and therefore the times most given to cannibalizing programs. How easy for the press to pin the responsibility and the blame on a single powerhouse, overlooking the corporate heads and boards that promoted him to successively more powerful positions until his bubble burst. The era of recombinatory excess took off in the Silverman seventies, and many industry old hands look back nostalgically to the presumably Golden Years, when patterns of imitation had not become so automatic. Grant Tinker harks back, for instance, to his earlier tenure at NBC, 1961–66, when "television was surely more varied, and because it was, I think people were hitting bull's-eyes a little more often. They weren't just clonishly following each other in a sort of futile game of program leapfrog, as we all seem to be doing now." But the trend preceded Silverman and outlasted him.

Cultural recombination is not simply a convenient if self-defeating way of concocting shows to exploit established tastes. It is part of the ground rhythm of modern culture.

Of course, networks and suppliers think they are being eminently practical when they order up recombinants and imitations. After all, they are bureaucracies trying to capitalize on and mobilize demonstrable tastes. If the success rates of recombinants are not very good, what routine procedure stands a better chance of fabricating hits with minimum risk of embarrassing flops? Recombination and imitation seem like low-risk ways of getting by. Executives in any enterprise, as the organization theorist Herbert Simon argues, aim to get by—he calls it "satisficing"—rather than seek breakthroughs on the odd chance of maximizing profits.

Recombinant talk is splendidly practical, too, providing signposts for rapid recognition, speeding up meetings, streamlining discussion about cultural goods that might otherwise seem elusive, unwieldy, hard to peg. Meetings have to be brisk, for the mass-cultural assembly line has to keep moving. Bertolt Brecht observed it in what he called the "mindless chatter" of an MGM executive in the forties: "the ongoing incest of what has been liked and bought with something else that has been liked and bought (simply rearranged)." Recombinant talk fairly begs to be parodied, but simply to parody would be shortsighted. TV executives are trying to gauge a show's appeal to consumers who, in turn, are going to make a snap judgment about whether to watch it partly, assumedly, on the grounds of whether it reminds them of pleasure and promises to repeat or extend it. But imitation too crude risks calling attention to imitativeness itself rather than the product being imitated. That is why crude imitations usually do less well than the originals. And thus the special appeal of recombination, which is imitation to the next highest power.

Beyond the immediate logic of marketability, recombinant thinking is rooted deeply throughout all modern culture and thought. Capitalism as a culture has always insisted on the new, the fashionable, the novel. Indeed, its first literary creation was precisely the novel; its second was the newspaper, with its artless juxtapositions. The genius of consumer society is its ability to convert the desire for change into a desire for novel goods. Circulation and employment depend on it. Popular culture above all is transitory; this guarantees not only turnover for the cultural marketers but currency for the customers. But curiously, the inseparable economic and cultural pressures for novelty must coexist with a pressure toward constancy. Nostalgia for "classics"—old movies, "oldie" songs, antiques—is consumer society's tribute to our hunger for a stable world. Consumers want novelty but take only so many chances; manufacturers, especially oligopolists, want to deploy their repertory of the tried-

and-true in such a way as to generate novelty without risk. The fusion of these pressures is what produces the recombinant style, which collects the old in new packages and hopes for a magical synthesis.

As Susan Sontag points out, imitation and recombination make up a cultural set that pervades Western life in the late decades of the twentieth century. Constantly we liken experience to other experience. We attempt to assemble scraps of memory and lore, cataloguing one phenomenon as a variant of others already in repertory. Comparison saturates not only public speech but private thought. The reader thinks that Ross Macdonald writes like Raymond Chandler. The tourist thinks that this landscape has the palms of Southern California and the broad beaches of the Atlantic coast. The doctor thinks that this case resembles that one, with a twist of the other. This style of thought limits risk and gain at the same time. It is the creativity of least resistance, a managerial way to navigate the flux of incessant stimulus. Recombination conserves the mind's powers under the unrelenting pressure of the new that modernity has opened up. Classification is the essence of modern science and everyday experience alike, and recombination runs rampant through the contemporary imagination.

The recombinant style is, of course, not new in the twentieth century. Arthur Koestler even argued that recombinant thinking, the ability to apply one intellectual framework in a different context, is always the essence of creative thinking in the arts and sciences. "The creative act," he wrote, "is not an act of creation in the sense of the Old Testament. It does not create something out of nothing; it uncovers, selects, reshuffles, combines, synthesizes already existing facts, ideas, faculties, skills. The more familiar the parts, the more striking the new whole. Man's knowledge of the changes of the tides and the phases of the moon is as old as his observation that apples fall to earth in the ripeness of time. Yet the combination of these and other equally familiar data in Newton's theory of gravity changed mankind's outlook on the world. . . ." But Koestler missed the fact that recombination as such brings forth a hundred or a thousand banalities for each striking new synthesis, and in the process degenerates into mechanical juxtaposition to suit the rhythm of consumption and fashion in consumer society. The executive raves "unique" or "special" many times a day; the producer says he is looking for "something new" and is jolted into his new idea by seeing *Smokey and the Bandit*. And when standardization threatens the integrity of new work by collapsing it into variations on the old, it stands to reason that connoisseurship requires and commands a proliferation of varieties: twenty different varieties of ice cream, French mustard, Cabernet Sauvignon. Discriminating taste counterbalances the imitative impulse. Connoisseurs adore nuance, yet often even nuance is expressed as recombination: this with a touch of that, a hint of the other.

The recombinant style now shapes not only the marketing of new toothpastes but the marketing of high as well as popular culture. Proust was not seen as "the new Balzac," but in 1984 a publisher will no doubt promote a serious novel as "the new *White Hotel.*" Willie Mays wasn't "the new Joe DiMaggio," but sports announcers now speak of basketball players who have "the speed of Dr. J. with the muscle of Willis Reed." Team owners would breed Mendelian hybrids if they could. The culture industry's sales effort, sharing in this fever, helps impose on us all a new language of shorthand. Shorthand is the semantic accompaniment of imitation and recombination. What they share is the tendency to reduce information to bits for rapid processing. Shorthand suits the computer age and the age of television, in which information comes in quick bursts, instant "hits," rapid cuts, what TV news people call "bites." If anything is communicated at all, it should be communicated quickly. By the same token, if it cannot be communicated quickly, it must not have been worth saying at all. In selling, moreover, shorthand is practical. A publisher's salesperson has thirty seconds to convince a bookseller to carry book X. Naturally, the blurb will have to tell the tale, and the sales force will prefer books whose "story line" can most easily be reduced to a thirty-second blurb, especially if the author's name is not an instant sell.

Even for the artist, in a world stripped of transcendent unities, the strategy of collage, of juxtaposition, makes the best of a bad situation. It is both recognition of, and romantic protest against, the idea that the world is finished, worn out. The best art coaxes a distinct unity out of juxtaposition; bad art deposits scrap upon scrap, endlessly reshuffling the cultural givens into pastiche, as in *Star Wars* and *Raiders of the Lost Ark.* Whether in *fin-de-siècle* assemblage or surrealist juxtaposition, in Rauschenberg or Larry Rivers, the style of conjunction is central to modern art. In poetry we see it in the fragments of Eliot's "The Waste Land" and Pound's *Cantos,* in John Ashbery's breathless swoops from image to image. The nervous editing style of most contemporary film has shaped every other art form. In the novel, we have the pop-cultural dumping grounds of Joyce, the luminous lists of Jorge Luis Borges; in architecture, the postmodernism of Michael Graves and Philip Johnson among others. In a single building, postmodernism shamelessly combines the classical (columns and pediments), the decorative (ornament and trim), and the Bauhaus (simplicity and angularity). In museums, as Susan Sontag points out, the Paris Beaubourg is built with movable partitions, so that the relations between distinct exhibits can be redefined at the curator's will. The high forms of popular music are unified recombinant albums—the Beatles' *Sgt. Pepper's Lonely Hearts Club Band*, The Who's *Tommy*—and more recently, Blondie's 1980 album *Autoamerican*, which contains songs in big band, reggae, rap, religious-portentous, and rhythm-and-blues styles. Such albums with their peculiar unity assert that order can be assembled only from the juxtaposition of shards. They echo Eliot's line, "These fragments I have shored against my ruins." In fashion, the New Wave extends the conventional assertion that all styles are born equal and juxtaposition amounts to wit. Anything goes with anything else—tuxedo jackets with candy wrappers, leg warmers with sandals—mocking and extending the recombinatory mode at the same time.

In the background stands the ultimate recombinatory form: television, the medium that perpetually levels, juxtaposing *Holocaust* to a soap commercial, news of cluster bombs in Lebanon to an appeal for hemorrhoid medicine, converting each bit into a sequel to the last and a prologue to the next, composing unintended and hitherto unimagined wholes out of parts and proposing that all images are related to all others. Scarcely a punk rock or New Wave album is complete without a song decrying television, satirizing the singer's dependency on it, skating along the slippery edge where irony and subjugation melt together. The fascination TV works on its most furious bewailers is the fascination of meaninglessness raised to a universal principle.*

Yet the mind-sets of network gatekeepers and New Wave songwriters may not be so different at least in one respect. They are both haunted by the half-felt premise that nothing is new under the sun. This is not, of course, the first cultural moment to suffer from, or revel in, a sense of exhaustion. At the turn of the century, the West did not know whether it was speeding toward universal utopia or running out of meaningful inventory. In his singular way, Nietzsche proposed both at once. At the same time, socialists and inventors and Cubists insisted there were great things to be done, a universal mankind was in the making, although Marx and the Wright Brothers disagreed over whether the instrument of universal oneness would be the class struggle or the flying machine. Both the political and aesthetic hopes of the Second International period were crushed by the First World War; for doubters and onetime believers alike, the old sense of clo-

---

*Consider "T.V.O.D." by the British group, The Normal:

> T.V.O.D. . . .
> I don't need a TV screen.
> I just stick the aerial into my skin.
> Let the signal run through my veins.

sure was now reconfirmed a hundred times over in the trenches of Passchendaele and Verdun.

This sense of cultural exhaustion has, if anything, swelled in the course of the century. Not unvaryingly or irreversibly: Artists are perennially animated by the hope for a breakthrough, or the allegation that they have already attained one. There have been moments of renaissance: Weimar Germany, Paris in the thirties, New York in the forties, and many places in the sixties. But without question the seventies represent the culmination of artistic weariness in more fields than television. Consider what Kennedy Fraser wrote about clothing in 1980:

> Fashion appears to have reached an impasse . . . has been atrophying for a decade or more. It may now simply have achieved the end toward which it has been tending: to short-circuit or completely foil spontaneity in its creators and its followers. The snag is that spontaneity is the whole point of fashion. . . . [M]ost collections both here and in Europe continue to be absolutely saturated with more or less direct borrowings from the twenties, the thirties, the forties, the fifties—and now the sixties as well. . . . Now that fashion has started reviving the nineteen-sixties, it seems clear that we've reached the end of some sort of line. . . . There won't be anything of the seventies to revive.

Substitute "pop music" or "painting" or "theater" or "movies" or "the novel" or "television" and those lines still ring true.

So Fred Silverman was not alone when he permuted the television programs of his early years. Recombination was and remains the fashionable mode. And Aaron Spelling was speaking for the *Zeitgeist* when he said, "There are only seven original plots." Many industry hands echo Spelling, with variations: There are eight basic sitcoms, seven basic mysteries, or, even more grandly, nine or twelve or fifteen basic dramatic structures in history, period. Didn't Goethe, after all, say there were thirty-six basic plots? Gatekeepers say they are gamely looking for something new, but secretly they doubt it exists. There is barely an idea that hasn't been tried, they say, barely a plot device that hasn't been done again and again. Even gimmicks have precedents: A show featuring a monkey is patterned after a show featuring a dog; *The Six Million Dollar Man* spins off *The Bionic Woman;* and they "work," don't they?

When network executives admit something is wrong with television, they invoke shortages. Novelty and quality are scarce, they say, because in the end talent is scarce. Call this jadedness or realism, it is strikingly the same claim made by publishers of books and magazines, by producers of Broadway plays, even by many critics: There is simply not enough talent to go around. Canny studio buyers and advertising men and worn-down series producers say the same thing. "We eat our children," says Brandon Tartikoff. "It's very tough to deal with the enormous appetite of television," according to Richard H. Low, executive vice-president in charge of Broadcasting Programming and Purchasing for Young and Rubicam. "You're not going to increase the water supply by adding more spigots. We're all for more diversity and more quality, the three networks are dying for more quality—granted, quality with the requirement of large audience. The search for new writing talent that can fit that special need is continuous and enormous. Another way to look at it is to ask how many plays of quality make it to Broadway, and how many of those would appeal to 20 million people or more."

Even writers agree: "It's not a mark against the creative community," says Larry Gelbart. "I just don't think ever in the world there have been that many talented people, all in one place, who could supply this kind of assembly-line demand." "The appetite is so voracious," said Grant Tinker when he was still at MTM, "that we wind up just feeding shit into it and that's what comes out. Nobody's setting out to make shit, but there are just only so many Jim Brookses and Allan Burnses.* Television would be wonderful if it were only on Wednesday nights."

The statistics are indeed daunting. Prime-time television takes up 22 hours a week on each network, for a total of 3,432 hours a year on all three. The comedy writer Michael Elias even argues that television looks so bad because so much of it is visible. If the equivalent number of oil paintings from a certain year were hung in full view, he says, painting in general might not look so stellar. The same might be said of all the new fiction published in the course of a year.

Of course, the point is arguable, unproved, unprovable and probably exaggerated. Talent is one of those mysteries, like intelligence or beauty, which is not a static national attribute like land mass. If talent is defined relative to the untalented, the argument is even tautological: Talent is always scarce. The fact is that network television works just well enough, as money-making machinery, to satisfy America's pop-cultural entrepreneurs. Whatever talent does exist, or might rise to the occasion under the right circumstances, the networks have no vast incentives to encourage it—and some to cut it to size, the size of network formulas. Writers in any form tend to write what they see: If they see formula, they learn to write formula, and forget they may ever have aspired to write anything else.

---

*Responsible, together or separately, for *Room 222*, *The Mary Tyler Moore Show*, *Lou Grant*, and *Taxi*, among others.

The television assembly line devours talent along with incompetence, not only because it runs through programs so fast, but because
the system prizes slick dialogue more than story, schematic story line
more than complexity, and, in comedy, jokes more than consistency
or intensity of character or situation. (Joke-writers are hired to
"punch up" flagging sitcom scripts; the norm is three gags per page,
which works out to three a minute.) Rainer Werner Fassbinder, Alain
Tanner, Michelangelo Antonioni, Federico Fellini have made important films for West German, Swiss, and Italian television, but in
American television there is no high-cultural reservation that is insti-
tutionally insulated against the pressures of mass-market thinking.
Even public television is far more interested in (and subsidized for)
the acceptably quaint or "high-cultural" productions of the British
than native forms.

As for the actual "creative community" of Hollywood, that quite
definite collection of a few hundred producers, writers, and directors
who get the lion's share of the work, most have been rewarded
handsomely enough and long enough for adhering to formula that it
is only painful to recall they may have hoped for more. They pride
themselves on what the industry calls "craft." Younger writers who
loathe the conventions will shirk the business altogether, or divide
themselves, writing episodes to order to make a living, while they
work on the side on more serious plays and screenplays. So the
business selects its own, and there is no shortage of craftsmanlike
writers looking at the screen, saying "I can do that!" and catching the
next plane for Los Angeles.

In the heart of the business are a hundred or so writers whose
names show up again and again in the credits, composing a recombinant mosaic all their own. Once they master the standard forms and
prove themselves reliable for the subdivided tasks of television writing—for "light" or "cops" or "family"—they are in demand. Routinely the networks come to them and ask if they would be interested
in doing a pilot on such-and-such a subject in such-and-such a style.
They wangle a respectful hearing when they "pitch" an idea back.
The networks dicker with them. They are the regulars, the ones who
have succeeded in internalizing the industry's values. Once in a
while they are strong enough and inventive enough and lucid
enough to break through the old norms and to keep control of a show
against all the network pressures to flatten it. Usually they lack either
the capacity, opportunity, or will to do more than get by.

The problem is not simply that in the heat of production the
writing is done by committee. With many hands stirring the broth,
the Hollywood studio system succeeded in producing not only
watered-down, derivative concoctions but quite a few fine movies in
rapid order. Steady production does not automatically debase art;

when skilled crews are kept under contract they can only help a serious repertory company, even in television. Insiders blame the pace of series production, which is more to the point. Rarely can a series stockpile enough scripts before the show starts shooting each season. The rest are being written while other episodes are being shot, edited, troubleshot. While the clock ticks away, each of the four acts of an hour drama may be farmed out to a different writer, as on *Hill Street Blues*, leaving it up to harried producers to yoke them together at the eleventh hour. Without doubt episodic television's ever-looming deadlines do damage the long-term quality of a series, but deadlines by themselves can't account for the shallowness of most pilots. Most network television is simply bad—inert, derivative, cardboard—because no one with clout cares enough to make it otherwise. It is good enough for its purposes.

Many of the most talented people in the business feel, or tell themselves, that they are serving their apprenticeship, or their time, making their money and their contacts, honing—or so they want to think—their craft, hoping to sell a movie script and move up into the big leagues of feature films to stay. But most television writers don't burn to do anything different from what they already do. They only wish they had more time to do it, with less interference. The going conventions work well enough for networks, advertisers, affiliates, producers, writers, and enough of the audience. No critical mass of writers demonstrates all at once the passion to say something different, the craft and ingenuity to make it mass-marketable, and the clout to sell it. Audiences are disgruntled with network television, but passively, and without any clear allegiance to a substantial alternative.

And so the sense of cultural exhaustion—whose most prominent symptom is the recombinant form—is at least in part self-fulfilling. In the early eighties, the networks flounder without anything that qualifies as an exciting trend even in their own terms. Old-timers proclaim that the spark is missing from the new shows, and wonder if they're only getting old. The networks whistle in the dark against the threat of competition from the new video technologies. While the official line proclaims that the networks will do fine—because ad rates are booming and the total number of homes using television is still rising even though the networks' aggregate market share is falling—in the industry's dark night more than a few executives wonder how much longer they can stay at the vital center of popular entertainment. There is anxiety about the networks' future, and the sense of a slow fadeout. It might turn out that television is not only a cause but the flickering exemplar of our larger cultural exhaustion.

The more sophisticated the numbers the executives play with, the safer the forms they employ—whether spinoffs, clones, or recombinants—the more cynical and disheartened TV's major players become, and the more their products ring hollow. The pursuit of safety above all else makes economic sense to the networks, at least in the short run, but success anxiety reduces many a fertile idea to an inert object, which usually also turns out to be a commercial dud. For all the testing and ratings research and all the self-imitative market calculation in the world does not produce that originality or energy that makes for much commercial success, let alone truth, provocation, or beauty.

In headlong pursuit of the logic of safety, the networks ordinarily intervene at every step of the development process. It is as if there were not only too many cooks planning the broth, but the landlord kept interfering as well. This presumably rational process wreaks havoc with shows, and confounds even the network's own logic. Far from a smoothly humming assembly line, the development process is clumsy, chancy political warfare. Eventually the network sets the terms, but doesn't always get the results intended. More often than not, commerce defeats not only art but commerce itself. The complex workings of network power, and its hold over production, are best pondered concretely. Consider, then, the travail of a single prime-time series.

C H A P T E R 6

"Another American Dream Gone Astray"

On Sunday night, April 26, 1981, from nine-thirty to eleven o'clock, ABC broadcast the pilot of a series called *American Dream.* This was one of thirty-one pilots ABC had developed for the 1980–81 season, and it was coming on late, as a backup replacement. *American Dream* was a quiet show about a white family, in middling circumstances, who move from the suburbs to an interracial city neighborhood, where they play out their domestic dramas amid problems of schools, crime, and racial hostility. It was the year's only new dramatic series set in a family, and the only show on television featuring an intact, modern-day, mom-pop-and-the-kids family. (*The Waltons* and *Little House on the Prairie* were set in the idealized past.) Like every other family show in television's history, it proposed that domestic life could be an adventure.

In a season heavy with situation comedies, shoot-'em-ups, and the sort of adventures Hollywood calls "tire-squealers," *American Dream* was also—along with *Hill Street Blues*—the only new series to make a serious approach to the edgy everyday experience of life in the heart of American cities. Top-rated shows like *Dukes of Hazzard* and *Magnum, P.I.* used automobiles as the traditional emblems of speed, prowess, and freedom, but *American Dream* showed them as burdens. Like most television series, *American Dream* told small

moral tales that left clear-cut virtues standing out in the open where
no one of ordinary intelligence could miss them. But this one
plunged the good guys into a recognizable world of choices rich with
political implications. It showed a decent middle-class family trying
to get traction in a world out of control.

The pilot was the "genesis" show, the episode that carries the
characters into the series' enduring situation. Shot in Chicago, it
opens with husband Danny Novak (Stephen Macht) stuck in a rush-
hour traffic jam. We soon learn that wife Donna (Karen Carlson) is
pregnant with their fourth child. With their two sons, fifteen and
twelve, already squabbling over the room they share in a suburban
house, Danny and Donna go looking for larger suburban premises;
but with Danny working in the sporting-goods department at Marshall Field and Donna taking care of the children, they can't afford
a house they like and don't like the ones they can barely afford. Fed
up with his long commute and annoyed by the casual racism of one
of his sons, Danny happens one day to pass by the inner-city neighborhood where he grew up. There he spots a big, beat-up, but eminently right and, it turns out, eminently affordable Victorian house.
Donna is skeptical of city living and dubious about the run-down
house, but Danny, with the help of the house's crusty old owner,
Berlowitz (Hans Conreid), convinces her that they need the space,
that he needs to break the habit of commuting, and that the children
will grow up more decent, spunkier, and more cultured if they grow
up with other races and close to the city's cultural bounty of museums and concert halls. The boys don't want to leave friends and
budding romances in the suburbs, but Danny thinks they are spoiled
and overrules them. The lily-white suburbs, he says, amount to
"nothing but shopping malls and crab grass." He was "conned" by
"the American Dream. To own your own home complete with ga-
rage, barbecue pit, lawn mower, and a two-hour ride to anywhere
remotely civilized. It's become a nightmare."

The Novaks move into the city and immediately run into trouble.
A Hispanic neighbor rebuffs Donna's friendly overtures because,
with middle-class whites moving into the neighborhood, he knows
his rent is going up. Then twelve-year-old Todd is mugged and
beaten up by a Hispanic tough in school. But the neighborly Hispanic
wife proves helpful; the Novak sons move closer together; Todd
begins boxing lessons with Danny's encouragement; and with her
father coming to live with them, Donna grows pluckier about the
urban adventure.

The pilot was soft, sentimental, obvious in many respects, but there
were some striking notes. For one thing, far from being TV's automatically adorable tykes, the Novak boys were whiny and obnoxious.
(The younger girl was cuddly and adorable, for relief's sake.) More-

over, the parents fought back: When Todd said to his brother, "It's that time of the month again. Look out!" Donna shot back, "That's the last time I wanna hear that expression. It's cheap and sexist!" When Todd whined that Donna's father was coming to live with them, Donna lectured him sternly, with her voice cracking: "You're a selfish, inconsiderate little boy and I don't like you very much right now."

The show confronted race tensions with liberal piety, yet acknowledged that people of color might have economic reasons for resenting do-gooding whites. When I saw the show, I was touched by Danny Novak's embrace of those liberal pieties, now in such bad odor, and impressed with the show's presentation of reasonable arguments among reasonable people on thorny subjects. I was pleased to see Chicago instead of Los Angeles for a change, and I shed some tears when the Novaks stood up for the American spirit of fair play.

The next night, ABC ran another episode of *American Dream*. According to Nielsen, the pilot acquired a 28 percent share of the viewing audience, which is about average. The second episode, the next night, drew the same share; the third, two Wednesdays later, did much worse; and the fourth, run off three weeks later, did worse still. Most reviews were favorable. But after four episodes ABC pulled the plug. *American Dream* disappeared.*

Only connoisseurs of Hollywood's behind-the-scenes dramas noticed that while the credits for the pilot listed Barney Rosenzweig as producer, the credits for the subsequent episodes listed Jerry Thorpe and William Blinn as executive producers with only a "Developed for Television by" credit for Rosenzweig. In the tale of *American Dream*'s journey onto the schedule and its brief moment before the public, the replacement of the show's guiding hand was the weirdest and least typical turn of events. But even this oddity reveals something about the network's safety-first logic, its *modus operandi*, and the ways in which producers cope with network power. So committed was ABC to shape *American Dream* into the object of its desire, it was prepared to take a show away from its authors.

American Dream was Barney Rosenzweig's idea. In fact, to hear Barney Rosenzweig tell it, "Danny Novak is Barney Rosenzweig. Those are my children. That is my dream. Danny Novak is a guy who is not particularly well educated, not particularly intelligent, but a caring and concerned and decent human being, an outraged guy, a guy who is totally nonplussed to discover that his twelve-year-old doesn't know that Paris is in France, who is totally pissed off that his

---

*In months to come, NBC expressed an interest in picking up the show, but nothing came of it. The networks are very reluctant to buy "damaged goods."

fifteen-year-old will not take a bus anywhere. Those things happened to me. My kids are all girls, but they are those kids, and they're not like me. They don't have my motivation; they don't have my push; they don't do things the way I do. No kids that I know do. And it angers me."

On the June day I called him, Barney Rosenzweig was also angry about the fate of his television program. Barney Rosenzweig was forty-three years old, a tall man who wore a neatly trimmed beard that, along with his sandy hair, was just beginning to gray. The curve of his career was typical. While still in his twenties, he had been the line producer—the functioning organizer of stories, schedules, casting, editing—on the long-running series *Daniel Boone*. After a reverse in the film business, in the late seventies he got the knack for converting commercial book and theater properties into television movies. In 1980 he produced the miniseries *East of Eden;* a high-rated TV movie, *Cagney and Lacey;* and the pilot for *American Dream.* In the small world that values the efficient production of "product," he was a known quantity, a pro. He knew how to bring in television programs on time, on budget, and to order. It didn't hurt that, in a town that relishes the tang and rhythm of fast, engaging talk, Barney Rosenzweig was a direct and passionate talker. Among buyers and sellers who trade in stories, he was a story-teller *par excellence.* And his talk was no bluster. He had a track record: By 1981, he had produced about 110 hours of prime-time television entertainment.

Like many other producers in Hollywood, Barney Rosenzweig had made the right connections early on. The right connections might not make you successful—that depends on many things, including talent—but they could usher you in the right doors to get a shot at proving yourself. He grew up in East Los Angeles, the son of a music teacher. (It never hurts to grow up in the company town.) As head cheerleader at the University of Southern California, he was bitten by the showmanship bug. Upon graduation, Rosenzweig went to work in the mail room of MGM's publicity department. The mail room is the easiest route to visibility in the networks, studios, production companies, and agencies, and so has long been a good launch point for a show business career. The first film he was put to work on, typing captions and such, was *Ben-Hur.* Rosenzweig knew USC, where the premiere was to take place, and wound up organizing a chariot race in the Coliseum at the USC-UCLA football game. But he hated the "anonymity" of being a press agent. He wanted his name on his work.

One break led to another. His father-in-law, Aaron Rosenberg, was a top producer at Twentieth Century–Fox and executive producer of, among other projects, the *Daniel Boone* series. Rosenberg put

Rosenzweig up for the job of line producer, and although Fess
Parker, the star, was feuding with Rosenberg, Rosenzweig impressed
Parker and got the job.

Rosenzweig made the most of it. While executive producers take
charge of quality control, budget, writing, casting, and hiring the
production crew, the directors, editors, and production managers,
the so-called line producer is the all-purpose organizer of the nuts
and bolts of production. At *Daniel Boone*, because Rosenberg was
busy with other projects, Rosenzweig was free to supervise the writing. Although no writer of lines, he proved adept at coming up with
stories for writers. Themes came out of his head, out of newspapers,
out of movies and plays that came his way. A good number of his
treatments were liberal, consonant with the leftward drift of educated opinion in the late sixties.

"I could steal anything and make it a *Daniel Boone*. I did *The Guns
of Navarone*, I did *Moby Dick* [with a white bear], I did Brendan
Behan's *The Hostage*," with the Irish Revolution transposed to the
American. He instructed writers to portray the Revolutionary War
by "making it Vietnam, with the colonials as the Vietcong and the
English as the Americans." Boone defended civil disobedience. Rosenzweig transposed the black studies controversy, then raging
across American campuses, into a story about Red Indian studies in
which Boone's son supports a Cherokee chief's son living in Boones-
boro who wants to learn about Indian culture. "What's wonderful
about it was that I wasn't preaching to the converted. *Daniel Boone*
was a hit in Louisiana. *Daniel Boone* was a smash in Arkansas. *Daniel
Boone* was number one in Kentucky. I wasn't preaching to a bunch
of liberals in New York or L.A. or Chicago. I was hitting people who
never had explored these ideas before. And they were digging it.
Some of them were getting angry. They were writing letters saying,
'What are you trying to do here?' I would write them back: 'Daniel
Boone was a revolutionary. If it wasn't for people like Daniel Boone,
we'd still be a colony of England.' "

Most people in television hope to rise into—or at least visit—the
higher-status world of feature films. Rosenzweig was no exception,
but he found *Daniel Boone* a hard act to follow. His attempt at a
blockbuster feature film, *Who Fears the Devil*, proved disastrous. He
retreated to television, made a TV movie, and got hired by Aaron
Spelling to produce part of the first season of *Charlie's Angels*. By the
late seventies, he realized that he needed a partner, "somebody to
politically run interference for me, somebody who had muscle," and
he hooked up with a one-time manager named Mace Neufeld who
headed a small production company called BNB Productions. As
head of the television department, he was ready to try a series of his
own.

The idea for *American Dream* germinated because Rosenzweig remained a USC football fan. He drove to every home game, and, like any savvy Angeleno, he liked to scout for alternatives to the jammed freeway. So, on streets where people of his class did not ordinarily travel, he would pass through block after block of old Spanish-style homes priced at an extraordinarily low $80,000 or $90,000. "Built by eastern builders before they understood what you could get away with in California. They're built like fortresses. Massive lawns. The problem is that they're all-black neighborhoods. It's the old part of L.A. that whites liked thirty years ago. Fifteen minutes west and you'd be paying a million dollars for the same house in Beverly Hills. I used to drive by those all the time, and I used to say, wouldn't it be funny, wouldn't it be an interesting series, to come up with a guy who is crowded in his house in the Valley, tired of fighting the freeway every day to downtown Los Angeles, and one day he gets off the freeway because there's a traffic jam, and he's driving all these circuitous routes, and he sees this place for sale, and it's got everything he needs: bedrooms, bathrooms, yard, five minutes from his work. What's the problem? Everybody in the neighborhood's black. And he says, 'Fuck it, I don't care.'"

Rosenzweig described his idea to the woman he lived with, a successful television comedy writer named Barbara Corday. "Initially we thought that it was a half-hour comedy idea," recalls Corday, "sort of the antithesis of what you might normally see on television." The idea was that a white family in such a neighborhood would be a fish out of water, a promising premise for a long-running series in need of a myriad of plot ideas. Since her normal writing partner was in Europe, Corday and Rosenzweig asked another comedy writer, Ken Hecht, to work with Corday.

Then came the "pitching." Rosenzweig pitched the comedy to CBS, which "passed" (a Hollywood euphemism for slightly softening the bad news of a No). The following week Rosenzweig took it to NBC's comedy development department, who said yes. The next morning Corday said to Rosenzweig, "I think we've pitched the wrong show."

"I woke up dreaming about it, and I said to Barney, 'This is not a comedy, this is a dramatic show, and I think what's going to happen if we do it as a comedy is that it will be a one-joke show, and it will wear thin very quickly.'" She was also horrified about the racist connotations of jokes about black images of whites and white images of blacks. Rosenzweig agreed and added a formal consideration. Half-hour comedies take place on two or three sets indoors. In his conception, on the contrary, "the star of the show should really be the neighborhood."

So Rosenzweig went to NBC's drama department and sold a new

version of the show as a dramatic series. But that afternoon the word came down that NBC chairman Fred Silverman had just put a freeze on buying. If Rosenzweig wanted to wait seven weeks, he would probably have a deal, but he decided to take the show to the last network in town. Rosenzweig's pitch to ABC was the same: "This is an American pioneer family. This is the recapturing of an American tradition. This is Daniel Boone in 1980. The family is a unit. They are warm, they care about each other. This is a bust-loose show. We are going to talk about the real America. The American dream no longer exists, or is a bare possibility, or may be recapturable. It's a populist kind of picture. It's an opportunity for a guy to see that the world is not working out the way he expected it to, that he's been sold a bill of goods, and he's going to take the bull by the horns, take charge of his own life, and despite all other odds is going to deal with his family and his life, and not let the bureaucracy, not let the society, not let the bullshit get him down. That's who Danny Novak is." And ABC's dramatic development executives, Clifford B. Alsberg and John Levoff, bought it.

"We all conceded from the beginning," says Rosenzweig, "including ABC, that this was a CBS kind of show"—reasonably realistic, reasonably serious, race-conscious. But CBS already had *The White Shadow*—a show about a white basketball coach among black players—on its schedule. ABC was a riskier prospect but a more exciting one, for ABC was then the top-rated network and *American Dream* wasn't its typical product. The chances of getting on the schedule were lower, but Rosenzweig figured that with the network's enthusiasm, once they did get on, they would be given a protected spot with a good, compatible lead-in at an appropriate hour. ABC's audience was younger and more urban than the other networks', just the sort of audience to which the show would appeal. Rosenzweig recalls, "The instructions from ABC were, 'Okay now, when you write this, we would like it to be in the idiom of *Eight Is Enough* [a light, successful, family melodrama about a large family]. We know it's tougher than *Eight Is Enough,* but don't make it too gritty. Keep it light, keep it gay.' "

Television writers normally do what they are told, and comedy writers "write light" without needing to be told, even when they are attempting the hour-long dramatic form. Their product is designed to go down easy. It has to be compatible with commercials. Advertising executives like to say that television shows are the meat in a commercial sandwich. Situation comedies above all are meant to propel the audience from one little crisis to another, each crisis erupting just before the commercial break, each fairly begging for a happy and accessible solution. Despite Norman Lear's breakthroughs in the seventies, sitcom characters are, for the most part, still what the novelist Herbert Gold once called "happy people with happy problems."

Accordingly, the Corday-Hecht drafts dwelt on the adorable children, assigning them signpost dialogue—another television staple—to advertise the show's themes. When the family was still living in the San Fernando Valley, for example, the father asked his little girl, "Do you know how to get here from our house?" To which she replied cutely, "Yes, Daddy. I get in the backseat and Mommy takes me." Coiled around the script's little laughs was the show's original purpose. The black neighbors suspected that the new white owner was a speculator; the next-door neighbor feuded with Donna's father, while the respective kids got along famously. Inside this sitcom script was a serious show straining to get out.

According to Rosenzweig, John Levoff read the script and said, "It's a wonderful show. I don't think it's gritty enough."

"Well," said Rosenzweig, "we were operating with your instructions. I agree with you. But if you want this show tougher, then we have the wrong writers." Levoff's boss, Cliff Alsberg, was happy with the script as it was, and Alsberg's boss, Brandon Stoddard, suggested only a minor scene change.

Then, suddenly, the network cast of characters turned over and *American Dream* was swept into a corporate shuffle. Executive mobility, both upward and lateral, is the industry's pulse; now top management was edgy about ABC's performance, and several executives spotted greener pastures elsewhere in town. Brandon Stoddard was elevated out of series and placed in charge of movies and miniseries along with ABC's new feature-film division. Alsberg left ABC to become president of Filmways Television, and Levoff went to Columbia Pictures.* To replace them, Marcia Carsey moved from daytime into the top position overseeing all series; Tom Werner, formerly in charge of comedy, was promoted to Stoddard's job heading both comedy and drama; and, beneath him, Jonathan Axelrod, formerly in TV movies, was placed in charge of drama.

The new team inherited ten development projects from Alsberg's regime. Normally, whenever executive turnover is so drastic, the new regime shrugs off the old. Old scripts are the stuff that lines new wastebaskets. But Axelrod, a young onetime writer and agent, and stepson of the screenwriter George Axelrod, liked the idea of *American Dream*. He and Werner, a thirty-year-old Harvard graduate formerly in research, asked for a meeting.

Rosenzweig met them at ABC's Century City offices, by far the

---

*A few years later, Alsberg became an independent producer and Levoff rotated to Rosenzweig's old job with the producer Mace Neufeld.

gaudiest of the West Coast network headquarters. Bright Southern
California light spills through skylights and keeps a forest of trees
flourishing indoors. The sofas are deep leather and the receptionists
glamorous. Werner and Axelrod told Rosenzweig they had thrown
out eight of Alsberg's ten projects but wanted to save *American
Dream*. They wanted to change it, though. The script was too much
like *Eight Is Enough*. They wanted "a tougher city show," and Axelrod wanted an eastern or midwestern setting. "Everybody knows
that Los Angeles is like this," Axelrod said, making a horizontal
sweep with his hand, "and a city is like this," making a vertical
movement.

"It was the only serious fight I lost on the pilot," Rosenzweig says,
quickly granting that "Chicago was fine. In fact, there was a certain
texture and verisimilitude that worked, made me happy about it. So
network ideas are not always bad." Rosenzweig was not thrilled,
though, when Axelrod damned Corday and Hecht. Rosenzweig had
on his wall a plaque a writer gave him, reading "The Producer Who
Helps Protects"—protects writers, that is—and he reminded Axelrod
that Corday and Hecht had simply written what the network had
asked them to write. But that was old business. Axelrod damned their
work and wanted a new writer. It was nothing personal. Simultaneously, ABC offered Corday a job as vice-president for comedy development. Everything worked out: Just before he married Barbara
Corday, Barney Rosenzweig fired her from *American Dream*. Corday was a pro and graciously yielded.

In the search for a writer or an actor, the network provides lists of
who is acceptable and who is not; the producer then finds out who
is available and decides whom he wants to work with. Axelrod's list
contained twenty names, but Rosenzweig had trouble finding the
right one. Some didn't want to write a show unless they could share
the coveted "Created by" credit with Corday and Hecht, a credit
that determines royalties for the rest of the show's life. Some weren't
available or cost too much. Moreover, Rosenzweig wanted another
writer: Ronald M. Cohen, with whom he had worked on a movie
about drug abuse among doctors and their families.

Cohen was from Chicago, where he had worked as a reporter, and
he had not been smoothed out much by Hollywood living. He had
never done a television series, but he had written eleven screenplays,
of which three had gotten produced. One was the Robert Aldrich
film starring Burt Lancaster, *Twilight's Last Gleaming*, which was
the most political film about Vietnam and its legacy to come out of
Hollywood. *Gleaming* had done badly and lowered Cohen's stock for
a while, because the industry considered it depressing. Cohen was
weary of waiting on stars who paid him handsomely to write movie
scripts they then didn't want to make—often didn't understand, he

thought—and now he was thinking about television series, because although he had no love lost for the industry, at least there was action in it. Television, he felt, was "a massage, a hypnotizing act between commercials. TV is for marketing, it isn't for entertainment. They'd put on twenty-four hours of commercials if they could get away with it, but nobody would watch. So they do the best they can—they put on a program between the commercials, but they don't want it to be too heavy, too provocative." Cohen had a reputation for feistiness: "I don't get along," he said with some pride. "I don't suffer fools easily."

Jonathan Axelrod knew Cohen—before moving to ABC he had been Cohen's agent, in fact—and he thought Cohen wasn't humorous enough, didn't have enough "heart" for a family show. So Rosenzweig settled for a writer on Axelrod's list who specialized in family shows. This man wrote twenty pages and it was Rosenzweig's opinion that he had got the story all wrong. "He wrote a very neurotic guy, a guy in midlife crisis. I said, 'Danny Novak is not in midlife crisis. He's not intelligent enough to have a midlife crisis. Danny Novak is a doer; he's an old-fashioned hero.'" Rosenzweig brought up Ronald Cohen's name with Axelrod again. This time Axelrod was receptive.

Under no illusions about the force of his argument, Rosenzweig attributes his success to the good fortune of getting to Axelrod just after Axelrod had finished a meeting with the producer David Gerber. Gerber was renowned as one of the best salesmen in Hollywood. "Dynamite," Rosenzweig said. "By the time David Gerber left his office, poor Jonathan couldn't get up for another argument. David had beaten him to a pulp." (Rosenzweig called Gerber later and told him, "I want one favor from you, David. I want your secretary to let me know whenever you're having a meeting, because I love going in after you.")

After a quick trip to Chicago, Cohen went to work furiously rewriting Corday and Hecht's script. Cohen says Rosenzweig is "exceptional at working with writers," that he doesn't compete with writers, doesn't denigrate them, doesn't confront them. Because Cohen trusted Rosenzweig, he let him keep his hand in. Their styles corrected each other. "I have a tendency to be a little bit tougher," Cohen says, "and Barney has a tendency to be a little bit soft, so together it's a good combination."

Rosenzweig agrees: "Ronald was too tough. His first script, I could never show it to anybody, and I softened it. I used to kid him about it, in fact. I said with his toughness and my *schmaltz* from *Daniel Boone*, we were together going to make a good show."

Cohen used the characters Corday and Hecht had written, but roughened their edges, filled out their emotional ranges, and outfitted them with histories that gave more weight to their feelings and conflicts. The husband, hitherto called Tony Weston, was now an

ethnic—first Mickey, then Danny Novak. He was also a onetime
All-American football player who had played professionally until he
hurt his leg; now he was trying to find his way back to the warm,
direct way things were when he was a boy. As Rosenzweig says,
Danny Novak "was brought up on the streets, among Latinos and
blacks, and he had no prejudice." He objected when son Casey called
a Mexican-American basketball player "a beaner." Rosenzweig insisted, though, that "Danny Novak is not liberal. In many ways he
comes from the Ronald Reagan school and the Frank Capra school
of populism. 'I can make a difference,' he believes. He's a flag-waver.
But he doesn't like his kid calling somebody a beaner." He stood for
the traditional family values that ABC said it was trying to tap.

Both Donnas were creatures of feminism, but Cohen's was
sharper. Corday regarded herself as a feminist—"I hope so, yeah. I
try," she said to me—and had set out to break the mystique of perfect
motherhood. She had violated the taboo that television mothers not
resent their children. She thought the women's movement had made
women feel guilty for choosing to be homemakers and childbearers;
her Donna was to be the new feminist housewife. On this there was
no disagreement. "Ronald," she says, "lives with a woman who is
extremely intelligent and has worked all of her life and has been very
successful and is a very interesting woman, and Barney has been
living with or going with me for seven or eight years, and I think is
as much a feminist as you could hope for in a forty-three-year-old
man."

Cohen's Donna was recognizably a rewrite of Corday and Hecht's,
but at the same time transformed. It was as if the same character had
attended a consciousness-raising group. In sitcom fashion, Corday
and Hecht's Donna—call her Donna 1—was cutely burdened by
household chores; Cohen's Donna—Donna 2—seemed more afflicted
by her men taking her for granted, diminishing her, trying to take
advantage. Both Donnas found cause to resent their boys, but Donna
2 was feistier, her conflicts with the men of her family sharper.
Donna 1 cried when she was frustrated; Donna 2 fought back or
stood fast. Both Donnas were liberal and college-educated, but
Donna 2 was more class-conscious. She told Danny that for him a
move back into the city would still represent progress from the slums
of his childhood, while for her it meant downward mobility. Donna
1 finally went along with the move in order to prove to herself that
she was no racist; Donna 2 changed her mind in order to challenge
her "spoiled, dependent brats."

The house and the neighborhood were changed in the same direction. Cohen's inner-city neighborhood was more threatening from
the start: The Novaks' car was stolen during their first visit to the
house. The new house was run-down and filthy, not spacious and

sunny. In the Corday-Hecht script, Todd was mildly intimidated and cheated by some school hustlers, but Todd was himself a junior-league businessman who admired such tactics, and quickly befriended two black girls who took the sting out of his hard times. Cohen's Todd was greeted by menace as well as malice. He was beaten up, and then set out to train himself for revenge à la *Daniel Boone.*

Rosenzweig and Cohen fought through their differences, and the first ABC executives to read the new script said they loved it. Of course, around Hollywood one often hears that "So-and-so loved the script," or "So-and-so said it was the best pilot he's ever seen." Such language is good for the morale of producers and writers, costless for executives, strengthens their arguments for changes in the script, and might even be meant. When it is not meant, it still has its functions. In the case of *American Dream,* however, there is no reason to doubt that the lowest-echelon prime-time development executives were royally pleased.

"I was a star for about five minutes," Ronald Cohen recalls. "It was amazing. The script went around ABC like wildfire. We would walk down the halls and people would come out and grab me—people I didn't even know—and say, 'This is the most important series that ABC is developing.' Tony Thomopoulos, the head of ABC entertainment, was on record as saying, 'If *American Dream* fails, our whole development season is a mess.' " Rosenzweig kidded Cohen that he had made him a star, and Cohen reveled in his five minutes of glory —on such records are further deals made—but still he had "an uneasy feeling, because I have always been very suspicious of that kind of attitude. I was just as good a writer a month ago as I was that day. A month ago I wasn't a star; now I'm a star. Why? It didn't seem real, and it didn't seem authentic."

It didn't last long either. Rosenzweig and Cohen were summoned to a meeting with Axelrod and Werner. "I had been tipped off that everybody loved it," Rosenzweig says, "and I came in there expecting congratulations. Instead of that, they started dumping shit on my head. We had an enormous fight. What could have been a fifteen-minute meeting lasted two and a half hours." Axelrod and Werner wanted the Novak kids to go to a private school, as if Danny Novak could afford such a thing. They wanted to soften a tough school-teacher based, in fact, on one of Rosenzweig's teachers. In the same spirit, they also wanted the Novaks' dilapidated new home spruced up in a hurry. Rosenzweig protested that the house was a continuing character tracing the Novaks' progress on the urban frontier. "I believed that for the first six episodes we could do *Mr. Blandings Builds His Dream House,* that we should take our time with that house, because the idea of refurbishing that old wreck is interesting, funny. Every week we could have been repairing another room, and having something going wrong." But Werner and Axelrod insisted that the house be prettied up before the image of dilapidation could sink in. As a result, the house was mysteriously fixed up, overnight and without comment, halfway through the pilot. Its filth and disarray were not cleaned up but simply banished.

Then there was the matter of the feuding brothers. "It was Tom Werner's idea that the brothers become reconciled at the end, give it an upbeat ending." Rosenzweig could see the point of affirming the brothers' bond, but on balance he didn't want to surrender the dramatic potential of a continuing tension between them. "They thought Casey was too abrasive. And so they made him too nice a kid, too early. I wanted that kid to be hostile; I wanted him to leave home twice. I wanted the parents to have to go get him. My point was, 'You're not going to leave us anything to do with the series, fellas. The series is about the urbanization of this family. If you completely urbanize them in the pilot, then what am I going to do with the series?' "

Rosenzweig worried that the show would stagnate into a run-of-the-mill family show. But he could understand why Werner and Axelrod were trying to pretty it up. "They have a problem, giving them their due. They have an audience, too. Their audience is their management in New York. They believe they have a clearer insight than I do as to what the group in New York will buy. Their job is to sell." To sell, a middle manager has to anticipate the objections of top executives, who fear that a show with ragged elements might raise anxiety and spread gloom. Headquarters believes that people watch television to lift their burdens, and that one prerequisite for burden-lifting is that the course of action come to a neat conclusion. "They kept wanting a nice little movie," Rosenzweig adds.

To get a picture commitment—a network decision to make the pilot—Rosenzweig and Cohen accommodated. Yet even then, differences remained. For line-by-line rewrites the script went to two ABC development executives, who reported, in turn, to Jonathan Axelrod. The main one was the executive in charge of drama development, Ann Daniel. Cohen respected Ann Daniel. She was not, he thought, one of those executives who bully writers and then, at the impasse point, pull rank by reminding them who's paying their salary. The network had the power, in the end, but it was crude and offensive to insist on it. Cohen saw Ann Daniel as the more intelligent kind of executive who tried to understand the writer's point of view and, moreover, got the point of *American Dream*.

Cohen thought Daniel was on the side of making the show "work." When they did tangle, the issue was always, in Cohen's terms, "How real should it be?" Most memorably, they battled over the issue of

Donna's birth control. In Cohen's script, when Donna told Danny she was pregnant, the dialogue went this way:

DANNY: How the hell could you do that?
DONNA: I suspect it's because we had sexual intercourse.
DANNY: But you're not only on the pill, you use a diaphragm. I mean, that's double. That's like a guy who wears a belt and suspenders.
DONNA: It was never impossible! Only improbable! I'm pregnant.
DANNY: What are we going to do?

Daniel, anticipating the reaction from the ABC censors, said the reference to a diaphragm had to come out; presumably it would offend too many viewers. Cohen wanted to keep the joke about double protection. Now came, in Cohen's words, "a tremendous fight." To make things more complicated, his solid front with Rosenzweig broke down momentarily. "You can't make a reference to the pill because it isn't safe," Rosenzweig told him. Without Rosenzweig's firm support, Cohen couldn't possibly win on the pill reference. Rosenzweig did convince Daniel to keep in "you use a diaphragm," only to see the ABC censors—called Standards and Practices—delete it later. But Cohen won on leaving in Todd's snide reference to Donna's "time of the month," although Standards and Practices tried to delete that, too. Now, after telling Todd his crack was "cheap and sexist," Donna added, "It's also a gross misrepresentation of the facts." The small feminist point was buttressed.

So it went, back and forth. Scripts can get picked over like this for months, right until shooting starts. "Some of the ideas the network has are good," Cohen says. "Some of them are not good. I ignored some of them. Some of them they forget, they don't bring them up again. Others they bring up again. And then you fight. . . . Sometimes I would get tired and Barney would fight. Sometimes Ann Daniel would get tired and she would stop fighting. But generally when we were working with Ann, everybody had a sense of humor. There's a certain kind of humor that people can have who fight with each other and who don't let it become personal." Rosenzweig later maintained that he had no real problems with ABC development—or, for that matter, with Standards and Practices, the usual butt of writers' disgust and producers' fury. Standards and Practices, though a tempting target, was, he thought, really a minor distraction. Al Schneider, the canny lawyer who is ABC's top censor in New York, "kept challenging me to come up with rougher issues," Rosenzweig says. "Standards and Practices is a straw villain."

The struggle over casting was different. Casting is often contentious precisely because the television industry traffics in phantoms.

The mass taste it aims to please is a convenient fiction. The culture-makers have no firsthand acquaintance with this entity that is not quite firm, that will always have spoken, in its confused murmur, long after the decisions have been made and the consequences have to be lived with. Faced with this abstraction, the networks are thrown back on the taste they know best: their own quick subjective takes. Disputes about casting in television are less over how well an actress acts than over whether she "has it," whether an aura of appeal mysteriously streams from her person. What better way to anticipate the phantom public's feelings than to sample one's own? But since everyone knows such judgments are subjective, there is no rational ground to exclude the opinion of any interested party. With $40 million or more resting on a single ratings-point's difference when stretched over the course of a season, the nervous networks have asserted steadily more control over casting and brought more executives into it. Casting meetings get crowded.

Casting *American Dream* was for Ronald M. Cohen "the most horrendous part of the whole experience. Casting was an ordeal. We cast for three months." The meetings were interminable, wearing, and clogged with experts. Rosenzweig was there with his casting directors, the freelance specialists whom producers hire to advise them. The network's own casting executives were there, along with the major development executives. Cohen was there; so were representatives of BNB, the company that owned the show. Each deposited two cents, each afraid to be left out of account. "Here were twenty people in a room," Cohen says, "discussing actors in the most inhuman manner that you can imagine. This one 'has no tits,' this one's 'not pretty,' this one's 'not attractive,' 'I wouldn't want to fuck him'—you would not believe how mature people talk."

Karen Carlson, Hans Conreid, and the children were cast without great difficulty, but Danny Novak posed a huge problem. "We were talking about a forty-year-old guy," Rosenzweig says. "Now, forty-year-old guys are either stars or something's wrong. They'd been in the business a long time and they never made it. We interviewed a lot of guys, we tested a lot of guys, we had a lot of fights about who should be in it." For a while everyone agreed on an actor named Joe Bologna, but Joe Bologna worked in movies and plays and didn't want to commit himself to a series. Then Rosenzweig's casting people found Stephen Macht, a former literature teacher. Rosenzweig thought Macht was perfect. Handsome without being pretty, intelligent and passionate, a family man himself, he seemed to intuit the character. Barbara Corday agreed. Excited, Rosenzweig tried him out on Tom Werner and Jonathan Axelrod. "Terrific," "wonderful," they said. Rosenzweig congratulated Macht. "It was one of those little moments in show business that you like."

The next day there was another meeting. Werner came in and said "I had a dream last night."

Rosenzweig said, "What do you mean you had a dream?"

Werner said, "Ned Beatty is the American Dream."

Ned Beatty's name had come up before. Beatty was not a first-magnitude star, but he had starred in *Deliverance, Network,* and *Superman,* among other movies. He was energetic and cheerful. But Rosenzweig, who admired Beatty, thought him inappropriate for the part. "You couldn't believe Ned Beatty as a former football player," he said later.

Cohen's reaction was "Are you serious? We've already cast Karen Carlson. Karen Carlson is four inches taller than Ned Beatty. What happened to Stephen Macht?"

"Well, we like him," Werner said, "but I'm really worried. I think we need a star."

Cohen saw disaster looming. "Ned is a terrific actor. He's off-center. He is not a handsome leading young man. They thought that was imaginative casting. And when we tried to bring up the fact that he's not urban, he's rural, he's from Kentucky, they couldn't deal with it. This happened because at the end of six months you are so exhausted, you are so bedraggled, that ultimately you give in. The network cannot say to a production company, 'You must hire Ned Beatty.' Or anybody." After all, the production company owns the show. Technically, when the network "picks up" a show, it is simply agreeing to pay the company a license fee for two broadcasts. "What they say is, 'We like this actor very much. If you hire this actor, we think he would be very good in your show. We'll promote the hell out of it.' Meanwhile, it's getting later and later in pilot season. If you don't start shooting pretty soon, it's going to be too late to get it to the network in time for their scheduling meetings. So they wait you out. It's really showdown poker. But the response should have been, 'We are not going to go with this actor, because we don't think he's right for it.' Now they have to make a decision. Either the network will decide to go with an actor that the producers are enthusiastic about, or they'll put the project in turnaround. For the producer the risk is tremendous. He wants to make the pilot because that's the only way he has of getting his show considered for the fall schedule, but if he accedes to the demands of the networks, then he might be destroying his show."

During the entire meeting, Rosenzweig had reason to believe the Beatty idea was moot. "Ned Beatty's deal was stiff, and I thought ABC would never pay it. He wanted a guarantee of a commitment to the series. He would do a pilot if we guaranteed him twelve episodes. You're talking about hundreds of thousands of dollars." Rosenzweig used up all his arguments against Beatty, but in the end, as he said later, "I was desperate to make the picture. I said, 'Look, you're not offering me chopped liver. I'm acquiescing'—but in the back of my head I know we can't make the deal with Ned Beatty, so I said, 'I tell you what. I'll go along if your number-two choice, if Ned Beatty won't do it, will be Stephen Macht.' They said, 'You have a deal.' I said, 'Terrific.' "

But Rosenzweig quickly realized he had been "finessed into a trap." To get Beatty, ABC agreed to guarantee him his salary whether the series went on the air or not. It was an offer Beatty could not refuse, and he signed up. Now Rosenzweig had no choice but to try to make the most of a *fait accompli*. "One of your jobs as producer," Rosenzweig believed, "is to keep the ship afloat, and to find ways to get your way, but to do it diplomatically, and to keep everybody working while that's going on. You cannot say, 'This is awful, and we're shutting down for two days while we figure out what's right.' That's not television." The enormous machinery of production had to keep moving. Beatty, for his part, lost some weight, came in for meetings, read his part with other actors, and Rosenzweig decided after all he was "charming" and "funny" and "terrific." Executives let it be known they thought Ned Beatty and Karen Carlson could turn out to be television's Spencer Tracy and Katharine Hepburn. Tony Thomopoulos told Rosenzweig, "You cast Karen Carlson and we will give you the *Tenspeed and Brown Shoe* campaign," referring to a vastly expensive advertising campaign on a failed series the year before. If anyone noticed the irony of ABC's invoking a series that had failed *despite* a major promotion, no one said so out loud. Rosenzweig felt the bitter pill sweeten in his mouth.

Shooting started in Chicago in March 1980. Each day the dailies —the results of that day's shooting—were shipped back to ABC executives in Los Angeles for scrutiny. Four days in, the executives were dismayed with Beatty's performance. Top executives flew to Chicago to meet with Beatty and the director, Mel Damski. Rosenzweig flew in from Savannah, where he was producing *East of Eden*. Charges and countercharges swirled for hours. When the dust had cleared, Beatty was let go.

Rosenzweig was ready to go again with Stephen Macht, but again the executives were queasy. ABC's head of casting, Tim Flack, told Rosenzweig, "I've had a lot of experience with these things. When things go wrong, you have to go with a safe person." Rosenzweig insisted he had an agreement on Macht. "I said, 'Listen, Tim. I went along with what you guys wanted, and you have failed. We are now going to do what I want to do. You must at least do me the courtesy of meeting this man. I want Marcie Carsey to meet this Stephen Macht.' " Carsey, the head of programming on the West Coast, was perched above Axelrod and Werner in the hierarchy. Up to this point, she had not been as involved as the other two. Carsey arranged to meet Macht, and then called Rosenzweig. "She loved him," Rosenzweig remembers her saying. "Why didn't she meet him before?" The next day, Macht was on his way to Chicago, and Rosenzweig was busy locating winter clothes in Chicago warehouses for an actor who owned none of his own.

The rest of the shooting was uneventful. Footage was carried back to L.A., and the director, editor, and Rosenzweig put together the pilot. The ABC West Coast executives screened it and proclaimed themselves pleased. At Preview House it tested very high, with audience ranking highest the lightest treatments of family tension, the show of affection between Danny and Donna, Danny's demonstration of adult authority, and his speech to the kids about family responsibility. The film was flown to New York for the scheduling meeting. "They were calling me from New York," Rosenzweig remembers. "I was the new genius filmmaker of all time. Jonathan Axelrod called me and said, 'Thank you.'" Axelrod said that Fred Pierce, the president of ABC Television, came up to him and raved to him about the pilot. Pierce said *American Dream* was the best pilot he had seen in ten years. He told Axelrod it was the only cassette he had taken home, and that his wife and he had both cried. There were New York programming executives who said the show had no chance, but Pierce said, "I don't care whether it's a hit or not. I want this show."

The schedulers were still nervous about the show's commercial potential, however. "It never was in anybody's mind," according to Rosenzweig, "that *American Dream* was going to be an immediate bust-loose hit. Everybody agreed it was going to have to take time and build. I was promised a protected time-slot. I was promised that they would not kiss this show off." Shows without trademark features like car crashes and infidelity jokes traditionally build slowly, and no one wanted to rush it into the wrong slot. Several executives felt that if the show were placed on the fall schedule, "against tits and ass and the World Series," as Rosenzweig puts it, it would fail. And so ABC decided to save it till the spring, and to make a short order of four episodes. Eventually the number was raised to six, with more backup scripts in reserve so that if the series did well, more could be filmed with dispatch. Ronald M. Cohen went back to work writing episodes.

Cohen's scripts did not, however, please the Current Programming department, the wing of the network bureaucracy—usually a training ground for younger program executives in the making—that takes over supervision from the development department once a pilot has sold. "The big problem," Rosenzweig says, "was the actors' strike. On the surface, it gave us more time to prepare scripts. The negative side was, it gave the network more time to read them. And it also meant that there was no pressure of an air date. Traditionally, there are two major departments that people on my level deal with at a network: Development and Current. The Development people kick me around, because they threaten me, if I don't pay attention to them, with not making the project. I get to kick the Current people around, because I threaten them with not being able to make an air date if they don't stop messing with me. That's true except when you have a brand-new show that doesn't have an air date. Then the Current people begin to sound a little bit more like Development people. They could not wait to get their hands on this show. This was going to be the best ABC show ever. And they became very nervous. The excitement of last May in New York was over. 'Now what are we going to do with these guys?' They kept calling us in for meetings. 'What are you planning to do? How are you going to do this? Can we see this?' They're just frightened people, basically. They don't make the shows, and so it's all a mystery to them. If you're Norman Lear, you can say, 'Go away and don't bother me.' Or if you're Barney Rosenzweig and not as powerful as Norman—and also, my style isn't like that—you can argue with them. I would treat them as equals and debate with them.

"They had reduced *American Dream* to a formula. They said, 'We want an A story, a B story, a C story, and runners.' An A story is a primary story. A B story, by their definition, is a story of equal length to the A story, and that ideally somehow ties in with the A story. A C story is shorter and has nothing to do with either the A or B story. Runners are like running gags. I had never heard of such a thing in my life. And they wanted stories that were minitriumphs every week. They wanted a John Wayne ending. And they always wanted the look lighter and brighter. And they also didn't want the show to be shot in the winter in Chicago. They didn't want snow. And I said, 'Well, you better stop wasting my time so that I can make the shows before it snows, because the way we're going, we're going to be in the dead of winter.' "

"I wrote over twenty hours of television that summer," Cohen recalls. "I must have written twenty scripts that were rejected." He thought he *was* writing scripts with victories at the end. "I don't end movies where people are lying in the gutter."

Cohen wrote one *American Dream* episode in which the virgin sixteen-year-old Casey meets a considerably older prostitute from Appalachia. He pays her, sleeps with her, falls in love with her, fights with his parents, and moves in with her. In the climactic scene, the prostitute tells Donna, "Relax. I just borrowed him for a little bit. Your son is a remarkable young man. You should be very proud of him. He's a loving person."

"All of a sudden," Cohen says, "what the show is really about is a mother who refuses to accept the emerging sexuality of her son. The network was panicked about it." "There's no hope in that story," one program executive said.

Cohen wanted to do another episode about Danny getting fired. "They said, 'Okay, but you've got to give him a job at the end of the show.'" The same executive said, "What he really should be doing is getting a promotion." Cohen said, "No, I don't want his identity to be predicated on a job. I want to do a show where Danny loses his job but regains his self-esteem. The network said, 'You can't do that.' Then I wanted to have him quit over a moral principle. The store that he works for is selling a motorcycle that's not safe, and he quits. 'No, you can't do that either, because then you're portraying American business as unsafe.' Well, we all know that American business is unsafe. I rewrote that same script five times. I wrote it where he gets fired, I wrote it where he quits, I wrote it where he loses his job due to a business recession. And it was never acceptable. Whatever I found interesting, they always found objectionable." The network wanted the Novaks' little victories to be material, not moral. Executives found Cohen's scripts "joyless."

Cohen came up with a story in which Todd swallowed a chicken bone, and his parents carted him from hospital to hospital until, twelve hours later, Danny finally took charge and found a doctor who would get the bone out. To Cohen, the point was supposed to be that "we must take responsibility for our own health" sooner than "wait for great god Doctor to save us"—hardly a radical critique of the medical system. But one programming executive saw the story as "really about urban decay as it affects hospitals. And it was a horribly depressing story."

Another executive insisted that the show vindicate the Novaks' move to the city. "There should be lovely things happening in the city," this man said. "It should be a reinforcement of his decision; it should be perceived that his decision was a winning one." He proposed to Cohen a story in which the little girl Jenny falls in love with the ballet. "You do a *Turning Point* type of story, where maybe she runs away for a day and they're afraid that she's been mugged, but in fact there she is, fascinated, sitting in the front row of the Chicago Metropolitan Opera. So you have a story that says to people, you can win and there are values in the city that are working."

In the midst of these skirmishes, Mace Neufeld, who owned the show, ran short of cash. With *American Dream*, the *East of Eden* miniseries, and a TV movie all unexpectedly in production at the same time, along with three feature films, he was running a $4 million deficit. Neufeld thereupon made a deal with the Viacom company, a large but at that moment not very successful supplier, who became his financial partners and took effective control. Viacom was headed by a former network executive named Richard Reisberg, who began attending meetings with Rosenzweig, Cohen, and the ABC current programming executives.

"I kept accommodating [ABC] as best I could," Rosenzweig says. But Reisberg says, "We were getting no place fast with the network. I think it got to where if they saw Ronald's name on a script, they'd throw it out on that basis. The network felt the scripts just were not good. It was a combination of personalities, coupled with what the show should be about. I think Ronald is a very good writer. I don't think Ronald can write for television, at least not that kind of a show. It was too hard. Too much grit. Stuff that you know they'd never let you do." When Cohen first proposed the episode about Casey and the prostitute, Reisberg thought the network would never let him write it. He felt the same way toward a Cohen idea about a Nazi march through the neighborhood, in which Danny would support the march, Donna would organize against it, and Berlowitz would turn out to be a Holocaust survivor who would rather duck the issue.

The network said yes to these story notions, but Reisberg didn't think they would ever put the episodes on the air. "There's no way you can resolve the Nazis marching down the street." Moreover, he thought that Cohen, inexperienced in series television, was writing scripts that would take eleven or twelve days to shoot, not the seven allocated to a weekly series. Cohen "couldn't deliver [the scripts] according to the network's standards," Reisberg says. "And in many of those cases, I agreed with the network. I didn't agree with them forcefully, because I basically believe in more of a producer's company. Their name is on the screen, not mine. I backed them as best I could, but at some point, in my heart, I really wasn't believing it." To Reisberg the point wasn't to talk the network into the initial six scripts, because "the name of the game was not producing six shows but producing sixty-six shows."

"At some point," Reisberg says, "I had a lunch with Tony [Thomopoulos], and Tony said, 'I don't think this is working. Do you?' And I said, 'Well, let's just say I've got some doubts.' Tony said, 'Do you think [Bill] Blinn and [Jerry] Thorpe could do this show?' I said, 'Yeah, in a minute. It's right up their alley.' "

William Blinn had written every kind of television drama, from *Brian's Song* and *Roots* to *Starsky and Hutch, The Rookies,* and the pilot of the very show that ABC executives saw as the prototype for *American Dream, Eight Is Enough.* Jerry Thorpe had produced *Harry O* and *Kung Fu.* As Reisberg says, "Viacom had an arrangement with them. And they had an arrangement with ABC: major commitments. I think the primary reason, however, was, I don't think Tony could have picked any better people to do that show than Jerry Thorpe and Bill Blinn. So they were brought in with the greatest of expectations." The idea was that there would be some sort of coproducing arrangement with Rosenzweig.

Rosenzweig was in Rome, supervising the music for *East of Eden*, when he heard the news from Reisberg. He flew back to L.A. to find that ABC was divided about Cohen's scripts, and when he told Reisberg this was the time to fight and win, Reisberg told him to stand aside. And Rosenzweig discovered that, under the terms of Mace Neufeld's sale to Viacom, he had no creative control. Rosenzweig was devastated. "I didn't object to [Blinn and Thorpe] before," he said to Reisberg, "because I was supposed to get more episodes out of it. I'm a whore like everybody else. I don't want to be rescued now. I am on the beach at Salerno, pinned down by enemy fire for three months, my men are bleeding and wounded, and finally the Nazis are in retreat, and you're telling me that Patton's coming in, and we have to wait to chase the enemy until Patton arrives with his newsreel photographers. Fuck you, I don't want to be rescued. They're going to do it without me."

ABC's Werner and Carsey called Rosenzweig the next day, invited him to breakfast, and asked him to stay on the show. Rosenzweig said to them, "When Jerry Thorpe says it's chocolate and I say it's vanilla, what flavor is it? If you don't want to ask Jerry Thorpe to work for me, don't ask me to work for Jerry Thorpe. I have great respect for him. Bill Blinn's a very talented guy. As a matter of fact, they're both more talented writers than I am. But I'll tell you something. It'll never be their show, and they'll fail. I just wish you a lot of luck with it." And he walked off.

Cohen stayed on for a while but now lacked the protection of a producer. "You must protect your creative people," he says. "if you send Ronald Cohen into the breach every day to fight with Marcia Basichis and Peter Roth [the Current Development executives] and Axelrod, it's just a matter of time until Ronald Cohen offends them. Once I offend them, they'll get rid of me. Grant Tinker does not allow his producers to go to the network and get bloody. He goes to the network. 'Look, you want to take a shot? Take a shot at me. Ronald's back at the office working.' Because I call them the way I see them, because I understood what this show is about, because I care about what I do and I have pride, I fought them. And at a certain point, they got rid of me. I became an irritant."

A few days after he quit, Rosenzweig threw a party to celebrate his wife Barbara Corday's becoming vice-president of ABC in charge of comedy development. "It was very tense," Cohen recalls. "Everybody knew that Barney was gone and I was on my way out. But I showed up. Naturally, I would. And I ended up in a discussion with Fred Pierce. Fred Pierce gave me the whole network philosophy that night, and I knew the show was doomed. The woman I live with said flat out to Pierce, 'This show is only going to work if it's real, if you deal with real issues.' And Pierce said, 'It has to be charming, it has to be warm, it has to be lovely, it can't get too depressing. We're not doing *East Side, West Side,* you know.' And she looked at me and I looked at her and I said, 'My God, we're going to get creamed.'" Soon afterward, Cohen was fired.

Bill Blinn and Jerry Thorpe started producing episodes of *American Dream,* some of them based on Cohen's and Rosenzweig's story ideas. They tried to accommodate the network, but their versions were still not "light," "bright," "warm," "lovely," and "joyful" enough for ABC's taste. At first, ABC gave the new team the same mixed messages they had given Rosenzweig and Cohen. "It was, from one executive, 'We want this to be the kind of show that people talk about the next day,'" says Blinn. "From another executive in the same meeting: 'But don't be so controversial that the audience feels like we're giving them a civics lesson.' We were told, 'Issue-oriented but not too issue-oriented.' 'Deal with social problems but not in a downbeat or depressing manner.' When we came out of the meeting I'd say to Jerry, 'You have a fix on what they want now?' And he'd say, 'No, I don't, do you?'" After another meeting Blinn made a list of network comments. They wanted outside characters involved, but the story should concern the Novaks. They wanted to make more use of Berlowitz, but not lose Donna's father. They wanted to show the city, but not make it look too gritty.

Reisberg remembers a meeting that ended with Jonathan Axelrod saying, "We're going to do issues but at the same time there is going to be a blend of entertainment and humor."

"Okay, we're going to hit the issues," Reisberg said.

Whereupon another executive said, "No, let's keep it soft, at least for the first six."

"Blinn is not weak-spined in the least," Reisberg says, "but he was basically at a point of saying, 'I'll give them anything they want. Just someone tell me what they want.'"

On balance, though, what they wanted was prettification and what Reisberg calls the "networkese" of "small victories." To satisfy both network programming and Standards and Practices, Blinn toned down his scripts. Casey's older prostitute-lover became a twenty-four-ish waitress. "It had to be shot," Blinn says, "in such a way that the network could say it is not definite that they slept together. We had one line where the mother says to the father, 'Boys like sex; I'm aware of that.' They wanted that changed to 'Boys like girls.' We didn't change it because it had already been shot by the time we got the note."

In another episode, a topless bar opens up in the neighborhood. Donna's father has written a letter to the editor in protest, espousing the virtues of what he called "Anglo-Saxon society," and signing off, "The Novak family." Danny is furious, and Donna agrees to go on a radio talk show with a woman who is crusading against the bar. She appears and leaves early. Then, on her car radio, she hears the other woman say, in Blinn's words, "It's a historical fact that white Christian people founded this nation. How many of your listeners know, for example, that the business Mrs. Novak's attempting to defend is located in a building that's owned by a Jewish man? I'm sure this Mr. Berlowitz is a very nice person, but I do think we have a right to question why Jewish names seem to crop up so often on the list of landlords, don't you?" Whereupon the host announcer says, "No, as a matter of fact I don't think so, and I doubt that our listeners will either. The reason I had you on is so our listeners can hear how harmful your views are. Let's open up the phone lines now." Thinking she has been used to legitimize anti-Semitism, Donna breaks into tears.

Standards and Practices told Blinn that the host had to come down harder on anti-Semitism. Blinn said that he does attack the woman's views. Standards said, "Yeah, but he says it in a very reasonable tone. We really have to come out foursquare, without any equivocation." Blinn didn't want to overstate the point, but he dutifully wrote stronger lines, which Standards approved. The host recorded the new lines, which were inserted over Donna's breaking into tears. Standards then said, "Her tears are because this lady's being attacked. Her tears are in sympathy with the anti-Semite." Blinn rewrote the lines again. In all, the host's lines were rerecorded five times. Blinn thought the network was trying not to offend its affiliates with an unflattering portrait of a radio announcer. Perhaps it was going out of its way to avoid offending the fundamentalist right as well.

In the last episode that aired, the Novaks' home was burglarized. Todd suspected his new black friend was involved, and after he hinted around to that effect, the stolen goods were returned. In the final scene, Todd told his friend he didn't have any evidence that made his involvement clear, so he would simply have to go on trusting him. But ABC wanted it crystal-clear that the friend had not been involved, so the scene had to be reshot with Todd saying, "I know you didn't do it." Ambiguity would not placate hypothetical protesters.

Network complaints continued to filter in even while these episodes were being shot in Chicago. According to Blinn, "The directors of episodes were getting phone calls from the network saying, 'Please try to stay away from graffiti on the walls.' 'No garbage cans in the alleys.' 'Why don't they have a dishwasher in the house?' We're shooting on location in a real gym in a real high school. 'The walls are too brown,' we're told. The thing that was said was, 'Well, when

I go to the Forum to watch a Lakers game, it's very bright and "up" and it's a wonderful Technicolor kind of experience.' But we're not in the Forum. We're in a sweaty, small gym."

Network executives kept saying, "We don't want *Eight Is Enough*, but we also do not want 'urban crisis of the week.'" Reisberg, who had favored softening the show, thought they were protesting too much. Blinn and Thorpe were supposed to have been the pliant alternatives to the troublesome Rosenzweig and Cohen, but by now perhaps not even Walt Disney could have flattened the show enough to suit the network.

Blinn concluded, "I guess it's like having a Reggie Jackson on your team. You want him to hit, but you don't want to put up with the problems involved with having him on your team." He thought ABC was especially "gun-shy" about anything controversial at a time when the fundamentalist right was lowering the boom on the networks. ABC's philosophy, he thought, resembled that of the salesman "who comes to the door and says, 'You don't want to buy any magazines.'" That year the network was more comfortable with law and order.*

Rosenzweig, Blinn, and Reisberg all agree that the scheduling of *American Dream* suggests that the network was dumping the show. The ninety-minute pilot aired at nine-thirty on a Sunday night in April, just after *The Phoenix*, a ninety-minute fantasy pilot with a young audience. *The Phoenix* drew a 32 share, *American Dream* a 28. Another episode aired the following night, Monday, against repeats, and drew another 28 share. The next day, ABC announced its fall schedule, with *American Dream* absent and *Strike Force*, *Code Red*, and *Today's FBI* present. The next episode of *American Dream* was aired eight days later, on a Wednesday night at nine, and drew a 21 share. Reisberg urged Tony Thomopoulos to put the show up against *Dallas* rather than scrap it entirely, but Thomopoulos said no one would sample it that way. Anyway, it was already scheduled. The show was then preempted for two weeks before a final episode was aired, again on a Wednesday. Viacom ran ads in the trade papers urging ABC to give the show another chance. Mace Neufeld, who still had an interest in the show, says he "bombarded" ABC with photocopies of hundreds of friendly letters from viewers. "I even wrote to [ABC board chairman Leonard] Goldenson. There was never a response. And I do business with them!" "I think they simply threw it away," says Reisberg. "You couldn't have found that show with a compass."

Barney Rosenzweig could bear to watch only two of the Blinn-

---

*See Chapters 11 and 12.

Thorpe episodes. He had his criticisms, but still thought "Blinn and Thorpe didn't make a bad series." He thought ABC had let the show sink because they were embarrassed by what they had done to it. The salient fact was that on Wednesdays it was dropped into the wrong audience, stranded between two Aaron Spelling shows, *Vega$* and *Charlie's Angels.* To one top ABC executive who would not speak on the record, the salient facts were that *American Dream* had been dropped into noncompetitive periods, preceded by fairly high-rated shows, and "promoted like hell." ABC's Ann Daniel says, "The public tuned out of the show, and came back to ABC after the show was over. That's unusual, to select out at that hour." Another executive put it more pungently: "People ran to avoid that show. There was a decided five-, six-point dropoff from its lead-in."

Daniel thinks that in time the ratings could have picked up, but time was precious. The juiciest time-slots had to be reserved for continuing shows. And by now it was May, a sweeps month, when ratings determine advertising rates for the following six months. This was no time to let an iffy show build. Executive attention was already turning to the fall schedule full of law-and-order shows—which also rated weakly, as it turned out, though they lasted out the year. *American Dream* had always been what one top executive called "a fragile concept." Another added that "there are only a few shows on the air that are dealing with contemporary problems. I happen to prefer them in comedic form." Anyway, this executive noted, "the success of CBS is not based on *Lou Grant*, it's based on *Dukes of Hazzard* and *Dallas.* This was an attempt on our part to develop our own *Lou Grant*, and I don't think it worked." *American Dream* disappeared.

Two years later, all the protagonists were still in the television business.

After getting fired from *American Dream*, Ronald Cohen couldn't find work for a year. He sued Viacom for breach of contract.* "Something like *American Dream* happens," he concluded, "and everybody gets frightened. Talent is important, but being able to get along is more important. If you examine television and see how lousy it is, so how talented are all these people? Modest talent. What's more important is, can you get along? I couldn't get along." Later, he wrote a pilot for Scott Siegler at CBS, went back to screenwriting, and in 1982 made a fifty-fifty ownership deal to write and produce series pilots at Paramount. One of his pilots was *Air Force*, a look at the politics of the sixties through the eyes of a military family, as based on a one-line idea from ABC.

---

*At this writing the suit is still pending.

Barney Rosenzweig concluded, "I had the rug pulled out from under me, not by the network but by the [suppliers]. The networks are the heavies, but they could not be the heavies without the corporate producers letting them be. We are collaborating in our own demise."

Rosenzweig went on to produce the movie *Cagney and Lacey* for CBS, starring Loretta Swit and Tyne Daly as two female cops in New York. After it took an enormous 42 share of the audience, he sold it to CBS as a series, and since Swit had a prior commitment to *M*A*S*H*, recast her part with Meg Foster. "Compared with ABC," he said before the series went on the air, "it's the difference between the Gulag and Tahiti." But that was before CBS made him drop Meg Foster as a condition for renewing the show, because testing told them she resembled Tyne Daly too closely and was insufficiently feminine.

Mace Neufeld also concluded that ABC was more likely to "look over your shoulder" than the other networks. He kept producing for all three. "You win some, you lose some," he ruminated. "This was another American dream gone astray."

Bill Blinn went to MGM, which assigned him to replace the original producer on the series *Fame*.

Richard Reisberg became the president first of United Artists Television and then of the combined MGM/United Artists Television Production division.

Tom Werner left ABC to go into independent television production with Marcie Carsey, who had left the previous year. In 1983 he produced two pilots for ABC.

Jonathan Axelrod left ABC for Columbia Pictures Television.

Barbara Corday left ABC to go into independent production.

Ann Daniel stayed at ABC drama development. The low numbers on *American Dream* disposed her to believe that the present-day audience would prefer light escapism to "a little bit of a harsh reality."

Tony Thomopoulos remained president of ABC Entertainment. He himself is a devoted family man, but neither personal experience nor predilections prevail against the logic of network television. Only once since *American Dream* has any of the networks scheduled a dramatic series featuring a mother, a father, and children set in present-day America.

2

THE TELEVISION-INDUSTRIAL COMPLEX

CHAPTER 7

Inside Tracks in a Small World

The language of the free market seems to imply that buyers set up shop and wait for sellers to beat a path to their door with the best, or at least the most salable goods. But because the buyers' calculations of marketability are necessarily crude and clumsy, they resort to sellers they've worked with before, sellers they're comfortable with. Buyers and sellers become interchangeable, and—as with the principals of *American Dream*—the same names keep showing up in the credits.

"It's a tiny little business," Grant Tinker said while still heading the MTM production company. "There is no question that [TV] is sort of a little closed society and very hard for the new guy to get into . . . [and] the product looks like it. It reflects that we are a limited crowd." "[Television] is such a small shop you can't believe it," says Esther Shapiro, co–executive producer of *Dynasty* and former vice-president for miniseries at ABC. "Here we have a country with two hundred million people, and a couple hundred people running the whole show."

This structure is normal when a handful of buyers dominate an industry. When it lets contracts for major weapons systems, the Pentagon goes to a handful of large corporate suppliers; the federal Treasury has even rushed in with loan guarantees to keep an important company, Lockheed, afloat. Recording companies looking for studio musicians, airlines looking for jumbo jets gravitate toward a relatively few reliable suppliers. All want to stabilize supply, and all can muster arguments to convince themselves that the favored suppliers are the best and most affordable to be found. Sometimes, indeed, they may be; and sometimes not. But in either case they have the virtue of being present, available, efficient, and large-scale.

In each of these enterprises, buyers and sellers congregate. Their conflicts of interest, however fierce, take place within a common universe of discourse. The executives of each are at home in their shared world. Sellers walk through revolving doors and become buyers; buyers go the other way round. Thus the small world perpetuates itself. Indeed, in the ranks of network executives, "failing upward" is so common that the term exists for it. Executives with passable records and good contacts slide through the revolving door and get good jobs as suppliers and studio executives. Once they have been in position long enough, they become fixtures of the industry. Rare is the failure who is booted out of the business in disgrace.

"What's the worst thing that could happen to me at NBC?" asked Ethel Winant, who at the moment I interviewed her was vice-president in charge of miniseries, and had been casting director at CBS before that. "They probably won't kill me, so they'll fire me. Well, that isn't the worst thing. I was fired from ten jobs when I started out in the business. Everybody's been fired. I think being fired is good for you. There's a kind of joke that you hear often in this business. The same people move in a kind of circle. It's a family. If I were fired tomorrow, I would get a job the day after. Maybe not a job I wanted or a job I would even keep, but because I have a lot of friends in the business they would rally round and [producer] David Wolper would give me a job or [Lorimar president] Lee Rich would give me a job or somebody would give me a job until I found yet my next job. I've become part of that little inner circle of people who have been around a long time—what I guess would be the old boys' network, and I don't know how I got into it because I'm not an old boy, but I'm part of that group. Which has very little to do with whether I'm good or bad. Because I am familiar and the devil you know is better than the devil you don't know. . . . I've paid my dues and I've spent enough years and I've worked with enough of those people. MTM would hire me because they owe me one, because I got their shows on the air when I was at CBS. That happens. The markers are out and you can call them in if you're in trouble." In fact, a few weeks after this interview Ethel Winant left NBC and went to work for Robert Wood at Metromedia—the same Bob Wood who had been president of CBS when she was casting director there.

The extended family even shelters its failures and miscreants. Executives may saddle the networks with heaps of programming mistakes, then bounce right into successful independent production, selling to that same network among the others. "It's a forgiving town," says one screenwriter. The most astonishing example is David Begelman, the onetime president of the film and television divisions of Columbia Pictures, who pled no contest in 1978 to felony grand theft for cashing a check made out to Cliff Robertson, drew three years probation and a $5,000 fine, and then in 1980 was hired to be chairman of United Artists, where he lasted thirty-one months. It took a string of box-office failures to squeeze Begelman out in 1982.

The industry's small world gets to be that way by getting along and mastering the unwritten rules; and its mastery of the game crystallizes the rules, making them harder and faster than they would otherwise be, which in subtle and not so subtle ways keeps interlopers out. The privileged suppliers are especially masterful at meeting specifications that they have had a hand in writing. Buyers can set the basic rules that define the nature of success; then the favored sellers can develop new methods, new lines of research, new technologies like the jumbo jet, which transform, if not the basic rules of the game, at least the industry's premium strategies for winning. In this sense, the industry's small world embodies its own rules and secretes them at the same time. Outsiders looking in often feel that the buyers and privileged sellers are caught in trust-making. Regardless of the precise strictures of antitrust laws, trust is the right word. Buyers and sellers get along; they speak each other's language and their common discourse is sealed in common ritual. The steady pulse of such a business is the refrain "I owe you one." Despite the fiercest internecine struggles, they attend to their common good.

Like the military and airframe industries, the television-industrial complex operates within an oligopolistic structure. After all the numbers are counted, the demographics heeded, the conventions deployed, the trends assessed, the networks still don't know how to make a successful show. Therefore, they turn to suppliers who have demonstrated they can deliver market success (though they may also have produced their share of failures). These insiders may have cracked the secret. They may not be the only suppliers in the world who could deliver, but after all they have delivered, and why look elsewhere when X and Y are tried and tested?

As former NBC programming chief Paul Klein says, "*Dukes of Hazzard* goes on the air, and it consistently gets a very big number. Now a bunch of people have leverage. Since CBS has no fucking idea in the world why that is succeeding, and nobody in that company ever watches that show—you've got to take this on faith—they don't know why it works. So everybody connected with that show has leverage. The writer has leverage. The line producer has leverage on

a hit. Because they don't know the reasons for the hit." Richard
Reisberg speaks for many production-company executives when he
says, "I personally think that who does it is almost more important
than what it is that's being done. I don't think that [the networks] get
that many ideas that are so remarkably different, but rather there's
a great commonality among the ideas, and I think to a great extent
it's who's going to do it. And I think that's right. I think that's the way
it should be."

So it is that a few score producers' names come up over and over
again, and a few major production companies dominate the network
airwaves. Some are the television departments of what were once
major movie studios and are now the centerpieces of corporate conglomerates: Universal, Paramount (part of Gulf + Western), Columbia (now part of Coca-Cola), Warner Brothers (part of Warner
Communications), Twentieth Century–Fox, and MGM (which now
owns United Artists). The studios own major production headquarters, the office buildings and sound stages that adorn extraordinarily
valuable stretches of Los Angeles real estate. They can afford to keep
producers and writers on payroll without specific projects. All but
Fox (wholly owned by Denver oil magnate Marvin Davis) are publicly owned. Otherwise, as business enterprises they are not much
different from the major so-called independent suppliers who have
pyramided a few successes into big production companies. All the
top suppliers are organized to parallel the networks. All of them are
key filtration points for mass culture: They have their own development executives who seek out "hot" producers, take pitches, read
scripts, chat with agents about new talent, keep eyes and ears open
for trends, serve as meeting points for gossip, idea-mating and deal-
making, and try to read, or anticipate, or less successfully to change
the minds of the networks. All enter into complex coproduction
arrangements with the producers who actually make the shows.
(Phrases like "in association with" in the credits signal one of these
deals.) And they sell, sell, sell.

While the studios tend to be eclectic, the major "independents"
specialize in the genres of their founding successes, with one or two
new genres added later. (Being privately held, except for Lorimar,
it is easier for them to resist the temptation to diversify.) The four
major independents that dominate the business today were launched
in the early seventies: Aaron Spelling (through two companies,
Spelling-Goldberg Productions and Aaron Spelling Productions)
began in police shows (The Mod Squad, The Rookies), then moved
to light escape (Charlie's Angels, The Love Boat, Fantasy Island).
MTM Enterprises, under Grant Tinker, parlayed The Mary Tyler
Moore Show into a higher-toned production empire that hired
writer-producers on their way up and gave them their heads. They

specialized in unusually literate comedy and comedy-drama hybrids centered in the workplace. Tandem/T.A.T. grew from Norman Lear's *All in the Family* to include all its "socially relevant" spinoffs as well as the "softer" *One Day at a Time* and *Diff'rent Strokes* and, for a few years, two nightly serials that were so "hard," violated so many network taboos about subject matter and form and language, they had to be sold directly to local stations: *Mary Hartman, Mary Hartman* and *Fernwood 2-Night.* Lorimar, headed by the former ad-agency executive Lee Rich, moved from the wholesome-family style of *The Waltons* and *Eight Is Enough* to *Dallas* and its serial spinoffs and copies, becoming so successful that in 1981 Lorimar was renting a good number of the sound stages on the MGM lot.

All the major suppliers thrive on series, which keep their large administrative staffs on payroll and promise the vast payoffs of syndication. They also do TV movies and the occasional feature. (In 1981, Lear's empire even bought a motion picture distribution system, Avco-Embassy, and became Embassy/Tandem). All are headed by formidable salesmen.

In the fall of 1981 and 1982, the studios and major independents, and their coproducers, supplied the vast majority of prime-time series to the networks, as follows:

Network Series by Production Companies, Fall 1981 and Fall 1982 Seasons[1,2]

	Number of shows		Number of hours	
	1981	1982	1981	1982
I. STUDIOS				
Universal total	8	6	7.0	6.0
Glen A. Larson Productions	3	1	3.0	1.0
Alone or with other producers	5	5	4.0	5.0
Paramount total	7	8	3.5	4.5
Miller/Milkis Productions/ Henderson Productions (Garry Marshall)	3	2	1.5	1.0
Weinberger-Daniels, John Charles Walters, Charles/Burrows/ Charles	2	2	1.0	1.0
Other producers	2	4	1.0	2.5

| | Number of shows | | Number of hours | |
	1981	1982	1981	1982
Warner Brothers total	5	4	3.5	2.5
Twentieth Century–Fox total	4	4	3.5	3.0
Glen A. Larson Productions	1	1	1.0	1.0
Alone or with other producers	3	3	2.5	2.0
MGM/United Artists total	2	3	2.0	3.0
David Gerber Productions	0	1	0.0	1.0
Alone or with other producers	2	2	2.0	2.0
Columbia total	2[3]	4[4]	1.5	2.5
STUDIO TOTAL	28	29	21.0	22.5

II. MAJOR INDEPENDENTS

Aaron Spelling Productions and Spelling-Goldberg Productions	5[5]	6[6]	5.0	6.0
T.A.T./Tandem and Embassy/Tandem	5	8	2.5	4.0
Lorimar	4	3	4.0	3.0
MTM	3	4	2.5	3.5
MAJOR INDEPENDENT TOTAL	17	21	14.0	16.5

III. UNAFFILIATED MINI-MAJOR INDEPENDENTS[7]

NBC Productions	2	2	2.0	2.0
Viacom	2	1	2.0	1.0
Alan Landsburg	2	2	1.5	1.5
Witt-Thomas-Harris	2	2	1.0	1.0
Stephen Cannell	1	2	1.0	2.0
David Gerber[8]	1	0	1.0	0.0
UNAFFILIATED MINI-MAJOR INDEPENDENT TOTAL	10	9	8.5	7.5

IV. OTHER INDEPENDENTS

IV. OTHER INDEPENDENTS	11	7	7.5	5.5

	Number of shows		Number of hours	
	1981	1982	1981	1982
TOTAL STUDIOS AND MAJOR INDEPENDENTS COMBINED	45	50	35.0	39.0
TOTAL SERIES	66	66	51.0	52.0

Sources: *Variety*, September 30, 1981, pp. 76–82; *The Hollywood Reporter*, May 7, 1982, pp. 1 ff.

Notes:
1. Projected prime-time series for the three networks, excluding news magazines, sports, and movies.
2. Not including 3.5 hours of replacement shows slated to start later in the year, of which 1.0 hour was from Lorimar and 1.0 from Johnny Carson Productions.
3. Not including one hour coproduced with Spelling-Goldberg.
4. Not including three one-hour shows coproduced with Spelling-Goldberg.
5. Including one hour coproduced with Columbia Pictures.
6. Including three one-hour shows coproduced with Columbia Pictures.
7. Independents who sold at least two shows to the networks for the 1981–82 and 1982–83 seasons combined.
8. In 1982 Gerber went into coproduction with MGM.

Year to year, decade to decade, majors may rise or sink. A onetime powerhouse like Desilu, fruit of the *I Love Lucy* phenomenon, can even evaporate. But the principle remains the same: A few companies are the top sellers. Not only do the majors and the networks breathe the same cultural air, not only do executives go to the same parties and read the same magazines, but they pitch new program ideas back and forth. Writers and small-time producers who want to pitch to the networks often find it useful to throw in with one of the majors. They give up ownership of their show and often a certain amount of control—and gain large and steady salaries. At Universal, for example, a producer might get a guarantee of $400,000 to $800,000 over a period of years, with all the fees he earns counted against it. A thirteen-show series might give him $10,000 per episode, for a total of $130,000 counted against a $400,000 guarantee.

For this handsome deal, Universal takes 40 percent of the network
license fee of roughly $700,000 per episode. The most successful
producers, like Glen Larson (*Quincy, Magnum, P. I., Battlestar
Galactica, The Fall Guy*), negotiate heftier deals and can even claim
profit shares—if their lawyers can prove there are any.

Even though this tracking system normally locks network television into its familiar ruts, it can on occasion have the opposite effect.
Since the networks don't know how to read popular moods and
therefore listen to established suppliers, an established supplier is in
a stronger position than a producer off the street to devise a fresh
show and sell it. Of course, most top suppliers have little interest in
new forms; the old forms work perfectly well for them. But if for any
reason—a new market intuition or the interest of a television star—
they become inclined to depart from the beaten track, they start
with advantages. Market power eventually rests on a record of continued success; but it can also be used, if anyone chooses to use it, as
a license to break the rules from time to time. In the end, however,
the networks are the ones who decide which violations of rules can
be tolerated.

In the world of suppliers, some inside tracks are more inside than
others. At a minimum, a Lee Rich or a Norman Lear is always guaranteed a serious hearing from the top network executives. Beyond a
commitment to a respectful hearing comes a commitment to "develop" a script; beyond the script is a pilot commitment; beyond the
pilot, the elusive on-air commitment. If a network believes strongly
enough in a producing-writing team, it may even make a commitment to put a show on the air without a pilot. Others get serious
hearings, even pilots, even a series on the air, but no prior commitments. Even many a commercially successful producer is shut out
most of the time. Herb Brodkin, a crusty New Yorker who produced
The Defenders and *The Nurses* and many "docudrama" movies including *Holocaust,* says that of all the ideas and outlines and scripts
for dramas, musicals, romances he submitted over the course of
thirty years, about 10 percent had gotten on the air.

The most precious of inside tracks lead to commitments, of which
there are various kinds: commitments to actors, to writers, to producers and production companies, to studios, and to former network
executives. From the networks' point of view, commitments make
perfect sense. They put the services of proven winners under contract. The favored ones who garner commitments are, of course,
delighted to have found a degree of stability in an industry otherwise
so chancy. Some even argue that commitments insulate them from
normal commercial pressures and generate higher quality than the
vagaries and hedges of the normal development process. But in a
closed market, favors to somebody are disfavors to somebody else.

The smaller producers and newcomers smell favoritism. These se-
cond-tier, marginal suppliers behold networks locked into contracts
that have, in effect, signed over large hunks of their schedules to
privileged big operators, and they feel frozen out.

Commitments to actors, to "talent," are the most common kind.
Such commitments are usually for TV movies, but once in a while a
network is so eager for a performer, a Mary Tyler Moore or Farrah
Fawcett, that they will guarantee a series, especially when the star
comes in the same package with a production company and writers
who also have good track records. The network then has to put the
series on the air or pay a stiff penalty. This is the so-called pay-or-play
commitment. (Occasionally, if the series is sufficiently misconceived,
the network chooses to pay; but usually pay-or-play means on-air.) So,
for example, *The Mary Tyler Moore Show* originated with a commitment CBS made after the actress pleased them in a special with Dick
Van Dyke, echoing her role as Van Dyke's wife in *The Dick Van
Dyke Show* of the sixties. *The Mary Tyler Moore Show* was a big
success and spawned commitments to Valerie Harper *(Rhoda)* and
Ed Asner *(Lou Grant)*. From all this was formed Hollywood's benign
empire, MTM Enterprises.

Robert D. Wood, the president of CBS during the heyday of the
Mary show and now head of programming for the booming Metromedia conglomerate, recalled how the *Lou Grant* commitment
sprang up. "The [*Mary*] show'd been on the air for seven years. And
when Mary decided that the show was creatively fatigued, and [writ-
ers] Allan Burns and Jimmy Brooks and Grant [Tinker] all concurred,
and they said to us, 'We're not going to renew,' and we knew the
show was going down, then what about the careers and the oppor-
tunities of the people in that cast? One of them was Ed Asner. So
Fred [Silverman, then CBS programming chief] came in one day and
said the man who represents Ed Asner was asking for a series commitment. Now those are very important assets. You don't give those
away very often. And my question was 'What is it for? A half hour
or an hour?' And they said they don't know yet, 'but if you want Ed
Asner, you're going to have to guarantee him a series.' I said, 'Give
it to him.' Eight months later there was a show with Lou Grant."
While Wood had no idea what the show was going to be, he "did
know that in Asner I had an extremely attractive personality that the
audience loved. I knew I had the auspices of MTM, who don't do
things casually. That's a hell of a shot, as opposed to doing a pilot,
putting a new cast together, spending all that money. . . . I'd rather
be out a lot of money with Ed Asner, with whom at least I felt we
had some kind of a shot. I said, 'We'll be damn fools if we let Ed Asner
get away from us, because he *is* CBS, he *has* been on the air, people

do know him. There's not a whole new thing you've got to do with
Ed Asner; he's *Ed Asner.*'"

It happened that Asner and his producers and writers wanted to
do more than transplant Grant's comic, crusty persona from one
office to another; and therefore for five years television got a singular
show. Whether *Lou Grant* and the *Mary* show would have gotten on
the air and stayed there if they had come up through the normal
development process, without commitments, is questionable. *The
Mary Tyler Moore Show* tested weakly. The *Lou Grant* commitment
may have coaxed CBS to give the show a full year to build its audience after a low-rated start. On the profits of the *Mary* commitment
have been reared some of network television's most inventive shows,
including MTM's *WKRP in Cincinnati* and *Hill Street Blues*, and
none of its worst. Let it be noted, though, that less impressive empires have also been built on pay-or-play guarantees, not least the
Spelling-Goldberg combine, from *The Mod Squad* to *Dynasty*.

The strongest case for commitments rests on MTM's record, and
it comes as no surprise that the strongest argument I heard for them
came from the founder of the company, Grant Tinker, who was,
when I first interviewed him, still the head of the company and
perhaps the most liked man in Hollywood, the only important man
about whom I heard not a nasty word anywhere. "You didn't ask
me," Tinker said at one point in his most graciously bluff manner,
"but I was telling you what I would do if I were suddenly running
a network. I would seek out the best people and I would say, 'Forget
pilots. Just tell me what you want to do, and if I think it's okay I'll give
you a series commitment.' And then the audience, of course, makes
the ultimate judgment."

Five months later, Grant Tinker was the head of a network, and
I read back to him that earlier quotation. "I feel exactly the same
way," he said. "When we can attract the right people—by that I
mean on and off camera; it could be a star and a writer in whom we
have confidence, whatever combination—we will frequently just
hold our noses and jump."

Networks are investors, and investors play the averages and try to
keep costs down. Out of ten comedy pilots at $450,000 a half hour,
only two might get on the air. Such costs weighed on Grant Tinker,
new head of a floundering network, but he also defended commitments as a way to lure better writers back to TV: "If we attract more
of those good people whose batting averages tend to be higher, we
will be on balance better off." For example, Tinker was trying to
tempt Allan Burns, co-creator of the *Mary* show and *Lou Grant*, back
to television from feature films.

For any writer or actor, a network commitment is an important
asset indeed. A commitment can set a performer up in business,

which means he or she is no longer simply a glamorous employee, flattered by producers, scorned by writers, and written out of the profits. Actors can be important enough to a show, and the show important enough to the network, to give them extraordinary leverage. Overnight they can negotiate the wherewithal to found their own production companies. They can bargain for development money, or guaranteed pilots, or movies; even, on the rarest of occasions, for on-air series.

Gary Coleman, a diminutive boy with a kidney transplant, was irresistibly charming, articulate far beyond his years, perpetually precocious, and a star. Since he was not only indisputably talented but black and his on-air "family" white, he could safely satisfy an audience's thirst for fair play. Gary Coleman was *Diff'rent Strokes*, which in 1980–81, its third year, was one of only three series NBC landed among the top twenty; the cute twelve-year-old with the sly delivery was not only the linchpin of a single show but, as the network reasoned, the "tentpole" of an entire evening. So Gary Coleman's lawyer got him a guarantee of movies and pilots, then worked out a money deal to swap his commitments to Twentieth Century–Fox.

Or take Johnny Carson, the definitive showbiz host with a following so great he could launch a line of suits and bargain about the length of his *Tonight Show*. NBC could ill afford to lose his late-night wit and aplomb, and consequently each time Carson renegotiated a contract he could ratchet his way up. In 1980, he bargained for more than $5 million a year for three years, longer vacations, and finally the establishment of Johnny Carson Productions, with NBC guaranteeing, over a three-year period, not only a number of TV movies, but up to ten scripts, from which would be made three pilots, from which not less than one series would get on the air.

Gary Coleman Productions, Johnny Carson Productions, Estrada Productions. . . . Commitments are a barometer of performers' leverage and network desperation in tandem. By the early 1980s, therefore, CBS was the least "committed" network, NBC the most. All over town the word was out in 1981–82 that selling movies to NBC was almost impossible. "Movies for television routinely have been that area of the network where the most diverse, interesting anthological programming is done," said thirty-five-year-old independent producer Len Hill, a former head of TV movies for ABC who had left with his own "back-end deal" setting him up in business as a producer. He added: "Under the Silverman administration, a pattern emerged where, in that handcrafted, Tiffany area of the network, the critical suppliers at NBC became such experienced producers as O.J. Simpson, Erik Estrada, Larry Wilcox, Gary Coleman—not as talent, not as stars in these pictures, but as primary producers responsible for story development and production design. And Carson had production commitments second only to Aaron Spelling. For two years, the NBC movie department hung out a sign saying, 'Closed for Business. Only Producers with Commitments Need Apply.'"

What had happened? Fred Silverman was the easiest, most immediate explanation. People all over Hollywood blamed Fred Silverman for bad taste, self-imitation, and, not least, pledging NBC to commitments stretching years into the future. The conventional wisdom was that Silverman was a splendid programmer as long as someone was sitting over him with the power to say no; his troubles were said to have begun at his third network, NBC, when he was granted the absolute authority of chairman. Few, however, wanted to admit that Silverman was also a creature of the system that hired him, glorified him, and promoted him from network to network, granting him more and more power all the while. Len Hill blamed the Silverman phenomenon at NBC on the increasingly panicky, short-term-profit mentality at the networks. "The tenure of a network executive [now] seems to be about two and a half years—even shorter if they've been given back-end commitments," said Hill, who was at ABC in charge of movies for almost four years.

Detroit, too, ran aground because too many auto executives cared too much about the quarterly bottom line for too long. "Everybody has to have a profit statement this quarter that's better than the last profit statement," says Norman Lear. "That's the social disease of our time. I think that's what we're dying of as a nation." Len Hill points to "the tremendous high stakes that they're playing for over the very short run. There was a willingness, as a result, on the part of some very capable showmen—Fred Silverman, I think, was a consummate example—to make terribly shortsighted decisions because the logic of this television season dictated that. Fred was willing to give away 1984 to Johnny Carson and Gary Coleman, if he could get through 1981." (Silverman didn't last through 1981, but NBC was left holding his commitments. Grant Tinker subsequently cut back on new commitments there, leading Len Hill to say in 1983: "It's a relief to the entire community of independent producers that the Tinker/Tartikoff administration has managed to dig out from under the Silverman commitments. The 'Closed for Business' sign no longer hangs from NBC.")

Commitments circulate and can be traded, bind loyalties, and attract talent. Commitments also multiply, as they did so disastrously at NBC. While a commitment may begin only with a star or a writer-producer who the network and major suppliers think is hot, top suppliers, production companies, studios, and agencies pyramid such deals into more deals. "We make sure," says agent Jerry Katzman of the important William Morris Agency, "that, when we make series deals for talent, we try to get additional commitments for the talent for TV movies to protect them if the series fail. That used to be the old Universal way of dealing with NBC. If you want to pick up a series of theirs, well, then, you had to give them more commitments." When Universal was riding high at NBC, it had been able to call those sorts of shots. "We kind of play the same game. And if they don't buy it, then we'll try someplace else."

As deals generate more deals, commitments can be banked or even swapped like chips. For years, for example, Universal Studios was knee deep in unfilled, blind commitments that had piled up as part of the payoff for hit series, especially at NBC. Universal then cashed in some of its chips by getting a profusion of less than luminous shows on the air: *The Incredible Hulk*, *Lobo*, *B.J. and the Bear*, *The Gangster Chronicles*, *Harper Valley*, and *House Calls*. Occasionally one would take off, a *Quincy* or a *Magnum, P.I.*, generating yet more chips for the studio to play with. For all its reputation in the industry as what the writer-producers Richard Levinson and William Link called "a sausage factory," Universal did have valuable chips it could offer writers, producers, and actors. With its seven-year contracts, Universal was the last holdover of the old studio contract system. Staff writers could move from one Universal show to another, and the studio was therefore known to be a good apprenticeship for younger writers. Steven Bochco, who served his twelve years on the Universal lot before he moved on to MTM and the classier act of *Hill Street Blues*, recalled frequent meetings with the president of Universal Television, where he would say, "'NBC or ABC or CBS wants a cop show and yada yada yada yada, and are you interested in developing it?' When you're at a place like Universal, you hope you get those phone calls, because the one thing you discover at a place like that is that to develop your own stuff and carry it upstairs is generally not a productive process. So you wait for them to come to you." Commitments might even be traded in; if a top supplier had an on-the-air show in trouble, it could give one of its outstanding commitments back to the network for a second-season renewal.

For a number of years, network executives also succeeded in bargaining themselves into the production-commitment business. The so-called back-end deal started when certain top executives took advantage of their presumed importance and growing fame, and convinced the networks to write into their contracts that when they left their jobs, the networks would underwrite office overhead for these executives-turned-producers, and/or buy from them a certain amount of material. In the course of the seventies, with this precedent set, the networks lost control of the back-end deal. Not only top-level executives like Bob Wood and Fred Silverman, but middle managers—vice-presidents for series development, or movies, or miniseries—could get them, especially at ABC and NBC. Agents liked back-end deals and promoted them.

The back-end deal institutionalized the ultimate revolving door. Many young executives saw the networks as way stations en route to, or back to, the creative community anyway. Some had previous production experience and some had none, but since the networks had become so thoroughly involved in assembling shows, all of these executives had learned something about packaging the elements of a program, and these skills were useful once they became suppliers; in fact, they were the essence of producing. It was as if deputy undersecretaries of defense could not only reasonably surmise that fine aerospace jobs would await them as soon as they left the Pentagon, but could sign contracts while still in the Pentagon itself, binding the government to underwrite their designs of new jet fighters, with an option to produce them later on.

"Most people take their back-end deals in groups of pilots, so they'll have more than one shot at getting on the air," Michael Zinberg told me in his office on Warner's Burbank lot. Like his friend Len Hill's, his story is typical of this period. In fact, Zinberg and Hill resemble each other. They are bright young men of medium height, compact of frame, no fat anywhere. Zinberg still has a Texas accent and Hill comes from Los Angeles, but both speak crisply and radiate confidence. They exemplify the take-charge network middle manager of the seventies and after. Among executives, Zinberg was unusual in having been a director first, working his way up through MTM and producing *The Bob Newhart Show* before Fred Silverman tapped him to head NBC's comedy-development department, where he godfathered *Hill Street Blues,* as well as many less notable shows. After straining against Silverman for several years, failing to get his shows out of development and onto the air, Zinberg took advantage of his back-end deal in 1980 and bailed out. NBC was now committed to buy several pilots and TV movies from him for three years. Zinberg could have exercised his option to go into business for himself as an indie prod—as did Marcie Carsey and Tom Werner when they left ABC in 1981, and Silverman himself when he activated his own back-end deal in 1981 on his way out of NBC. But Zinberg really wanted to make movies, so he took his commitments to Warner and traded them in for the chance to write features—only to go back to TV later because that was where the action was.

The boom years of the sixties and especially the seventies were boom years for middle managers like Zinberg. The networks filled up with layers of such gatekeepers. Herman Keld said that when he started as a junior research executive at CBS, in 1955, there were four executives separating him from Chairman Paley in the pecking order. In 1981, he was a vice-president for programming and there were five layers standing between him and Paley—and CBS's was the most streamlined of the three entertainment divisions.

"When I worked at NBC [in the sixties] and I was in charge of the West Coast in Burbank," said Grant Tinker while still at MTM, "I didn't have any program-development people. I went home every weekend and read myself blind. Now they've got bodies on bodies they don't need. I mean the layers starting with the drones; then you go to senior drones; and managers and director and vice-president [the standard executive ranking in all network development departments] and senior vice-president. Not only are they a huge drain just fiscally, but I claim they get in the way of good, clean, decisive judgment." But as Tinker discovered when he went back to NBC as chairman in 1981, it was not so easy to break down a bureaucracy once it was entrenched. He kept not only most of the top people, but their positions.

More layers in the hierarchy means more executives with the power to say no, and the proliferation of that power means more executive involvement at every stage of decision-making and program production. "There is a curious corporate principle," according to Len Hill, "that says a person with a vice-president's title will find enough work to fill the day. There's a producer's axiom: Beware of networks that have too many vice-presidents." Many producers share this lament, and more than one remembers when executive Hill himself stood in the way of a pet project at ABC.

The structural surplus of executives and network interference is hard to trace to any one source. In any industry dominated by a few manufacturers, each seeks to regulate as much as possible both supply and demand. Bureaus multiply, tasks get subdivided, efficiency gets defined with an eye to parts of the overall process rather than the whole. As the networks took over direct control of programs from sponsors and ad agencies in the sixties, they gathered more and more authority in their own hands. This structural tendency toward a centralized bureaucracy was accelerated under the successive reigns of Fred Silverman. As Barney Rosenzweig says, "In the early seventies, the programming people were all making very little money: thirty-five, forty-five thousand a year. The people they were doing business with were making a hundred, two hundred, three hundred thousand a year. So the one thing they had going for them was power: They could tell a guy making three hundred thousand dollars a year that he couldn't make a picture. That was their compensation. Because they certainly weren't making, by show-business standards, very much money. Barely making a living. I mean, even a bad writer makes thirty-five thousand a year. So what Freddie did was he elevated that. He started paying more money to executives. So now it's not uncommon for a network executive to make seventy, eighty, a hundred thousand, a hundred ten, a hundred fifty thousand dollars a year. So the envy aspects have been minimized because of that. And that was a good thing Fred Silverman did. But the bad news was that in doing that he told them, 'Now that you're getting all this more money, I want you more involved. Tell these people how to make pictures.' I happen to like [executive X]. I think he's very bright. What his qualifications are to tell me how to make a movie, I'm not so sure. My wife Barbara Corday is, I think, the only major network executive on the Coast who had a successful career in show business before she went to work in the network. She was a successful writer. But even with her qualifications, what right has she to sit there, anonymously—because her name doesn't go on the screen, her fortune is not at risk, her job is not in jeopardy, she is secure—what right do any of them have to sit there, in their anonymity, behind their secure desks in their corporate façade, and tell people who are willing to take that risk how to make pictures?"

The growing authority of middle managers made them more and more valuable investments for the networks. Meanwhile, middle managers had their own ambitions. The founding fathers of the television networks were broadcasters who came from radio. They were canny investors in a marketplace that had been reserved to private capital by the Radio and Communications Acts of 1927 and 1934. "They've become enormously successful," as Rosenzweig tells it. "Now, when you become enormously successful, when something wonderful happens to you at Berkeley, you go out and buy a new suit. When I become enormously successful, I go out and buy a new car, or a new house. What happens when a corporation becomes enormously successful? They buy a new building. They build a building at Century City, right? They build a building on Sixth Avenue. What do you do with a big building? You fill it up with executives. So they began to hire more people. One of the great myths about the business is how you have to pity the poor network people because their jobs are in such jeopardy, and they're under such pressure. Nobody ever gets fired from a network. You really have to have your hand in the till or be an idiot to get fired from a network. It's the closest thing to total job security that ever happened in show business. They don't fire anybody, and they keep adding people. Now, who are they adding? Are they adding broadcasters? No, they're not. Are they hiring people who are even particularly interested in broadcasting? Are these people interested in climbing the corporate ladder at ABC or NBC or CBS? My observation is no. It turns out who they're hiring are people out of universities, colleges, and film schools, and people who are interested in film. People who want my job. They're interested in using this experience and this power base as a training ground to further their own ambitions. Think about the potential conflict of interest. Is this network executive making decisions that are best for the viewer or the corporation that employs him, or is he, or she, making decisions that will further his or her own career ambitions? Is the executive dealing with the best picture makers, or rather those suppliers who are in a more favored position to further that executive's private ambitions?

"The scenario is, these people come to work for a network. They are trained by the network and they stay there for two or three years. They've been very visible in the industry, they've wielded a lot of power, they've made a lot of friends. Then they say to the network, 'I'm leaving.' The network says, 'No, no, we don't want you to leave. Please don't leave. We've taken all this time to train you, you're so good at your job now.' 'Okay, I'll stay another two years, or another year, but at the end of that time I want to be "an indie prod with a multi-pic pact," ' as *Variety* would say [for an independent producer with a multiple-picture contract]. So they leave the network with a guaranteed commitment of a pilot, or four pilots, one must go on the air, or two movies of the week. They are making these people instant millionaires."

Back-end deals and other commitments bother even some of the beneficiaries, including Len Hill, who says, "I don't think they serve the industry. I think a professional organization of trained network executives, whose goal it is to work over the long haul for the best interests of the corporation, is going to be better off than a network whose executives see themselves having a two- or three-year crash course in the network programming ranks, only to leave. And I cite myself as an indication of what's wrong. It would be in the public good to create certain antitrust provisions that said, among other things, that the network could not give to department executives guarantees of production. In the best of all possible worlds, we'd have a free television market that was not encumbered by long-term exclusive pacts that guaranteed production to a hand-picked privileged few."

Recently, recognizing that they had locked up too much money and too much of their schedule in commitments, the networks started phasing out the back-end boom. Perhaps they were also beginning to see that in their high-flying years they had simply tied themselves to too many humdrum projects, projects that, no matter how competently produced, lacked a commercial spark. By 1981, the networks had ceased to make new back-end deals and were trying to cut back on other major production commitments. NBC and ABC were busy trying to meet the commitments they'd already made.

The small world of network executives finds its counterpart in a small world of top suppliers. The major fixtures of the seventies and early eighties are the Spelling, MTM, Tandem/T.A.T., and Lorimar companies, which like the studios maintain their own stables of producers and writers. Just a cut below them in market power are the independent producers I am calling mini-majors, master managers of formula like Garry Marshall and Glen Larson, who have produced shorter skeins of hits and are enmeshed in complex coproduction arrangements with the studios. The mini-majors have established track records, but it would be truer to say that they have devised formats so popular and so lucrative that the biggest have laid out their own tracks. As long as their records hold tolerably well, they are in a position to ask not only for money but guarantees—to keep their tracks perfectly manned and maintained.

More often than not, the mini-majors and majors have started out producing comedy, where it is easiest to keep control and make a financial killing. The reason is economic. The amount the networks pay in a license fee for hour-long drama is almost always less than the cost of making the episode; the difference has to be made up by the backer who owns the episodes and who, once the network has aired them twice, is free to release them abroad and, much more importantly, to syndicate them to local stations, where the vast profits lie. The studio or major supplier that provides this deficit financing gets ownership and, with it, control. Comedies, almost always half an hour long, are relatively cheap enough for smaller independents to produce without having to go into deficit financing. But in comedy, drama, or action-adventure, the mini-majors find that the more hits they make, the more money they make for both networks and backers, and the more control they can keep over their product.

Among the most prominent mini-major producers is the Ed. Weinberger–Stan Daniels–Jim Brooks group, who wrote The Mary Tyler Moore Show at MTM and then formed their own production company, affiliated with Paramount, and produced Taxi and Best of the West (a Weinberger on-air commitment for ABC), and Cheers for NBC. In 1981, Weinberger was so deeply involved in Best of the West that, although he was credited as neither executive producer nor director, he stepped in to direct episodes. Power over employees is usually coupled with a certain power to resist network control. On the same show, Weinberger told an employee to refuse to accept calls from ABC's Standards and Practices censors. Weinberger's clout at ABC ran out when the network refused to renew Taxi in 1982, but NBC broke precedent to pick up this ostensibly damaged merchandise.

Most successful of all the comedy mini-majors is Garry Marshall, the ageless adolescent at Paramount, whose Happy Days finished among the top four three years running, Laverne and Shirley four years running, with Mork and Mindy a hit alongside. Three hits at a time, a hat trick only Norman Lear has also managed—and not, like Marshall, on a number-three network, ABC. Marshall's hits actually helped carry ABC to number-one status, making him all the more valuable a commodity and Fred Silverman, then at ABC, all the more grateful an executive. On that strength, every fixed star in the Garry Marshall galaxy could bargain a commitment. As Barney Rosenzweig puts it, "When you make a deal for *Happy Days* you make a seven-year deal. At the end of the seven years, the show is still a hit. Now ABC says, 'We want two more years of *Happy Days*.' Henry Winkler [*Happy Days*'s Fonz] says, 'No, I don't want to do it anymore.' Garry Marshall says, 'No, I don't want to do it anymore, I'm tired.' Paramount says, 'We don't want to do it anymore because we want to put the show in syndication. It hurts us to have it on the network now.' 'We'll give you more money,' says ABC. 'We don't want more money.' 'What do you want?' Well, Paramount gets a picture commitment for every episode, or every ten episodes; Henry Winkler gets a guaranteed picture commitment and a pilot commitment for every year he stays on the show; Garry Marshall gets [pilot commitments in exchange for an exclusive deal with ABC]. . . . Well, what happens, you see, is all these commitments eventually have to be paid off, and the free marketplace is reduced in the process." Understandably, other indie prods felt frozen out by ABC's commitment to Garry Marshall & Co. Marshall had the inside track. When ABC was riding high, he had even been able to sell them *Mork and Mindy* on a phone call, with no pilot at all. But what the indie prods tended to overlook was that even Garry Marshall, with his exclusives and pilot commitments, had no on-air guarantees; his pilots still went through the scheduling mill.

Garry Marshall is a slow-moving, slow-talking man, free of evident spleen; yet he says in the unreconstructed Bronx tones made familiar by his sister Penny, better known as "Laverne," "[The networks] spend millions of dollars on research, don't trust it, and then copy movies or plays. Typical of them is, three years ago, I had a show called *The WACs*. I spun it off *Laverne and Shirley*. Their research said nobody wants to see women in the army. They showed me all this research. 'We checked, and it said forty percent don't want to watch.' Then *Private Benjamin* came out, and they called me back, with no shame, and said, 'We want that army show now.' I said, 'But you said it was no good.' 'Yeah, *Private Benjamin*'s a big hit.' 'I'm not doing it,' I said. 'You missed your chance for me. I can only get excited at a certain time, fellas. Don't you see, I'm not excited now. Now it's going to look like I copied *Private Benjamin*.' I didn't do it.

"I did *Odd Couple* for five years. That's what I did, period. They said, 'Very nice, but we don't want you to do that any more. We want you to make a lot of shows, so you'll have so many shows you won't have time to do any of them well, and you will run around like a crazy person.' They did that to Norman [Lear] and David Gerber and everybody else. They give you so much work that you can't do any of it very well. And then they keep coming, more, more, more." At this precise moment the phone rings: time to go off to look at a rough cut of a *Mork and Mindy* episode. In the screening room across the Paramount lot, all eyes turn to Marshall as he questions a scene, assesses the jokes, gives instructions for the final cut. Then back to his office to read a glamorous actress for a bit part, in a shamble so slow it must be a sort of bracing against the fragmented speed-up of his days. Garry Marshall is overextended. While he shepherds three of America's favorite shows through their paces, he must continue to spin off new shows to fill new commitments. However, his more recent pilots seem like the wan babies of what's gone before. Garry Marshall is imitating himself.

Like other successful producers, Marshall still stares at the specter of failure. Producers don't keep title to their inside tracks forever. They have to keep producing and succeeding; otherwise, they can be consigned to the outer reaches. Back-end deal, pilot commitment or no, the producer is still subject to the network mentality. As Michael Zinberg says, "You work in conjunction with the network, because they have scheduling authority. So I can go off and say, 'Hey, I want to make this pilot,' and they probably would let me do it if it wasn't really just terrible—I wouldn't be in the position of making something just terrible—but if it's not something that they're going to want to schedule, what the hell do I want to make it for? Collect a few bucks in a production fee? That's not the object. The object is to get on the air." Even producers with pilot commitments consult with the network about subject and characters; in practice, ABC could "consult" Garry Marshall out of a pilot.

Although the networks don't own the shows, they keep tabs on the writers and lead actors whom producers hire. Like top producers, the successful writers also make up a small world. Although anyone with persistence and credentials of competence can find a network executive to pitch an idea to—Stu Sheslow at NBC said he would see "anybody" and took three to five pitches a day—some writers are more equal than others. The insiders are known quantities. Once a writer breaks into this charmed circle, as the writer Michael Elias says, "you have to be legally sociopathic for them not to hire you." Once considered reliable, a writer may be minimally competent, minimally appropriate, and still land a plum writing assignment simply for being known to "give good lunch" or "give great meeting." "Once you have a life in this business," Michael Kozoll of *Hill Street Blues* says, "no one goes out of his way to break your rice bowl. I've seen people hired on the basis simply that somebody's coming to take

the house away—which is really an amazing largesse." But unless
they ascend to the top ranks, writers can get stuck in the farm-team
leagues of episode and occasional pilot writing. Only a few hundred
writers are regulars, most of them on the staffs of series. Fully half
of prime-time television is scripted by only 10 percent of the Writers
Guild's 3,000 active members. The marginal writers, even those who
have sold a script and joined the Guild, complain of trouble getting
assignments. The regulars have head starts, and moreover the continuing series routinely return unsolicited scripts unread. (There can
be legal trouble if a rejected writer claims that a story point was lifted
from his or her script.) Yet even insiders usually pitch without guarantees. Typically, David W. Rintels, the former president of the
Writers Guild of America–West, writer of many episodes and TV
movies, says, "I win some, I lose some, some get rained out." (A
network executive said to him about one recent script, "You're
gonna get ten awards and I'm gonna get a ten rating.")

Indeed, chance is the residual category on every seller's lips.
Whether a script or a pilot sells depends on who exactly is on the
buying end, who is the packager, and who is in the package; but only
a handful of top producers and writers can count on on-air guarantees for long. Everyone else weathers the vicissitudes of fortune.
Producers who have tasted enough success to feel ready for more
tend to blame network commitments to the top suppliers for clog-
ging the inside tracks; the less successful people are more inclined to
shrug their shoulders and blame bad fortune. "It's a crapshoot," goes
the common refrain. The metaphor is revealing, in one way, for the
odds are finally on the house's side; but it obscures in another sense,
for TV sellers, unlike most gamblers, get someone else to subsidize
their losses. In any event, so many chance elements are irreducible.
The year a supplier tries to sell a show, the network may be oversup-
plied with that genre; the sponsoring development executive may
have just revolved out of the network; the show may get on the air
opposite a blockbuster, and sink fast; the most suitable time-slots may
be filled. (By the same token, the network may tell the producer his
pilot was terrific but there was simply no place on the schedule for
it, as a polite way of saying, "No thanks.") So attributing lack of
success to bad (or average) luck is not only accurate to some degree,
it also soothes the much-afflicted ego. The idea of luck is balm.

One day I was interviewing Richard Reisberg, then president of
United Artists Television, when the door of his office opened. Another executive walked in, flipped a coin in the air, and jokingly said
to Reisberg, "Heads or tails? Heads? Okay, we'll make that deal."
When the networks regularly boast of their success in reading the
public mind, and the next minute cancel last week's confident predictions and replace them with new ones just as confidently, reading

the network mind translates readily into such jokes. Production-company scuttlebutt knows how arbitrary network decisions are, and all at once acknowledges and mocks its own rock-bottom uncertainty.

Because the networks dominate a buyers' market, they also shape the small world of the big writers. "For the most part," says Michael Zinberg, "I'm not going to be in business with anybody who the network doesn't want to be in business with as well." The same applies to casting, although contractually the producers keep the prerogative. "You go in and you have a conversation," Zinberg says. "Ultimately, they're the ones with the money, so, yeah, they can bend your arm. . . . And you've got to keep the larger picture in mind. You know there's always more to a relationship than just this one part. So it's a give-and-take affair."

"People going to parties and knowing each other is not all that important," says the agent Bill Haber. "Along with extraordinary talent, which doesn't happen too often, the most important thing is that people have good working relationships with each other. Because you will always go back there if you can work with them. I may see you at a party and have a great meal and think you're great, but if I had a bad experience with you on a series, I don't care if you're my best friend, I'm not interested."

One exemplary career suggests how commitments can pyramid and, in the process, transform the face of television. Aaron Spelling is in a class by himself. He came up the hard way, a Texas boy who moved from odd jobs into acting and TV writing, and proved a prolific hand at series formula. Spelling hooked up with Danny Thomas at Paramount, coproduced *The Danny Thomas Hour* and a curious, forgotten western, *The Guns of Will Sonnett*, in which an old scout and his grandson scoured the countryside for the boy's gunfighter father. Spelling had an eye for trends. It seems a former vice-squad cop had written a pilot script about an undercover unit in the fifties. However much of a series idea came from that script (which had rattled around for a while) and however much from Spelling himself—the retired cop did get the valuable "creator" credit—Spelling saw an appeal in it that bypassed everyone else. When he brought *The Mod Squad* to ABC in 1968, most of the executives were doubters, but Spelling got the enthusiastic backing of ABC programming chief Leonard Goldberg. By the 1969 season *The Mod Squad* was the only dramatic series ABC could land among the top twenty-five shows. At a time when the network was mired in a distant third place, Spelling parlayed his success into an exclusive contract with ABC.

One hit later, Spelling took on Leonard Goldberg, who had left ABC to head Screen Gems, as a partner. But no old-boy network could have kept Spelling on the air if he hadn't kept grinding out hit shows. Between them, Spelling-Goldberg and Aaron Spelling Productions ran an extraordinary streak through the seventies: *The Rookies, S.W.A.T., Starsky and Hutch, Charlie's Angels, The Love Boat, Fantasy Island, Vega$,* and *Hart to Hart,* each of which finished among the top twenty-five shows for at least one year.

For upscale viewers and finicky critics, there was Spelling-Goldberg's more tasteful and realistic *Family,* but mostly Aaron Spelling produced what he called "fast-food entertainment": high gloss, glamorous settings, shot in bright, primary colors, with plots, lines, and gestures stamped out so predictably they look as if they have been programmed by a home computer that not only carries out the programs locked in its memory but has been programmed to write variations. "Spelling wants tennis-match dialogue," said one of his former producers: a simple line from A, shot over B's shoulder; a simple counterline from B, shot over A's shoulder; another simple line from A, from over B's shoulder. Spelling himself was known to have called his products "mind candy." Certainly, he did have a distinct style. Barney Rosenzweig, who produced the second half of the first season of *Charlie's Angels* for Spelling, calls it "show and tell." On a Spelling show any plot point important enough to signal once is signaled twice. "He shows the scene," Rosenzweig says, "and in the next scene everybody talks about what was just seen. 'You'll never believe what just happened! This just did this and this just did that.' You know, when you do television episodes, especially action-adventure shows, you have a tendency to remake all the old great movies. Well, one of the episodes I was doing was sort of a mild ripoff of *Foreign Correspondent.* It took place at a resort. The Angels were going up for a week of sun and swimming in the pool and playing tennis. And as they're driving up, we see Kate Jackson in the back, reading *Time* magazine, and on the cover of *Time* magazine is this Henry Kissinger–like character, Theodore Bikel, the man of the year. He's going to be at this resort. God, wouldn't it be terrific if I could meet him, says Kate Jackson. They're all kidding her about how she's got this crush on this erudite political intellectual.

"And so they arrive at the resort, and Farrah goes off to get her tennis racket fixed, and Jackie Smith goes off to buy a new swimming suit, and Kate's kind of unpacking in the room, and she goes out on the balcony, and across the balcony she sees Theodore Bikel. He's there with the FBI and the CIA and a lot of other people, and she kind of waves at him. And he waves back. He's kind of a cocksman, and she's an attractive woman. So when the FBI leaves, he crawls over the balcony to her apartment. And they sit, and they have a nice discussion. And while this conversation is going on, he's smoking cigarettes. He's got a cigarette lighter. And he says, 'Listen, I have to get back. I have to make a speech. I'll see you later.' And he leaves. He goes off by the balcony. Kate runs downstairs to the swimming pool, finds Farrah and Jackie, and says, 'God, you'll never guess who I just met, it was so incredible.' 'Oh, yeah.' They don't believe her, right? She says, 'I'll prove it to you.' And here he comes, walking along, and she says, 'Hi, how are you.' And he doesn't acknowledge her. She says, 'Wait a minute, he knows me.' Well, something's wrong, right? That's what the whole thing's about. There's been a switch made, and nobody believes her. She goes back to the apartment, pissed off that her friends don't believe her, and she sees on the dining room table the cigarette lighter. Very distinctive cigarette lighter. Picks it up. Aha! Evidence that he was here.

"Now, we're running the rough cut, and I say to Aaron, 'I'm going to get a close shot of the cigarette lighter, and Kate's hand will come in and pick it up and light it, so it will be one shot, instead of just an insert. So we'll have that tie-in.' Aaron says, 'Good idea, good idea.' Then he says, 'Listen, when you do it, get the insert earlier with Theo's hand, showing him putting the lighter down on the table.' So we go on and we run the rest of the picture. He had a few other notes. I said, 'I like your notes. We'll accomplish them,' I said, 'but one I have to really disagree with violently.' He said, 'What's that?' I said, 'I really don't want to put in that insert of Theo Bikel putting the lighter down on the table in the previous scene. It's a real red flag. I mean, it just says to everybody, Uh-oh, look out!' And he says, 'Well, of course, but you must do that.' I said, 'I don't understand. Look, to me, everything I've learned about picture making is to go for revelation, to learn about something through the eyes of a principal. Don't intrude the camera in to have the audience see something that our cast doesn't. It's much better to learn about it through Kate.' Big argument. Finally he said, 'Look, just do it.' Aaron was the boss, right? He owned the store."

That night at a party, a friend reminded Rosenzweig, who was complaining bitterly, of the conventions of children's theater: "The villain walks out onstage and says, 'Heh-heh-heh, I have the secret matchbook, and I am going to hide it. I am going to put it behind this basket, and the heroine will never find it. Heh-heh-heh! And he walks off. Now the heroine comes out and says, 'Where oh where is the secret matchbook?' And all the kids in the audience say, 'It's behind the basket, it's behind the basket!' That's what Aaron does. He believes that that's what the American audience is, you see." And, by any network standard, it all works.

ABC didn't brag about the magnitude of their commitment to Spelling, but it was reported to be two pilots a year, with one guaranteed to go to series, as well as a number of TV movies. If at least one series did not get on the air, the network would have to pay millions of dollars. Spelling's track record was unmatched, though in 1981 even Spelling's eye for the right marriage of formula and the cultural moment seemed to be failing him. That year, he got two series on the air: *Aloha Paradise,* a spring recombinant that dry-docked *The Love Boat* on *Fantasy Island* under the hostess-ship of Debbie Reynolds; and a fall rough-tough, mow-'em-down show, *Strike Force,* starring Robert Stack. Both rated badly; neither was renewed. But who knew when Spelling might concoct another runaway hit? In 1982, he bounced back with a successful cop show, *T.J. Hooker,* starring William Shatner of *Star Trek.* Even those who felt iced out by his special position at ABC thought him "incredibly talented," as one indie prod put it, "and I mean that sincerely."

Spelling embraced the form's simplifications so fervently he left his personal impress on the medium. In the 1967–69 *The Guns of Will Sonnett,* a son was looking for a father while a father was looking for a son. Not only was the genre wrong, an outdated western, but the father was a bad guy. In *The Mod Squad,* though, Spelling got his formula right: a team of young, attractive undercover police, once in trouble themselves, bringing other errant souls into line under the firm hand of a paternal captain. Father and sons were still in evidence, though now one of the sons was black and one a daughter; and everyone was on the side of the angels. The sons had located the father they deserved. *The Mod Squad* could appeal to dismayed parents who wanted to think the best of their errant children while seeing their authority approved in the end; to teens who imagined that if they ever stepped out of line they could step back in and authority would lend a hand; and to the law-and-order-minded of all ages who saw in the kids' plain clothes not simply the hang-loose garb of the young but the disguises of effective law enforcement.

Next, Spelling tried to carry the youth market one step farther, splitting the social-reform motif away from law enforcement. In 1969 he produced *The New People,* created by Rod Serling, whose premise was that forty college-age kids returning from a goodwill tour to Vietnam had crash-landed on a South Pacific atoll left uninhabited after years of nuclear tests. The young now got to see if they really could (as in the old IWW slogan) bring to birth a new world from the ashes of the old. But Spelling's utopia failed to ignite enthusiasm, and sank after a season. Perhaps the elements simply weren't right. Perhaps Spelling needed adult authority to get his elements right.

In any case, after *The New People,* Spelling returned to law-and-order teams, his young more acceptably offbeat. Sometimes the team consisted of tough-minded peers, as in *S.W.A.T.* and *Starsky and Hutch,* patrolling the street nasties and keeping recalcitrant, childish reality under control. Sometimes the team was supervised by a sage and authoritative elder as in *The Rookies* and *Charlie's Angels.* Either way, Spelling's formulas worked wonders in the ratings. His idealistic, hip plainclothesmen of 1968 evolved into his fun-loving but career-minded Angels of 1975. The mod trio's forceful Captain Greer softened into the Angels' avuncular boss Charlie and indulgent eunuch Bosley. *Angels'* glamor and bright colors were the transition to Spelling's next winning formula, the upbeat Day-glo look of the romantic semicomedies in which he retained his two-generation pairings. *The Love Boat*'s captain watched genially over his crew, which in turn presided over the romantic adventures of the passengers; and *Fantasy Island*'s Mr. Roarke dispatched his midget helper Tattoo to help wishful visitors come to terms with their childlike desires. Neither Spelling, his aides, or the executives who came and went at ABC were given to speculating much about the sources of Spelling's touch, but the network was certainly willing to build the grandest barnyard and set out the finest fodder for their golden-egg-laying goose.

The cultural power of major suppliers like Spelling attracts projects the way political power attracts jobseekers. As Spelling became a powerhouse at ABC, big-time producers began to bring him shows they might otherwise have produced themselves but had trouble selling. The point was to jack up the odds, for the odds of selling a pilot were slim. Clout brought Spelling-Goldberg not only movies but whole series. Esther Shapiro, a writer who served for a time as an ABC executive, had a commitment from a back-end deal. In the wake of *Dallas*, she and her husband Richard wrote a full-blown treatment for a serial about business and family intrigue in a Denver-oil dynasty. An innocent might think that a well-regarded writer fresh from ABC executive circles, paired with an experienced writer-producer, would choose to develop such a hot project on their own. But the Shapiros needed production facilities, and even with a back-end development deal they also needed clout to get on the air. So they brought their project to Aaron Spelling Productions, where it became *Dynasty*. Esther Shapiro appreciated Spelling's "fairness." He was willing to share not only hypothetical profits but the lucrative here-and-now investment tax credit.* The so-called ITC is a government rebate of about 6⅔ percent of production costs granted to the owners of series and movies. With the majors' penchant to charge all conceivable overhead against future profits, profits might or might not materialize, and years later if at all. But the ITC means dollars

---

*The 1976 Tax Reform Act extended the Kennedy-era investment tax credit to include all movies and TV shows except those it called "topical or transitory"—later deemed by the IRS to include variety shows and daytime serials aired only once.

in hand in the next tax year, and can be applied toward previous or future tax years. With a series costing $700,000 an hour, the ITC can be worth a million dollars in a single year. Other majors would have been slower to share that bounty.

Many indie prods still resent the politics of these deals. The indies need to maintain regular production in order to keep their staffs on hand; when they make only an occasional TV-movie deal, it is hard for them to maintain continuity. They feel the classic disgruntlement of a small operator up against a giant corporation. "I think there is the beginnings of hardening of the network arteries," says Len Hill, "a hardening that's brought on by a diet of commitments." Hill doesn't dispute the networks' right to judge a supplier by his reputation or experience. The problem is "the fact that they've given away so much that no matter how much they trust you and want to be in business with you, there just isn't any more space on the schedule."

The marketplace is not sealed up airtight. In fact, a year after this interview, Hill and his partner Phil Mandelker sold a short-lived series, *Tucker's Witch,* to the least commitment-laden network, CBS. The most important thing, though, is that the networks' marketplace has come to be dominated by the simplistic conventions of glamorous look and banal dialogue, blunt action and crude comedy. Newcomers are free to compete for space in the uncommitted part of the schedule, but on terms set by the going conventions, at which the established suppliers excel. In the early sixties, before the major suppliers cornered the market, independents like Herbert Brodkin *(The Defenders),* David Susskind *(East Side, West Side),* and Herbert Leonard *(Naked City)* had produced prime-time series of considerable ingenuity and merit. But by the late seventies, with a few notable exceptions, the comic-strip conventions were so deeply installed that most independents' shows closely resembled the majors'. Given the networks' structure and mentality, opening them up to more suppliers would not necessarily change the face of prime-time television. "Independent" is a business term, not a description of the product.

Most of the indie prods can't afford to indulge their outrage at the privileges of the majors; usually they swallow their resentment or mute it to get along. They are realists. In the end they might well have to cut the best possible deal with the powerhouses. If they are unseasonably liberal or middle-brow in their tastes, their ideology is unlikely to forbid the necessary adaptations. After all, they believe in the business system; they only want a fair chance to sell their wares in the mass market. The range of "production values" considered commercial is narrow indeed, and established and would-be established alike are ambitious go-getters. Off the screen as on it, slick and quick get the job done. Indeed, the indie prods as a group are aggres-

sive men (almost always men) in a business that uses "aggressive" as
a term of high praise. Their brisk, wisecracking style is mirrored, in
fact, by their vigorous hero-creations, from Kojak to Magnum. Like
the young executives at the networks, the producers relish talking on
the phone, doing business at lunch, seeing and being seen. They are
bright, glib, and persuasive; selling is their *raison d'être* and half their
battle. Admiring success before all else, they admire a winning style
even if it does them a bad turn, for that winning style is something
they will have to learn to emulate if they are going to stay on the
track long enough to acquire a record.

Barney Rosenzweig, for example, appreciates Aaron Spelling's
achievement. "It is not villainy," he insists. "Aaron's been very successful for that network. It's perfectly logical that they want to be in
business with him. They're paying a fortune to keep him exclusive.
Aaron could make more money if he wasn't exclusive to ABC. If he
could have NBC and CBS competing for his wares, he would do
every bit as well or better. So ABC does have a special relationship
with him, which has worked very well for ABC, not just for Aaron.
It isn't because it's that good old boy club." On the 1983 fall schedule,
Spelling and his coproducers were responsible for fully one-third of
ABC's prime-time hours.

That "special relationship" exemplifies the structure of commercial television, but much more is at work than tennis-playing, party-
going and back-scratching. Behind the old-boy club lies both capital's
logic and the shared pleasures of the joint expedition in pursuit of
formula treasure. A rising social class is always united by personal
bonds and a mesh of reciprocal interests as well as rational calculation. Across the industry spreads a culture of ingratiation. To a few
victors go the huge spoils, but there is enough left over to keep
everyone else scheming and dealing and hoping. "The theory," says
Barney Rosenzweig, "is that, if we keep hanging in there long
enough, we will become part of the inner circle." Overriding their
conflicts of interest, the creators of the culture that blankets America,
and much of the rest of the earth, make up a little society at one with
itself.

CHAPTER 8

The Deal Is the Art Form

In this little world, the personalized license plate is an inexpensive form of conspicuous self-promotion. NOO YAWK, 2HOT4U, an EX POOR Rolls-Royce and a 40 SHARE Jaguar affirm the industry's paramount values. Like prime-time itself, the spirit of these signs is: If you've got it, flaunt it. So it is that down Beverly Drive in Beverly Hills drives a new white Jaguar sporting the plate TEN PER.

TEN PER is a talent agent's plate, a sign that he ranks high around town and is not abashed to advertise the fact. Indeed, he insists on it, for his business rests on the general understanding that he is indispensable. In any industry, competition breeds middlemen who specialize in drawing together the loose strings of influence, centralizing a marketplace that would otherwise be more chaotic, bidding up the value of scarce goods.

In Hollywood, writers know they had better hook up with the right agent if the right doors are going to open, if a script is going to be read by the right people. After all, it is one thing to be read by a low-paid story editor at a studio or a production office, and quite another to be read by the top dog. The networks, studios, and top producers, in turn, need to be spared the nuisance of having to read the most amateurish scripts, so agents perform a real service as screens. Moreover, producers, actors, directors all need masterful attention to their amazingly intricate contracts. Indeed, at more advanced stages of their careers the talent often turns to the even more elite entertainment lawyers.

Once agents have positioned themselves at the gates between buyers and sellers, they become useful to the buyers themselves. Agents advise network executives on their own contracts, their career moves, and until recently, their back-end deals. They circulate ideas for programs, try to make matches, and sometimes launch projects. Building on their power as middlemen and brokers, the top agencies even become entrepreneurs themselves. If the deal is the art form, as is said in Hollywood, the agent is Hollywood's master artist.

Writers sometimes complain that agents have usurped too much power. But if agents did not exist, they would have to be invented, because the market mentality that fuels the networks fails to answer the key question—What is going to work on TV next season? While, as we have seen, executives live and breathe by the numbers, they cannot truly rely on an abstract, statistical market to make decisions for them. The anonymous audience does not knock on their door requesting a show with three attractive young women, one blonde, one brunette, one redhead, all working for an unseen detective. The market's numerical voice is slurred, ambiguous, after-the-fact. If executives waited for it to tell them what it wants, they would have to wait too long. Meanwhile, there are a thousand specific questions that need to be answered fast, and strict reliance on commercial values breeds a special anxiety.

In this blur of possibility and doubt, agents are a kind of solution. Agents are, in the words of *Dynasty* executive producer and former ABC executive Esther Shapiro, "people who are very strong and very confident and very rational dealing with frightened network executives who don't really know that much about this and that. And [some agent's] screaming at you, 'All together! Ready-made! Here!' " As a result, in Los Angeles, the top agents rank high in the social hierarchy, and are much consulted and much chatted up. Of course, writers, producers, and former executives also mutter, mostly off the record, about the power and wealth and sometimes arrogance of these wheelers and dealers. When I told Esther Shapiro I couldn't get through to one of the top agents in town, she quipped, "Neither can most of his clients." When outsiders come prying, the agents usually prefer to stay in the background. One young agent said she would be glad to talk to me—I had been referred by two of her writer clients—but by new company policy all interviews would have to be cleared through a vice-president, who refused, saying, "Our clients want publicity; we don't."

The agent has been a conspicuous operator in Hollywood for half a century, but became a powerhouse relatively late. For more than twenty years the film studios held the elements of production in their own hands. With stars, producers, directors, writers all under contract, and studio-owned theater chains providing a captive distribution system, the studios were the companies who ran the company town. The agents were little more than hard bargainers for their clients' salaries, as immortalized in a line attributed to H. L. Mencken: "There's enough sincerity in Hollywood to fill a peanut shell and still leave room for an agent's heart." But in the late forties the old system came unstuck. The Justice Department forced the studios to divest themselves of their movie houses, and simultaneously television began to rip into the old guaranteed movie market. The studios were late to shift to production for TV; by the sixties they had decayed into mere physical plants where preassembled movie packages were financed and produced. The studios found more money in real estate than in movies; the Century City complex was built on Twentieth Century–Fox's back lot. Paramount and United Artists sold out to conglomerates, Gulf + Western and Transamerica respectively. Financially, MGM became an auxiliary to a Las Vegas hotel. Now it was independent producers who scooped together the elements and formed complicated distribution and coproduction deals with the studios.

The agents were perfectly positioned to take up the slack, as they began to negotiate not only fees but shares of the profits. They bid up the asking price of the "talent"—the actors—and at the same time seized the loose reins of power. They were already in the selling business; why not put together film packages themselves? The most skilled, best-organized and -connected agents emerged as impresarios, "the new czars of Hollywood," as the screenwriter John Gregory Dunne put it, "allocating to their clients the profits and perquisites that once had belonged solely to the studios."

In the late forties the established studios resisted television and refused to traffic with it. Television was the enemy, keeping people home from the theaters. But first one agency, then others, began to smell opportunity. The success story of one top agency, MCA, tells the tale. MCA began as the Music Corporation of America, a booking agency for big bands in the twenties, but by the late forties, under the leadership of a young agent named Lew Wasserman, it had gobbled up the top Hayward-Devereaux agency in Hollywood. While the studios were shying away from television, Wasserman drew a bead on production. "MCA," as Bob Gottlieb has written, "moved aggressively into the void, initially pushing its clients onto network shows, frequently packaging entire programs, complete with writers, directors, producers and actors, all from the MCA client list. And, most importantly, MCA decided to get involved in television production itself." But a Screen Actors Guild bylaw provided that agency involvement in production amounted to conflict of interest. At this key juncture a longtime Wasserman client named Ronald Reagan, a director and former president of the Guild, helped get a waiver for MCA. "By the early '60s," Gottlieb writes, "MCA was responsible for more than 30 hours of television—either as producer or talent representative." MCA bought the huge Universal City lot in the San Fernando Valley, then gobbled up the Universal Studio itself. When the Justice Department finally brought an antitrust action, forcing MCA to choose between the agency business and production, Wasserman closed down the agency. MCA had transformed itself into a major production entity.

MCA was only pursuing a logic of power. As the old institutions crumbled, the top agents moved into the breach: They knew packaging and the ins and outs of business. A good number of studio heads were former agents. The television networks are also studded with executives who started out that way. David Gerber is one major television producer who began his career "agenting," and others still come along.

Agents are the outriders of the star system. They are preeminent movers and shakers because the business presumes, with reason, that characters—and therefore stars—are central to a show's success. "We like to think of ourselves as the development arms of the producers and network executives because we represent the talent," says Jerry Katzman, and he is not alone in his opinion. Katzman is an affable agent at William Morris, which is, along with Creative Artists Agency (formed by five top agents who split off from William Morris in 1975) and International Creative Management, one of the supreme agencies making things happen in television. "I think that we have a tremendous influence on what does and doesn't get on the air. I see it stronger and stronger. Today we hear nothing from the networks but 'Who is the talent? Who are the writers or stars that we can develop something for?' And I have been witness now to all three networks in the last two months saying, 'Please don't come in with ideas. Come in with pieces of talent that we can develop for, or writers we can rely upon.' "

In a capsule history of the agent in American commercial television, the main story would go like this: In the early years, advertisers and their agencies developed most of the shows and sold them to the networks. Theatrical agents dealt directly with the ad agencies. Sometimes, as in the case of MCA and William Morris, the theatrical agency "created the package," put together "the elements," then went to the ad agency. "You developed your friends at the ad agency," as Jerry Katzman puts it, "and they would buy the shows from you."

But the networks began to fight to wrest power from the advertisers and ad agencies, and succeeded by the early sixties. "Then, as everything happens," Katzman goes on, "the network became a little bit more possessive. And they said, 'You know what? We can develop our own things. We don't have to rely so much on what the ad agency wants us to buy.' Moreover, the shows became too expensive for single sponsors to buy, undermining the power of the ad agencies. So then the theatrical agencies, being astute, realized that they also had to become closer to the networks, and became extensions of the network development process. We would find out what kind of shows do they want to develop. They can develop them by spending money on the scripts, but we have the talent. So if we can get the writer-producer that we represent, together with the talent that we represent, we can bring it in to the network, and they'll buy it. So they haven't had to do any development at all."

The commercial bleakness of the 1981–82 season afforded the agencies a golden opportunity to prove indispensable as last-minute packagers of star series. Cost pressures were working in the agencies' favor, too; for the higher costs go, the more the networks want the surer things the agencies stand for. In 1977, each network developed about 150 pilot scripts for fifty pilots, of which perhaps ten would get on the air. In 1980–81, each was down to about thirty scripts for fifteen pilots. Meanwhile, the costs of pilots had risen to roughly $450,000 for a thirty-minute pilot, $1.5 million or more for a sixty-minute one. "We have to come in with many more packaged projects" for the networks, Katzman says, "because they can't afford to develop as much and hope that they can get the five or six main stars to do these shows. They would like to know up front that they have a show for Cheryl Ladd," to name the actress who played one of Charlie's long-running angels. The networks don't want to go to the trouble of developing two or three projects and taking the chance that one will turn out "right" for Cheryl Ladd.

Once an actress has soared into one of the hit constellations, and turns out to be possessed of the mysterious pizazz called "star quality," of course she tries to parlay the privilege into role after role, in salaries running into five figures per week and a chance at profits. The agents have helped bid them up. Stars, according to Katzman, used to say, " 'I won't read anything, I won't show any interest unless you have an offer [from a network]. Give me an offer and I'll read it and let you know what I think of it.' Now talent is more interested in starting with the project, so that they have some kind of ownership position in the project, or they have some meaningful participation in the project." The stars become "their own entrepreneurs." All the more important for a writer to have the right agent. Ordinarily a star won't read a script without a cash offer "up front," but if writer and star have the same agent, the star will make an exception.

As agents and stars have thrived together, the top agents have become their own entrepreneurs. When the agency "packages" the whole project, instead of collecting its normal 10 percent off the top from star, writer, director, and each of the rest of its clients, it collects an overall packaging fee. William Morris charges the top commission, 10 percent divided "five and five": 5 percent off the top, and another 5 percent deferred, to come out of future profits. There are extraordinary amounts of money at stake. Suppose, for example, the agency packages an hour-long series that gets a license fee of $700,000 per hour. Twenty-two episodes are sold per year, for a total license fee of $15.4 million per year. Each year the show is on the air, the agency collects $770,000 up front, and another $770,000 out of profits. If the show goes into syndication, the agent's cut balloons. For a one-shot TV movie that pays a license fee of $2.2 million, the five-and-five packaging fee adds up to $220,000. Smaller agencies take lower packaging fees, at least for favored clients, but William Morris holds the line at five and five, and justifies it as equal treatment. "Whoever it is, if it's Robert Redford or if it's Clint Eastwood or if it's Jerry Katzman," says Jerry Katzman, "they all pay the same commission at William Morris. Our feeling is that nobody is a second-class citizen around here." At the top agencies, packaging fees have become a major source of income.

Jerry Katzman insists that the packaging fee is earned, because packaging is an art, nothing unfair about it. "In packaging, you don't necessarily use your own clients. More times than not, it's not your clients. It's lucky for your clients if you can put those elements together [from your client list], because they pay no commission, but you always reach out for the best and try to make a project happen. You're usually using your writer, because it's usually your writer's idea that has made it happen. Yet you may not be using your star, because the stars that we have here may not be right for the kind of project that's being done, or the people that we have here have been turned down by the network. We usually try to put our talent into it, but maybe the network will say, just hypothetically, 'We don't want X for this, and we want you to go out and get Lana Turner.' So they will again dictate, sometimes, what elements go into the package. By the time you put all of the ingredients together, of having done all the business affairs for it and all the accounting for it, and all the sales into it, there's probably about a one and a half to two percent profit margin on every show. That must be amortized over all the losses"—the agents do not collect commissions in the development process, or on half-hour pilots, or two-hour movie scripts. "It's a very big number in successes, but it's not a big number in its total profit margin because of all the failures."

Obviously, the agent's main business is to represent clients, and Creative Artists's Bill Haber's important clients are legion: Aaron Spelling, Angie Dickinson, and James Clavell, among many others. He is frequently mentioned around town as the most important agent in the television business. "We will take fifteen pilots into New York in April," he says, "and out of fifteen pilots we will get four shows on the air, at least." Creative Artists packaged 170 hours of long-form television, movies and miniseries, in 1981. The receptionist in Creative Artists' Century City offices tells me she once logged ninety incoming calls in one minute there.

The trim, high-pressure Haber, still in his thirties, occupies a corner office with a parquet floor and one of the lushest views in Los Angeles: Outside, an angular glass high-rise floats off to one side, while the Santa Monica hills roll out behind. There is a bentwood rocker, stylish wicker chairs and table, a super-realist statue of a washerwoman, and a coffee cup marked with dollar signs. "Usually we're into development with our clients from the very beginning," Haber says. "The only time we really begin to pull back on a project is after it's very successful and it's been on for two years, because then they really don't need an agent around. But in the first year of a project, there are all kinds of problems."

Most of the time, Haber says, his clients come up with the ideas. "They're writers. We don't pretend to be writers. For every idea that I may have that Aaron Spelling likes, Aaron Spelling will have ten." Other times the networks are the ones who initiate. "My job is to implement what the network feels and to assess what it is they want to put on, not to disagree with them." In 1981, he privately disagreed with the networks about their brief swing toward law-and-order shows. "I never believed [Today's] FBI would work in this country," he says. Haber stays in touch with the networks and immerses himself in media—he reads three newspapers a day, the trade papers, and ten popular magazines. Each agent in the company circulates items of interest from other magazines as well. Perhaps 10 percent of the time, "which is a nice even number," Haber himself finds the germ of a series or a TV movie.

"I went to a screening one Saturday night at Aaron Spelling's house," he says by way of illustration. "A social screening. And we ran For Your Eyes Only. That was during the course of the time where ABC was telling us, and we knew, that they needed eight o'clock programming [for a younger audience], and that there was a need, maybe, for some kind of a superhero, which is good eight-o'clock programming. I realized, based on the screening, that the thing everybody loves in a James Bond movie is the moment between James Bond and Q, where they sit and do all the inventions. So the next Wednesday we had a staff meeting. Out of that staff meeting evolved a project that ended up being called *Massarati and Q*, which was the story of a guy who was like a soldier of fortune, not a secret agent—it's all in the United States—who's a guy for hire, who has a friend who's a genius who can invent anything for him at any time. One of my associates said, 'Why don't we have the friend be a thirteen-year-old genius kid inventor?' And Aaron said, 'You're right, that's a terrific idea.' Out of which then came *Massarati and the Brain*. We called ABC. We made a suggestion of a writer who's a client of ours. He said Okay. He wrote maybe four drafts before we turned it in to the network. They said great, and two days ago they ordered it. Now I'm trying to get a director client of ours to do it. And that's the show. It's an eight-o'clock show. It has a fourteen-year-old kid in it, a very attractive thirty-year-old star, and a lot of lightness, bigness, helicopters, boats, things exploding, things kids love." The pilot didn't sell, and ABC ended up "running it off" as a summer movie, wherein the network recoups its pilot costs by selling its normal ads on the air.

The power of agents shines forth most visibly in movies for television. "TV movies are TV talent," says Jerry Katzman. "The subject matter of all these movies you can list. There's only ten or fifteen story lines that they'll use. And there are twenty or thirty artists that they'll want. It's television's own stars. Motion picture stars generally do not do well in television movies. So they'd much rather have Larry Hagman in a TV movie than, say, Dustin Hoffman. I'm not saying they wouldn't want Dustin Hoffman in the right piece, but Larry Hagman can get anything off the ground, where Dustin Hoffman, I believe, would have to be in a particular piece of material that would stand on its own."

Bill Haber says television movies are more often developed by concept than by star, but in either case a top agent helps the sale. Jerry Katzman takes particular credit for selling politically charged material. "I've been responsible," he says, "for packaging two shows that got critical acclaim, but in each instance were disasters in the sweeps ratings." One was NBC's three-part 1978 miniseries *King*, about Martin Luther King, Jr.; the other, the three-hour 1981 NBC movie *Kent State*. Both ran during sweeps months, the periods when local stations measure their audiences with special precision to set new ad rates. (Therefore, these months—November, February, and May—are when the networks run the special projects calculated to rate highest.) Neither *King* nor *Kent State* had a big-name star. How did Katzman buck the networks' aversion to political controversy? In the case of *Kent State*, he played up writer-client James Michener's book on the subject ("it gave them class") and screenwriter-client Gerald Green's reputation *(Holocaust)*. And then, both times, "We didn't let it die." Access and persistence are the elements of "agent-ing," a trade and a style all its own.

"We have another project that we made happen that I think was a tremendous bit of agenting," Katzman says with obvious pride. "And that's *Will*, Gordon Liddy's book [represented by William Morris]. Now, I don't know whether that should ever be on the air. I don't know whether Gordon Liddy should ever capitalize off what he did. I'm not morally thinking about that. But as an agent I knew that there was one way of having it happen. I do know that there is one person in this community who can get anything off the ground that he wants to, and that's Bob Conrad [formerly star of *Hawaiian Eye* and *The Wild, Wild West*], and I knew that Bob Conrad would love to play Gordon Liddy. So I went to him with the book, and sure enough, he was all but strangling me, saying, 'If I don't get the rights to this material, you will not walk out of here alive.' That's how much he wanted to do that." Just the sort of thing Gordon Liddy would appreciate; actor imitates perpetrator. The usual phrase is "He'd kill for that role."

"Now, Fred Silverman [then at NBC] will do anything that Bob Conrad wants, but when push came to shove Silverman didn't want to do that story. He, too, had a moral questioning about whether this show should be done. So what we were able to do as the agent is go to the sales people at NBC, find out what they anticipated that they would be able to sell, in terms of time on the show, went back with this as information, and that, to the programming people, justified putting it on the air." Katzman says it is unusual to go to such lengths to sell a show. "But we know all the angles that it takes. And if we don't know, we'll be given clues, because we have friends there. I knew that was the way to sell Silverman. But I didn't know because I'm so bright! I knew because someone there had told me. The next thing we knew, the picture was picked up."

Packaging is the latest wrinkle in the agent's growing ability to shape the product. Many actual and would-be producers complain about the packaging fee, even resort to end runs around their agents to avoid it. "I have nothing against it," says Ronald M. Cohen, who wrote the pilot for *American Dream*, "if you really put up a package. If an agent comes up with an idea, he goes to CBS. Now he sells it. He says, 'Ronald, I want you to be writer-producer.' Listen, they're enti-tled; they came up with the idea. Or if they put in an actor. Say CBS likes your idea. Now [the agent says], 'We're going to put Loretta Swit in it, and you'll have an instant deal. Right now they'll give you a picture commitment.' All right, that's a package. Then they've con-tributed something. But they don't contribute anything half the time, or three-quarters of the time. That's really the objection."

Even writers and writer-producers who own points and collect salaries that almost any American would drool over, resent the agent's packaging fee mightily. It offends their sense of justice. Esther Shapiro, who has worked both sides as both network executive and writer-producer, agrees that agents can be helpful, but notes this essential unfairness: "Writers can make ten thousand dollars an episode, and they have to be writing, writing, writing. And somebody's getting ten to fifteen percent of the series license fee, in perpetuity, for negotiating that initial thing, and very low servicing. I object to people getting paid for not working. After the first year, after they package it, does it deserve that much money? Where does it say that it has to be ten percent or fifteen percent? Why not one percent, why not two percent? Does it deserve more than all the creative people involved in it? And all that money doesn't go on the screen."

Ronald M. Cohen puts it this way: "Five percent of seven hundred thousand dollars is thirty-five thousand dollars per episode. As a writer-producer I might make fifteen thousand dollars a week. The packaging fee in Hollywood is a scandal. This town is run by and for the lawyers and the agents. Not the creative people. I know agents who make six hundred thousand dollars a year, every year. For a writer to make six hundred thousand, it's almost unheard of to do it, and to do it you have to own a significant piece of a hit series. It would be a once-in-a-lifetime deal. But agents—they've got a guy at C.A.A. [Creative Artists Agency] who's building a two-and-a-half-million-dollar house in Brentwood. Just cash money, two and a half million. You say, 'What the heck is going on here? Who created this system?' It was created by the agents for themselves, because they understood that writers and creative people aren't too bright about business; they don't understand the intricacies of an extremely complicated business; and they live with desperation."

Television writers like Cohen acutely measure discrepancies in income because, sumptuously paid as they are when things are selling, they can easily measure their exploitation. However much money they make, someone nearby is always making more in a visibly easier way, especially someone who owns a piece of the project. It is usually someone they see at parties or on the tennis courts, someone they may even call a friend—and this well-positioned soul is often doing something visible with the spoils. The sense of exploitation is never absolute, but relative. People paid in five figures per week grind their sense of justice exceeding small. If they work hard for their Mercedes, why should someone else get a Jaguar for a few phone conversations?

Hollywood cultivates such a vivid sense of exploitation because most writers are treated with a customary contempt. Even the rich work for The Man, and they are frequently reminded—as their lines are blue-penciled, their projects killed, their offices repossessed—that they are still, as Jack Warner once said, "schmucks with Underwoods." Whether they live in Beverly Hills or the San Fernando Valley, they are possessed of an equally vivid sense of the infinite possible gradations of income and prestige. Their little world is minutely stratified yet lacking in conspicuously rational reasons for its remunerations. Talent is not necessarily rewarded, bad judgment not necessarily penalized. To make matters more complex still, above the minimum payments established for different categories of work by the collective bargaining of the craft guilds, every deal generates its own individual terms. Most practitioners rub elbows; secrets don't stay secret long, especially with agents trundling new projects all over town. Gossip hums steadily. No matter how much money anyone makes, there is always room, and opportunity, for resentment.

To critics of the agenting trade, agents seem to have wedged themselves into an undeserved indispensability. Esther Shapiro emphasizes that agents and network executives are congregating with each other constantly. "It's like a soap, really," says this executive producer of a prime-time soap. "You just begin to see how incestuous it all is. They socialize. Tennis is very important. They play tennis together at home, or they go down to Malibu." They vacation in Palm Springs, at the La Costa resort near San Diego, and in Colorado. "They own Aspen," says Esther Shapiro. "I mean, if you go skiing in Colorado, it's like going to another network meeting, with the condos. And there's Hawaii, of course, for the powerhouses. You know, just another palm tree, another hors d'oeuvre. But it's all kind of business."

Shapiro maintains that business as usual brings agencies and network executives even closer together than socializing would require. "The agents are the confidants of the heads of the networks." Most extraordinarily of all, she, like other Hollywood producers, maintains that certain top agents represent network executives, *pro bono,* in their own intricate contract negotiations with the networks. After all, the executive is a private contractor, too. By calling on the friendly agent's expertise, Shapiro warns, the executive puts himself or herself in "a very vulnerable position." For the agent inevitably accumulates power in the process. "Naturally this guy has made this terrific deal for you. If he calls up, he's going to get preferential treatment." The executive then wonders, she says, "Did you buy a thing because of that?" Not that the agent can automatically sell the next project, Shapiro cautions. "Otherwise," she says, "they'd have everything on the air."

The influence of top agents has become a sensitive point in the industry. "On series," ABC's Ann Daniel says, "when you get down

to 'Are you going to make the show or not?' the financial ramifica-
tions are so far-reaching that some people would suggest that agents,
through their relationships and so on, can get shows on the air. I think
that their influence is felt far before then, and is less significant at the
point where you are actually committing to a series." It can be felt
in development deals, "getting writers committed to shows, directors, actors. Then an agent can be very helpful or damaging. The
producers feel that more than we do. We get it secondhand."

No one is willing to say that top agents are *never* decisive at the
crucial junctures. "I suppose the agent could push something over
the last hill if it was already close," Daniel grants, "depending on
what he or she can bring to bear on that particular show—commitments of other writers, directors, or actors in the agency, for example." But Daniel insists that the identity of the agent does "not
usually" influence her in deciding to develop a series idea. She suggests, too, that an agent's enthusiasm, if too routine, can cancel itself
out. "I remember distinctly," she says, "the day I decided I particularly trusted one agent. We needed a specific writer for a special
project. I called and was told that he was unavailable. After explain-
ing the nature of the project to him, I asked for other suggestions. As
we chatted a bit, I could hear him going down his list of clients, and
finally he said, 'No, I don't.' I thought, okay, that one I trust. I like
being told, 'No, I don't have anyone available and appropriate.' Generally it's, 'How tall is he?' 'How tall do you want him to be?' "

"I get very very antagonistic," says one top agent, "when I hear of
agents in this town representing network executives. No member of
[his agency] has ever represented a network executive for commission." But he acknowledges the truth of Esther Shapiro's claim that
agents are confidants of the executives. "We are privileged sometimes," he says, "to advise them on certain aspects of their career."
He gives the example of advising an executive whether he should
consider setting up an independent company in the event he leaves
the network. "If [this executive] said he was thinking of making a
deal with MGM or Warner Brothers, we would advise him on that.
How can you have a business in which people who know each other
so well don't advise each other on such matters?" He adds, "Incidentally, if the people at the network are your friends, it also makes
business easier to do. That's incidentally."

This sort of friendly mutual aid would be hard to banish in a town
as small, as unremittingly anxious about success, as Hollywood. The
agents, after all, are business experts. What they know best are the
arts of deal-making, at which they are far more successful than are
the executives at their task of making successful programs. In return,
the executives offer something the agents need: the power to decide.
The circle draws round. Agents counsel the executives they bargain

with; the revolving door conveys agents into studios and the networks (though rarely back again), network executives into independent production. They do business with each other, hire each other, protect each other from the consequences of error, not so much because they are buddies or, as some would say, cronies, but because they share the industry's values. This mutual regard is the cushion against commercial failure. Each player recognizes the others as carriers of a common competence. Despite the different strategies of buyers and sellers, what they all aim to do is to deliver the standard goods.

Whatever their private tastes, television's power elite are not connoisseurs of subtlety, complexity, or astonishment. "Quality" comes to mean mastery of the conventions, the ability to execute the standard formulas with "high production values," seamlessly. In such a setting, playing for high stakes, the powerful people gravitate toward each other and make their deals. Those who trust each other to slip into the conventions and deliver the agreed-upon goods collect into nodes of power. It should not be surprising that they often like each other, play together, advise each other, and sooner or later fill each other's positions. In any elite world—in business, government, or the professions—power goes with sociability and mutual aid.

But the power of these elites is not absolute, for they have to adhere to the rules of the game. The products of these comfortable working relations must be able to pass as readily mass-marketable. If Aaron Spelling brought ABC *Che Guevara's Angels, Harold Pinter's Family,* and *The Leonard Bernstein Hour,* he would no longer be Aaron Spelling. If Bill Haber represented him in these projects, he, too, would lose credibility. The inside track can provide real advantages: exemptions from needing to produce a pilot, for example, or from having to test it favorably, or from having to prove itself against *Dallas* or needing to manifest quite so clear-cut a success before getting renewed for a second season. Inside tracks do not found new sports.

Friendship and favoritism have other uses, though. The old-boy networks binding executives, agents, and top producers amount to a curious kind of solidarity. Outsiders charge corruption. Women and minorities charge that the old boys are boys, and almost entirely white boys at that. All this is true, and no one can doubt it affects the product's stereotypes. Women and minorities in key positions would be more likely than white males to collect their mass audiences by affirming female and minority characters, even through counter-stereotypic stereotypes. (One network series development executive, for example, told me she had made sure that every female lead in that season's pilots was a working woman.) But it may be doubted whether gender and color are more powerful than the formal con-

ventions of network television, just as it may be doubted that executives of working-class origin generally show special tastes. Whatever
the origins of the old boys, even if they were black or old girls, their
small world secretes a culture more powerful than personal origins.

This culture embodies values that stand against both the imperson-
ality and the unreliability of marketplace calculation. Favoritism is
complicated. It rests both on assumptions of mutual obligation and
on the crudest computations of the market values of those obligations. In the television-industrial complex, favoritism is also the system's way of compensating for the inscrutability of the mass
audience. Since mass-market failure is the norm, and no one really
knows what will "work," why not trust Aaron Spelling or Garry
Marshall? From this mesh of trust springs Hollywood's home-grown
counterbalance to the feverish competition it cultivates.

Cronyism, mutual backscratching, behind-the-scenes favors, revolving doors, musical chairs, careers made by failing upward, the
"amazing largesse" given to favored members of the "creative community"—all this knits together what might otherwise fall apart in
the skirmish of all against all. The same names may stay in circulation
for years, or decades—sometimes because a rare competence will
out, but more often because beneath the hell-bent pursuit of the
fugitive audience, and the smooth logic of taking the fewest risks,
old-boy networks bind this savage business together against its own
ignorance and against its centrifugal whirl.

C H A P T E R 9

Movies of the Week

The television-industrial complex manufactures not series alone, but the one-shot movies that vary the networks' weekly routines. Each year, the three networks together underwrite more original movies than all the studios combined. In 1982–83, ABC, CBS, and NBC scheduled some ninety movies that they had ordered, financed, and shaped explicitly for television; and that number was down from earlier peaks. In sheer volume, the network departments of TV movies and miniseries (which the industry calls "long form") have therefore become the mass-production studios of this time. Their pictures no doubt make less of an impression on society than series, for they don't stay long enough to inspire sustained identification. Rather than producing personality cults, they exploit them. These B movies come and go, leaving who knows what traces in the consciousness of our time. They are the pills and modules the networks drop into their schedules for relief from the series habit. But whatever their precise consequence, they add up to a considerable portion of the prime-time schedule. Although they did not become staples of the schedule until the mid-sixties, they took up twelve and a half hours a week in 1980–81, or almost 20 percent of the prime time. The corporate deputies who develop and license these regular stopgaps are the functional equivalents of David O. Selznick, Louis B. Mayer, Irving

Thalberg, Samuel Goldwyn, and Jack Warner, although their names don't circulate through American households the way their products do.

If the economics of production determined content all by itself, TV movies should be more diverse in style and ideology than either feature films or series, for they are far cheaper and therefore less risky as business propositions. In the early eighties a two-hour TV movie cost about $2 million, compared to an average of $9.4 million for a feature film and $14.3 million for a season's worth of an hour-long series. There is enough money in TV movies to pay for months of writing and about three weeks of shooting, making possible in sheer technical terms more complex scripts, more sophisticated direction and editing, more accomplished acting. Between the lure of money and the chance for less standardized material, TV movies attract not only the major suppliers but forty or fifty low-overhead independent producers, most of them in Los Angeles and a few in New York. Indeed, the long form lends itself to the indie prods, who should be—and sometimes are—more adventuresome than the major suppliers. Because TV movies don't syndicate well (although they often go into theatrical distribution abroad), they theoretically wouldn't have to look like the money machines that series promise to be. And their very evanescence means that characters don't have to survive intact for next week's resuscitation. They can be killed off, or descend to bad ends, making tragedy possible at least in the technical sense. Months and years can elapse. Upheavals and revelations can interrupt and transform a character's life. Since movies are usually singular, any producers so inclined ought to be able to carve out some freedom from formula. Since they are transitory, they have less chance to offend that offendable public the networks are always so concerned to protect. And so, one might think, the definitions of permissible subject matter and form should be free to open up.

At times, of course, the networks do take chances, largely for prestige's sake. The format of the "docudrama"—or as some in the industry prefer to call it, the "motion picture based on fact"—has taken on subjects foreclosed to series. In recent years CBS has aired *Fear on Trial*, about TV's own blacklist, and *Playing for Time*, about Auschwitz; ABC has put on *Roots*, *Attica*, and *Friendly Fire*, which explored anti–Vietnam War sentiments; NBC, *Holocaust*, *Kent State*, *Bitter Harvest*—about chemical pollution—and, in a much different spirit, a version of G. Gordon Liddy's *Will*. Yet what stands out about most docudramas is how unexceptional they really are. Mostly they are special events made routine—precisely by the same network system of market calculations that dominates series. TV movies, like series, are deficit-financed. Overhead and huge interest payments pile up long before there is any prospect of income. In effect, the networks are banks, and for their cash they exert control. Since, as ever, the networks seek the sure accumulation of maximum audiences, TV movies become just another set of predictable interruptions in the series stream.

Because movies are rarely aired twice, though, they pose a special marketing problem that radically shapes the networks' decision-making process. As posed by Stu Samuels, the energetic, outspoken young vice-president for TV movies at ABC, the question is, "How are you going to get people into the tent?" Each episode of a series advertises the entire season; the early episodes of a miniseries can build interest in the later; a regular feature film can do well on word of mouth, reviews, and multiple viewings; but the one-shot TV movie cannot advertise itself. Therefore, network executives in charge of movies think first and foremost about promotability.

Since the networks are their own best advertising medium—with *TV Guide* and the local newspaper listings second, newspaper ads and critics' columns third—network executives focus not so much on how the movie will look as a movie but on how its "summary" will play. A TV movie, it's believed, has to have a story line that can be summarized in a line or two in *TV Guide*. As examples of clear concepts, the agent Bill Haber offers "Mine collapses, family separated," or "Train hijacked over Alps."

"If you can't define [a TV movie] in a television log line, how can you get the audience to it?" says Deanne Barkley, former vice-president for movies at NBC and ABC, summing up industry wisdom on the subject. "You've only got one shot to get them, you know. It doesn't matter how good it is or how bad it is. *Jaws* is a perfect television movie. If you can describe it in one sentence so they know what they're coming to, and it stars Angie Dickinson, or someone that they've heard of, they'll come to it."

Since marketing is of the essence, it seems only reasonable that one of the most successful executives in the field of TV movies should have begun his career in advertising.* Uncustomarily for television, Brandon Stoddard is a white Anglo-Saxon Protestant who came from a Connecticut lawyer's family, went to private schools and Yale. He worked at the Grey and BBD&O ad agencies for nine years before making his way through every major department in ABC's programming hierarchy. Starting at daytime in 1970, Stoddard headed both daytime and children's programs, next TV movies, then dramatic series development and movies, and finally, beginning in 1979, all ABC TV movies, plays, miniseries, and its newly developing theatri-

---

*Nor is it surprising that one of his successors, Stu Samuels, came to television from eight years at *TV Guide*.

cal films as well. "The most important thing for a television movie," he says, "is the capacity for a movie to be understood by an audience after watching a ten-second film clip. The problem—or advantage— of the television movie is that an audience decides whether they're going to watch it or not watch it, a huge audience of fifteen million people, in roughly four days, which is miraculous, and they do it primarily off the on-air promotion. So if you have a movie that takes a long time to explain, or it is a movie that is somewhat diffuse, you're going to have a very very difficult time telling the audience about it."

The second most important factor in the selling of TV movies is the star, who by himself or herself may be the magnet drawing that audience in. That is why the network's favored stars have such leverage. A commitment from Ron Howard or Sally Struthers can get a project made that otherwise might fail to reduce neatly to the ten-second clip or the *TV Guide* blurb. As CBS vice-president in charge of movies for television Steve Mills said, "There are only so many different story lines. Let's just say a picture where a man in a midlife crisis has an affair with a younger woman is not a new story idea. We have done it many times, and everybody else has, too. That's okay; it depends on how you do it, how you cast it. We did it last year with Ed Asner having an affair with Meredith Baxter Birney while married to Anne Jackson, and we could predict that it would do five share points higher than if we did it with a non–television star; and it did. If I had to predict what that would do, a midlife-crisis man having an affair with a younger woman, I'd say a thirty-two, thirty-three share. But Alan Alda or Ed Asner* in it and I would say a thirty-seven, thirty-eight share, getting up into the forty range."

Finally there are the prestigious exceptions, projects that some network executives may have especially cared about and all make a point of singling out. "You sometimes say," as Brandon Stoddard puts it, "All right, I really love this movie. It's not very easy to sell it in a promo or in an ad, but we're going to make it because we really care about this idea, and we are going to spend a year selling it, publicity, promotion, screenings, teacher's guides, and all the rest of that kind of stuff. *Friendly Fire*'s a pretty good example of that. Now that was also helped by Carol Burnett in her first dramatic debut on television. But *Friendly Fire* was an example where we just decided we really want to make that movie. We felt it's a really important movie, and we spent a great deal of time and effort selling it beyond the normal four days and the *TV Guide* ads."

In fact, the 1980 ABC version of C. D. B. Bryan's popular book

---

*This was before Asner's press conference on behalf of Medical Aid for El Salvador, and the cancellation of *Lou Grant*.

Friendly Fire was launched by Stoddard's friendship with Bryan, going back to college days at Yale, and ABC produced it itself through its own movie department, ABC Circle Films. But the typical development process is more elusive. "We put into work a hundred and fifty to two hundred scripts a year," says Steve Mills of CBS. "We probably have five thousand ideas pitched to us in various forms, in oral presentations, an idea at lunch, or over cocktails, a few pages prepared by a writer or a producer, sometimes a step outline, sometimes a completed script." Eventually those 5,000 ideas and 150 to 200 scripts will generate fifty or sixty movies. (ABC takes as many pitches, develops about half as many scripts, and makes twenty to thirty movies a year.)

Mills, like Stoddard, says that, important as the star is in attracting the requisite numbers, "Very seldom do we have a star or a director and then start off and have to find something for them to do. We go the other way. We go for material first." Even commitments to current or former series stars—and CBS has forty or fifty of them—rarely determine what the movie will be about. "When we do make that kind of a commitment, as in the case of Liz Montgomery," Mills says, "we know that from our batch of one hundred fifty or two hundred scripts we will find at least one property that a woman in her thirties or early forties can play very well." But which projects to develop in the first place, which scripts to commission? As with series, there is no neat logic for generating salable stories. The networks want "good stories," yes, but what are they? "Usually it's something that I respond to on a gut level," says Janey Rosenthal, who works under Steve Mills and, in her early twenties, is probably the youngest high-ranking woman in network entertainment. "Is it intriguing, is it interesting, is it entertaining, is the character sympathetic, or do I want to watch him because I'm curious about him and want to know more and want to go deeper?"

Even when they talk up light entertainment and escape, the executives in charge of movies operate under the sign of a distinct form, which might be called television realism. Always they want "high concept," clear stories that tell viewers instantly whom to care about and root for. Movies have to be "believable" and sensational at the same time. The characters have to fit the familiarity of the home screen. The network idea is that people will venture out to movie theaters to be voyeurs of other worlds, but if they stay home they want stay-at-home figures. It's felt spy stories don't work on television, for example, because spies are not the folks next door. Industry lore also has it that the audience is fickle and expects instant clarity. The finger is always poised near the dial, so all salient elements have to be established with breathtaking haste. In network logic, it follows that characters have to be stripped down to unequivocal moral emblems; their troubles spotlit; their traits, like trademarks, leaping out of the screen.

The rare historical dramas are no exceptions to this rule. Abraham Lincoln strides into Ford's Theatre; FDR or JFK or Richard Nixon sits behind his desk in the Oval Office: These are the moments to be immortalized as History. The rest of historical time is an unpopulated void between the great moments. Private life is best consigned to the present. History-as-pageant is normally reserved for the realm of special miniseries and movies: There are the adventures of the imperial explorer as outsider and hero *(Shōgun, Marco Polo)*; the docudramas of pivotal moments in the lives of presidents *(Truman and MacArthur, Eleanor and Franklin, The Missiles of October)*; the Watergate shows *(Blind Ambition, Washington: Behind Closed Doors, Will)*; and tales of tyrants *(The Bunker* and *Inside the Third Reich)*. The "docudrama" was aptly named, for it exists not to comprehend but to document, to authenticate the validity of surface detail, to establish that this really happened.

Docudrama is melodrama whose stereotypes, however, sometimes disclose the point of view of historical victims. Whatever its limits as historical chronicle, the 1977 *Roots* was not only an unanticipated record-breaking ratings blockbuster, but a national purgation that kept blacks and whites alike tuned in in acts of moral witness, of expiation as well as curiosity and compassion. *Holocaust* in 1978 had sufficient impact to seize the moral high ground not only in the United States but in West Germany, where it helped mobilize public feeling for an extension of the statute of limitations on atrocity crimes.

Roots got on the air partly on the strength of Alex Haley's bestselling book and partly because of a favorable run of network circumstances. Aside from making money by appealing to the largest audiences, *Roots* producer Stan Margulies says, the networks have consciences. He also recalls, as "a joke that had some truth in it," telling ABC while it was wavering, "What have you got to lose? You're number three. If *Roots* fails, you'll still be number three. But what if the show takes off? Since there's nothing else like it on the air, that's a possibility. Maybe the novelty of it will drive everyone crazy."

ABC had already committed to its first, precedent-setting limited-run miniseries, *Rich Man, Poor Man*, which was to run once a week for twelve weeks. Stan Margulies gives credit to Fred Silverman for what he calls the "very daring and yet safe maneuver of scheduling *Roots* during a single week." "We first started talking about it as five two-hour shows," he says. "Half in jest I said, 'Why don't we have a *Roots* week?' And someone at the network said, 'Because if the first show doesn't do well, we've lost the whole week.' I thought, Well, that made sense. So it was considered that it would run probably five consecutive Sunday nights, or whatever. When we got down to where they really had to schedule the show, that's where I thought Freddie Silverman showed a touch of genius. [ABC was] breaking new ground by doing the show. Why not break new ground by finding a new way to show the show? And so, what Silverman did that was incredible was he scheduled the show so that we were a one-hour show on certain nights. It meant a lot of reediting. On those nights, he therefore protected the known hit shows, so that if *Roots* went straight down the toilet he still wouldn't lose the week, because he had not affected *Laverne and Shirley* and *Happy Days*. By putting us on at ten o'clock, he kept his eight to ten schedule intact; he knew he would win those nights, and, if *Roots* did nothing, what the hell?"

The networks came to regard the successes of *Roots* and, later, *Holocaust* largely as flukes. Executives concluded nothing more than that anything might work once. If the miniseries form made for success, or if socially charged material made the difference, why had later "relevant" miniseries like *Loose Change* (campus radicals in the sixties) and *King* rated badly? Stan Margulies, who produced *Roots*, noted that *Roots* was upbeat while *King* ended in assassination. Indeed, ABC's promotion department had billed *Roots* as "The Triumph of an American Family." But public curiosity is not so simple: The hardly upbeat *Holocaust* rated splendidly.

Executives might conclude that miniseries and movies do well when they create identification with families, so that audiences can enact in ritual what they feel in reality: anxiety about family stability in a churning world, sweetened by a message that family feeling persists amid the most atrocious conditions. Or they might conclude that *Roots* and *Holocaust* were national rites of exorcism and expiation, with a touch of the soap opera version of the theater of cruelty. (The Hollywood joke was that in the South, *Roots* was shown with the episodes in reverse order.) But instead of theorizing in this vein, most network executives and advertising agencies and many producers did what managers and gamblers always do: They simply went right back to what they saw as the low-risk gamble. They decided that the successes were not precedents but unrepeatable exceptions in violation of the odds. Perhaps they worked because they were pioneering; perhaps they belonged to singular historical moments like the liberal upwelling of the early Carter administration. Such arguments may be plausible. What is certain is that network belief has made them self-fulfilling, for no one will ever know how other serious historical dramas might rate as long as the networks refuse to invest in them.

If the networks like a dollop of controversy now and then, they usually want it manageable: social significance with a lifted face. This normally means little personal stories that executives think a mass

audience will take as revelations of the contemporary. To spot em-
blematic stories when they see them, the executives have to stay
current—by their lights. "I look at television commercials to look for
a trend," says Deanne Barkley. "Or places where money is spent, not
free stuff like television. What's on the cover of magazines? What are
advertisers using to sell soap? What are they saying about what's
going on in the country?" To her, AT&T's "Reach out and touch
someone" campaign is a sign of growing desire for family connection,
a desire she faults current executives for failing to tap. Other executives find inspiration in commercial television's own "reality" forms.
Brandon Stoddard says that the idea for *Pray TV*, a 1982 movie about
a television evangelist, was launched when he watched a piece on the
subject on ABC's news magazine show, *20/20*.

Stu Samuels looks at it this way: "It's not just a question of giving
the people what it wants. That's a gross oversimplification. Sometimes you don't know. It's not a science. Anyone who tells you it is
is a fool." Then what do you do? "You look at what worked before,"
he says. "You look at what's just happening, so you come in on the
crest. And you look at fundamentals: acting, directors, and so on."
When I asked Samuels how he knew "what's just happening," he fell
back on Deanne Barkley's reasoning, but with a more explicit rationale: "In a free society, in a free capitalist society, the public pays for
what it's interested in. They buy what they're interested in."

Like all half-truths, this one is notable for what it omits. Gatekeepers like Barkley, Stoddard, and Samuels select; so do commercial
makers, magazine editors, and *20/20* producers. From the great pool
of demonstrable and potential public interest they choose and recir-
culate those images that match their sales sense and their own values.
From among these the public chooses, but they can't choose what
they don't know exists.

I asked Stu Samuels to give me an example of the normal development process at work, and he described the origins of a TV movie
then in development this way: "About forty-eight hours after the
hostages came home from Iran, the story started to break that Vietnam vets were disgruntled. About three months before that, there
was a little tiny segment on *Real People* about a reunion of World
War II veterans. These were guys who had been in some German
POW camps, and I think there were also people who'd been in the
Japanese theater. It started off very nicely, and then, halfway
through, started listing some of the aftershocks—some of the injuries,
some difficulties they had getting benefits. I saw it in my home. I got
very angry and very moved. I came in the next morning, I called in
somebody in this department, and I said, 'I want to do a story about
two generations of vets, World War II and Vietnam, about how
they're not getting what they're entitled to.' The piece that we're

doing is called *A Little Piece of America*—that's a phrase used in the *Real People* piece. Now I'm betting that if we do a show about two generations of vets, I think we're going to strike a nerve with that picture."

I asked Samuels if he had thought about the plight of veterans before he saw the *Real People* piece. He shifted from his own feeling to his politically couched assessment of what the traffic would bear. "I'd heard stories," he said. "But something said to me that this country is swinging to the right. And I thought that with this swing to the right we could possibly strike a resonance here with viewers. But I'm not talking about something political, I'm talking about something emotional. . . . Reagan is touching the patriotic impulse, saying, 'Don't be ashamed about patriotism.' I want to do a film that will ask you to take a look at your government, at agencies like the VA, and say, 'You don't like it? Change it! Make government respon- sive to the people!' " This traditional fusion of feeling for nation with hostility to government bureaucracy was precisely the right-wing mixture Reagan had brewed for his own mass medium, the American electorate.

Network executives are not, themselves, right-wing. Samuels's best guess, and mine, is that in 1980 they supported John Anderson in disproportionate numbers. (So did many top producers, including Norman Lear and Grant Tinker.) These people admire getting the job done; they thought Jimmy Carter was inefficient, and between Anderson and Reagan, as Samuels says, "Anderson probably repre- sented pragmatism, and network people are pragmatic."

Efficiency and pragmatism are core values for all managers. At the center of their lives efficiency and pragmatism funnel into the great and enduring American drama of personal success. Network execu- tives are skilled in negotiating the heights of the corporate bureauc- racy. Their own hard-won skill testifies to the possibility of personal triumph. Their own lives are "upbeat." If this sounds like a television movie, there is good reason for it. Men and women of this character gravitate toward the upbeat formula, partially because they believe it's what the mass audience desires, but also because their own expe- rience enshrines it.

If an idea rings bells for subordinate and chief alike in a network TV-movie division, then they go after producers and writers to write scripts. Ninety percent of the time, though, producers and agents pitch their ideas first. Either way, the network has the upper hand. It knows what it doesn't want even if it doesn't know what it wants. Producers have to tailor their pitches to the standard conventions, and eventually the script has to match the network's version of the dramatic verities—characters should be simple and simply moti- vated, heroes familiar, stories full of conflict, endings resolved, uplift apparent, and each act should end on a note of suspense sufficient to carry the viewer through the commercial break. Wherever the idea originates, the development and approval process is the same. Aspiring producers and writers learn that it makes sense to arrive for the pitch meeting with appropriate article or book in hand, certifying that the project comes already equipped with mass popularity and significance.

When a project snakes its way into a producer's hands from more obscure sources, it is harder to sell, though not impossible. When the project is out of the ordinary and the sell is harder, then the television-industrial complex must come into play, and personal connections count all the more heavily. The disposition of a single executive or a star might make all the difference. The production company has to have a solid track record. The paradox is that when all these usual elements are in place, the product stands a chance of being unusual. A case in point is *Bitter Harvest*, a 1981 movie made for NBC, based on the actual poisoning of most of Michigan's cattle by a mispackaged chemical, and loosely derived from the 1978 book of the same name written by a Michigan farmer, Frederic Halbert, and his wife, Sandra.

Bitter Harvest starred Ron Howard, onetime child star in *The Music Man* and the long-running *Andy Griffith Show* and later a teenage star in *Happy Days*. Howard played a farmer whose cattle sicken, whose child develops rashes, and who gradually, against the lassitude and callousness of the state's health bureaucracy, traces the illness to a toxic fire retardant, polybrominated biphenyl, PBB, that had been mistakenly mixed into cattle feed. More children and adults sicken; the state still refuses to quarantine the poisoned cattle or ban their milk. Finally, to alert the populace, the farmer kills his own cattle. The show drew a good Nielsen rating of 18.0 and a handsome 29 percent share of the viewing audience, although promotion had been botched* and major affiliates in Philadelphia and Dallas didn't carry the movie at all. It drew four Emmy nominations. The writer won a Writers Guild award, among others, for his script. Yet the picture came within inches of not getting made.

Bitter Harvest began with an earnest, unflashy young man named Richard Friedenberg, who had directed, among other films, a feature called *Grizzly Adams* he thought so contemptible its enormous box-office success filled him with disgust. He had also directed on televi-

---

*NBC promotion and scheduling were in chaos that year. The network decided on *Bitter Harvest*'s May 18 screening date only two weeks in advance. By that time, Ron Howard had gone on three talk shows giving a previously announced date of May 11. The switch also cost *Bitter Harvest* any chance at a cover of *TV Guide* or the newspaper logs.

sion for a while until he lost interest, whereupon he decided to see
if he could write. In his diffident way, Friedenberg admired Italian
neorealism, especially DeSica's *The Bicycle Thief* and *Umberto D*,
from which he extracted the idea that TV movies could tell small
personal stories that revealed the larger society. Like most young
Hollywood writers trying to get noticed, he wrote "spec scripts,"
scripts on speculation, and sold nothing. "I have a totally uncommercial mind," he says, and so he was unemployed for months on end.
Whenever he came up with an idea, his agent told him, "Forget it,"
and Friedenberg started looking for a new agent.

Friedenberg was a loner, a conscientious objector to the Hollywood glad-handing circuit; and he had the odd habit, from a Hollywood point of view, of reading a magazine called *Country Journal*,
where one day in early 1979 he noticed an article about a Michigan
farmer, Ric Halbert, who had campaigned to get the state to do
something about his poisoned cattle. To Friedenberg this sounded
like a television story, a large issue on a small scale, but his old agent
was as usual less than enthusiastic. Friedenberg liked the Michigan
idea well enough to try it out, among other ideas, on a sympathetic
agent named Norman Stevens.

Any television deal brings a producer, a writer, and often a star
into conjunction with an executive, often through the mediation of
an agent, and all at the right time. Accidents happen, yet even
accidents have a history; happy accidents happen to people who get
into the right places often enough at the right times. Friedenberg's
new agent happened to intersect with a bright young producer,
Tony Ganz, who had been to Harvard, worked in documentaries on
PBS's *Great American Dream Machine*, and then gone to work for
a successful producer named Charles Fries at the Metromedia conglomerate. When Fries went off and set up his own company, Ganz
went with him as a producer. Charles Fries Productions became one
of the pillars of the TV-movie business, and over the years sold some
forty movies to the networks.

In the spring of 1979, just as the Love Canal chemical dump was
becoming national news, Three Mile Island was stopping the national
heart, and *The China Syndrome* was growing into a national media
event, Charles Fries happened to go to a meeting that Fred Silverman also attended. Within Fries's earshot, Silverman turned to Norman Lear and said that the Love Canal story was interesting and that
someone should do a movie-of-the-week about it. The next day Fries
sent a note to Ganz and Malcolm Stuart, his partner in the Fries
Productions development department, repeating this conversation
and saying, "Is this of any interest to you? See if you can follow this
up."

Ganz knew barely anything about Love Canal, by his own account, so he did some research that convinced him Love Canal "wasn't the right story, but a story about chemical pollution seemed like an exciting idea."* He began talking to Hollywood agents, writers, and New York agents who handled new nonfiction manuscripts. After several months of looking, he had failed to find anything that lent itself to the dramatic boundaries of a small-screen movie. "One day —this is where the accident happened—" he recalls, "I went into Malcolm's office, and he was on the phone, so the man who was sitting in his office had no one to talk to until I walked in, and his name was Norman Stevens, and he was Friedenberg's agent—I guess he had just signed him. None of this would have happened if Malcolm hadn't been on the phone, because I would have asked him what I was going to ask him and left. Stevens said, 'What are you looking for?'—typical agent kind of question—and usually the answer to that question is 'Jesus Christ, anything I can, anything that's interesting that I can sell.' But in this case I had a better answer." Ganz told Stevens he was looking for something like Love Canal.

The next day, Friedenberg was in Stevens's office reeling off a list of possible story ideas. Halfway through the Michigan cattle story, Stevens stopped him. "Hold the thought," he said. Stevens picked up the phone, dialed Tony Ganz, and set up an appointment.

Ganz didn't treat his first conversation with Stevens all that seriously until Friedenberg came in and told him Ric Halbert's story. Then he paid attention, for he heard Friedenberg tick off what he thought were the hallmarks of a workable story: character, visible consequences, visible accomplishment, and the symbolic accoutrements of a morality tale. "I thought it was one of the best stories I had ever heard, period," Ganz says. "It had at its center a character, which was crucial and something that was missing in most of the

*Another producer, Robert Greenwald, independently sold CBS on a movie about the Love Canal housewife, Lois Gibbs, who led the neighborhood in a movement to get government help. Greenwald, who had a considerable track record with TV movies like *Lady Truckers*, *Portrait of an Escort*, and *Portrait of a Centerfold*, was shifting his territory to liberal morality tales. On the strength of his record, and the interest of a big television star (who later lost interest), Greenwald persuaded CBS's Steve Mills to buy what he called "the story of a woman who'd do anything to protect her children." He pitched for fifteen minutes, in fact, before he let fall the words "Love Canal." Mills could see the tale as an uplift piece about personal triumph over adversity; it also borrowed from the woman-in-jeopardy genre. To Mills—as to Greenwald and Gibbs herself—it was a little Frank Capra movie, *Mrs. Smith Goes to Washington.* There followed months of haggling about casting, with Greenwald arguing for an actress with "an everywoman quality," "not a movie star." In the end, CBS settled on Marsha Mason, who was no one's first choice, and finally committed to the movie. Like *Bitter Harvest*, it was framed as hero-versus-heedless-government, not hero-versus-corporation. *Lois Gibbs and the Love Canal* aired February 17, 1982, and for whatever reasons rated a miserable 12.5, with a meager 20 share.

other stories that I had heard. They tended to be group efforts at
stopping chemical dumping, and that sort of thing. And there was a
victory involved, but it wasn't too pat—I mean, it was a sort of hollow
victory, or Pyrrhic, in the end. Nine million people were contaminated. There was just this guy, who at least sounded the alarm,
and made certain connections that everyone else refused to believe
in. And it had strong central characters. And it was in the middle of
the country, which is a landscape that appealed to me."

Ganz has his own recombinant repertoire of movie precedents. "It
was the same landscape as *Friendly Fire*. I didn't think *Friendly Fire*
was a masterpiece . . . but I loved the way it looked, and I loved that
it wasn't New York or Los Angeles or on either coast. I went to school
in Vermont, so I knew cows a little, and I liked cows. They're big,
stupid, and dumb. They're sort of like us, in fact. They do what
they're told. They don't fight back. In the end, they go into the pit,
and they get slaughtered, which is what we're doing to ourselves.
The cows also made visible the effects of the poison. In most of those
other stories no one really gets sick. It's an *it*, in the water table, or
where there's radiation leaking from a *China Syndrome* plant, and
you can't really dramatize it. The cows got sick, and you had to take
them out back and shoot them, just like in *Hud*. It was a terrific story.
It just all worked."

The idea went first to CBS, where executives passed, saying that
the *Lou Grant* series had already done an episode on the PBB poisoning; they didn't want movies to duplicate series.* *Bitter Harvest* then
went to ABC, where an executive said she liked the story but, after
all, the switch of the fire retardant for the cattle growth additive was
an accident, so where was the drama, where were the good guys and
the bad guys? Reasoning of this sort has the effect of prohibiting TV
movies from depicting the social structures that make accidents routine, even, paradoxically, predictable. A company that permitted the
two chemicals to be packed in similar sacks, one pile next to the
other, could not be held accountable by a dramatic form that refused
to recognize the normality of evil.

NBC, the third buyer in town, was widely believed to be so over-
loaded with commitments and so short of capital that there seemed
no sense pitching to them. The idea of *Bitter Harvest* therefore
languished for several months. Then it received the blessing of the
Hollywood gods, who move through revolving doors.

---

*Interestingly, that *Lou Grant* episode had been scheduled to air the night before the
1978 Michigan gubernatorial primary in which then Governor Milliken was being
challenged in part on the ground that he had not acted swiftly enough to stop the
spread of the PBB infestation. The *Lou Grant* producers had decided to delay the
show a week in order not to affect the primary results.

One of Ganz's producer colleagues at Fries Productions was an experienced TV hand named Irv Wilson, a magnetic, gregarious man who had shuttled through every cranny of the TV business, from ad agency to Universal Studios to talent agency to the NBC programming department. In fact, Irv Wilson had helped pioneer the development of TV movies at NBC. He was not always averse to TV fluff. He owned up to having devised *The Harlem Globetrotters on Gilligan's Island* during his second tenure at NBC, and while he was there NBC aired *Enola Gay*, a romance about the bomber mission that dropped the atomic bomb on Hiroshima. But Wilson was possessed of an uncommonly active social conscience. Born into a Depression-era working-class family in the Bronx, he had been instructed by the social-problem movies that Warner Brothers produced in the thirties and forties. He had worked for Henry Wallace in the presidential campaign of 1948. Although Wilson was no longer committed to any particular political position, he did think television entertainment had a responsibility to be more than entertaining, at least some of the time.

While still with Fries, Wilson bought his *Los Angeles Times* one morning and read the first in a series of articles called "The Poisoning of America." "It was incredible," he recalls, "and Tony came in one morning, and we were talking about it, and he said he had met a writer who had a story that he had heard, Richard Friedenberg, that was a true story, and he thought it was fantastic. I said, 'Gee, you ought to do something about that.'"

Then Fred Silverman tapped his old friend Irv Wilson to run NBC's West Coast specials department, which was to include whatever Wilson could pass off as "a special movie." As soon as Wilson told Ganz about his impending move, Ganz enlisted him for an unusual sort of pitch meeting at NBC with an executive named Dennis Considine. "Dennis," as Ganz put it later, "was in the curious position of being pitched to by the man who was about to be his boss, and he knew it. So at the end of [Friedenberg's] telling the story, he looked at Irv and said, 'Well, what do you think?' And Irv said, 'I think it's great and we should buy it.' I had never been in a meeting like that; it was really fun."

Wilson was sold by the time he got to NBC, but NBC was piled high with movie commitments that extended back years. Ganz kept calling Wilson and Wilson kept saying, "Someday I'll get it through for you," but right now NBC was only making movies to fulfill existing commitments. There was no money for new deals. Six more months passed. Dick Friedenberg gave up for the second time, and busied himself with other futile projects. But Wilson was biding his time. Then *Time* magazine came out with a cover story called "The Poisoning of America." As Wilson remembers it, "On the cover of *Time* was a guy being swallowed up by this crap in the ground. And I showed it to Brandon Tartikoff, and he says, 'All right, write the script.' " Wilson was sure that the *Time* cover had made the difference.

Ganz and Friedenberg were jubilant, but almost immediately they had to worry about possible network censorship. As soon as NBC headquarters in New York learned of the project, they "red-flagged" it as a possible legal risk. Ganz didn't know how seriously to take New York's concern, but he decided to test the waters. He called up an NBC attorney named Barbara Hering, whose job was to inspect movies based on fact for potentially litigable issues. He found Hering to be, as he put it, "at once supportive and pleasant and, on the other hand, guarded and realistic that it was not going to be an easy project." Ganz made an astute decision. He decided to level with Hering. "If you're too careful in the beginning and you write a sort of compromise script keeping one eye open for legal problems, you won't even get to test the legal problems. So I said to her, 'Look, it seems to me, unless you disagree, that we should just proceed now as best we can, being somewhat careful but writing the story as it happened.' And she said, 'Yes, do it that way, and then let me see it.' " Ganz was still apprehensive about how to handle the company, the governor, and the Michigan bureaucracy, but decided to save his worries for later. "It is impossible to get reliable, consistent answers from anybody about what you can and cannot do. So if you react too soon you could be reacting to the wrong thing."

Instead of handing in the usual first or second version, Friedenberg and Ganz were inordinately careful and handed in a fourth or fifth draft. NBC program executives waxed enthusiastic, asking them only routine questions about dramatic structure: What was the proper balance between the time before and after the farmer ascertains the source of the illness? Couldn't there be more scenes between the farmer and his wife? "They asked a lot of questions," Ganz recalls, "and I think without exception they were questions that we had asked ourselves and tried eleven different ways."

Irv Wilson knew, meanwhile, that success would depend on the hero's appeal, and had for a long time been thinking about Ron Howard, a sure-fire TV draw. Wilson later thought his major achievement at NBC was to have nudged Ron Howard's career toward serious drama. The first movie Wilson had pushed through at NBC was *Act of Love*, a movie about euthanasia committed by one brother on another. He had persuaded the producers that Ron Howard had just the kind of likable image to sweep the audience into sympathy. And—all-important to getting a movie about euthanasia made— NBC had commitments to Howard.

Now Wilson saw Howard as box office again: "The first time I met him I loved him, because he reminded me of today's Jimmy Stewart. Every Frank Capra picture you want to make, you could recast Ron Howard, and it's smashing, because he is the all-American boy who is so pure and so fucking honest, and good, and decent." *Act of Love* should have been depressing, by TV standards, yet it garnered high numbers, a 21.7 rating and 35 share. So in the case of *Bitter Harvest*, Wilson's argument for Ron Howard met no resistance. "Jimmy Stewart could have played that part, right?" Wilson said. "*Bitter Harvest* was a Frank Capra movie," one idealistic, responsible man against the system. Karen Danaher, a forceful and socially conscious former junior-high-school teacher and TV newswoman whom Wilson had brought into the NBC movie department, had the same feeling. "When I read the script," she says, "I knew we had to get a TV star that people could trust." When Ganz saw a cassette of Howard's dramatic performance in *Act of Love,* he was convinced. Wilson fired the script off to Howard, and he was sold on it immediately.

So the *Time* cover made possible the writing of the script; the script garnered Ron Howard; Howard sold the show. For the smaller part of Howard's farmer neighbor, NBC brought up Art Carney, another piece of offbeat casting. Carney was expensive, but the network was willing to spend the money for what, in effect, was insurance. Howard's agreement, and Carney's, neutralized the opposition of the affable and cautious Perry Lafferty, NBC's West Coast senior vice-president for programs, who reported directly to Brandon Tartikoff. "I had a lot of reservations about it," Lafferty says, "because I didn't know whether the audience would be interested in such a disagreeable subject. It's got Ron Howard and Art Carney and you can make a good promo on it and take a good ad. But for me, I thought it was very tough, and material that I've heard about before." Novelty that was *too* novel was out of bounds; novelty not novel enough was stale. "You've had the chemical wastes and all that stuff over and over and over. I didn't think it was going to be that big a ratings-gatherer." Lafferty had often been a conservative voice in high NBC circles; he had resisted *Hill Street Blues* as well. This time he was overruled.

From then on, *Bitter Harvest* went through the network screening process without much tampering. Ganz remained apprehensive, but Hering was satisfied. "They really did a first-class job on the hard facts," she says, "whether there had been real negligence bordering on reckless negligence in the factory, which led to the mix-up; whether the Agriculture Department had really been bound down by red tape, or whatever the cause, but failing to do what was necessary to take strong steps to stop a problem that was clearly very serious. All of those things were very, very heavily substantiated. You get into charges like that, and you have to worry a little bit, because you're making serious claims against important institutions and organizations. If justified by the facts, the program performs a public service, but if the facts are not as portrayed, the possible undermining of the public's faith in their institutions would be not only unfair to the institutions but a real disservice to our audience. It's not the same when the story is about a guy who is truly anonymous, in that he might be any one of hundreds of people, and whose story, however interesting, is simply personal."

A few changes were dictated for legal reasons. For one thing, Fries Productions' insurance company demanded that the name of the state of Michigan be taken out. Ganz wanted to keep Michigan, for verisimilitude's sake, but NBC backed the insurance company and Ganz went along. Michigan became "the state." Later on, Ganz regretted the sacrifice of realism. But it could equally well be argued that the very generality of "the state" made the story more universal and more powerful. This poisoning did happen somewhere, but it could have happened—it could still happen—anywhere. The names of the Michigan Chemical Co. and Michigan Farm Bureau Services, Inc., the companies responsible for the chemical switch, were also changed, but this was Friedenberg's doing. Even the earliest outlines Friedenberg worked up for Ganz used the pseudonym United Chemical. Ganz felt no particular moral outrage toward these particular companies. After all, they had paid millions of dollars in claims. So he did not care about this change, any more than he cared about the change in the farmer-hero's name from Ric Halbert to Ned De-Vries. Such changes are standard in the movie-based-on-fact format. They afford legal protection and may even contribute to the movie's aura of familiarity. If the audience knows that a character is no more than "based on" a living person, the character comes closer to Everyman. The farmer Ned escapes from the singularity of Ric Halbert and is pulled closer to Ron Howard playing Ned, and therefore to Ron Howard, the trustable, Jimmy Stewart–style actor.

Hering intervened on only one script issue. Late in the movie comes a scene in which Ned tries to alert another farmer, a tense and conscience-stricken man who has unknowingly—or so he says—sold his poisoned milk on the market. The farmer pulls at his son's hair to show Ned—it is a wig. There are bald patches all over the child's scalp. Barbara Hering questioned the accuracy of this vignette. "If the bald patches and wig were true, they could be shown; but not otherwise." Ganz was also asked not linger on this shot, "because," he was told, "we are not out to scare people needlessly." No matter. Brief as it is, the moment in the film when the farmer pulls away his child's hair remains shocking. Real people were really hurt. That was what happened when Michigan was poisoned.

As the script went through refinement after refinement, though, one potentially troublesome line kept nagging at Ganz. When Ned finds out the nature of the toxic chemical in his cattle feed, he races home, triumphant, to tell his wife about PBB. "What on earth is that?" she asks. In early versions of the script, Ned answers, "It's a fire retardant. It's used for TV sets so they don't burn up. . . ." Ganz knew that RCA, which owned NBC, also manufactured television sets. "I knew NBC would say something." He consulted with friendly West Coast programming executives. Although Barbara Hering had never flagged this line—it was a problem of corporate public relations, after all, not the law—one executive feared that someone above Hering in the New York chain of command might raise a fuss. Knowing that the red flag of controversy was already flying over the project, and not caring exactly what PBB was used for, Ganz decided on discretion—self-censorship, some might call it. "I was concerned," he said afterward, "that something like that could blow the whole goddamned project." At a late stage of the script he changed the line to: "It's a fire retardant. They put it in plastics or something."

Another political point flattened during the shooting was a borderline case that couldn't be laid at the door of the network—or, for that matter, the audience. Dr. Freeman, Ned's medical angel, testifies before a state committee in favor of a cattle quarantine. In the middle of a long speech about the effects of PBB—about its permanent presence in the bodies of those who eat the meat or drink the milk from the poisoned cattle, about effects that might even skip a generation—the script had Freeman say, "And don't think it's an isolated case. There are thirty-five thousand other chemicals out there that are unsafe, and they're being spilled and dumped and buried all over the *planet*." During the shooting in the dairy country of Northern California, at the last minute, Tony Ganz and the director, Roger Young, decided Freeman's speech was too long—almost a minute and a half. These lines seemed to them the most expendable. "We didn't want to get didactic," Ganz said. "It seemed too much a documentary statement. We felt that, given the reality of that little courtroom in that little town, nobody was thinking about anything but the nightmare of one particular chemical." Friedenberg agreed. To him the issue mattered so little, in fact, that when I asked him about it just after the shooting, he couldn't remember whether the line had stayed in or not. But Richard Dysart, the actor who played Freeman, was disturbed about the cut. He thought this was the one moment when *Bitter Harvest* generalized from PBB to make a larger point about the chemical industry. Freeman was speaking directly to the audience. After the cut, was the story of PBB narrowed into a single dreadful exception, "an isolated case"?

Ganz and Friedenberg thought not. They believed they made the larger point by hewing close to the story of PBB. They adhered to the prevailing aesthetic of small scale, in which the general point is inherent in the particular, and indeed their claim cannot be dismissed out of hand. True, any cut, in a literal sense, changes the meaning of the whole. To make this simple point is my bias; it is the bias of all close readers of texts, especially those who aim to ferret out the traces of political censorship or the virtues of political expression. But I confess I am not altogether convinced by the literal-mindedness of such criticism, especially as it bears on a medium that rushes lines past us at an irreversibly fast pace. Lines that break radically with the expected level of discourse might be more memorable, therefore more effective, especially when they come from the authoritative Freeman; or conceivably a general message buried amid the specific, in the context of the small-scale story, goes by so fast as to be lost with or without such individual lines. The tools for assessing the effects of lines are too crude to tell us anything.

Whatever the effect of this or that line, it is clear that Ganz, Friedenberg, and all other "docudramatists," simply by accepting the conventions of their form, are committing a kind of self-censorship. Television docudrama abhors what it considers polemic, didacticism, speechifying. Convention clamps a tight frame around the story. It doesn't want the larger public world leaking in. The soapbox is forbidden furniture. This convention of the small, restricted, realistic story has ideological consequences. It has the effect of keeping the show compact, narrow, simplified. Indeed, coherence is defined as narrowness, and not just in the thinking of the writers but audiences, too. It is the dramatic aesthetic that prevails in this culture. Such conventions are shared, not imposed. When they are shared long enough and deeply enough, they harden into the collective second nature of a cultural style. True, against restriction there arises a counterconvention based on audience identification with the normal. If Ron Howard is Everyman and if his fictional state is Everystate, and if Ron Howard's cows and child and neighbors are at risk, then in imagination everyone is at risk. But there is still a difference between saying that PBB is in the body cells of virtually everyone in Everystate, and warning that there are thousands of other dangerous chemicals—that PBB is, in a way, Everychemical.

Bitter Harvest further restricts the meaning of the problem of chemicals. What, after all, is the source of Ned's troubles? It is expressed most pointedly in NBC's promo, where the voice-over says breathlessly, "And now: Ron Howard in *Bitter Harvest*, the true story of one man's triumphant battle against the bureaucracy. His cattle were dying and no one would help." This accurately defines the movie's main line of tension: Ned's care played off against the heedlessness of the agricultural bureaucrats. The state is no true guardian of bucolic peace; from the opening shot—acoustic guitar and flute sounding a sweet, wistful melody over a shot of Ned and his wife feeding their calves from giant baby bottles—we understand that Ned is that guardian. Later, when the cattle start drying up, Ned gets the bureaucrats to conduct tests, which come out negative. The bureaucrats outrage Ned by suggesting that he is guilty of bad management. These unkind and uncaring men claim knowledge, and impugn both his skill and his care. But Ned has been to college and can't be so easily intimidated. He fights to reclaim his title to both knowledge and care.

The question the movie poses is, Who really knows and who really cares? When Ned presses the agricultural inspectors to undertake further tests, they protest that they aren't a research laboratory. In other words, they really aren't in the business of knowing. He has to shame them with direct evidence. He trusts his intuitions about his cattle and his methods; while bureaucrats play by the book, the farmer and lover of animals is the real investigator. Persistence leads Ned to direct action. Behind a wall in his barn he finds a pile of rats that have died from eating his feed; and when the bureaucrats continue to put him off, he dumps the rats onto their conference table. Ned's devoted search for the truth pays off when he shames a state technician into performing one more test. This gives him the data to find help in the person of Dr. Freeman, the good scientist freed from bureaucratic fetters, the crusty spirit of truth-seeking incarnate. In the end, though, even antibureaucratic truth-seeking proves insufficient and Ned has to take direct action again. The cost is terrible, all those cows shot down; but even at this traumatic moment Ned demonstrates he is closer to the cows than any remote bureaucrat.

The written text ("crawl") and simultaneous voice-over that follow give Ned credit for a victory but indicate that bureaucrats will still be bureaucrats: "After Ned DeVries killed his herd, public pressure forced the state to start testing livestock for contamination. Over five hundred farms were closed. Thirty thousand cattle were driven into mass graves and slaughtered. It was not until two years later, in 1976, that testing was finally begun on state residents. Ninety percent of the people tested showed levels of PBB. Another year passed before a law was enacted to eliminate all contaminated meat and milk from the marketplace. It is now estimated that eight million men, women, and children carry the toxic chemical PBB inside their bodies."*

---

*Until the last minute Ganz wasn't sure exactly what to put in the crawl, or whether to accentuate it with a voice-over. He thought of resurrecting the point he had earlier excised from Dr. Freeman's speech, about the proliferation of dangerous chemicals

Ned expects the state to help; he is a citizen and he feels entitled to public health. When the bureaucracy derails his rights, he crusades. But never in *Bitter Harvest* does he couple his fury against the state with any comparable attack on the company. There is one scene in which he joins a state team investigating the factory where the PBBs were substituted for a cattle feed additive. Ned shows disgust, but he never takes up the cudgels against the company. He claims no entitlement against the private economy. The corporate decisions that produced PBB and similar chemicals, the mentality that relies on them, the slack shop-floor conditions that permitted such substitutions are never mentioned; by the convention of the hero-centered narrative, the corporate bureaucracy remains invisible.

Ned, and the movie, accept the political-economic division of labor: The company should manufacture, the government should regulate. This keeps the movie on the normal side of American ideology—yet without making it conservative, as Americans measure the term. The corporation is more forgotten than forgiven, while the most visible blame is the government's for not regulating well. Although Ned is a lone hero, his rugged individualism departs from the kind celebrated in the speeches of Ronald Reagan. In fact, *Bitter Harvest* cleverly turns the Reagan view of the world on its head. In Reaganism, "bureaucracy" and "regulation" are inseparable evils. In the movie, bureaucracy, not regulation, is to blame. Ned shows that the public urgently needs regulation, while bureaucracy obstructs it. Citizens then have to act to force the government to live up to its legitimate calling. If this sounds familiar, it is not only the Frank Capra formula of the thirties, but also the crusading image that brought both Jimmy Carter and Ronald Reagan to power. All hail to the outsider who takes up the call to clean the Augean stables! The hero's foray into politics brings about the public good. In that sense, *Bitter Harvest* was deep in the grain of American political mythology.

If the forte of everyday American screenwriting is the short, flat line, *Bitter Harvest* put it to good use. The movie was moving, understated, sharply directed, and well photographed (including a lovely sequence of the live birth of a calf)—in short, one of the best of its breed. Shot in a breathtakingly intense and under-average eighteen days, on a budget of $1.8 million—at the low end of the TV movie

---

in the environment, then decided against it. After he satisfied Barbara Hering about the validity of the facts he finally selected, his version was the one that ran.

In April of 1982, the results of fuller tests on Michigan residents were released, showing that an estimated 97 percent of them carried PBB in their bodies five years after the contamination.

range—it didn't look as if it had been prefabricated on the back lot. On the weakest network, even without two major affiliates, Philadelphia and Dallas–Fort Worth, the show won its time-slot handily.* As a rural show, it had the advantage of a lead-in from a rural series, the popular *Little House on the Prairie* (from which, significantly, it lost no audience). It beat out *M*A*S*H* and *Lou Grant* on CBS, and another serious movie on ABC.

Under such conditions, an above-average share might have suggested that Americans were concerned about major social issues and interested in straightforward dramatic representations of likable Americans grappling with them. Yet *Bitter Harvest* made barely a ripple on network consciousness. The day after it aired, I overheard one ABC executive say to another, "They claim this *Bitter Harvest* was high [i.e., clear and simple] concept. What high concept? All it was was a bunch of sick cows." Robert Greenwald, an independent producer who was pushing hard to make a CBS movie about Love Canal, grumbled that the networks would attribute *Bitter Harvest*'s success to Ron Howard, period. The networks were more comfortable drawing negative conclusions from the ratings failure of a run of social-issue movies than taking the chance of offending their nervous affiliates, or advertisers, or any other powerful institutions, or blocs of viewers. Only an executive with conviction would have bothered to use the success of *Bitter Harvest* to fight such a drift toward the bland; and politically committed executives, even politically interested ones, were rare. Indeed, within a year of going to New York as NBC's senior vice-president for programming, Irv Wilson was on his way back to Los Angeles as an indie prod, and by then the projects he was pitching were less political than ever before.

The reasons were a little obscure, but constant frustration was certainly one of them. Wilson's imagination didn't usually transcend the normal TV-movie conventions, but one project he pushed at NBC was an uplift story called *300 Miles for Stephanie,* based on a true story of a Hispanic policeman in Texas, father of a mortally ill little daughter, who decided to run three hundred miles to declare

---

*To beef up May sweeps ratings, the Philadelphia NBC affiliate, in the nation's fourth-largest market, ran the movie *The Night They Raided Minsky's,* ironically the last feature product of television's Mr. Social Consciousness, Norman Lear. The Dallas–Fort Worth affiliate, in the eleventh-largest market, ran a baseball game. When Tony Ganz heard about the Philadelphia decision, a few weeks before air date, he called up the affiliate to try to change its mind. NBC's affiliate relations and promotions departments were so chaotic that the Philadelphia man hadn't been told that Ron Howard was the star. "*Act of Love* got a thirty-five share," Ganz said to him. "If I told you about a movie in which a guy goes into a hospital room and blows his brother's brains out with a shotgun, you wouldn't think it would get big numbers, would you?" He failed to convince the Philadelphian.

his faith. Wilson wasn't religious, but he liked the fact that the movie was going to star Hispanic actors exclusively. At a certain point, he sensed that the other executives, including Fred Silverman, were stalling. "I screamed at Fred and everybody else. I said, 'If you don't order this movie, they're going to burn the building down. If I was a Mexican, I would bomb this fucking building, because we're doing shit for any of these people. It's our responsibility to do it.' Then I knew that I was in big trouble, because I had a big mouth, and they don't want anybody rocking the boat."

When less passionate executives than Wilson feel twinges of social conscience, they can buy indulgences with heart-warming stories of non-Hispanic people struggling to overcome handicaps: affliction stories, the kind of movies that one industry influential calls "crip-flicks." As one network executive points out, "The networks are always mistaking real social issues for little human-condition stories." For weeks, whenever I told executives I was trying to understand how television dealt with social issues, they proceeded to tell me about movies dealing with alcoholism, cancer, drugs, crippling illness, death and dying. Writer-producer Carol Evan McKeand (*The Waltons, Family, Second Family Tree*) said she had judged the 1980 television movie entries for the Humanitas Prize, a high-prestige Hollywood award: "They were all about death and dying." If the preferred stories give us "deviants" at all—homosexuals, criminals, fundamentalists, people of color—the principal attitude they recommend is mild tolerance, which is the cement of a plural order that can't abide basic criticism for fear the fragile cultural balance will tip and the mythological national community decompose.

Network pressure against a political definition of social problems is automatic—so automatic that executives don't construe it as pressure at all. Not only is "innovation" clamped within the iron embrace of the little personal story, but even that category is routinely depoliticized. I mentioned to CBS's Jane Rosenthal, for example, a story the *Los Angeles Times* had been following for several days. A black Pasadena couple wanted to adopt a sixteen-month-old white infant they'd cared for since she was three months old. A court-appointed psychologist said that the child, whose natural mother was of Armenian descent, should be given to an Armenian couple, that she would have a hard time if brought up by black parents. This seemed to me ideal material for a TV movie: potentially gut-wrenching conflict on a small family scale. I asked Rosenthal whether this was the sort of story that would be suitable for CBS. Without missing a beat, she replied that CBS had in development a story about a child whom a court wants to take from its deaf parents. "It has similar kinds of elements," she said. "We've sort of done the adoptee story, where the court's trying to take the child away. It just sounds like we've seen it before."

Thus do stories about racial conflict get sidetracked or bleached. In late 1976, the screenwriter Richard Kletter went to ABC to pitch a TV movie about civil-rights workers Robert Moses and Stokely Carmichael and the transformations in the southern movement in the early sixties. Kletter said he had lined up a top television director and was ready to get any two black actors in the world. ABC said, "There is no package in the world that will get us to make that film." Shortly thereafter, the smash success of the miniseries *Roots* seemed to change the rules of the game. Briefly, blacks could be admitted through prime time's front door. But there followed the catastrophic *King,* which slammed the door again. Unlike Moses and Carmichael, Martin Luther King was the incarnation of a national consensus after the fact, but the show did so badly that the networks took it as an excuse not to do any more movies about contemporary racial issues. To make matters worse, black dramatic series also did poorly. *Roots* producer Stan Margulies says he thought *Roots* would "certainly open the door to continuing shows about blacks that were more than situation comedy. The networks did two shows: one with Lou Gossett, who played a cardiologist [*The Lazarus Syndrome,* ABC, 1979], one with James Earl Jones in which he played a policeman [*Paris,* CBS, 1979]. Both shows failed. The word is, 'They failed because no one wanted to watch Lou Gossett or James Earl Jones. They weren't interested in a black show.' In network terms, they gave Lou Gossett a shot and they gave James Earl Jones a shot, and they didn't deliver."*

Ethel Winant, in charge of miniseries at NBC, said, "I don't think you couldn't do a dramatic show about a black, but I think you probably would not do Martin Luther King again. You would probably do the Josephine Baker story with Diana Ross, because maybe that would do better. Or if I want to get the Thomas Jefferson Society angered, I'll do Sally Hemings, Jefferson's slave mistress. I just happened to read the book and thought, 'God, that's a great story.' And I thought, 'Oh, God, that's all I need. The DAR and everyone will kill me, because I will soil the image of another American.' But at the moment I don't have any money so I can't buy it anyway, so it's a moot point."**

---

*The general lore among producers, by contrast, is that the Gossett and Jones shows were simply dull shows. So believe Steven Bochco and Gregory Hoblit, for example, whose opinion is interesting because they produced *Paris* and went on to produce *Hill Street Blues.* *The Lazarus Syndrome* was produced by William Blinn and Jerry Thorpe, later the second producing team on *American Dream.*

**Before Steve Mills's arrival in the CBS movie department, in fact, CBS had a Hemings-Jefferson miniseries in development, and this one was one of the few cases in which they felt direct pressure from affiliates. "We got a lot of indications from some of our southern affiliates," says Mills, "that they would not look kindly on carrying a

By late 1979, the success of *Roots* less than three years earlier had been consigned to another era. Now the networks believed that most versions of black reality would fatally divide the mass audience. NBC's Perry Lafferty says, "I think the mass audience likes to see blacks in roles that are not threatening." Michael Warren, who plays Bobby Hill on *Hill Street Blues,* adds, "Now we're in the eighties and we're back to the passive look, one that says, 'Oh, he's pleasing to look at.' I know when I'm on the screen, some little white lady in Minnesota or Montana is not going to rush to turn off her screen because she's fearful that I may come in and do whatever."

In 1980, in the same spirit, David Gerber produced the Civil War romance *Beulah Land,* which many black actors and the NAACP felt was rife with happy, subservient slaves. After a black actor went to the press with protests, NBC got nervous, delayed the air date, hired a black Yale historian to advise Broadcast Standards, and changed a number of lines. Around the same time Gerber produced the excoriated *Beulah Land,* he also produced a movie called *The Neighborhood,* based on a Jimmy Breslin idea, about black couples integrating a white community in New York. NBC took two and a half years to put this one on the air.

To the charge that the networks have lost interest in blacks, ABC's Stu Samuels said, "Nonsense," and in the next breath added, "It's very hard to find properties about blacks that can also be appreciated by whites." He mentioned *Roots,* its sequel, and a TV movie about Satchel Paige, starring Lou Gossett. But he acknowledged there are not many others in development at ABC. "It's a white country," he said, "and a commercial business."

However, even the fear of dividing the mass audience with racially charged conflict doesn't altogether explain the breadth of network taboos on the subject of race. For long periods the networks' conservative market calculations seem to have decreed that blacks are inherently controversial. In 1979, for example, NBC took delivery of two TV dramatic movies featuring well-known black actors playing middle-class roles. One was *Sister, Sister,* a version of Chekhov written by Maya Angelou, starring Diahann Carroll and Irene Cara among others, executive-produced by Irv Wilson. It had originally been commissioned as a series pilot by Peter Andrews, a black producer now at MGM but previously, as NBC's vice-president for dramatic development, the highest-placed black executive at the networks. *Sister, Sister* was family drama targeted for a female audi-

---

show about Thomas Jefferson having a black mistress, even though he had one and it was documented. Fortunately, the script wasn't good, and we abandoned it and didn't have to test the water."

ence; the family happened to be black. The other movie was *Sophisticated Gents,* a whatever-happened-to-the-old-gang piece adapted by Melvin van Peebles from a novel by John A. Williams. NBC stored both for three years, eventually suffering a bad press before finally airing them during the 1981–82 season. True, in the meantime NBC shelved a few other movies that weren't easy to promote. True, opinions varied about the quality of these shows; Irv Wilson himself thought the critics bent over backward to be kind to a weak *Sophisticated Gents* when it finally saw light. But during those three years the networks did not shy away from broadcasting lily-white mediocrity. The key fact was that Fred Silverman, desperately trying to yank up the ratings of his faltering network, was disinclined to take a chance on driving away a considerable share of the elusive audience. Perhaps most whites wouldn't accept serious black actors as members of their televised quasi-family, although the great success of blacks in sitcoms *(The Jeffersons, Benson, Diff'rent Strokes, Gimme a Break)* shows that blacks are still entertaining as comic relief.

Although even at best, blacks never had anything but trouble on TV, by the early 1980s the networks were quickly retreating to a sort of racial self-censorship that the enlightened seventies were supposed to have abolished. The so-called Golden Years of the fifties were actually white, as Ethel Winant, who then worked in casting at CBS, recalls: "We never had any blacks on television. We never had a porter in a show. If a bag was carried, it was carried by a white conductor." The motives for whitening TV may have shifted since then from crude racial prejudice to a kind of market calculation, and the power from advertising agencies to the networks themselves, but the consequences are not so different.

A typical fifties story went something like this: In 1955, Rod Serling was intrigued by the story of Emmett Till, a black teenager from Chicago who was killed by two white Mississippians because he had whistled at a white woman. Or more precisely, Serling saw a story in the way the white community backed his killers against a hue and cry from outside. By the time Serling took the idea to the Theater Guild for production on the *U.S. Steel Hour* anthology series, he was already trimming. In keeping with the psychologizing of the time, the victim was now an old pawnbroker, the killer a neurotic. But Serling mentioned to a reporter that the play was suggested by the Till case, whereupon the Theater Guild, the BBD&O agency, and U.S. Steel got into the act. To avert the slightest hint that Serling's unspecified location might be the South, the executives insisted the show open with a shot of a white church spire, New England style. Coca-Cola bottles were banished from the set; so were all traces of southern accents. The TV historian Erik Barnouw tells us that Serling was "a realist and eager for acceptance" from the beginning; it is useful to remember that, in the climate of that time, the first step toward "realism" and away from the race issue was Serling's own. Consider that the executives changed Serling's script less than Serling had already changed the Till case. When such self-censorship has become deeply ingrained, the culture industry rarely requires the blue pencil.

David W. Rintels, an established television writer and former president of the Writers Guild of America, West, has testified to similar experiences in the mid-sixties:

> I was asked to write [an] episode of *The FBI* on a subject of my choice, at about the time [1963] . . . when four little black girls were killed by a bomb in a Birmingham church. It had been announced that the FBI was involving itself in the case and I told the producer I wanted to write a fictionalized account of it.
>
> The producer checked with the sponsor, the Ford Motor Company, and with the FBI—every proposed show is cleared sequentially through the producing company, QM; the Federal Bureau of Investigation; the network, ABC; and the sponsor, Ford, and any of the four can veto any show for any reason, which it need not disclose—and reported back that they would be delighted to have me write about a church bombing subject only to these stipulations: The church must be in the North, there could be no Negroes involved, and the bombing could have nothing at all to do with civil rights.

Even with the coming of the new maturity and presumed youth-minded realism of the early seventies, Rintels recounted, such censorship did not disappear:

> [In 1971] John Bloch was story editor on an ABC–Paramount Studios series called *The Young Lawyers*. He wrote a script in which the white male Young Lawyer was to be shown having a drink in a public place with the black female Young Lawyer. Just drinking and talking, with perfect and total innocence. Six times the producer, acting under the explicit direction of the Paramount Studios censor and network liaison man, Henry Colman, requested that the black girl be rewritten into a white girl; six times Bloch refused. Finally he was promised that the change would not be made. His option was not picked up by the studio and, after he was let go, the film was shot—with a white girl playing the part.

After testifying thus to the Senate Subcommittee on Constitutional Rights, Rintels found himself unable to work in television for a couple of years. Producers would bring up his name; network executives would say, "Not him."

People of color aren't the only ethnic minorities to run afoul of network and advertiser timidity. Given the large number of Jews who hold top positions in the networks and production companies, it seems surprising that Jewish characters are scarce on the screen. But television is still a site for the great American drama of assimilation, and the ethnicity of executives and suppliers doesn't necessarily determine characters. In the end, the networks fall back on their sense of marketplace predilections, compounded perhaps by self-protectiveness against any real or conceivable anti-Semitic charge that Jews are too powerful in the media. When I asked Brandon Tartikoff, the president of NBC Entertainment, about the scarcity of Jewish characters, he first came back, "Barney Miller's Jewish"; then agreed that Jewish characters were scarce, though he didn't think the omission was conscious; then added, "People perceive Judd Hirsch [in *Taxi*] and Jack Klugman [in *Quincy*] as Jewish." An explicitly Jewish show like *The Goldbergs* of 1949–54, he said, "would not work today." It worked when television was new, television sets expensive, and the owners were disproportionately middle class in major cities; that is to say, disproportionately Jewish. "Suppliers are probably self-censoring," he said; they know as well as the networks that a large part of the audience prefers its Jews Gentile. Tartikoff added, though, "I wouldn't put it past a network executive to say, 'We don't want this because it's Jewish.' "

In a market society, taboos are usually justified on market grounds: what the traffic will presumably bear. No offense is the best defense. Ethel Winant recalls that the early days of television were "crazy." "I remember some guy from [a top advertising agency] telling me he wanted his shows to look like the covers of the *Saturday Evening Post*, and I said, 'You mean you don't want any Negroes or any Jews.' (In those days they were 'Negroes.') And he said, 'Well, no, I mean, but I, you know, I want it to look like the covers of the *Saturday Evening Post*. . . .' You saw very few Jewish actors who looked like Jewish actors. I'd cast Jack Carson and they'd say, 'He seems ethnic.' There were all these wonderful euphemisms. He certainly didn't look like the cover of the *Saturday Evening Post*."

When big advertisers were the sole sponsors of shows, it was especially easy for them to impose their authority. Once, for example, in the late fifties, the producer of a variety show was told flatly by the sole sponsor's advertising agency not to use a certain supporting actor, on the grounds that the star was pretty and "they don't want unattractive people." The producer's agent finally told him that somebody, somewhere thought the actor in question was Jewish—although, in fact, he wasn't. Only the producer's threat to quit, and the star's threat to quit if the producer quit, beat the agency back.

Writers also fought back using transparent disguises. "In the old days," crack docudrama writer Ernest Kinoy remembers, "in the days of live television, you'd come into Studio One, or NBC, and Philco, and you'd tell them this long story about this marvelous Italian family. And they would say, 'It's too Jewish.' Because they knew very well that it wasn't an Italian, it was a Jewish family. Paddy Chayevsky did it a number of times. *The Catered Affair* is about an Irish family: In a pig's eye it's about an Irish family! Marty, the Italian butcher. . . . It was because a number of the Jewish writers would come in with material, and the networks would say, 'It's too Jewish. The rest of America won't understand.' They're always worried that some slob, somewhere around Chicago, isn't going to know what you're talking about."

The same premise persists into the present. According to Oscar Katz, once head of CBS programming in New York, Carl Reiner's original scripts for what became *The Dick Van Dyke Show*, in the sixties, were originally written for Reiner himself as the lead. "They de-Jewishized it," Katz says, "Midwestized it, and put Dick Van Dyke and Mary Tyler Moore in the leads." Then, in 1973, looking to capitalize on Watergate, NBC asked Ernest Kinoy to write a script about the Dreyfus case. When Kinoy tendered his script, an executive said, "My God, does it have to be that Jewish?"

A year later, comedy writer Danny Arnold, with the collaboration of Theodore Flicker, wrote a pilot script about a Greenwich Village police captain named Barney Miller, who was the hub around which revolved an Asian, a black, a German, a Pole, and other various and sundry New York types. ABC ordered the pilot. "We got into casting discussions," Arnold remembers, "because of course the networks always have, by contract, final approval of everything—casting, director, writer, and so forth. Whether they exercise it or not is also dependent upon who it is they're dealing with. If it was Norman Lear, obviously nobody exercised any of those prerogatives. I started casting. I had seen Hal Linden in New York, in [the play] *The Rothschilds*, a couple of years before, and I had sort of filed him away in the back of my head." He liked Linden's "sensitivity," and "the ethnic/nonethnic quality about him. I didn't particularly want a Jewish policeman. I wanted a legitimate, intelligent sensitivity, and a sense of humor that came out of an understanding of the human equation."

Linden signed on. "So I went to ABC," Arnold continues, and I said, 'I have the fellow for Barney Miller,' And they said, 'Who?' And I said, 'Hal Linden.' They said, 'Who's Hal Linden?' I said, 'He won the Tony for *The Rothschilds*.'" One network figure said, "What does he look like?" Arnold said he would show them a dramatic pilot

Linden had made, based on the film *The French Connection*. Some executives thought Linden acceptable, but the dubious executive "particularly hated" him—"personally," Arnold says, "I think because he was Jewish." Not that the word "Jew" was uttered. "They just said, 'Well, the guy's got a moustache, and he doesn't have the right look.' But I knew what that meant." "Did they say what the right look was?" I asked Arnold. "They don't say that," he replied. "What they do is suggest other people. And the people they suggest are nice, clean-cut, Aryan-looking, you know, obviously WASP: the sort of people who are not going to offend anyone out there in the great unwashed mass." But in the end the dubious company man removed himself from the matter, Arnold stuck with Linden, and eventually, though the show tested badly and didn't get on the fall schedule, it was ready to be called up as a midseason replacement and became a hit.

Stereotypes float. To my eye, moustaches are meaningless as ethnic pointers (indeed, five years later, Tom Magnum's moustache is an emblem of virility), and Hal Linden doesn't look so "Jewish" to me. The character was not, after all, Barney Goldblume to be played by Woody Allen. "We never said Barney was Jewish and we never said he wasn't," Arnold told reporter Sally Bedell. "We deliberately called him Miller because it was an ethnic/nonethnic name."

But in network and advertiser parlance, "the market" is still personified as a hypothetical anti-Semitic midwesterner ready to switch channels at the first sign of a Stein. Top-level squeamishness is particularly important when a potential movie carries a prestige look and seems a ratings risk. Then sponsorship by a single image-conscious oil or electronics company might be the only way to get it produced. In a 1981 meeting, an NBC executive tried to convince one of these blue-ribbon companies to take on the story of Moe Berg, a baseball player, linguist, and war hero who had infiltrated enemy lines in World War II. Said the company man: "It's too Jewish." The NBC executive, astonished to hear this out loud, said, "Excuse me?" "I don't know if all America could identify," said the company man. The same year, the advertising agency for the same company was offered yet another politically charged script. When the script came back to the producer, the account executive had written in the margin: "Change Jewish to Italian or Greek."

The quest for the surest possible maximum audience explains why the networks are cautious yet, in their limited way, pluralist at the same time. Executives want to play it safe, but there are two important qualifications. They are not expert at knowing just how to play it safe. And if they succeed in playing it too safe, they may bore their audience to the point of indifference. From these qualifications flow whatever diversity the networks maintain. The quest for the offbeat, or for high demographics and prestige, sends them after new material, satisfying some of the creative drives of some writers and producers; then the quest for the mass market clicks back in, flattening that new material, striving to reduce it to standard proportions.

This dialectic of difference and sameness generates the form and style of the television movie, but both ends have to be kept in mind. If we forget the drive to difference, we fail to understand why the networks sometimes have use for executives like Irv Wilson and Karen Danaher; we also fail to understand the rise of social-comment movies in the seventies. If we forget the drive to sameness, we fail to make sense of a million tales of direct censorship, self-censorship, and the censorship imposed by style and convention and the moment's prevailing view of what the mass market will bear. We fail to grasp why, according to some Hispanic actors, NBC, when it made a movie of *Evita*, refused to hire actors who had Hispanic accents; or why one liberal producer, considering a story about a Chicana political organizer, told the writer that the show didn't have a chance at the network unless Joanne Woodward was interested. Television has become "the last bastion of the social-comment film," as Richard Friedenberg says; but the social comment it makes is enfolded within shows that are simplified and flattened—not because network executives* are either "conservative" or "liberal," but because they don't want a show to jar the expectations of the regular TV audience, which they take to be uneducated, distracted, and easily bewildered. The producer and writer may care mightily about a social issue, but the network views the issue mainly as an occasion for the hero to strut his or her stuff.

The network's anxiety about holding its audience can extend even to overseeing the film's look. Take the case of CBS's 1980 *Playing for Time,* the story of Fania Fenelon, a woman who survived Auschwitz by playing in an orchestra the Nazis set up. CBS interested itself directly in the style of the shots. According to the playwright Arthur Miller, who wrote the script, "there was a constant struggle going on between CBS, who had seen the daily rushes, and the cameraman, who had a very powerful feeling about this picture. They demanded close-ups, close-ups, close-ups." One is reminded of ABC Sports (and later News) chief Roone Arledge's formula for the success of ABC's football coverage: "up close and personal." Whether in sports, entertainment, documentaries, or news, the networks believe that what glues the audience to the tube is invariably this personal feeling for the characters. Most television producers, directors, and camera peo-

---

*Or producers. Herb Brodkin, who produced *The Defenders, Holocaust, Skokie,* and much other "relevant" television, is a Republican.

ple would agree. Certainly long shots lose their panoramic potential on the small screen, though it doesn't follow that close-ups actually have the effect claimed for them. The networks have undertaken no empirical research, even in the experimental terms they value, to test the idea. Still, the conventional wisdom goes unchallenged. As Marvin J. Chomsky, who directed *Attica, Holocaust,* and *Inside the Third Reich,* puts it, "Our audience is the guy who's used to walking around and getting a beer. We've got to reach him. He's a guy who hasn't made much of a commitment to give his rapt attention to what we're offering, right? We're going for the eighty million who will watch something. An infant in a cradle likes to watch things that move. So, there you are. We go in for close-ups and we try to find the conflicts."

But in *Playing for Time,* the cameraman was unusual. He didn't want to reduce the piece to a set of personal sagas. Inasmuch as scale, form, and budget allowed, he wanted to convey something of the monstrous whole. "He refused to do the close-ups, and persisted and persisted, and won," Arthur Miller recalls. "He did not want that Ping-Pong game [of close-up to close-up] to start in his picture. Because it would, so to speak, 'televise' Auschwitz. He had almost a moral aversion. Now, if you see that film, I think part of your belief in it comes from the fact that it is a dialectic between the environment and the people."

Low budgets by themselves can also flatten TV movies, with the same consequence as an excess of close-ups: a diminishment of the social dimension of things. When Miller wrote the script for *Playing for Time,* for example, he included a scene in which the orchestra was forced by the Nazis to play for hundreds of Auschwitz victims as they were led out to be gassed. To Miller and the producer this grand, pathetic sequence was the climax of the piece. But to shoot it would have taken several hundred actors, several extra days, and therefore scores of thousands of dollars. The picture had already gone over budget several times, and CBS was now holding the line on costs.

On top of the normal budgetary pressures, CBS was nervous about the political controversy swirling around the casting of the outspoken Palestine Liberation Organization supporter Vanessa Redgrave in the lead role. Several Jewish groups clamored against the choice of Redgrave; the flesh-and-blood Auschwitz survivor Fenelon herself denounced her, and influential Hollywood liberals like *Roots* executive producer David Wolper joined in. Once Redgrave's role was announced, CBS held fast: partly, at least, to resist the appearance of caving in to political pressure; partly because the Jewish lobby wasn't enormous; and partly, too, perhaps, because such huge advance publicity might end up boosting the show's ratings. But the network was also trying to cut potential financial losses. So the producer reluctantly cut the grand orchestral sequence, and Arthur Miller had to find a way around it.

Miller had never written for television before. He didn't know the conventions and didn't want to know. "I told them when I started, I don't know how to write a television thing. I don't know what that means. It will be written for the screen." So he wrote details of concentration-camp existence in many quick flashes, random shootings, for example, that established the context of Fenelon's immediate travail. The point was to underscore the everyday, arbitrary enormity of a concentration camp. "That stuff is on the minds of everybody in the orchestra," as Miller puts it. "If they hear a shot, well, who's next?" But these context shots also got dropped for lack of time and money. Still, Miller thought a decently funded feature film of *Playing for Time*—no best-seller as a book—would probably never have gotten made, Arthur Miller or no.

Every year the networks mount a few movies for conscience's sake. *Playing for Time*, on September 30, 1980, was one, and it demonstrated two important points: that serious subject matter isn't necessarily at odds with big numbers, and that big numbers don't necessarily cancel out commercial risk. For the Redgrave controversy had the drawback of bringing some advertisers to the panic point.

In an effort to keep commercial disruptions to a minimum, CBS had trimmed the number of spots to start with. Normally they would have sold forty-two thirty-second commercial slots for a three-hour movie. In *Playing for Time* they decided to group them in four two-minute clumps, with four more minutes at the beginning and four minutes at the end, for a total of only sixteen minutes, or thirty-two spots. So, from the start, they were losing out on almost one-quarter of their normal commercial load. When the pressure against Redgrave began to mount, CBS did lose some sponsors. "I had a [pharmaceutical] client who was going to buy in," a CBS vice-president for sales told me, "and whose sales manager came to him and said, 'You can't buy in that, because a lot of the drug wholesalers are Jewish, and we can't take the chance. We've had guys say, "We won't put your product on the shelf." Maybe they would or wouldn't, but I'm not going to take a chance.'"

Publicly, at least, advertising agencies said that the real reason they would hesitate to recommend the film to their clients was its "depressing nature." "It's one low line of depression," said Bruce Cox, executive vice-president of Compton Advertising, to a reporter after a sales screening. "I think it's the kind of thing the networks need to do. It's honest and frightening as hell, but I just can't see a client who has a selling job to do placing his spots after scenes that consistently end on such a remarkably low point. I went home after seeing the picture Thursday and got drunk immediately."

In the end, CBS didn't lose money, though the commercials brought only half the normal prime-time rate. Since the show drew an enormous 26.2 rating and a 41 share, with the audience share actually rising as the movie wore on, the advertisers got a bargain. CBS might have concluded that commercial success is not automatically ruled out when the central conventions of the form are violated. There was, after all, nothing upbeat about *Playing for Time.* But corporate managers are most concerned with what economists call "opportunity costs"—how much more money they might have brought in with a less controversial movie. They found it more convenient to conclude that millions of viewers, alerted by a media storm, tuned in this time simply to see what Vanessa Redgrave would do with the role. (Later, though, they didn't test this logic so far as to reason that Ed Asner's *Lou Grant* series might be worth keeping on the air precisely because Asner might prove more draw than liability.)

Meanwhile, no sooner had *Playing for Time* aired than the networks reverted to their normal approach to history, movies like CBS's *The Bunker* and ABC's *Inside the Third Reich*, which portrayed Nazi Germany from the executioners' point of view. Among other commercial virtues, such ritual exorcisms don't inspire boycott threats. The vociferous Jewish organizations have been more exercised by Vanessa Redgrave's support of the PLO than by television's banal humanization of Hitler and his cohorts. Despite the enormous success of *Holocaust* and *Playing for Time*, the networks' commercial wisdom points toward a mindlessly "documentary" form: Nazism relatively uncluttered by visible victims.

The high-rated May 1982 *Inside the Third Reich* was based, of course, on the memoirs of Hitler's architect and minister for war production, Albert Speer, supplemented by hundreds of hours the writer-producer spent interviewing Speer. And this is precisely the point: The movie's vision retained the blinders that led Speer into the Nazi movement and kept him there. Speer's motives were pared down to the television-sized staple of Faustian ambition, revealing nothing of Nazism's historical mainsprings: inflation, nationalist panic, anti-Semitism.* For the sake of balance, Speer was issued an anti-Nazi wife, but by Part II she had degenerated into the familiar

---

*Writing in 1954 about a television play about a fascist dictator, T. W. Adorno criticized "the spurious personalization of objective issues. . . . The impression is created that totalitarianism grows out of character disorders of ambitious politicians. . . . In order to deal with the concrete impact of totalitarian systems, it would be more commendable to show how the life of ordinary people is affected by terror and impotence than to cope with the phony psychology of the big-shots, whose heroic role is silently endorsed by such a treatment even if they are pictured as villains."

nagging *Hausfrau* whose principal objection was that political meetings were pulling her husband away from his family nest.

A year earlier, ABC movie chief Brandon Stoddard had been mindful of the criticism that CBS's *The Bunker* had presented Nazism without victims. "We've made a big effort to show the victim," he told me. "Speer didn't know, or put it this way, he avoided knowing. That has to be filmed; that's the fiber of that book." *Inside the Third Reich* did open with newsreel footage including the dread images of heaped corpses found in the death camps at the end of the war. The movie proper included some valuable reminders that Hitler's rants and Goering's bluster were responsible for mass murder. But the bulk of the movie was family angst, petty palace intrigues, and pageantry passing for historical understanding. ABC's expensive European locales simulated authenticity without challenging Speer's world view, which was that he was mysteriously trapped by Hitler's charisma. Here Hollywood reverts to the style of Cecil B. DeMille's Biblical spectaculars, this time featuring the veneer of authenticity rather than the painted backdrops. When Hollywood approves the look of a movie, it raves that "All the money is right up there on the screen." In *Inside the Third Reich* and its equivalents, the money is what shows.

When American commercial television renders history, money buys details, which are the façade of authenticity. Producers contract with special agencies to check the most trivial script details.* But money can buy neither a sense of historical structure nor a feeling for human freedom. The convention of docudrama naturalism titillates the audience by feeding its propensity for hero worship. Some of this naturalism is encouraged by the small screen as such. Actors cease to project, for otherwise their every gesture would seem grotesquely magnified. Even British noncommercial television is devoted to underplaying, except for Shakespeare and other classics. "In Shakespeare the very language requires projection," Arthur Miller says. "You have to breathe deeply in order to say those long lines. But those are exceptions. Any modern little thing tends to be diminished. And I think that's got to do with the medium, fundamentally. I think

---

*The memos from these agencies warn against anachronisms; factual errors; possible copyright and trademark violations for songs, quotations, and products; fictional names that happen to duplicate prominent historical names; and commercial product identifications. A typical memo for one half-hour show lists twenty items, including: "The word ['carpeting'] is anachronistic for the period." "The concept of 'salad' would be highly unlikely for the period and locale. Snapping beans or shelling peas would be better." "Prop note: a fitted, squared mattress, please; two large pieces of fabric, seamed on all sides and stuffed with feathers or other appropriate material would be suitable."

that you'd have a hard time combating it. You could combat it, but the director, the cameraman, and the actors would have to take special care."

The use of television as a living-room advertising medium accelerates this tendency to reduce the scope of the social world on the screen. Only a few personal decisions count; society becomes their backdrop. With the occasional exception of a *Bitter Harvest,* television presents history without alternatives, an inevitable world without politics. By the terms of its convention, *Inside the Third Reich* could not possibly convey, for example, that if the Communists and Social Democrats had combined forces in the late twenties and early thirties they could probably have defeated the Nazis. Arthur Miller calls the naturalist form "simply recognition of activity." All it says is, It happened this way. Historical inevitability and the possibility of personal transcendence, these are the choices posed by television. When history is spectacle, a larger-than-life fate that befalls humanity, personal escape becomes all the more tempting. Fortunately, the viewer never has to wait long; a commercial is always looming, to show how the desire for freedom or pleasure or status can be realized through the purchase of appropriate things.

The triumph of American TV naturalism, in fiction as in the news, is the revelation of familiar figures visibly coping with public troubles, *right here in the living room.* Raw pictures of stillborn calves or bodies piled high—the actual consequences of social decisions— are the medium's most potent messages. But the price of familiarity is diminishment of the scale of things. As always, the images of socially inflicted damage are softened and blurred—literally blurred— by the size and imperfect resolution of the glass screen. If a movie has force, much of it—most of it?—dissipates on the home box. Panoramic images of social process are hard, though not impossible, to cram into 221 square inches of blurred image. Muddy sound makes it all the more difficult to convey the buzzing cross-purposes of society. These are no small factors in gauging the meaning of even the most vivid TV films.

The poor quality of the image is especially scandalous. The current American television signal generates a picture from 525 horizontal lines. Although it can be blown up to a large size by expensive projectors, the enlarged video image washes out colors and magnifies the flaws. By comparison, the Europeans, who developed television later, use a 625-line standard. The more lines, the more precise the image. Recently, the American networks have filed with the Federal Communications Commission for permission to use certain frequencies to enable them to go to a technologically feasible 1,125 lines, at which the video image looks like that of 35-mm. film and giant TV screens begin to make visual sense.

The current TV sound is even worse than the picture. Soon, though, Sony and other manufacturers will have stereo television on the market, making the wretched quality of television sound technologically—if not economically—obsolete. Should the improved equipment get cheap enough, it could impel television producers to upgrade their production standards at least to *Hill Street Blues* quality, much as the spread of relatively inexpensive home-stereo equipment in the sixties coaxed rock producers and musicians to pay more attention to the tonal qualities of their records. But one fears that the brave new world of technical feasibility will only heighten the industry's fascination with special effects—at the usual expense of historical texture, which is believed by George Lucas and his imitators to distract from the "production values" of "pure cinema." The technological fix may be used mainly to make Albert Speer more compelling, to take us deeper "Inside the Third Reich."

In principle, technical improvements in the video image might help a movie like *Bitter Harvest* achieve its effects. Paradoxically, the small scale of the human-interest story should loom large if it is to have its full sway. The image of a stillborn calf a few inches across will never be able to match the—I was going to write animal—force of the same image blown up larger than life. But even an improved *Bitter Harvest* probably could never be as powerful emanating from the furniture—our minds occasionally drifting toward the familiar objects of the household, if toward anything at all, while we wait for the next commercial—as it appears when projected on the big screen.

In any event, the comparison is moot. Only the invited Hollywood audience saw the film in that powerful form. The movie business won't put a *Bitter Harvest* into theaters. "No producer is going to make a feature about sick cows," as the movie's director of photography, Gayne Rescher, puts it. There is simply not enough payoff for the corporate hit-hunters. "A feature about sick cows" would do nothing for the mass youth audience that has become the prize target for blockbusters. It hasn't the pseudo-epic adventure or the horror or jeopardy or cuteness or whimsy or uplift that big-time producers and studios want to invest in. It is "only" the equivalent of the social-problem films that inspired Irv Wilson when he was a child.

Not even its producers make any vast claim for *Bitter Harvest* as either art or edification. Well acted, well directed, and well photographed, it radiates a quiet power. It takes mass-produced suffering seriously; it suggests, in however limited a way, that social arrangements can be hazardous to the public health; it proposes that something might be done, but doesn't mislead about happy endings. *Bitter Harvest* represents the outer limits of today's television movie as a politically insurgent form, and if more movies like it got on the air, and "mature themes" came to signify more than sexual titillation, more people might be prompted to write maturely and modestly. "Movie made for television" might cease to be what it ordinarily amounts to today: mass culture's equivalent of the squarish, hard-skinned, tasteless tomato grown for quick, reliable, low-cost machine harvesting, untouched by human hands.

The trend is otherwise, however. By the time *Bitter Harvest* aired in May 1981, the networks, under severe financial pressure in a declining economy, were listening with a new intensity for political tremors. The fundamentalist crusade against smut was reinforcing advertisers' caution in the face of other threatening material. Tremors seemed to be growing into an ominous roar during the sweeps month of February 1981, when the social-issue trend of the late seventies happened to deliver four TV movies one after another. Right on the edge of sweeps, on Saturday, January 31, CBS ran *Thornwell*, an MTM docudrama about a black soldier whom the CIA used as a guinea pig for experiments with LSD. The next night, ABC ran *A Whale for the Killing*, with Peter Strauss, the former star of *Rich Man, Poor Man*, as a man who tries to save a stranded whale. On Thursday, February 4, CBS ran *Crisis at Central High*, with Joanne Woodward as a Little Rock teacher caught in the integration wars of 1957. And on Monday, February 8, NBC ran *Kent State*, another Irv Wilson project, this one straining to embrace the viewpoints of both radical students and National Guardsmen. The ratings and shares were as follows:

	Rating	Share
Thornwell	16.0	25
A Whale for the Killing	19.1	27
Crisis at Central High	14.4	22
Kent State	12.1	17

In network terms, these were miserable numbers; *Kent State* dipped so low it approached the level at which producers indulged in gallows humor: "That's not a rating, it's a shoe size." There were some extenuating circumstances—*Kent State* ran opposite the vastly popular *East of Eden*, for example. Neither *Thornwell* nor *Kent State* had a star, though the others did. None was outstanding, true, but then neither were many movies that rated much better. It was virtually automatic, however, that network executives would resort to a conservative extrapolation. ABC's Stu Samuels derided *Whale:*

"three hours about a big fish." In the words of Richard Levinson, who cowrote *Crisis at Central High,* at the end of that week executives were saying, "It's a new time, it's a new era, back to entertainment, folks, back to style and lightness and happiness." Levinson reconstructed their inductive logic: "The perception at the network has to be: Two shows deal with blacks a great deal. They all deal with the recent past, and they all deal with social unrest. . . . I heard agents and other people saying, 'I wouldn't walk into the networks right now with something of a recent past social drama black orientation.' "

Didn't the numbers speak for themselves? Never mind that *A Whale for the Killing* rated higher than *The Harlem Globetrotters on Gilligan's Island,* and *Thornwell* higher than *The Babysitter* (a film sold on the basis of its title alone). For that matter the previous fall's *The Women's Room* drew a 45 share, higher even than the phenomenally successful *Jayne Mansfield Story.* The networks were aiming at the surest and least troublesome 30 shares. With advertisers fidgeting about controversy, the networks gravitated toward the theory that the country had shifted to the right, or, what with economic misery, toward escape, or both. In any case, it was safest to err on the side of puffery. Whatever projects smacked of controversy got scrubbed.

In 1980, an independent producer in New York had read a chapter of Studs Terkel's book *American Dreams: Lost and Found* about a North Carolina man named C. P. Ellis, a working-class white who was "exalted cyclops" of the Durham chapter of the Ku Klux Klan. He threw himself into terrorizing blacks, but found that the white elite still scorned him. Roped into an interracial group concerned with race problems in schools, he found himself spurned by his racist white friends, just as a black woman in the group found herself isolated among civil-rights workers. The two became friends, and Ellis became a populist union organizer committed to racial equality. The producer saw the makings of an uplifting television movie about race relations here, and made a deal with NBC, which committed to a script. "It has a nice ending," Brandon Tartikoff told me. "We'd just as soon represent positive viewpoints." Ned Beatty was interested in playing Ellis.

The script got to NBC the week after *Crisis at Central High* drew its 22 share. The movie department was enthusiastic, but higher management said the project was "too controversial." Still recoiling from bad publicity over *Beulah Land,* NBC first said that if they were to make the Ellis movie they would have to hire a political adviser from the NAACP or some similar group; then they said it was the wrong time altogether, and passed. The script went to CBS, which responded in much the same way: "We don't want to deal with the Ku Klux Klan." ABC said the same. It didn't matter that the story was, in the producer's words, "a story about the possibility of change in the human spirit"; in Terkel's words, "an upbeat story, a story of redemption, about race reconciliation, almost *religious.*"

Around the same time, Steve Mills of the CBS movie department had concluded that, although America wasn't moving to the right, the presumably unitary public now wanted escapism, not the personal-problem stories that had made up the bulk of the network's "serious drama" in recent years. When I interviewed him in April 1981, he said, "I think the last couple of years, we've done more serious social drama—affliction stories and Love Canal–type of stuff—and although we'll continue to do those, I think in the balance of our mix, if ten or twelve of our fifty-five movies this year had to do with very serious social drama, we'll probably do only six or seven next year. If we did a couple of romantic comedies this year, we might do four romantic comedies next year." Partly because of the Reagan election, he said, "we just got the feeling that maybe it was right, now, to lighten up a little bit."

Mills added that the Reagan election and "the mood of the country" had only crystallized what he felt the previous October, after looking at what he calls "the daily report card" of movie ratings. He read me the figures. *Private Battle,* about the writer Cornelius Ryan's battle with cancer, got a 20 share; a year or two before, he thought, it might have gotten a 30. Two nights later, *Children of An Lac,* about the rescue of fifty orphans from Saigon in 1975, got a 20 share. Then movies about an autistic child, prisons, and a boy dying of leukemia all pulled shares in the 20s. "You get hit in the face a couple of times with a two-by-four, and you start noticing that maybe the public is looking for escapist stuff. We did a light piece with Lucie Arnaz, her first television movie, and we thought it would get a 25 share. It got a 32 share. We did a little frolicky piece called *The Pleasure Palace,* with Victoria Principal and Omar Sharif, all about a gambling casino in Las Vegas, and it got a 32 share. We did *Jayne Mansfield,* and it got a 39 share. . . . We did one with Linda Gray, who is the costar of *Dallas,* called *The Wild and the Free,* all about training and domesticating chimps—it got a 30 share. So we felt that there was a swing in that direction. And I'm only talking about things on our network. On the other networks, the same sort of things were happening. We could see Sophia Loren get a big number on NBC, and other things like that."

Projects that might divide and annoy the apparently skittish majority audience got stuck in the pipeline. Ernest Kinoy, with his knowledge of black history and his considerable track record, had written a script for CBS about the first blacks to be integrated into the army air force during World War II. He had come across the story of this unit, based in Tuskegee, Alabama, while researching *Roots II.* No book had ever been written about them. He compiled his own oral history of the events, and wove the 1943 Detroit race riot into his composite narrative. *Roots* producer Stan Margulies was to produce. But by the time the script was written, CBS had concluded that the audience wouldn't be interested. The Ku Klux Klan, race riots, and integration were equally taboo. Where blacks—and other controversial subjects—were concerned, the networks had slid into what Daniel Patrick Moynihan once called benign neglect.

And the same thing happened to unsavory women. That same spring of 1981, NBC developed a script about teenage prostitutes. "It was the kind of project where you can lure viewers and educate them," said one executive, adding that there was nothing sexy or glamorizing about the representation; these hookers used heroin to numb their feelings. Women who read the script thought it was excellent. Male executives, suddenly scrupulous, said it was exploitative. The executive who advocated making the movie thought opponents were actually identifying with the tricks. At the same time, the network went ahead with the far more sensational *Dorothy Stratten Story*, about the Playboy centerfold model who was murdered by her estranged husband. This was one of those films that could capitalize on "profamily" Puritanism and a kind of sensationalist feminism all at once; ABC had turned it down as unethical. "I know these prohibitions have to do with the Moral Majority and affiliate pressures and the advertisers," this executive says. "Who are the large advertisers? General Electric, IBM,* the oil companies, Procter & Gamble. What I'm told about the prostitute movie is, 'Sales will have a hard time with this.' When you look at what Procter & Gamble's interested in, they're not your rock-the-boat projects. They're biographies; they're human-interest stories, but not the kind that will contribute to social change."

By winter of 1982, the tidal shift on the screen was unmistakable. When painful social reality obtruded at all, the new movies were no longer flirtations with controversy; now they were ritual exorcisms of general social catastrophe. Without being aware of it, the networks were discovering they could get far better numbers by uniting the audience in fascination with an overwhelming, transhistorical, apparently external threat (Nazism, the Bomb, the Russians, the Peo-

---

*Tony Ganz had in fact tried to interest IBM in sponsoring the whole of *Bitter Harvest.* Producers of TV movies hanker for the single institutional sponsor who will not only sway a wavering network to make the picture in the first place but will take fewer commercial breaks, help promote the movie, and give it the cachet of the out-of-the-ordinary. "I sent the script to Mike Dann for IBM," Ganz said. He said, 'I love it, IBM loves it, but they'll never sponsor it.' It's too tough for anybody."

ple's Temple) than by dividing it by pointing up conflicts in American society. This was the same principle that the makers of horror,
disaster, and sci-fi feature films had happened upon in the fifties, then
rediscovered in the seventies. Whatever the differences in tone and
ideology among *Earthquake, The Towering Inferno, The Exorcist,
Jaws, Star Wars,* and *Alien,* they all brought to the surface deep
terrors about dangers to the entire community, whether altogether
fictional (vampires, extraterrestrial monsters, killer wolves, Darth
Vader), or natural (the great white shark). *Masada*—about "Jews and
history," two "downer" subjects in industry terms—could nonetheless be a hit because, despite rising anti-Semitism, there was no national constituency for the Romans.

I asked an Emmy-winning writer-producer with a strong record in
politically-charged TV movies what he would do if he were a network executive. "If I cared about keeping the job," he said, "I suppose I'd do the same thing they do. In World War II, if you wanted
to get a bottle of Canadian Club you'd have to buy six bottles of rum.
A very smart network executive does a lot of shows that give them
a 35 share, and they say, 'We'll give him one.' As for me, I pitch
projects all the time, and I get turned down. I've written scripts I
can't get produced. There's nobody who has the secret anymore. I've
written all these years and I don't understand the patterns. I am now
known. I can get in the door. But I start over every time; the battle
is fresh every time." I asked him whether he thought political lines
were being drawn overtly. "You never really know," he said thoughtfully, then paused and added: "That's evasive. We know what the
rules are and we try to stretch them. But there comes a point where
you can't stretch them. And the rules aren't the same for all of us.
What you hope for is that the people with the power will fight for the
quality."

The transition from social problem to universal menace reached a
high pitch of equivocation in NBC's September 1982 two-night miniseries, *World War III,* which fused antiwar sentiment and jingoism.
It had started out otherwise. When an agent first brought the project
to NBC, said Ethel Winant, the network's vice-president for miniseries, "I didn't want to do it, because I thought it had to be done very
responsibly. I was not going to do a thing where the Soviets were the
bad guys and we were the good guys." But top management had
picked up public anxiety about nuclear war, and directed her to find
an acceptable script, whereupon she contracted with a writer she
considered responsible: Robert L. Joseph, who had written a number
of things she considered "all major," including a miniseries called
The Word, and, among others, the TV movies *Flight of the Maiden*
and *Charlie Chan: The Cradle of Hercules.* Winant asked Joseph to
do two things—avoid a good/bad dichotomy and see that the missiles

were launched in the end. "I don't want a happy ending," she said. "The moral is that if you allow these kind of shibboleths and prejudice and hysteria, if you allow a war machine to be built, it can be set off." She herself worried about Washington talk of "limited nuclear war," about the new generations of destabilizing missiles, and about the real chance that the ultimate catastrophe could be ignited, haphazardly, almost anywhere, even from such an improbable event as a runaway KGB unit dropped into Alaska to cut the oil pipeline in retaliation for an American grain embargo.

Originally, Joseph's *World War III* was to begin in 1984. Europe is starving; the United States is refusing to ship grain; European terrorists seize the Alaska pipeline to force an end to the embargo; one thing leads to another. . . . The scenario was improbable enough, but the point was that any set of miscalculations could trigger the ultimate war. NBC's law department objected only to one small point, which was that 1984 would fall within the current administration and so seem to be impugning a sitting president. The date was changed to 1987, but by the time the film was made, the Cold War was back with a vengeance, and Winant, independently, was leaving NBC for Metromedia. Now the invaders of Alaska became Russians bent on presenting the peace-minded Russian premier with a *fait accompli.* The American president (Rock Hudson) was peace-minded, too, but events had their own momentum. Neither he nor his opposite number was any match for the tricky, implacable red dogs of the KGB, whose "mole" had even penetrated an American radar unit. While the invaders lay endless and improbable siege to an American outpost, and two of the Americans renewed a long-gone love affair, the chiefs of state frantically tried to negotiate a face-saving rapprochement. But the KGB men undermined their talks, and eventually, as the American and Russian leaders stared eyeball to eyeball at the prospect of peace, the KGB assassinated the Russian premier. In the end, they tricked Hudson one fatal last time and launched a first nuclear strike.

It was a kooky recombinant scenario, with old-style infantry maneuvers and frontier romance superimposed onto a *Strangelove* image of plausible nuclear holocaust. The Soviets were the more duplicitous and aggressive side, but on both sides, men of goodwill stood helpless. What prevailed was the movie's electronic score, steadily pulsating like the inhuman music of a system that thrives on suspense and never lets up for a minute. Whatever the reasons, *World War III* found a huge audience. Considering that the networks believe a love interest to be the obligatory sugar coating for an occasional bitter pill of social realism, it is striking that the show's ratings rose consistently as suspense about whether the missiles were going to fly gradually replaced the early romance. The movie gained in market shares each half hour of its two nights, starting at 27 and ending at a smash 40. The total audience also grew steadily, although normally the number of TV viewers dwindles as the night wears on: People were switching over to *World War III* from the competition. Evidently flashes of suspense about the end of the world proved alluring. Foreign movie distributors thought so, too: At the Milan convention of the world's buyers that fall, *World War III* was the biggest sell.

As *World War III* was shooting, ABC announced a commitment to its own forthcoming thermonuclear-war movie, *The Day After.* Where NBC chose the origins, ABC, perhaps in a competitive division of labor, chose the consequences, setting out to dramatize the effects of a Russian H-bomb explosion on Kansas City. The political implications were again equivocal, but the balance of iniquity belonged to the Soviet Union. An official of the Federal Emergency Management Agency, in charge of the Reagan administration's civil-defense planning, read the message this way: "The principal characters in the movie survive. And that's what we've been trying to get across. No matter how bad nuclear war is, we're not all going to get wiped out." This was the year, after all, when ABC, even more than the other networks, was proclaiming the conservative temper.

At the 1981 affiliates meeting bedazzled by the just-landed astronauts of the space shuttle *Enterprise,* and a profusion of American flags in wide-screen slide-show glory, ABC Television president Fred Pierce told local station executives, "There's an evolving mood in the country now. It's based on a renewal of traditional values: home and family, courage and honesty, respect for authority and teamwork." What could be more "traditional" than the spirit of self-reliance? Network television had spent a good part of the seventies opening up television to the egalitarian and antiwar spirit of the time, after its fashion, but in the first year of the Reagan administration the networks' antennae were swinging around and facing right.

3

THE
POLITICS OF
PRIME TIME

CHAPTER 10

The Turn Toward "Relevance"

What comes across the small screen amounts to an entertaining version of the world—to ideology, in a word—but whatever conspiracy theorists may think, this is not because the networks are trying to indoctrinate the helpless masses. No, the networks generate ideology mostly indirectly and unintentionally, by trying to read popular sentiment and tailoring their schedules toward what they think the cardboard people they've conjured up want to see and hear. If they concoct a hit, for whatever reasons, competitive bet-covering dictates that it be imitated *ad nauseam,* creating the sense of a rampant trend. If this is cultural tyranny, it is a soft tyranny, operating through stripped-down formulas that the networks selectively abstract, via other media, from mass sentiments. These sentiments themselves are already heavily shaped, of course, by the immense weight of mass culture's formulas as they have accumulated over the years.

The network antenna is always rotating because, in the end, all the testing and copying and recombining and inside-track planning in the world aren't conclusive. Nothing can dissolve the network's dependence on certification by a mass audience. The trick is not only to read the restless public mood, but somehow to anticipate it and figure out how to encapsulate it in a show. No one comes to such arcane work innocent of ideas about what the market will bear, ideas that circulate constantly through the standardized channels of executive culture. The executive "instinct," much praised in the industry, is a schooled instinct, formed in experience and concentrated by that common culture.

Whatever their differences, network executives tend to sample the media in common. CBS's Scott Siegler, for example, claimed one of the wider ranges. He subscribed to the *New York Times* and *Los Angeles Times,* to *Time* and *Newsweek,* to *National Review, Mother Jones, Esquire,* and *Rolling Stone,* to *Emmy, TV Guide* and *Panorama* (*TV Guide*'s short-lived monthly), as well as to the ubiquitous trade papers. "I haunt newsstands," he said. "I go there every day." Most executives read less—skeptical writers think they really skim, or look at the pictures—but the majority I asked said they read the two *Times*es, along with *Time* or *Newsweek* or both; after these, the periodicals they mentioned most were, in descending order, *Esquire,* the *Wall Street Journal,* the *New Yorker,* and *TV Guide. People* is much in evidence, though not so frequently flourished before inquiring professors. If the executives read books at all, their taste runs toward best-sellers. Endlessly, though, the executives attend private screenings of the movies that are their town's most prestigious products; they dissect them, analyzing the elements that "work" and don't, while taking little if any interest in films produced outside Hollywood.

The reading habits of writers and producers are not so different. Defending the industry against the writer Ben Stein's argument that TV entertainment is subversive because the producers are themselves liberal cosmopolitans, Norman Lear, who once employed Stein, actually confirmed to me that the industry stays within the banks of a relatively narrow, cosmopolitan ideological stream: "I think he's wrong, for the simple reason that we all get our stimuli from the same wellspring. Whether you write in Spokane, Washington, or Hartford, Connecticut, or Los Angeles, California, we all watch the same network news. It's exactly the same, wherever you are in this country. We all read whatever we read—*Time* or *Newsweek* or whatever. There are no local newspapers, except for really small towns. The *Los Angeles Times* is a national newspaper; it's full of UPI, AP, it takes a lot of the *Washington Post* service. They're all the same, the big newspapers. And that's where we feed, writers. We feed and drink from those wells."

The ideas about public opinion circulating through these channels are the ideas that find their way into network offices. By keeping up to the minute, executives try to stay flexible, but their flexibility is bounded by the conventional wisdom that circulates through their favored media. Their periodicals put issues on their mental agenda. They also certify vague ideas, or fragments of personal experience, as potentially marketable ideas worth taking seriously.* Ideas form about the ebb and flow of popular feelings, and the genres that might or might not correspond to them.

The structure of power works toward uniformity. By the time of the scheduling meetings, consensus has usually jelled. At CBS, according to longtime executive Herman Keld, a significant division of opinion about a pilot arises in only one of every four or five cases. "Don't forget," he says, "we all live in the same world, we all have the same experiences." And occasionally, from that "same world," there also arise grander notions of larger demographic and ideological shifts in the public. Such occasions are rare, and their impact on programming correspondingly great—whether these notions are accurate or not.

I began working on this book at one such moment, when many top network people thought that a rightward swing in public opinion, combined with deep economic trouble, called for a shift in the tone of entertainment programming. America, they concluded, wanted law and order on the one hand and straight-out escapism on the other. Presumably, what it didn't want was the likes of *American Dream*. On the whole this time, the networks guessed wrong, and their errors were writ large across the screens of the early eighties. To appreciate the network mentality that could lead to such a sweeping miscalculation of public desires, we have to understand the limits of executives' intuition and the sources of their misreadings. To do this, it is useful to contrast the present period with one exactly ten years earlier, when a single network made a brilliantly correct guess about public moods and how to package them for TV consumption. That was trend-spotting in its moment of commercial glory, and much of Hollywood still remembers it fondly as the moment when television threatened to grow up.

In the early seventies, CBS's top executives decided the market ground was shifting under their feet, and took a calculated risk. It was an extraordinary moment for CBS. The network was stuffed with rural successes like *Gunsmoke, Mayberry R.F.D., The Red Skelton Hour, The Beverly Hillbillies, The Glen Campbell Goodtime Hour,* and *Hee Haw,* ranked number two, four, seven, eighteen, twenty, and twenty-one, respectively, in the 1969–70 season. It had *Green Acres* and *Petticoat Junction* on its schedule as well. CBS was the number-one network and then some, but demography was starting

---

*So, for example, *Los Angeles Times* and *Time* magazine stories about chemical pollution played important parts in selling the 1981 TV movie, *Bitter Harvest.* See pp. 170–171. Sociologists have long noted that the mass media certify ideas, trends, fads for the general population; they have not so carefully looked at the ways media certify ideas for the elites themselves.

to turn against it. As the pungent former CBS president Bob Wood put it to me, "The wrinkles were beginning to show on the face of the CBS network. It was becoming an aged, or aging, network."

By the fall of 1971, *Mayberry, Skelton, Beverly, Hee Haw, Green Acres,* and *Petticoat* were gone, and CBS was broadcasting *All in the Family* and *The Mary Tyler Moore Show.* A year later, *Campbell* was also gone, and *M*A*S*H* was a CBS fixture. This shift from cornball comedy to expressions—however ambiguous—of liberal ideas, was engineered by an executive who described himself as a political conservative. The same Robert D. Wood who put *All in the Family* on the air also canceled the Smothers Brothers show in 1969 because they wouldn't submit their programs sufficiently ahead of air dates for the Standards and Practices department to screen them. The tidal shift to "relevance" was made possible by a curious fact of broadcasting's corporate life: The companies that run television networks also own stations, and the economic interests of the two sectors don't always neatly coincide.

In 1969, Robert D. Wood was forty-four years old, a driving, powerfully built graduate of the University of Southern California whose arguments resounded with the force of hard salesmanship. He had started his career in sales, in fact, for the radio and television stations CBS owned in Los Angeles, and worked himself up to running the five VHF television stations that CBS owned and operated. These so-called O&Os were the only stations the FCC would permit each network to own. ABC, CBS, and NBC owned one each in New York, Chicago, and Los Angeles, and then two in other major cities, the exact mix depending on which network had bought which stations when. These fifteen O&Os were the bulwark of network profits, accounting for fully 70 percent of total network pretax earnings in 1970.

Then-president Frank Stanton of CBS, Inc., the corporate empire of which CBS Television was the central division, takes credit for promoting Bob Wood. As network operations swelled and became routine in the 1960s, and CBS, Inc., took on more and more subsidiaries, Stanton came to deplore the distance between top corporate management and the everyday operations of the broadcast division. Gone were the days when Stanton himself, or chairman William S. Paley, could stay in touch personally with the thinking of the local stations. An astute manager with a broad view of the industry, Stanton determined, as he put it years later, "deliberately to use our company-owned stations as the training ground for network executives. They were closer to the ultimate consumer. What the hell did I know? I was like an oblong blur suspended from Los Angeles to New York.

"I had no roots. Living on Madison Avenue doesn't give you any feel for what's going on in Peoria. The station manager, the man who worked in the station and grew up in that environment and became a manager, had not only to have a sense of the public's interest and demands and needs, but he knew the political science. He knew how to get along with City Hall. He knew how to negotiate a labor contract. He knew how to deal with breaking events in terms of news. . . . All of those skills he had in microcosm. Although they didn't seem like microcosm to the manager, these were all a microcosm of what he had to face if he was going to be a manager on a network basis. But by the time a man becomes a specialist in the network, he doesn't know these other things exist out there. So you want a generalist. And that was the rationale, if you will, for why I went to the company-owned stations for the bright young men who were coming in. (And I say men because in those days there weren't very many women who wanted to work in the field, and they didn't get much attention.)"

Running CBS's owned stations, Wood was keenly aware that, for all CBS's preeminence in the ratings, the network was not doing that well in the big cities. "We operated stations in New York, Chicago, Los Angeles, Philadelphia, and St. Louis," Wood recalled. "Except for St. Louis, these were large, urban, and I guess, to some degree urbane centers in the United States. And while the network was number one, it was number one largely because of the strength from which it drew in the C and D counties [industry shorthand for the less populated areas]. Moreover, the audience that was the most loyal to CBS was, by and large, the post-fifty-year-old group. I complained of the paradox that the network could on the one hand be the leading national network, and on the other hand CBS could own stations in major cities that weren't competitive. Because the programming that made the network number one was making our stations in the large markets number two or number three."

At this point in his account Wood thought better of his verb "complained." "Let me just say," he went on, "that I made several professional observations to the management about this paradox. But at CBS as well as the other two networks, the interest that always will prevail will be that of the network. My interests were obviously insular, or reduced to the welfare of our stations. I recognized that *Gunsmoke* and all these rural shows were doing terrifically nationally. It just wasn't doing much for the company-owned stations division."

Then, early in 1969, Wood found himself president of the entire network. "The first inquiry I made is, what can we do to maintain the leadership of our network while at the same time putting it through a test—of changing the character of the network from more bucolic material to more fresh or updated, contemporary, whatever you want to call it. The broadcast schedule of '69–'70 I inherited; that had already been set. So the first tinkering that I could do would be in the midseason of that particular broadcast season, and more fully, with what we could do as of the '70–'71 season. And so that's when we made some adjustments in the thinking. Shows that had done well did come to an end on the network.* I can remember Johnny Carson, at the Emmy Awards that he emceed: 'You know, the only time you're in serious trouble on CBS is when you have a show in the top ten.' "

Salesman Wood also knew that advertisers were beginning to care more precisely who was watching the shows. From the beginning of the Nielsen ratings, advertisers for the most part had been satisfied to know how many households were tuning in. But Paul Klein at NBC cleverly began to clamor that it was individuals who bought products, not households, and that it was the precise *composition* of the household—age, sex, and income—that counted. Advertisers had known the obvious all along, of course, but they hadn't acted on it. However, when the trailing network let the ad agencies know that they could get a quality buy at NBC, it changed the rules of the game. Before, as CBS vice-president Herman Keld said, "If you're number one by a sufficiently large margin, as CBS always was during those years, you're also number one in the preferred homes." Now NBC's fewer customers began to look relatively more valuable because they earned more and spent more. The agencies now wanted CBS to tell them how much purchasing power their ads would avail them. With advertising rates taking off, CBS had to pay heed. "It's always growing competition that makes you do things," Keld says.

So at just the time Bob Wood assumed the presidency of the CBS network, the sales department, as he remembers, was "undergoing a lot of pressure, or competing forces, let's say, from advertisers. As the rating services started publishing more and more data about who this audience was, it didn't take the sales department long to realize that advertisers were not altogether influenced by who was number one. 'Number one *how?*' became an important question to them. And the sales department, though they never really brought much to the decisions that were made on the program side, I was very much aware of their general feeling. What can we do to improve the demographics of the network? About a third of every advertising

---

*Bob Wood's programming lieutenant Fred Silverman told the *Glen Campbell* producers they could save their show by converting it to a big-city format. The writers argued that Campbell's countrified personality couldn't manage the move, but they were persuaded that with a few concessions they could procure another season. They made the concessions, according to writer Rich Eustis, and that way outlasted the other country shows by a year.

dollar spent is spent on the products that go to people fifty and over. So we were doing very well in that category. But where were the other two-thirds?"

So Sales sided with Bob Wood when he announced he wanted to go young, urban, and more "realistic." Meanwhile, CBS's programming chief, Mike Dann, insisted that nothing succeeds like established success. Who could doubt the CBS record? "Here we are, the number-one network, and are we willing to jeopardize that while we tinker with a hit? . . . A lot of things I did, probably, in the first two or three years, were things that I would have paused a little longer had I had seven or eight or nine years behind me. And I suppose by '75, '76, I might have been a bit more cautious, because I was more aware of the downside risks after I knew more about it, than I was early on. . . . [but] I was absolutely convinced that I sensed fatigue in the network schedule, and I was convinced in my own mind that left unchecked, if we had just permitted things to go on, that we could have been number three with those very same shows."

Of course even strong-willed managers don't make big corporate decisions on their own. It didn't hurt that CBS was a strong number one, with a certain obvious reserve of strength on which to calculate its risks. Most of all, if William S. Paley hadn't gone along, Wood couldn't have prevailed. As CBS executives like to say, "It's Mr. Paley's candy store." Paley had founded CBS and transformed an advertising vehicle for his father's cigar business into a national cultural force field. In Herman Keld's words, "Paley had that which only sons of wealthy fathers have: confidence that is bred by the knowledge that no matter what they do wrong, Daddy will bail them out. People of money, they have confidence because they have fuck-you money."

If anyone in American broadcasting ever had an instinct for showmanship, Paley had. When he first took over a fledgling radio network in 1928, he had been the man to edge out music and put comedy and vaudeville on the air, keeping some classical music purely for prestige. He signed Kate Smith and the Mills Brothers to meteoric radio careers. He maintained later that he signed up Bing Crosby after hearing his voice on a recording, but before learning of the crooner's growing popularity, and that he signed Frank Sinatra after hearing him sing, without billing, with the Tommy Dorsey orchestra.

Most of his programming executives over the years agreed that Mr. Paley had a keen eye for talent, that he knew what a popular genre needed. Unlike his opposite numbers at the other networks, founding fathers David Sarnoff of RCA/NBC and Leonard Goldenson of ABC, Paley never delegated the business of composing the schedule. Even as he grew preoccupied with the burgeoning conglomerate

operations of CBS, Inc., in the sixties and seventies—records, stereo
equipment, musical instruments, books, toys, and for a while the
New York Yankees—he never missed the final network scheduling
meetings, where he liked to play devil's advocate, pressing his programming executives to defend their shows, holding his veto power
in reserve. Never, according to Bob Wood, did he say, "That show's
going to get on the air over my dead body." A solid phalanx of
opposition was even known to change his mind. At the 1981 scheduling meetings, for example, Paley held out for one adventure series
which, according to one staff member, "tested very bad, below toilet
level. People hated every single character. Paley liked it. The executives spent all day talking him out of it."

Bob Wood's great shift of 1970–71 fell on receptive ears. Paley was
"a hundred percent supportive to the whole idea," Wood recalled,
"probably as outspoken on that subject as any that I can remember
during the years that I worked with him." Indeed, Paley later wrote
that he had understood as early as 1965 that CBS was becoming the
prisoner of its successful schedule, its top-rated shows locking in an
aging audience. Paley credited Wood with "taking the idea and im-
plementing it."

So top management got Bob Wood's point about the market shift.
Advertisers did not have to be persuaded. There was only one group
in the network chain of acceptance that remained to be convinced.
"I know there was resistance on the part of our affiliates," Frank
Stanton recalls, "because of two things. They had a success on their
hands, and they were getting unknown product. And you know the
fear of the unknown. It's just as virulent in the manager of the
Denver station, with his country-club pals, as it is in any other area.
And these guys, they didn't *know*. They were taking Bob Wood on
faith."

How, then, were they persuaded?

"Well, you showed them the product, number one. And now here's
a good example of the philosophy of having somebody running that
network who ran . . . one hell of a successful station in Los Angeles.
. . . When Bob stood up in front of the affiliates and pledged that this
was going to work and so forth, [he was] very persuasive, and had a
hell of a string of credits behind him, and that stood him in good
stead. Freddie Silverman never had that kind of management skill.
He had programming of a different kind. Bob Wood knew what it
was to go out and meet the advertisers and the audience in his own
community."

Bob Wood's sense of the drift of his moment was not only demographic but cultural. "Remember too," he said, "that in '69, '70, '71,
this country was undergoing considerable sociological changes and
points of view." He was talking about the youth revolt, about hippies

and Woodstock, about the antiwar movement; and he was one of those executives who paid attention to polls like the one conducted by Daniel Yankelovich, Inc., and published in *Fortune* in January 1969, noting, for example, that although only 11 percent of the college-student population identified with the student movement, fully 48 percent thought the police action at the 1968 Democratic Convention unjustified, more than half again as many as those who supported it. Something was happening and, Bob Dylan notwithstanding, Mr. Jones thought he did know what it was; knew well enough, anyway, to program for it. Wood's recognition of oncoming change was not subtle, not analytic, just deep enough to catch a chord of anxiety abroad in the land, perhaps a chord of hope, even better their combination. "It just seemed to me that if there was a parade going by, you couldn't be content to sit on a rocking chair on your porch and watch it, you had to get into the parade, and you had to elbow your way to the front of the parade." A nice description of ideal network strategy: Locate the cultural avant-garde and follow it, one step ahead of the rest of the public parade, pulling it along. *All in the Family* producer-director Bud Yorkin had a similar idea about that show's success: "Coming out of the sixties, the climate was right, the kids were letting it all hang out, the kids didn't want to see Doris Day: 'Quit jerking us off and give us something real.'"

However, cultural entrepreneurship was complicated. CBS discovered the youth parade just as it was passing out of politics into fashion on its way to oblivion. The young rebels did not watch much television anyway. The two new "realistic," "relevant" dramas in the 1970–71 schedule, *Storefront Lawyers* and *The Interns,* both flopped. Perhaps they were too youthful, too earnest; perhaps they failed to give their rambunctious young professionals either the senior target who would keep the elders viewing, or a youth rebellion plausible enough to lure the young. In any event, Wood's lasting shows enfolded the concerns of the young in a different way. Far from depicting active, concerted rebellion, *All in the Family, The Mary Tyler Moore Show,* and *M*A*S*H* were comedies; and they all depicted younger people bearing "sixties values"—anti-authoritarianism and the desire for the authentic—while trying to get on with their lives under rules imposed by arbitrary authority. This had long been a theme in American culture, but television had usually said that when push came to shove Father rather than Mother, Son, or Daughter knew best. Now less soluble generational conflicts moved to the center of the show and comedy made them bearable. But what really made these comedies work was their gift for making light of the quandaries of young humanists and elder authorities alike. How would Mike and Gloria Stivic cope with Archie Bunker's fulminations? How would the single career woman, Mary Richards, get on with crusty Lou Grant and pompous Ted Baxter in the world of work? How would army surgeons express their humane impulses in the midst of war?

Not that *All in the Family, Mary,* and *M*A*S*H* were devised with ideological strategies in mind. The founders, Norman Lear, Allan Burns and Jim Brooks, and Larry Gelbart, each in his different way wanted to nudge the real world toward center stage, but they were first of all showmen. When Lear Americanized *All in the Family* from its English prototype, he says, "I was one hundred percent interested in creaming an audience. This was a comedy, and I wanted to make an audience laugh. I also have a great proclivity for placing tears and laughter side by side, I guess because I was influenced so much by Chaplin and Preston Sturges in film, and because laughter and tears, as I grew up, were always side by side. I used to laugh at a lot of conflict in my family, which was very difficult for other people in that conflict. But my defense was to find the humor in it." Lear adds, "I've always had a social conscience." Already in college he was in the habit of firing off telegrams to members of Congress. His liberal interests primed him for a theory of comedy: "I've always considered that an audience laughs hardest when they're concerned most."

Lear made his original pilot for ABC in 1968. It tested terribly (relationships aggressive, Archie too nasty), got recast, and Lear made a second pilot. In the meantime, ABC went on the air with a comedy-variety called *Turn-On,* a bawdier and more scatological version of *Laugh-In,* devised by the same producer, George Schlatter (later the inventor of *Real People*). *Turn-On* was a turn-off, rating abysmally, driving Bristol-Myers to cancel sponsorship and many ABC affiliates to refuse to air any future episodes. *Turn-On* was the shortest-running series in history: a single episode, February 1, 1969. "That experience," says ABC programming vice-president Sy Amlen, "left management shaken by anything that would bring down the wrath of the community on its head." Whereupon ABC said no to the second pilot of a show with a foul-mouthed, bigoted lead.

Lear went to CBS, where Bunker's strange dissonance was music to Bob Wood's ears. "I really thought the pilot was very very funny. And it was in the vanguard of the kind of thinking that I've just been telling you about: How do you get in that parade and how do you get in the front of the parade? I thought, Well, it may be too far in front of the parade. You never know till you put the thing on the air. The jury, after all, is the audience. But it sure seemed to me to be a terrific way to test this whole attitude about the network." The show went on the air in January 1971, started slowly, and took sixteen weeks to take off. Wood anticipated trouble from the affiliates: "The first time the show went on the air, we alerted the switchboard in New York, and we sent teletypes to all of our affiliates saying, 'This show is different, and it may cause some kind of community reaction, pro or negative or whatever, and you might be alert to the fact that it's going to be a different kind of an on-the-air experience than you've probably had ever.' We were all geared for a big onslaught of reaction, and precious little of it came in. I knew most of the affiliates, or a lot of them, and I had made speeches before *All in the Family* went on the air—not about *All in the Family*, but the fact that we got to move this network out a little bit. They knew I was serious about it. They were friends of mine. By and large, most of the affiliates gave me their philosophical support to go ahead and toy with the schedule and see what I could do, and so nobody was against *All in the Family*."

In the interminable fights with Standards and Practices about "hells" and "damns" in the scripts, about whether Mike could be impotent and whether a toilet could be heard flushing, Wood usually stuck with Lear, and Lear stood fast. The director-producer Bud Yorkin remembers Wood "defending our position against Program Practices, against their legal advisers, against Bill Paley, sitting up above, who said, 'I don't want somebody called yid on my station.' 'Well, Bill, if you call somebody else a mick, you've got to call him a yid.' "

"The rest, as they say, is history," said Bob Wood. "*All in the Family* spawned so many shows, like *Maude* and *The Jeffersons,* that the sum total, I believe, changed the face of television." Enough so, at least, that by the early eighties Lear had become the Antichrist of the fundamentalist right, the man who put the abortion issue and birth-control references on prime time and let Maude's husband Walter erupt with an unprecedented "son of a bitch!"* Lear's abrasive comic style caught the tone of American resentment during the Nixon years, and gave Bunker and Stivic fans each something to root for. Later experimental studies in the United States and Canada seemed to show that although Archie may have lost the arguments, viewers took away whatever attitudes they brought to the show; racists felt confirmed in their racism, liberals in their broad-mindedness and sense of superiority. But Lear might have had a point in believing it was healthier for the society to flush out its rancor than

---

*Although Lear was permitted this special dispensation, among others, censors in later years were at pains to say that Walter would not have been allowed to use the phrase as a description—only as an exclamation.

to evade it. Giving vent to the various grievances of class, race, sex, and generation, Lear's formula did indeed help to keep wrenching conflicts "all in the family."

Bob Wood's second new show on CBS approached the same generational divide in a milder, if still comic, way. *The Mary Tyler Moore Show* began with a commitment to the actress herself because she had been a smash hit in *The Dick Van Dyke Show.* Moore's producer husband, Grant Tinker, coaxed Allan Burns and Jim Brooks, who had worked together on *Room 222,* to write the show. As Allan Burns recalls, he and Brooks "realized that first of all we couldn't possibly have her married, because that would bear too strong a comparison to the Van Dyke show, which at that time I thought was about as good as any situation comedy had been." Enter the idea of divorce: "Every writer I knew of," Burns says, "had this idea for doing the first series about divorce. And we thought, we can get away with it with Mary, because people will accept her where they might not accept somebody else."

When Burns and Brooks brought the idea to the executive dining room at CBS Television City, Perry Lafferty, then CBS programming vice-president, shook his head and said, "Fellas, they're going to think she's divorced Van Dyke. We can't have that." "Perry was not a bad guy," says Burns. "He was just doing his job, and he knew that we were in for rough sailing back in New York." New York was equally displeased. "CBS won that round," Grant Tinker remembers, "and Mary Richards, instead of being divorced, became a girl arriving in Minneapolis just coming off a failed four-year affair, which sounds to me a little more tarnished than a divorce, but they liked that better." The network feared that the mass audience wouldn't accept the proposition that an attractive and competent woman on the far side of thirty had never been married. And far from being in the cultural vanguard himself, Allan Burns recalls, "It tells you a little bit about our own lack of awareness of the women's movement at that time, which was just starting, but our feeling was that if a girl was over thirty and unmarried, there had to be an explanation for such a freak of nature as that."

But the *Mary* show borrowed from cultural change in two quiet ways the creators had barely intended. At the core of the show, Mary was a career woman. She was also the heart of a workplace group. Burns had a theory that long-lasting comedies were "well populated"; they didn't depend on the radiant talent of a single star. For this purpose the workplace group was ideal. (One problem with the *Rhoda* spinoff later on, Burns thinks, was that Rhoda did not have enough noteworthy company.) A woman no longer had to derive her *raison d'être* from family embroilments; she could find emotions and personal dilemmas on the job. The WJM-TV staff was a quasi-family, really, with Lou Grant as the gruff, sentimental father and Mary as the good daughter, a woman independent enough to have her own life and thus appeal to younger women, but sufficiently pliant to entice and not threaten the males and housewives who stayed home Saturday night to watch her. No feminist pioneer, Mary still came from the shadows of the women's movement, while the workplace quasi-family comedy streaked with serious real-world issues became and remained a staple of the prime-time schedule because it drew energy from popular desires to find meaning on the job. Most women who worked—and watched—worked in factories, salesrooms, and clerical jobs, of course, but television appeals less by mirroring statistical reality than by evoking and satisfying plausible desire. All the better, then, that Mary's job was a bit glamorous, though far less so than the actress herself. Meanwhile, shifting middle-class mores were making it harder for Hollywood writers to imagine—and probably harder for mass audiences to accept—the nuclear family as an arena for weekly excitement.* The quasi-family workplace therefore not only matched a new cultural mood, and met the formal requirements of a successful sitcom, it also rushed into a vacuum.

In short, *Mary* would not easily have been conceived five or ten years earlier; less likely developed, given producers' notions of the state of the mass market; least likely scheduled; and probably not so ardently watched before working women, the women's movement, and the sensitivity-culture currents of the late sixties—call this ensemble of change the feminization of work—disrupted the older values and, indirectly, network executive culture. No one should argue, though, that the show's cultural fit by itself is what pushed it among the twenty-five top-rated shows for six years running. Certainly, at the beginning, the carry-over from Mary Tyler Moore's previous popularity must have helped enormously. The sparks that flew between her and Ed Asner's Lou Grant—"some twisted kind of love," Burns calls it—also carried an unanticipated charge. And scheduling certainly played its part in the show's success. Mike Dann had originally slated it for Tuesday nights at eight-thirty, between *The Beverly Hillbillies* and *Hee Haw*, and opposite the popular, youth-minded *Mod Squad*. When Dann quit, his latitude and up-

---

*Another sign of shifting tides: the transmogrifications in *The Doris Day Show*, once an automatic symbol of the kind of squeaky-clean show that writers like Allan Burns wanted to avoid. In 1968–69, Doris Day was a widow with two sons who had moved back to the family ranch from the big city. In 1969–70, foreshadowing Bob Wood's urban shift, she got a job as a secretary at a San Francisco magazine, and shuttled daily between farm and city. In 1970–71, she moved into the city altogether and began to write for the magazine. In 1971–72, aping the success of the *Mary* show, she shed her family altogether while continuing to write.

ward mobility blocked, Wood and the new programming chief, thirty-two-year-old Fred Silverman, listened to appeals from the *Mary* staff, not least from Mary herself, whom Wood had known since she was a child. (She was the niece of a KNXT executive he had worked with years before.) Wood and Silverman relocated the show to Saturday nights, where it was eventually joined by *All in the Family* and played to full houses for seven years.

M*A*S*H ultimately played on CBS for eleven years, ranking in the top ten all but two of them. More raucous and blatantly anti-authoritarian than *Mary,* but more genial and collective than *All in the Family,* it is also one of the most widely syndicated shows in TV history. Alan Alda's Hawkeye Pierce is a singular hero for television, since the functioning of the quasi-family of army surgeons doesn't depend on his leadership. But this long-running saga of antiheroes got onto the Wood-Silverman schedule in 1972 not because it sprang full-blown from the cultural mood, but because Twentieth Century–Fox and CBS were capitalizing on the smash success of the 1970 Robert Altman–Ring Lardner, Jr., film of the same name. In this sense *M*A*S*H* was "presold," and all the more so because Larry Gelbart agreed to write it. Gelbart was a prime comedy writer, with credits going back to the Sid Caesar–Imogene Coca *Your Show of Shows* and Bob Hope. In his early forties, and living in London, Gelbart was tempted back into television by the prospect of a serious series. Wood's CBS had already signaled to Gene Reynolds, a contract producer at Twentieth Century–Fox, that it might be interested in *M*A*S*H* under the right circumstances. Gelbart liked the movie, and after what he called "a lot, a lot, a lot of years being a pure comedy writer," his "internal gyroscope" was pointed toward something more serious. "I came to that time, not where I wanted to play or write *Hamlet,* but where I felt that comedy should have more than just the one dimension—it certainly should work on that level but it should also express feelings and emotions and situations that an audience really cares about." Gelbart had left Hollywood for England in 1963, and says, "I wasn't very active in expressing my feelings about the war, except for the odd demonstrations in Grosvenor Square, which hardly counts. So I think perhaps I was drawn toward something that would let me get this sort of tardy negative vote in."

Reynolds was an experienced, skillful producer, and Gelbart was pure gold for the network. Years later the NBC executive Perry Lafferty, who had been at CBS with Wood and Silverman, said that if someone else had come to him with an idea for a show about American doctors in the Korean War, he would have said, "Never. Bad concept. Terrible. What are you talking about?" The show sold without a pilot.

Obviously *M*A*S*H* was launched on a wave of antiwar sentiment. "We wanted to say that war was futile," Gelbart said, "to represent it as a failure on everybody's part that people had to kill each other to make a point. We wanted to say that when you take people from home they do things they would never do. They drink. They whore. They steal. They become venal. They become asinine, in terms of power. They get the clap. They become alcoholics. They become rude. They become sweet. They become tender. They become loving. We tended to make war the enemy without really saying who was fighting." Gelbart's favorite line was when Klinger, under fire, said, "Damn Truman, damn Stalin, damn everybody." *M*A*S*H* and its cast were so lovable, the American right never saw much payoff in blasting it for dangerous pacifist tendencies. "It was chic to be antiwar," Gelbart says. "You couldn't offend anybody."

After four years and ninety-seven episodes, Gelbart wearied of the grind and left the show. Over the years the cast turned over, but the attitudes represented by the ensemble remained the same. Later Gelbart feared that "by routinizing an acceptance of war, year in and year out, it essentially defeats the original purpose of the series. I would almost hope that there would be a way to be even blacker about what war does to people, rather than just to say—and I'm afraid it does, as it always did, but in the tenth year much more than in the first—that listen: Given the right buddies, and the right CO, and the right kind of sense of humor, you can muddle through."

*M*A*S*H* could indeed have been called *The Joy of Muddling Through.* Like much of mass culture, it attracted people for complex, even contradictory reasons, and was capable of reinforcing all manner of human motives. Mike Farrell, who played B. J. Hunnicutt, told me he got a couple of letters "which say, 'Boy, you guys make war look like fun,' and/or, 'After watching your show I've decided I'm going to sign up.' I read those and I kind of shake my head, and I've written back and said, 'I don't quite understand how you can watch our show and come to that conclusion.' We also got a wonderful letter from a kid who said that he had intended to be a professional soldier, and after watching our show over the years he had seen that that's not what he wants to do, and as a matter of fact he's decided to become a priest. We get an avalanche of letters that say everything."

The point was that, at the very least, gung-ho enlistees could watch *M*A*S*H* without being offended; as could authoritarian fathers and youthful liberals delight in *All in the Family;* and career women and sexist men in *The Mary Tyler Moore Show.* TV entertainment takes its design from social and psychological fissures: That is the deep, unspoken reason why writers always look for conflict at the heart of the tale. If the messages are susceptible to divergent interpretations, that is no failure for television. On the contrary, a show that couldn't be interpreted variously would slide into what Larry Gelbart calls

"electronic pamphleteering," whose left-liberal form is the archetypal violation of the television conventions. (Right-wing shows like
The FBI, though, could get special exemption.) This taboo unites
virtually the entire industry, even most critics and the regular audience. The so-called creative community shares with network executives the desire to entertain the maximum audience; the tension
usually comes when writers come up with racier, riskier, more idiosyncratic ideas of *how* to do it. Producers and writers as well as
network executives normally don't deliberate about how to market
a show to diverse audience segments, but the successful ones claim
to know in their bones how to do it. They acquire Gelbart's "internal
gyroscope," mandatory equipment in the world of popular entertainment.

In 1970–72, Bob Wood must have had such a gyroscope. He tore
up the CBS schedule and reassembled it well enough to carry CBS
to ratings victory through 1975. Like Norman Lear, like Jim Brooks
and Allan Burns, and Larry Gelbart, he half-recognized that in television success often comes from finding the main fault lines of value
conflict in the society, and bridging them. The successful shows
found ways to enshrine, confirm, finally to soothe even acute psychological conflicts: the ones that inhabit the same breast.

Sometimes research gave Bob Wood clues about how to do it. *The
Waltons,* for example, originated as a TV movie that Fred Silverman
spotted for series potential. Some executives wanted star insurance
—Henry Fonda was prominently mentioned—but Fonda wasn't interested. At this point, William Paley supported the series because he
thought its wholesome family sentimentality carried prestige. It
didn't hurt, though, that Oscar Katz, a longtime research executive,
embraced the show. At this point in the scheduling meeting, Katz
recalls, Bob Wood turned to Paley and said, "Oscar Katz here has an
interesting theory." Katz, who had a degree in psychology and had
been hired by Frank Stanton in 1938, made it his habit to read the
Yankelovich studies of campus attitudes in the sixties showing that
campus radicals were the precursors of communitarian, egalitarian
youth majorities. He saw youth as almost universally disaffiliated,
riddled with identity crises, laboring under the burden of a protracted adolescence. He observed that *The Last Picture Show* and
Romeo and Juliet were hit movies. Therefore, he was looking for a
program "where kids would learn what it was like to be a kid in a
different culture." That "different culture" was Walton's mountain in
days gone by, an idealized America tempered by Depression, when
a family could unite and the older generation helped the young
through their awkward stages. *The Waltons* would be a TV series
that smothered adolescent problems in soft-focus romanticism. It
could also appeal to the older, rural audience that was CBS's residual

strength. Even if Katz's argument served only to legitimize Paley's desire to have a single "prestige" show—which at this juncture in television history might have meant nothing more than no sex and no violence—it played its part. After a slow start, *The Waltons* went on to rank among the top twenty shows for five straight seasons.

Wood made his mistakes. "Relevant" realism didn't fly. His *Beacon Hill,* saturated with class distinctions in the manner of the British *Upstairs, Downstairs,* failed quickly. But his regime was singular in television history, and his successes changed the tone and texture of television comedy. What made Bob Wood a master marketer was his grasp of the elementary but elusive point that mass appeal was the sum of specific appeals—if not within each show, then in the schedule as a whole. "I never felt it was safe to be represented very strongly in one category at the expense of all other age categories," Wood said. "The idea is, if you can, to distribute your audience in equal incremental parts. You know, the young, the thirties, the forties, the fifties, the sixties. If you can spread it like peanut butter, even, across the bread, that's terrific."

A decade later, network executives still admired Wood's audacity, but forgot the particulars of his demographic strategy. They were losing their grip on the intricacy of public moods. Moreover, the rules of the game were now working against unusual shows, especially slow-starting shows that aimed to capitalize on cultural conflict by dredging culturally repressed material up to the surface.

Although *M*A*S*H* and *Archie Bunker's Place* (as well as the Lear spinoff *The Jeffersons*) were still hits after ten years, the producers' conventional wisdom was that neither *All in the Family* nor *Maude* would have gotten on the air in the Reagan years. Whether or not public sensibilities had changed, executives had grown more cautious, more impatient for quick results. Lear himself thought *All in the Family* could still have made a debut in the early eighties, but surmised that in the era of overnight ratings and network panic for quick results, it might well have been dumped after a month.*

In general the networks were taking fewer chances now. Like the country as a whole, their motto might have been: When in doubt, shift right. But this time the networks displayed the limits of their

---

*M*A*S*H had seen a weak first year, too, but was granted executive grace to "find its audience," which it did in a new time-slot the next fall. A few years later, the *Mary* spinoff *Lou Grant* also started poorly, and post-Wood CBS tried to soften the show. A few weeks into its first (1977) season, according to Allan Burns, CBS executives told the producers at a showdown meeting, "Fellas, fellas, what you're giving us is the *New York Times,* and what people read is the *Daily News.*" "Ed is a loser," another executive said. "He's not heroic enough." "They wanted Kojak," Burns says. But MTM chief Grant Tinker stood behind the show's essential premise, and CBS relented.

acumen, even as they define it. Where Bob Wood had distilled a marketing strategy from a cultural shift and found the right programs to make it stick, his successors in the next decade, with equal confidence but a more advanced anxiety, gambled on a new public mood and went awry.

CHAPTER 11

Shifting Right: Yesterday's Vietnam, Today's FBI

During 1979 and 1980, the network antennae were swiveling every which way in search of political omens. Among other projects, each network was developing a situation comedy set in long-taboo Vietnam. Scripts were being written for three potential series, of which two went to pilot in time for the 1981 season. But by the time the pilots were ready, a good number of network executives thought they had gotten hold of a hotter trend. The long-playing hostage drama was on in Iran, and ABC News was getting unexpectedly good ratings with an eleven-thirty news show called *America Held Hostage*. Amid widespread panic about Soviet military might, and a widely heralded national recovery from the agonies of the Vietnam War, Ronald Reagan was elected president in a landslide. Like much of the nation's media elite, many network executives in charge of series thought the country was moving to the right and television entertainment ought to move with it.

In the spring of 1980, CBS's young vice-president for dramatic program development, Scott M. Siegler, commissioned a pilot script for a proposed series to be called *The CIA*, and said "the time is right" for such a series. "America's moving to the right," he commented. "America will become more antiforeign, more tolerant of the U.S. protecting its interests abroad, no matter who is president." *The CIA* went through two implausible jerry-built pilot scripts, and got rejected.

At the same time, Siegler also ordered from Lorimar a pilot from a script by Sam Rolfe called *Quarrel,* about an American spy being tripped up, unbeknownst to him, by a Soviet mole who has penetrated Washington headquarters. Once a liberal, Rolfe had written *Have Gun, Will Travel* (including an episode allegorically denouncing the blacklist) and the détente-minded *The Man From UNCLE,* but had now moved toward neoconservative politics.

At a dinner party the following September, 1980, Brandon Tartikoff, the president of NBC Entertainment, realized that Ronald Reagan was going to win the coming election, and decided on the spot to buy the series *Walking Tall,* based on the movie about a law-and-order sheriff who walked softly and carried a very big stick through a small town in Tennessee. NBC had already committed to a new-style tough-cop show that came to be called *Hill Street Blues.* And when the network needed last-minute star vehicles to fill the 1981 schedule, James Arness, who had played Marshal Matt Dillon for twenty years on *Gunsmoke,* obliged with a series called *McClain's Law,* about an officer who comes out of retirement to avenge the death of a buddy.

In May of 1981, ABC decided to drop *American Dream* and to schedule for the fall *Today's FBI* and an Aaron Spelling series about a no-nonsense special tactical police unit, *Strike Force,* starring Robert Stack. "I think the country is looking for heroes," ABC Entertainment president Tony Thomopoulos told me not long thereafter, "looking for the belief that there are organizations that bring this country back to some basic national values." Thomopoulos quickly repeated the universal network premise about the need for general appeal: "You don't program to one group of people, and that's the difficult part of network programming. But what we're trying to get across is the message that there is a spirit in this country that is looking for a return to some basic values." At all three networks, as we've already seen, the new slates of TV movies reflected the same premise. All these executives thought these new tactics, among others, could push them to the front of the eighties' biggest parade.

This thinking did not go unchallenged in network programming offices. Scott Siegler's immediate boss, Harvey Shephard, a former advertising and CBS research man, told me that spring, "I'm not really sure that the country has moved as much to the right as people believe. I'm not sure whether [Reagan's landslide] was really a move to the right, or whether it was really a rejection of Carter. Oh, admittedly, the country has moved somewhat more to the right, but I really am not sure that that really translates into the public's unconsciously saying, 'Now that the country has moved to the right, I'm in the mood to watch John Wayne, I'm not in the mood to watch Burt Reynolds." He thought "economic hardships, inflation, and things like that" were more important than the country's political direction, and that they would whet the public taste for fantasy, "as evidenced by the types of movies that are doing well."

Meanwhile, at NBC, Scott Siegler's counterpart and good friend, Stu Sheslow, like Siegler a veteran of the antiwar movement of a decade before, had been pitched *The CIA* first, and turned it down. "They've been villains too long," he said about the CIA. "I hate the CIA. Everything that was wrong with Vietnam was the CIA. They were not nice people." On the other hand, he approved a pilot about a rebellious international freelance operative who contracted to do dirty work for the CIA, then thought better of it, and ended up fighting against them. (This pilot, *The Seal,* didn't sell.)

At ABC, right after the affiliates' meeting, the movie powerhouse Brandon Stoddard noticed that the projects he'd chosen for 1981 and thereafter didn't fit the John Wayne pattern top management had triumphantly announced. He chuckled, wondered if this meant "big trouble for this office," and told himself, "I just sort of make them the way I see 'em, and about trends and things like that, I don't know. It's kind of difficult to go build a show around the mood of the country. We tend to go with a movie that we think is interesting and exciting and different, and is easily promotable. It's very hard to come up with those under any circumstances, much less match the mood of the country, whatever that mood may be. The other thing is, you're constantly surprised by the mood of the country." He also thought executives sometimes simply like a show and justified the choice by saying, "Weelll, I'll find a reason for it called 'the mood of the country.'"

This skepticism retarded the rightward trend, but didn't stop it. It wasn't an orchestrated party line, but a soft tendency, the latest in a long string of improvised, *ad hoc* theories. Nonetheless, the shift right swept through the 1981 development season. What came of the shows that resulted? Only one of the Vietnam series got on the air, and succumbed quickly. Meanwhile, two drafts of the pilot scripts for *The CIA* were so wooden the pilot was never made. The *Quarrel* pilot was judged stiff, and the series didn't sell. *Walking Tall* went on the air in midseason, rated badly, and was dropped by NBC by late spring. The James Arness show did poorly as well. And although ABC's rhetoric outdistanced the programs based on it, *Today's FBI* and *Strike Force* did go on the air in the fall of 1981, only to rate low enough to be canceled within the year. What was supposed to be the year's big trend was a commercial bust, while the Vietnam shows, leftish and otherwise, didn't get much chance. And, as we shall see, NBC's *Hill Street Blues,* which the networks might have interpreted

as a distinguished (and eventually successful) way to capitalize on
law-and-order sentiment in a more or less liberal fashion, was instead
defined as an inimitable fluke. No one emerged as the Bob Wood of
the eighties. By the end of the fall season of 1981, the same executives who had affirmed the rightward shift were buying Harvey Shephard's reasoning and repackaging the latest hits: fantasy à la *Raiders
of the Lost Ark*, and male "hunks" à la *Magnum, P.I.* The trend was
dead, long live the next.

With so much politics in the air, the early eighties were an abnor-
mal moment in television history, but from the workings of the short-
lived rightward trend, much can be learned of the everyday methods
of an industry helter-skelter in search of phantom popularity.

In network culture, opportunism is the cardinal rule. "There's not
a very deep commitment out here to ideas, ideals," says the writer
Larry Gelbart in the definitive Hollywood understatement. But precisely because Hollywood's movers and shakers are more committed
to saving precious metals than to saving souls, they cannot afford to
neglect the available clues to the mystery of mass interest. Not only
executives but most of the "creative community" deem it an occupational liability to be committed to any particular set of ideas about
the world; they are wary of being afflicted by blind spots, and losing
touch with the verities of convention and the signs emanating from
the marketplace. That is why most program executives say that they
try to keep their own politics, if they own up to any at all, out of their
work. "I have politics," commented NBC's Stu Sheslow, "but I don't
bring them to work with me." Even more typically, ABC movie chief
Brandon Stoddard says, "I really don't have much political attitudes."

"In college I was apolitical at a time when everybody else was
political," Brandon Tartikoff told me. Even those who were antiwar
in college, like Sheslow and Len Hill, learn to adapt to a network
environment in which national and international politics are not
much discussed, let alone synchronized. (When asked about politics,
executives are liable to assume that what is meant is office politics:
who has it in for whom, who is gaining on whom, who has the inside
track.) In such an atmosphere, vague notions about the public mood
slide by unexamined, and the networks get panicked by predisposi-
tion and whim. Notions about mood and marketable genre tend to
swing quickly out of control.

Executives try to stay loose, but after all they also stay attuned to
the tone top management is setting, a tone that may barely, if at all,
be stated as "policy." All junior executives develop a corporate radar,
of course, but I suspect the culture industry cultivates a specially
refined sense of what top management seems to want. Dissent, when

it occurs, is customarily muted. The in-house radar matches the external equipment that points toward the target audience. An industry devoted to satisfying abstract audiences does not usually attract individuals with firm moral positions in the first place. This industry that thrives on getting its products liked is inhabited by managers who advance by being liked. Before they ever needed to harmonize with a show-business style, the vast majority grew up in middle-class homes, where both child-rearing and education emphasized "getting along with people" from an early age. The veteran executive Ethel Winant criticized the business for selecting people who care too much about being liked, "people raised to reason and be flexible and listen and get along," she told me wearily. What results is a culture of ingratiation, in which sweeping assumptions about entertainment easily become inflexible and executives drift equally easily into market miscalculation.

The gregarious, self-marketing, jokey style is standard. Executives whirl from meeting to meeting, and even alone they are rarely alone: There are executives and even producers who routinely take seventy-five or a hundred phone calls a day. As in all sales worlds, they know at least the rituals of being tuned in to others; they can simulate speaking other people's languages. This quintessential occupational skill does not appear to be authentic listening to another human being, not real and reciprocal empathy, for the most part, but a mechanical function that the business requires. It is the "male" function of listening-for-a-purpose, not the "female" listening that goes with authentic recognition. Executives and producers gain reputations for "giving good phone."

Corporate radar is mandatory equipment for the long career through the industry. Although writers can get away with being a bit reclusive as long as they deliver their scripts on time and to order, program executives will have trouble exercising power if they don't know how to be sociable, and how to avoid giving offense. In these upper reaches of interpersonal marketing, the highest form of sociability is ingratiation. As they work their way up, executives strain to keep from offending anyone important: their bosses, top producers and studio executives and agents, the hottest writers, even competitors. Last year's competitor, B, might be this year's boss, or crony. Next year, A might have taken advantage of his back-end deal and gone into business as an indie prod; now he has to pitch his project to B. This behind-the-scenes culture of ingratiation matches Hollywood's larger and more public culture of ingratiation, with its innumerable awards, its mutual admiration societies, its exaggerated public gestures of affection, its indiscriminately effusive adjectives ("Fabulous!" "Very fabulous!") and exclamations ("Love it!"), all masking the supremely competitive cattiness of private feeling. The networks' attunement to the market is altogether pragmatic. A likes individualism, but it's not that he's especially interested in moving the country rightward, only that, as a businessman, now, today, at his desk, he faces the irreducible question of what notions to float, what concepts to put into development. The much-wooed audience does not make "demands." Groups don't fire off telegrams asking for a sitcom about waitresses working for a gruff diner owner; people don't tell pollsters they're pining for intelligent comedy about irreverent army doctors in Korea. The proverbial mass doesn't say that "it" wants to think about the war in Vietnam, or that "it" prefers not to. Public opinion, such as it is, speaks with a vast silence, or with a background yammer that is incessant, indecipherable, contradictory. What kind of guidance is this for cultural suppliers?

The yammer guarantees, though, that executives, producers, and writers are going to turn their antennae to the murmurs of public concern that come home to them, to the preoccupations that seep into their private worlds. They do not often go looking for issues; it would be more true to say that the issues go looking for them. If an issue makes headlines in the *New York Times* for months and years, if it makes the cover of *Time* or *Newsweek*, if one starts hearing about it at the tennis courts, if the neighbors' kids are into it, if one's wife hears about it at the hairdresser's in Beverly Hills, if one's daughter comes home from Berkeley for Thanksgiving and is talking about it, then no mystery about it: The issue is going to seep into the common lore, fairly begging to be concocted into the stuff of entertainment. And so it happens that the networks are often developing shows on similar themes, even with similar approaches. During his incarnation as a top supplier, Grant Tinker said, "There are always these coincidences. I mean, you just try to do a show about a one-legged clerk in a department store, and you are stunned to read in the trades that somebody else is doing that. I never understand how it happens but it happens a lot." It happens routinely in a small, dense world; the themes come out of the same cultural air.

Inevitably the "creative community" thought about the Vietnam War. Some marched against it, gave money to campaigns against it. A few signed newspaper ads against it, and a few spoke up for it. But while the war was on, the controversy was so fierce that the networks could never bring themselves to find a fictional container for it. News was different: The news could even be permitted to displease Washington, for the news was charged with the responsibility to inform. But no one running network entertainment believed that entertainment bore much, if any, responsibility for enlightenment.

During the years of mass demonstrations and counterdemonstrations and ever more violent polarization, no one could imagine how

to broach the unbroachable without offending at least one large bloc
of potential audience. No series set in Vietnam, or centrally concerned with the way America lived out the war, got even to pilot
stage at the networks while the war was going on. The closest was
M*A*S*H, a belated symbolic Vietnam set against the backdrop of
Korea, a war on which strong American feelings had long since
subsided. "Vietnam was like a plague," says the TV writer Howard
Rodman (*Naked City, Harry O*). "If anyone touched it, your arm
would rot away." Nor did a single made-for-television movie touch
it. Even Hollywood features ducked the war. Only John Wayne was
at once ideologue enough to let his political commitment outrun his
business sense, and bankable enough to raise the capital to make a
Vietnam movie; but his *Green Berets* failed dismally. The war was
like smog: simply there, taken for granted, outside the frame.

But it was also inevitable that, once the air had cleared, the networks would sidle up to the subject. The war had usurped an enormous part of the consciousness of millions, especially the generation
who, by the late seventies, were moving into middle management at
the networks and starting to make a name for themselves as producers. After the war finally ended, without resolving, in 1975, they
went to see *Coming Home*, read books like Michael Herr's *Dispatches* and Robert Stone's *Dog Soldiers*, and observed their considerable if not blockbuster success. Finally, *Apocalypse Now* and *The Deer
Hunter* broke commercial ground. As Grant Tinker said, "The Vietnam thing lasted so long, it's such a hunk of our recent history, that
it isn't surprising that everybody finally got around to it."

The networks got around to it in the sitcom form, which imposed
a distance from the grinding horror of combat itself. And stunningly,
each network sitcom that went into development in 1979–80 revolved around characters who *reported* the war, interposing still
another filter between the audience and the agony of the war itself.
Five years after the war had lurched to its ignominious, strangely
anticlimactic end, the sting was leaving; yet the war was still live
enough as material that each network, calculating independently,
thought it better to err on the side of a relatively inexpensive trial
than to commit the potentially costlier error of missing out on a gold
mine. "There was a time before that," ABC's Tom Werner said,
"whether it was a year or two or ten, that I think the feeling was that
the situation still was so raw that it couldn't be dealt with in a way
that would be comfortable and successful." The muffled, distanced
sitcom format seemed a good compromise risk with a high potential
payoff. In this sort of calculation, each network has to keep an eye
cocked toward the competition and their likely reactions. The networks are like three oil companies who, after all the research is done,
take note of where the competition is drilling, on the theory that

maybe someone knows something we don't. They subscribe, in effect, to the same geological newsletter, which has just noted the presence of huge reserves off the coast of, say, Guatemala, whereupon they each, "independently," lease large pieces of Central America. The creative community reads the same cultural newsletter.

Gary David Goldberg was a child of the sixties, a onetime Brandeis student and actor who, with his lover, had trouped around the world and then started the Organic Daycare Center in Berkeley. He had started writing comedy scripts "on spec," then wrote for Bob Newhart and the Tony Randall show at the MTM company, and moved to regular writing at *Lou Grant,* where he was responsible for some of the most wrenching social dramas, including one about an unemployed Vietnam veteran. Next, Goldberg developed a short-lived comedy, *The Last Resort,* based on his experience as a waiter. "When you do a show," he said, "you're spending twelve, fourteen hours a day on it, and I wanted to do comedy that had some substance to it." He liked the idea of the romance of journalists in Vietnam, he said, "and when I started going around, doing the research, [reporters] said that really it was funny over there. As black as it was, there was tremendous humor."

Goldberg proposed his Saigon news bureau idea to Grant Tinker, and Tinker appreciated the fact that there were, in his words, "*M*A*S*H* suggestions in the thing." "I had confidence in Gary," he went on, "so we went over to CBS. They had much more reluctance, certainly, than I had, and they wished that Gary would come back with something else. Gary is a very independent guy, and he said, 'No, this is the one I want to do.' And ultimately they said, 'Okay, if you feel that strongly, try it.'" In fact, CBS was sufficiently impressed with Goldberg's work that in 1979 they were ready to offer him and MTM together a series commitment, "pay or play," meaning that they would go to pilot and pay MTM for a full thirteen episodes no matter how many or few were aired.

Goldberg wrote what was to have been a half-hour script for a show called *Bureau*—actually about twenty-two minutes—but it came out much too long. At this point Tinker suggested that rather than make "brutal cuts," Goldberg open it out to an hour. After all, the style was really too serious for a sitcom. "I went back to CBS," Tinker said, "and I made a very good case for it. I had sold myself and I sold Gary and I sold CBS and I can sell myself sitting here now that it was a good idea." Tinker at MTM was without doubt "a topnotch salesman in the field," said CBS's Herman Keld, "with his velvety voice—a master of the sales pitch."*

---

*In fact, Keld thought that if Tinker had still been running MTM in 1982, he could have sold CBS on renewing *Lou Grant* for one more year.

Goldberg thereupon wrote an hour-long version of *Bureau*. In the MTM style, workplace relations were central. In something of a reprise of *Lou Grant*, the main characters in this news bureau were the grizzled managing editor, Matthews, and a spunky, go-getting young male reporter, Hartman. Hartman along with other reporters liked to bait the army's buffoon colonel at the daily press conferences universally known as "the 5:00 Follies." Hartman said he was in Vietnam because it was the biggest story going, and because he believed in Frank Capra movies—he wanted to tell the people the truth. He got his tips from a friendly, whining army press attaché from Princeton.

The *Bureau* pilot didn't cohere. It lurched between moments of pathos—Matthews lugubrious at a party: "When all is said and done, war sucks"; a GI dying on the battlefield—and moments of broad comedy. "Something about the balance of it wasn't right," Tinker said later. "CBS was not quite sure what it was. It wasn't a situation comedy and it wasn't a dramatic show. And they had the reservations about Vietnam." Some roles were indifferently cast; the actor who played Hartman was "kind of heavy," Tinker thought. The show tested Below Average, with three major criticisms included in research vice-president Arnold Becker's report: "First and foremost, viewers simply found *Bureau* a dull, slow-moving program . . . too much talk and too little action . . . story lines jumbled together." Second, "the program sermonized. Most of the talk was on one subject: War is hell. The third major criticism came from those who said they would have preferred to put the discomforting subject of the war in Vietnam behind them." If *Bureau* were to be salvaged, Becker wrote, "it is extremely important that each episode include a fully developed central story line. . . . Credibility should probably be enhanced if the Bureau contingent, most notably Hartman and Matthews, were not so totally consumed with the moral dilemmas of their time, and . . . the military personnel . . . [did] not emerge as a bunch of single-minded automatons." Becker told me later he thought *Bureau* "was so anti-Establishment as to be, I would imagine, offensive to the average American. There were no heroes; the army was the villain. The good guys were the villains and the bad guys were the heroes."

B. Donald ("Bud") Grant, the head of CBS Entertainment, agreed. Even at the script stage, he thought *Bureau* was not only antiwar but also "antigovernment, anti-army. It wasn't balanced at all. I had problems with that. We talked with them about it and I think Gary Goldberg felt that we were overreacting, that it would be handled in dialogue and softened in performance. But it turned out that it wasn't." The film, he said, was "very well done," but perhaps he was simply being kind.

"I personally liked *Bureau*," said another program executive, "but I don't think I would have put it on the air." He didn't speak up for it in executive councils. Herman Keld thought the pilot "preachy" and "heavy-handed." "I cannot think of anybody who liked it" at the scheduling meeting, he said. His personal reaction, moreover, was that *Bureau* "attacked the integrity of the military" and "was rather a low blow," although he insisted, "I'm not exactly a warlike person. I thought I would rather have the West Pointers, the people who have Honor, Duty, and Country as their motto, than this character who produced the movie, on my side. I was rather upset about the whole thing." The tenor of the scheduling meeting was that America was simply not going to be entertained by a show set in Vietnam. "You could rèad the subtext [of the discussion]," one executive said, "as really, deeply, about the war." In short, nothing militated for *Bureau*.

Tinker and Goldberg concluded that the one-hour version was a mistake, but CBS was still sufficiently impressed with Goldberg and MTM that they were willing to try a half-hour version—with the stipulation that it be "balanced." For Bud Grant, this was a question of market appeal as well as principle. "I don't think that we should advocate on television any one particular point of view: social, political, whatever. I think that we ought to examine both points of view. And by examining both points of view, we have conflict, and conflict is the essence of drama or comedy. I think if it were just a polemic it would be propaganda, and I think it would also be soft; I don't think it would have that necessary conflict. The conflict between Archie Bunker and Meathead, let's say. I don't think that *All in the Family* would be as successful if it didn't have that conflict: if Mike Stivic was a member of the American Nazi party." I pressed Grant to say to what extent he was expressing a *moral* position about television's uses, to what extent a *market* position. "I think it's basically what I think is marketable," he said. "I mean, I have my own values. Everybody has their own values. The guy who is making Chevrolet cars, let's say, may have Cadillac tastes, but he's making Chevrolet cars because he knows that that's what's marketable. And that's basic. Business is a business. We are out to reach the most number of people in a wholesome manner." Of course, "in a wholesome manner" is also a moral position. And while Cadillac tastes may yield to Chevrolet marketability, any General Motors executive who denounces the private automobile and advocates a crash program for mass transit will find himself out of a job.

The CBS program executives laid down the law specifically to Gary Goldberg: Build up the army press attaché. As Bud Grant put it, "What we came up with was a gimmick whereby the press attaché would say to Alan Hartman, 'On the record or off the record?' 'On the record' means army all the way: 'No, we're not napalming that village.' But 'off the record' with Alan Hartman, there would be that humanity that would show him not as a totally committed army officer but someone who does have some basis of humanity."

Bureau II was written to suit by two MTM contract writers Goldberg hired, and it was jokey sitcom with the obligatory sound track. The original Hartman begged off to act in NBC's *Kent State* movie, and Tinker and Goldberg went to a much lighter actor. Hartman was now milder, sweeter, and less cynical about the war. The bureau sported a new, ingenue reporter. The press attaché was now so "humanized" he was wholly implausible, going far beyond the line of duty to help Hartman get his story. The colonel was no longer covering up for army policy in Vietnam; he was now the cliché army brass of every American war comedy. The plot was as frothy as it was simplified: Greedy Vietnamese soldiers were switching toasters for grenades shipped to the front, leaving the infantry—including one GI who saved Hartman from enemy attack—ill equipped in the foxholes. "It's a situation that could be in any war," said Richard Dysart, the character actor who played Matthews. "It had nothing to do with Vietnam."

No one was happy with this second version. Badly directed and "not hard funny," Grant Tinker thought. "A shitty half-hour pilot," he called it, then corrected himself to call it "an okay show but not good enough." Goldberg didn't like the second script himself. To make matters worse, after all the changes, *Bureau* II still tested Below Average. Arnold Becker's report said: "Although viewers had no strong objections, neither did they find it particularly enjoyable or entertaining." They found the show "slow-moving, without enough action or humor"; the plot, though simple, still confusing and disrupted; the plot resolved too soon, and resolved, to boot, by the army, not the hero. The only character who tested well in both versions was the press attaché. In short, the show had lost its political edge without becoming commercial. *Bureau* was dead.

NBC's entry in the half-hour Vietnam sweepstakes was the only one to get on the air. It started when Norman Steinberg and Marvin Kupfer met at a party on New Year's Eve, 1979, and discovered they were both fans of Michael Herr's Vietnam chronicle, *Dispatches.* Steinberg was a comedy writer, vintage Mel Brooks. In fact, he had worked with Brooks on *Blazing Saddles* and a short-lived Robin Hood send-up, *When Things Were Rotten,* for ABC. Kupfer, a former *Newsweek* correspondent in Biafra, was producing *The Paper Chase,* which despite good reviews was coming to the end of its rope on CBS. The two men talked about doing a black-comedy feature film about the press corps in Vietnam. "However," Steinberg recalled later, "at that exact moment in history, [the film director] Arthur Penn was in the Philippines looking for locations for a Larry Gelbart film that was to be done at Columbia, called *Film at Eleven*, about the foreign press corps, and which never got made. So we said, 'Well, that ain't going to work. So let's do a television thing.' " They did some research on the armed forces television staff, people they conceived to have kept "a certain sense of antic comedy" to get through the war. They sold the idea to Warner, where Steinberg had a deal, and Warner in turn sold it to NBC.

"Our conception was always that it was a drama with comedic overtones," Steinberg said, "that we would never trivialize this war. The enemy would always be out there; there would always be people dying, albeit you're not going to see bodies falling out of the control booth. It's not a situation comedy." Nevertheless, *6:00 Follies* was developed in NBC's comedy department under Michael Zinberg, a hard-driving Texan who had been in the army himself. Step led to step: Zinberg approved the pilot script, Silverman liked the cast, and NBC made a short order of six shows.

The concept became more blurred in production. Kupfer, who had never done comedy, tended to be serious, along with three of the four staff writers, while Steinberg was more prone to fun. The producers and writers had strong differences, although positions were fluid.

On one occasion, Steinberg had the idea of making a story from the fact that one of Vietnam's major exports was duck feathers. One of the *Follies* people would get the staff overinvested in duck-feather futures, whereupon a major duck farm would be overrun by the North Vietnamese army, and the market would collapse. Steinberg turned the idea over to staff writer Erik Tarloff, who thought that it was "comic gold," that it would be "as dishonest to try to make this premise serious as it would be, generally, to treat the Vietnam war frivolously." Accordingly, Tarloff proposed a romp episode in the manner of *Duck Soup*, including kidnapped ducks and a ransom note containing a feather snapped in two, only to have Steinberg shoot the idea down as "too silly." The network wanted to show what Tarloff called "one big happy family, like Mary Tyler Moore in Vietnam." Writer John Steven Owen, who had been on a gunboat in Vietnam, wanted to convey the troops' "camaraderie," their "desperate humor" along with their "sense of futility" ("we never did understand why we were there"); he wanted "*M*A*S*H* in Saigon." Tarloff thought Kupfer and Steinberg wanted to evade the rights and wrongs of the war. " 'War is horrible' was the line." He thought it ended up "wishy-washy liberal"; Owen called it "a little silly." Meanwhile, the network was pressing to lighten the show, to cut back on combat footage, stay away from jokes about the Thieu regime or discussion of the enemy's rationale, and to highlight T&A from Candy, the bosomy weathergirl. Zinberg, a conservative, thought "it was too put-downish, too sarcastic" about the army, and moreover it wasn't funny enough. "It fell apart in the execution. The characters all were cardboard."

Cable and Preview House tests agreed. "It tested terribly everyplace," reported NBC research executive Al Ordover, "the pits." Fred Silverman decided to stitch together two episodes to make an hour-long premiere, and ran it opposite Mikhail Baryshnikov in April of 1980. "We thought it would go through the roof against Baryshnikov," Ordover said. Dance is supposed to be forbiddingly elitist and "low concept." Baryshnikov drew a low 22 share, but *6:00 Follies* was sunk nevertheless.

Steinberg blamed promotion. Ads ran nationwide the day before the airing, saying: "Meet those wild and wacky guys who brought you the news in Vietnam." His guys weren't wild and wacky, but they weren't much of anything else. Weak anti-Establishment jokes affirmed that there was racism in high military places and the government lied, but the characters were as fluffy as the gags. The show was long on dead stretches, long on exposition to set up the gags, long on high-pitched cackles, and short on vitality. Timing was ungainly even by television standards, and some of the acting was remarkably amateurish: One southern accent kept melting away like wax in the sunshine. The shots were all symmetrical, the camera immobile, the dialogue static.

The network ran off some of the six episodes during the summer, in order to recoup losses with advertising revenue,* and settled into desultory postmortems. Perry Lafferty, who had opposed the show all along, felt vindicated: "I don't think people want to hear about Vietnam. I think it was destined for failure simply because I don't think it's a funny war." Stu Sheslow, promoted to replace Zinberg as head of NBC drama development, agreed, and also extemporized that there was no one to root for: "The war is fucked up, and we're doing a show about a fucked-up war. Whereas *M*A*S*H* is a story about a family of surgeons who are trying to save lives. They are skillful doctors in a crazy situation, but when they go into that medical arena, they are the best. . . . The *6:00 Follies* was a lie to start with. It was what the army's point of view of the war was. What they were reporting was a lie. They were trying to get the truth across, but the

---

*To make back their investments of up to $2 million in development and production costs, the networks usually run off their failed pilots during the summer. For some reason, though, CBS never aired its *Bureau* pilots.

truth was a lie. Everything about it was convoluted."

"It convinced me," Norman Steinberg said later, "to get the fuck out of television." He went back to work on a screenplay about the good old days of television comedy, *My Favorite Year*.

ABC was the late entry in what the comedy writer Michael Elias calls "a Vietnam sweepstakes." Early in 1980, NBC was about to air *6:00 Follies*, and CBS had already developed *Bureau*. "ABC had to have one," Elias says, "because the higher executives are going to look at the program development people and say, 'Where's your show about Vietnam? What is this? How come we don't have one?' All right, they'll get one." They went to Elias and his partner, Rich Eustis, and commissioned a pilot script with the working title, *Bringing It Home*. "I don't think they ever had any intention to put it on," Elias said later. By the time I interviewed ABC executives about *Bringing It Home*, a year later, they had trouble remembering the entire affair.

This practice of defensive buying is not uncommon, although network executives don't like to speak of it. Network A may decide to develop a project because B is known to be doing something like it; A may try to get to the finish line first, or simply hold the imitation in reserve, keeping start-up time to a minimum. Or A may reason it can fox B into abandoning its halfhearted attempt. In the spring of 1981, for example, one well-known writer got a call from a high-ranking network executive asking him if he wanted to write a script tracing the story of a young man from the ghetto struggling to grow up within the law. The writer was a liberal who had been urging the networks to discover everyday black life, and so he listened avidly as the executive went on in considerable detail about what was evidently a specific story about a specific youth. Details of the young man's life piled up as the executive went on to say that one day this youth, on the verge of success, was going to . . . disappear, whereupon his body would be found: He was one of the victims of the Atlanta child-killer. Around the same time, an indie prod, also a man of the left, heard that a different network was planning to develop a movie about the Atlanta child-killings. Independently both writer and producer were horrified; couldn't the networks depict the lives of urban blacks, in dramatic form, without such ghoulish exploitation? The producer set out to try to talk his executive friend out of this cruel idea. Don't worry, the executive told him, it's only a defensive buy. The man didn't want his boss in New York to call up and say, "So-and-so is developing a movie about the Atlanta killings, why aren't we?"

Elias and Eustis were plausible choices for an entry in the Vietnam sweepstakes, and they took the project very seriously indeed. These prolific, experienced, commercial comedy writers were in considerable demand for screenplays. Elias was credited on the money-making

The Jerk and *The Frisco Kid;* the two together on *Serial.* Eustis, a
Canadian, with earlier partners had written episodes of comedies
ranging from *The Beverly Hillbillies* and *Green Acres* to *The Dick
Van Dyke Show,* and written and produced variety shows for Dean
Martin, Glen Campbell, and John Denver. Elias was a thoughtful,
rabbinical-looking man in his early forties with a worn, unsmooth
face. He was on the left, well read, and indeed something of an
egghead by Hollywood standards. He read the *New York Review of
Books,* and the day I met him The Clash's *Sandinista!* was set right
next to his cassette player. He had gone to St. John's College, worked
as an actor and nightclub comic, and done a political cabaret act
funny and commercial enough to get him on the Johnny Carson
show. Elias wrote episodes of *All in the Family* and *The Mary Tyler
Moore Show,* and produced one of Norman Lear's short-lived comedies, the politically disputatious *All's Fair.* Then he teamed up with
Eustis to produce and write an even briefer 1977 sitcom called *Szysznyk,* starring Ned Beatty as a retired marine sergeant running a
ghetto community center. Elias and Eustis were no strangers to
network political wars.*

Network executives are loath to tell outsiders why they contract
with anyone in particular, yet surely what must have interested ABC
was above all Elias's and Eustis's substantial track records as comedy
writers who were comfortable with political issues. ABC's tack, as
Elias remembers it, was to say, "We want a hard-hitting show, like
M*A*S*H, about the war in Vietnam, about the people who covered
it." The network was already sitting on a property, a treatment
optioned by two Paramount producers about correspondents in Vietnam, written by a former Saigon reporter. And so, in a not uncommon Hollywood deal, the network arranged a marriage, or in this
case a merger. Elias and Eustis, properly concerned about where
power would rest, were assured of creative control. They would be
in charge as executive producers, with "created by" credit and thus

---

*In one early episode they wrote, Szysznyk had to cope with the brother of one of the
ghetto regulars, a black youngster who had been away a long time . . . because, it
turned out, he had skipped out on the marines during the Vietnam War and hastened
to Stockholm. Szysznyk, learning the truth, threw him out of the community center.
Eventually the two of them happened to meet in a bar, got into a serious political
argument, and Szysznyk eventually saw the young man's point of view and forgave
him. It was substantial and touching. One CBS executive had tried to talk Elias and
Eustis into delaying this episode until later in the season, when the show would be
"better established" and the audience would presumably accept such goings-on from
a familiar character. "We said, 'We're not making things up,' " Elias recalled. " 'It's
something that exists. It's not radical. It's consistent with the amnesty program. People
accept it from President Ford.' " (After the episode aired, the CBS executive told them
it had been a good idea after all.)

a dominant financial position. The other two producers would be Ed Palmer, an experienced hand, and Stephen Dart, the son of the millionaire businessman, free-enterprise crusader, and longtime member of the Ronald Reagan kitchen cabinet, Justin Dart. Stephen's politics, Elias thought, "were more moderate than his father's," and though periodically there were differences inside this network-made marriage, this was not to be a big problem for Elias and Eustis. "Both were swell fellows," said Elias later, and in the initial backing and filling negotiations about the form of the show, Dart and Palmer were supportive. All Elias and Eustis had to do was keep some semblance of the original characters.

From the start, Elias recalls, "We made clear [to ABC] what our politics were, how we felt about the war and America's involvement, and it didn't seem to bother them. They echoed in fact: 'Oh, it was awful.' We said, 'Our characters are funny, and the situations they find themselves in are funny. It's black humor. But also, it is very important that the characters have opinions about the war. M*A*S*H is fine, it's really terrific, and it's made a real contribution. Our show has to go a step further, which is that the characters have to discuss and be involved in the politics of that war. Otherwise it's timeless, it's mindless.' "

Rich Eustis remembers dickering about the form of the show, telling ABC, "We're terrified of taking something as important as Vietnam and trivializing it with a twenty-two-minute sitcom. We don't want to be known as the guys who have turned Vietnam into another cute comedy, you know. So we said, if we're going to write it, it has to be an hour. That will give us time to develop characters and themes to a certain extent, and it was going to be an hour, single-camera film. And they said okay. But before it got written, we had more meetings, and they kept on saying they wanted to do it as a half hour. And we kept saying no. And then the project sort of died for a while. We finally were convinced by them that we could get what we wanted accomplished in a half-hour single camera film."

The point at issue seemed technical rather than political, but Eustis thought the show's purpose was at stake. Shooting with a single camera is like shooting a movie; every shot is set up independently, making it possible to do scenes of any length. There cannot be a studio audience, because it would get into the shot when the camera changes point of view and direction. The standard half-hour sitcom format, on the contrary, is shot with three or even four cameras rolling at once, from different angles, on a single set. The shooting goes much faster because the action doesn't have to stop for new sets, new camera setups, and the protracted relighting new scenes entail. In the three-camera style, as Eustis says, "You've got to do a scene that's at least three or four minutes long, and you've got to keep repeating the same sets, and so everything has to play like a little stage play." Three- and four- camera shows are shot in front of studio audiences, and initially, at least, that is what ABC seemed to want. "They saw it still as a bunch of wild and crazy guys in Vietnam, with three hundred people sitting there, and a live laugh track." They finally agreed on a compromise; a half hour shot with a single camera, like *M*A*S*H*.

Elias and Eustis went off to write their script, and it was not about wild and crazy guys in Vietnam, though as a onetime writer for Steve Martin, Elias certainly knew how to write those sorts of guys and their gags. This show involved a houseful of more or less authentic journalistic types in Saigon: Devlin, a wise-guy independent (the hero); a newly arrived female; a German photographer; a self-dramatizing TV reporter. The house was owned by a Vietnamese businessman whose brother was a Vietcong colonel. When asked, "Ever hear from him?" he replied "Oh, sure. Whenever he in town he call me. We have dinner."

The pilot script was a crisscross of episodes, thick with the average kind of gags, saturated with characters who were, well, *characters*, definitely sitcom. However, the serious story line concerned Devlin's discovery that the United States Air Force was secretly bombing Cambodia. Devlin's investigation of the bombing and the coverup was based loosely on the true story of the *New York Times*'s William Beecher and his report on that bombing in 1969, much amplified later in the British journalist William Shawcross's account, *Sideshow*. While this part of the script took up only three out of forty-five pages, in Elias's mind it was central, as in fact Beecher's report, though not followed up in the American press, was central to the journalists' achievement during the Vietnam War. Indirectly it was also a step toward Watergate, for Nixon and Henry Kissinger read it, called in J. Edgar Hoover, and together set in motion the administration's first leak-plugging wiretap operation. "It's a great moment," as Elias said, "really juicy."

The other threads dangling through the main narrative seemed almost to obscure it, though only direction and editing would have told the tale. In one thread, the self-dramatizing TV man, scratched during combat, recreated his skin-deep martyrdom for the cameras. The main subplot concerned a young truck driver who worked at transporting paper goods—forms, towels, napkins, and toilet paper —to government offices in Saigon. A reporter built a story about the kid, saying he risked his life to deliver sensitive papers to the highest diplomatic levels. Toward the end of the show, the kid tried to talk the reporter out of filing the story. He was no hero and didn't want to offend his Quaker parents. The kid got in his truck, hit a land mine, and was blown to bits. The reporter filed his cliché story about the inadvertent heroism of innocence. And then back to Devlin, who closed the show at a military press briefing asking, "Why are American B-52s bombing Cambodia?" Freeze frame.

A vast innovation the show was not. Most of its criticism was loaded into the war-movie convention that GIs are mistreated heroes and the brass at best dangerous buffoons. But within the limits of a half-hour show, I thought it was a funny, poignant, and honorable job, more intelligent and public-minded than most other sitcom scripts I've read.

Eustis was unusually excited. "We had gone away with everybody's blessings, and done what we thought was something pretty good. You get to be a grizzled veteran in this business, you don't expect anything, but we really did find ourselves thinking, Boy, I can't wait till they read this and call us and tell us how great it is. And we can't wait until ABC gets it and says, 'At last, a Vietnam series with some balls.' "

"They hated it," Elias said. "People at Paramount, Palmer and Dart, and everybody at ABC, fainted," Eustis remembered. They said, 'Holy shit! What have you guys done to us?' "

The ensuing meeting was extraordinary even by network standards. Eustis's recollection was as vivid as executives' recollections were faint. "We had one of those emergency meetings at the network. Everybody's face is the color of paper. Twelve people crammed into an office where usually you have a meeting with four or five people. This was wall to wall people, and it was like a friendly kangaroo court, they were always very friendly, and Michael and I were the defendants. And everybody filed in, there was a lot of shuffling of papers, and then somebody says, 'Well, let's just talk about how we feel about this.' . . . The charges were not well defined, but I think it was something to do with 'too political.' "

"They loved everything else," Elias says, "but they just hated that [Cambodia] story. 'How can you do a thing about bombing Cambodia?' And we said, 'The guy is a reporter. A real reporter did exactly what this guy did. Everybody agrees that the United States bombed Cambodia.' 'Yeah, but come on, there's no proof.' And we said, 'Sideshow,' you know. 'Read the New York Times. Watch television. Remember.' And, 'Well, okay, all right, so it's true, but Jesus Christ, you guys, come off it. It's just too rough.' " The story was a bummer; people wouldn't want to watch it.

"We said to these executives, 'You're wrong. Your conception of what America thinks about Vietnam is all wrong. It's all in your head. The polls don't support it.' " Elias rattled off figures from a study commissioned by the Veterans Administration, showing an overwhelming majority of Americans who thought the war had been mistaken.

"They really do have preconceived notions of what people think," Elias said. "I think they make them up out of their own fear, or to justify what they hear as somebody else's political opinion. A lot of it has to do with keeping their jobs. You hear things like, 'Oh, Christ, they'll hate that. You don't know what it's like in, you know, Iowa.' There's a mythical farm, there's a mythical Iowa. They think they're liberal and everybody else is right-wing. They don't know how unliberal they are. If you told them, for instance, that there's a tremendous history of, say, working-class politics across America, that has nothing to do with Hollywood—Wobblies, violent miners' strikes in Colorado —they wouldn't know what the fuck you're talking about. 'Huh? Where?' " Elias knew that one of the program executives had been active in the antiwar movement. "I was really naïve. I thought going in, well, she's certainly going to be an ally." But she was no help either.

"And then they said we've got to do more human stories," Eustis continued. "And we were saying, 'Well, what's more human than being in North Vietnam and bombs falling on you? And what's more human than a guy who is a reporter who suddenly begins to see that there's many facets to the situation? Etc., etc.' 'No, what we mean by human is'—and I swear to God, the birthday story came up!" The former antiwar activist mentioned that they could use "something like the birthday story." (As Eustis describes "this old sitcom standby," "Somebody forgets Dad's birthday. 'Why is he so grumpy today? Holy shit! It's his birthday! We all forgot!' ")

Elias said, "All right, we'll do Ho Chi Minh's birthday." " 'Oh, come on, guys, oh, stop kidding around.' " (Unknown to all, *6:00 Follies* had already done a birthday show.)

Eustis and Elias found themselves suddenly enrolled in Sitcom I. "There was a large discussion of how a sitcom functions by having all the characters in a room together at the beginning," Eustis chortled. "And we said, 'Well, the point of this was we didn't want it to be like other sitcoms.' 'Oh, it will be great! It will introduce the characters!' And we said, 'The characters get introduced.' They still had in the back of their minds getting in front of an audience with four people in a room telling jokes."

The point Eustis took away was, "We're not saying not to have any balls. We're just telling you we don't want to do bombing Cambodia. We said, 'We'll go away and think.' We didn't want to give them a chance to shoot down our other favorite idea," which Eustis described to them simply as "one of the funniest things that ever happened over there." The characters and subplots would stay the same, and all the characters would gather together to start the show, as requested. "Love it! Write it!" came the executive response.

Eustis and Elias didn't say that the new story was going to revolve around another actual event: an antiwar demonstration by American soldiers in downtown Saigon. In a week they wrote the second script, in which a GI reporter on Armed Forces Television blurted over the air the news of the demonstration. He got yanked off the air and shipped to the front for his pains. Devlin caught up with him just as he was ordered into action. "Tomorrow," an officer told him, "you're walking point." "Right," said the GI, who turned to Devlin and asked deadpan, "What's 'point'?" That was the last we saw of the GI. The texture of this second script was essentially the same. Lacking the tension of an unanswered question at a last-act briefing, the ending was now muffled, I thought, with male and female reporters clutching each other while Bob Hope entertained the troops on their television screen. This was still sitcom with serious overtones, some fun in hell, an ensemble of good kids making the most of a bad war and subverting its official pieties.

"This was the greatest script ever written, as far as Paramount and Palmer and Dart were concerned," Eustis recalled. ABC, in Elias's words, said, "It's great. We just love it. We just have to find a good time-slot for it. We're going to look at it, suggest a few changes, nothing serious, but God, we love it." The network paid for the second draft and put up the money for a casting director and a location manager, who started scouting locations. The script went out to agents, and thence to actors, who started expressing interest. Henry Gibson was interested in playing the self-dramatizing network correspondent, Meg Foster the female lead.

"And then it died," Eustis said. "The reason we think it went away is not because they had a distaste for the politics of it, but because the 6:00 Follies came on NBC, which was truly a trivialization of the whole thing, and it died the death of a dog. From our point of view, here in the trenches, they can't seem to differentiate between a shitty show that bombs and a good show on the same theme. 6:00 Follies died, therefore all Vietnam comedies are destined to die."

Barbara Corday, who ran ABC's comedy development department, confirmed that "the main reason that it didn't get shot was because NBC was already shooting 6:00 Follies, and CBS announced that they were picking up whatever the Gary Goldberg show was called, the Bureau, and we just said, Well, we've been through this already with Animal House,* and why be last? Who wants to do the third version of the Vietnam half-hour show?" But other ABC execu-

---

*The prototype of three unsuccessful network copies in 1979.

tives sounded a different tune. "It just wasn't very good," said Jonathan Axelrod, then vice-president for drama. "One reason that the [Vietnam] comedies didn't work," said Tom Werner, "is they bore much resemblance to *M*A*S*H*. It's a little bit hard to escape that comparison, with a comedy." *M*A*S*H*, of course, was exactly what ABC had asked for at the start.

Sometimes explanations for a failure are like the blind men's descriptions of that misbegotten elephant. By my lights, these less-than-brilliant scripts were funnier and more interesting than scripts that have gone to pilot and gotten on the air. But *Bringing It Home* did not come equipped with a major television star, let alone a network commitment. And the two scripts did demonstrate that the show meant trouble. "I would surmise," Elias said later, "that they were just as happy to get rid of it, because it was going to be a difficult show for them to do. It was going to be: 'Oh, God, every week, politics!' "

ABC, leaning toward "traditional values," didn't give up immediately on the commercial potential of Vietnam. For a while it tried marrying its hunch about the war to its sweeping sense of the country's rightward motion. The result was a one-hour drama project called *Fly Away Home*, developed by the TV and movie veteran Sterling Silliphant. *Fly Away Home* went as far as a two-hour pilot that was meant to be a kaleidoscopic view of the war through the eyes of a black enlistee, a cameraman, two gorgeous dancers, an ideologically anti-Communist pilot, and a South Vietnamese woman with a North Vietnamese brother, among other characters. The drama was perfunctory, the dialogue lame and often anachronistic; the show lacked an edge. Even a patriotic tone couldn't save it. "A good pilot, not sensational, there were a lot of flaws in it," Tony Thomopoulos said diplomatically, but those aside, *Fly Away Home* fell afoul of scheduling problems. "It's a ten-o'clock time period show," Thomopoulos explained. ABC had locked up virtually all its ten-o'clock slots: Sunday went to movies; Monday to football; Tuesday to the successful *Hart to Hart;* Wednesday by default to the promising *Dynasty* (otherwise it would have to go up against *Dallas* Friday nights, "which would be suicide"); Thursday to *20/20;* and Saturday to *Fantasy Island.* Tricky material like Vietnam, however neutered, however uncritical, however clichéd, would need a protected time-slot, not the suicide position opposite *Dallas* on Fridays, or so network executives felt. So *Fly Away Home* was grounded, the pilot run off as a one-shot summer movie. Silliphant tried to mobilize public pressure to give the series a chance, but to no avail.

The fall 1981 season came to pass without any Vietnam series on network television. The usual extenuations were heard. The notion was premature, the war still too fresh, too raw in the American imagination. Some thought the right formula might come along any

day, might work in the right hands. "Somebody will do it," agreed
Grant Tinker at MTM. "I still think *Bureau* could have worked. This
is not going to be a brilliant new thought, but the best comedy plays
against that kind of background. *M*A*S*H* is the perfect example,
obviously, but there are lots of others that have been done." "Somebody will one day do a show set in Vietnam that will be successful,
and we're still trying to come up with a show that can work," said
ABC's Tom Werner. "There's no shibboleths."

In the meantime, the war that first entered America through its
living rooms would remain repressed. Commerce, along with politics
and much of the public, was content to leave America's longest,
ugliest war in the closet.

Instead, out in the open, the airwaves were rife with shows cele-
brating law and order: one-third of the new network series, the
greatest such saturation since the police boom of 1973–78. Not only
did the networks glimpse a public swing toward duly constituted
authority, but they were playing up "action" to compensate for declining "jiggle" as the fundamentalist crusade struck home. (The
fundamentalists included "violence" in their unholy trinity of sex,
violence, and profanity, but no one in the industry thought they
really cared about violence on television. Traditionally, that had
been a liberal issue.) ABC Television's president James Duffy said, "I
see more action. Some people might call it violence—it's a matter of
definition. But you can't have a screen full of people standing still."
"While sex will be less evident," said one advertising man, senior
vice-president William H. Lynn of Ketchum, McLeod & Grove, Inc.,
"there will be no lack of violence on the small screen—but it will be
of the 'acceptable' form as law-enforcement heroes beat up, and
otherwise maim, the bad guys." Writer-producer Nigel McKeand
(Family) noted a resemblance to an English practice: "In the music
halls, when a comedian is going in the toilet, he always says, 'All right
now, and let's all sing "Rule Brittania"!' Everyone sings, and they all
cheer. It really does deflect. You can't boo the queen of England."

In this network mood, no project could have been more welcome
than a new version of ABC's 1965–74 standby, *The FBI*. The producer David Gerber says the inspiration was his. Gerber, everyone
agreed, was a driven worker, face animated, hands constantly in
motion, his sprawling conversation masking an astute sales sense. A
former Hollywood agent and Columbia television executive, originally from Brooklyn, Gerber had set up his own company, produced
the successful *Police Story* and *Police Woman* series, and made himself one of the thriving independents in the business. He joked that
he had inherited his work from his father, who had worked as a

salesman in a slaughterhouse: "I figured that was perfect for this business."

Gerber got into cop shows both because he felt an affinity with cops and because cop shows were a marketable convention. "I grew up in a different era," he says. "Most of my friends were civil servants, so they were cops, firemen, or what. The greatest thing in my life was on Saturday afternoons, we had to go underneath the fence of the public school because it was closed. We used to get kicked out by the cops. And we got older, some of our own guys became cops. So the greatest thing that ever happened, I knew there was a new era in my life, is when we went underneath the fence, the cops that came around were our people—see, they had gotten in uniform. So we never got in trouble again." Years later, Gerber was at Columbia, which had bought the rights to Joseph Wambaugh's best-selling novel *The New Centurions*. In 1973, he jumped at the chance to produce what started out as a few TV movies and became *Police Story*. "I had a feel for these people," he says. "I respect them."

Gerber not only read the public mood, he internalized it. "We were close to chaos, close to suspicion of institutions in the early seventies. The blue line was there to preserve what was left, what was the semblance of what used to be one helluva government when it served the people." *Police Story* toed that thin blue line. "I thought we were on the way to success when, about the second or third year I was at UCLA, some kind of a seminar, and a woman came up to me and said, 'You're just as bad as they are.' A young college girl. I said, 'What do you mean?' She said, 'You're making them like human beings.' And I said, 'You gave me a compliment.' I showed the warts and the pimples, I showed them being brutal because they were frustrated and not just being brutal because they were brutal people. . . . I showed alcoholism, I showed the high divorce rate. People don't realize the kind of life they live. See, they thought they were the minority. They felt they had to cluster together in a group, nobody understood them. And I showed where they could be damned and vilified, but soon as you're in trouble you yell for the police, not the firemen, not anybody else, *the police.*"

But Gerber took to cop shows not only because the police were society's blue line but because they could be the networks'. In the industry jargon, they afforded a franchise—a hero's right to interfere every week in the lives of others. "In television there are a certain amount of franchises," Gerber points out. "What do you got? You got doctor, lawyer, and chief. Throw in some Indians, for westerns. So doctor, lawyer, and police; the westerns are gone. You try to do something offbeat—*White Shadow, Paper Chase, American Dream* —and you get shot down. So you stay with the franchise or you take a chance. In June the networks have patience with anything. The flowers are blooming, hooray, hooray. Come September, they lose patience, because they're in a competitive race."

In 1979, his antennae up, Gerber read a magazine article about the FBI in the era of director William Webster. He thought, Here is a new FBI, hiring minorities and women, cooperating more with local police, using sophisticated weapons. "It gives a whole new spin to the FBI, rather than the old FBI, which was sort of inflexible." The FBI, unlike the CIA, he thought, had never lost its appeal to the American mainstream. "It's like Lincoln, apple pie, and a dog." In addition, ABC had an attachment to its old FBI franchise, since the original series had been a winner during ABC's grim third-place years. Even Leonard Goldenson, the board chairman, loved the idea. But ABC got wind of two other producers pursuing a similar idea, so Goldenson and ABC Television president Fred Pierce, in a rare act of top-level involvement, went to the FBI to ask them to wait for Gerber's script.

"I wrote a hell of a presentation, a letter to Judge Webster," Gerber says. He wanted "to do it with a sense of reality, I want to do it today," he wrote, not "pristine, plastic, or making guys look like superheroes. My letter, as I understand it from some people in the FBI, the judge liked so well he said, 'Even if we don't do it, you ought to frame the letter.' It gave a philosophy of the FBI of today. And being the executive producer of *Police Story* didn't hurt me at all; there was a tremendous respect for that in a law-enforcement agency. They said, 'Fine, we'll do it.' " In exchange for official sanction and access to FBI files, Gerber granted the Bureau approval of the stories and the casting of the FBI agents. According to a *New York Times* account, an FBI spokesman "noted that Mr. Webster had granted his legally required permission for commercial use of the FBI's initials and official seal only after seeing and approving a film of the pilot episode. He could withdraw this permission if he does not like subsequent episodes."

In exchange for its cooperation, the FBI procured an image of law-abiding agents—a thoughtful middle-aged man (Mike Connors, once the star of *Mannix*), a young woman, a young black—going out of their way to get warrants for their wiretaps. The benefit wasn't lost on the Bureau; its spokesman told a reporter that "the effort is part of an overall attempt by Mr. Webster to 'do a better job in trying to get the word out to the public' that the FBI today is a group of dedicated professionals who operate within the law, use sophisticated techniques to combat crime and terrorism, and deserve public respect and cooperation." In the new mode, they were also vulnerable humans; the pilot, for example, which concerned the old standby of waterfront racketeering, had an eager young undercover agent succumbing for a while to a charming bad guy.

Did Gerber see *Today's FBI* fitting Tony Thomopoulos's model of the new hero fighting to "bring this country back to some basic national values"? "I used it as a sales technique," he said. He also hoped an audience that had recently lost interest in cop and private-eye shows might gravitate toward the "comforting factor" of a "legalized, national, federal institution looking after you." To keep that image clean, *Today's FBI* would be careful to avoid Bureau burglaries and illegal wiretaps. "I'm not living in the past. All those accusations and/or acts were done prior to me getting there. I'm not out to lift up garbage lids on cans and look for something incriminating against them. We're looking for heroes, and without thinking you have to be jingoist or opportunistic or nationalistic in some form, there's nothing wrong with this country having some heroes. Just as long as they're not artificial heroes, brutal heroes, comic heroes. I think the public's had all they can of antiheroes and negativism. I don't think there's anything wrong in attempting to show the FBI in an honest, heroic light. Now if you ask me, do we go into the Abscam, yes, . . . but certainly I'm going to see it from the FBI viewpoint, although you'll hear the other viewpoint."

"You start out as a liberal," Gerber said, "you end up as a moderate." Gerber's belief was also the belief of at least some ABC executives. Jonathan Axelrod expressed it this way: "I like shows that are about institutions that we look up to. In a country where crime is exploding, things like the FBI become more important to people. When you think of the amount of kidnapping that's going on, and murder, it's very important. So you do a show that hopefully makes people feel comfortable with the FBI, so they'll use them more and relate to them."

Didactic purpose and commercial hopes pooled together. ABC and the FBI hoped that Gerber's experience and skill could accomplish the common objective. Once on the air, though *Today's FBI* may have been cleaned up, they had lost their punch. The show finished forty-eighth (out of 105) for the 1981–82 season, and did not get renewed; nor did Aaron Spelling's *Strike Force*, starring Robert Stack as an uncleaned-up police commander, which came in seventy-sixth; nor did NBC's *McClain's Law*, worse still at eighty-fifth.

A few weeks into the fall season of 1981, word was already going around L.A. that the tilt toward the right had been a mistake. "Everyone in the television industry," said Bill Haber of the powerful Creative Artists Agency the following January, "knows at this moment that this big push to law and order didn't work. Every single law-and-order show that's been put on the air is not working. What the country seems to be attracted to for the moment is fantasy, escapism, *Love Boat*. They don't want to hear about the mugger on the streets, they want to be on a ship in the Caribbean. And it's reflected in the ratings. We misassessed the country's mood. On the very highest level at the networks." With alacrity, the industry disengaged from its mistakes and started trend-hunting again. David Gerber went to work producing the musical series *Seven Brides for Seven Brothers*. A few months later, NBC's Brandon Tartikoff told an executive at Johnny Carson Productions, "It's time for a daffy female."

The question is why the boomlet arose and then so quickly subsided. The network antennae were poorly pointed, their readings of public trends simplistic. The executives miscalculated the nation's mood not so much because they were themselves growing conservative, although some were, but because they had trouble grasping the ambivalence and fluidity of the public mood. It was easier to grasp at slogans about a mass taste for powerful authorities. Personal politics—Leonard Goldenson's relations with the FBI, Jonathan Axelrod's argument about crime, Herman Keld's feelings about the military—entered into scheduling insofar as these reinforced marketing arguments, and sometimes even helped shape those arguments. The Reagan landslide in particular generated some powerful simplifications, tempting executives—along with many journalists and other Americans—to make quick sense of elusive and contradictory facts. Selected facts mixed with a certain executive mood to congeal into a "trend," and too many executives, eager to make their mark in the eighties as Bob Wood had done in the seventies, stretched their hunches too far. But one could not point the finger at nervous management alone. The guiding structure for such mistakes was the oligopoly structure of the industry, which tended to harness each party to the other's miscalculations, the way the Big Three auto companies had for so many years assured each other that America "demanded" big cars.

In the end, such popular moods as did exist weren't engagingly channeled into shows. The whole industry was exhausted, feverishly cannibalizing and cloning and splicing shows from its own lengthening past. Television was saddled with its own history, and even the best writers seemed to be imitating themselves. Neither networks nor suppliers were working up new forms to suit a new public mood —with the exception of the makers of *Hill Street Blues*. No one in television conjured up the contemporary equivalents of the angry sitcoms and black humor of the Wood era. In the "creative community" as well as the networks, concoction was doing the work of conviction; the shows were being muscled into existence. However shrewdly executives and inside-track producers and agents sold each other on the law-and-order trend, the products turned out half-hearted. The industry as a whole failed to have the courage of its lack of conviction, and to make shows about *that*.

CHAPTER 12

The "Far Righteous" Shake the Temple of Commerce

The networks' early eighties programming jitters were a case of normal malaise getting out of hand, compounded by the intrusion of a new force: the fundamentalist right. For whatever the vagaries of the marketplace, the essence of network cultural power was that no one else could tell them how to manage the national airwaves. True, they had to pay attention to outside forces. Each network had to court and cater to its two-hundred-odd local affiliates; for none, after all, was bound to broadcast the networks' programs. The affiliate-network relation was contractual, based on a division of total advertising time and revenue, and since the affiliates' ad rates depended on the popularity of network shows, the affiliates had a significant stake in the networks' programming choices. They would make their pleasure and displeasure known; in a pinch, if a network declined, it could even lose some affiliates to the competition. Affiliates had local tastes and taboos, but in the main they wanted what the networks wanted: the best possible coverage for the advertisers, who financed the entire operation. Still farther in the background there had always loomed the abstract threat of federal regulation if the networks got too far out of hand—and now in the Carter and Reagan administrations, there was the luminous promise of friendly deregu-

lation in the network interest.* All these forces had achieved a kind
of equilibrium that ceded the networks their considerable programming power. But now there arose a lobby that challenged the networks' very ability to program as they saw fit.

The fundamentalist crusade to "clean up television" was founded
on a recognition that television entertainment amounts to politics
conducted by other means. For if the networks muffle controversy,
they also delight in the semblance of it. Again and again television
acknowledges social and cultural conflicts, if only to tamp them down
in the process of "resolving" them. But no matter how it muffles and
oversimplifies controversy to go with what it sees as the tidal flows
of public taste, television cannot help but generate conflict of its own.
The fault lines in American culture run too deep to permit television
to go its merry way, especially since television's trick is to try to
amuse its audience with flattened images of its own desires. When
those desires point in opposite directions, the drive for a mass audience imports cultural antagonisms into the shows. Indeed, the industry never ceases to insist that a kind of conflict is the essence of
drama. Which is only to say that television can hardly avoid staking
out *de facto* political positions: about who has power, who deserves
it, and by what values.

That is why television entertainment, beneath its consensus on
uplift and the well-appointed life, has become a contested zone. As
long as television shows are packaged more than written, the process
is automatically political more than artistic, with network standards
departments acting as political brokerages, antennae always thrust
into the wind for trends. Their polling process softens most sharp
lines, one reason why the shows usually lack the conviction and the
sense of internal proportion that mark real art. These shows are
registries of symbols, central bulletin boards on which the looks of
social types get posted.

In an age of image, every social group practices the politics of the
look. Prestige in modern society rests on it—as do disgrace and danger. In a world of strangers and a diffuse sense of threat, people's
images of The Other are heavily influenced by the public array of
images. The steady barrage of images is not only received but in-
spected and criticized. Everyday conversation makes plain that most
people who watch television are also critics of it, although not everyone can articulate criticism on either the aesthetic or the ideological

---

*In 1970, for example, the Federal Communications Commission had issued a rule
barring the networks from the right to share in the enormous revenues from program
syndication, or to own portions of programs independently produced. Since there
were enormous profits at stake, the networks were lobbying the Reagan FCC for a
repeal of this rule.

plane. We like this, we don't like that, and we think the other is or is not a fair representation of a type. The audience is sophisticated enough to recognize that media images are stereotypes, and don't hesitate to complain that some stereotypes are the wrong ones. As the media world becomes virtually everyone's secondhand world of reference, any group sensitive to its social standing makes claims on this national registry of symbols. The aggrieved party may not credit the image, but believes that other people do, which spurs him or her to take it seriously indeed.

In short, the public no longer takes television for granted as if it were natural, or a wondrous gift of beneficent science. A society that delights in its media, and hangs on their every word and picture, also runs rife with suspicion. In recent years, minorities, feminists, PTAs, the fundamentalist right, big business and labor, and several presidents have all campaigned to shape selected Looks. Year to year, some win, some lose; no evident pattern emerges in the rising and falling curves of pressure groups, except that all share the belief that image is central to their strategies of dignity and power, and an apprehension, for which there is much evidence, that while TV (not only news but entertainment) may not tell people what to think, it does confirm which topics are important and what is a sensible way to think about them. It relays a common discourse from coast to coast, and overseas as well. It specifies the limits of legitimate thought. It helps us define our place, and the place of others, in an imagined world.

When many people turn on television, whether outside the Bible Belt or in it, they feel invaded by an alien force, lurking in the furniture. The time is gone, probably for good, when network television could lord it over the common stock of images unopposed. Since World War I at least, publics have been suspicious of propaganda and disposed to see it whenever images offend them. Americans have long been predisposed to purity crusades, rooted in a deep feeling that native-born folks are being shortchanged. The long-standing buzz, insecurity, and self-doubt of American life is both fuel and product of individualism. In the sixties, first blacks, then white youths, then other ethnics, women, and homosexuals began to formulate their restless drives for dignity and self-improvement in collective terms. As political and cultural consensus dissolved, scarcely a social group was willing to rest content with its position.

Just as sexuality is usually at the core of repression and social management, it was at the core of the upheavals of the sixties. In an ever more lavish service economy, the body could be freed (relatively speaking) from labor; money could be spent for pleasure. Birth-control technology made it still easier to convert the body into an instrument of pleasure. The Emersonian ideal of self-expression bubbled to the surface again, loosening the bonds of the patriarchal family and community—which were already being undermined by the seductive freedoms of goods-laden consumerist hedonism. With the twin verities of patriarchy and Puritanism crumbling, a very American moral panic came to the surface. It was an old story: moral crusades to police the mass-cultural order. When the movies were young, in the early part of the century, nativist Puritans mobilized to check the titillating extravagances of the ethnics, often Jewish, who were quick to see the industry's potential for both business and pleasure. In the thirties, the Catholic church and others organized the National Legion of Decency to police "films which portray, approvingly, concepts rooted in philosophies attacking the Christian moral order and the supernatural destiny of man." Hollywood's semi-official Hays Office Code lasted until 1966, when it was replaced by the far less restrictive G-PG-R-X classification scheme.

Prominent figures on the fundamentalist right had for years expressed disgust with network television's growing "permissiveness," its display of flesh, and its extramarital innuendo, but the new crusade gathered real momentum and publicity with the election of Ronald Reagan. Much of the press held the Moral Majority and other New Right groups responsible for a good part of Reagan's landslide, and the New Right "social issue" groups—antiabortion, antifeminist, antirevolutionist, and proprayer—went on the offensive. The fundamentalist right could already speak directly to national television audiences through its satellite-relayed gospel shows. In network television, however, it recognized a national target of opportunity. The assemblage of groups that the Hollywood writer Larry Gelbart calls "the far righteous" had a keen sense of how to play the press, and eventually got a huge boost from panicky advertisers. When the dust cleared, the networks, sensing no real audience counterpressure, had retreated from their high-water mark of sexual titillation, indeed from controversy in general.

The pivotal figure in this successful surge was the Rev. Donald Wildmon, a Methodist minister straight out of a bicoastal network executive's grim dream of a benighted Middle America. In his early forties, Wildmon had for several years operated a National Federation for Decency from a tiny office in his home town of Tupelo, Mississippi. It was as if the respectable citizens of Tupelo were finally going to get revenge on their native-born pelvis, Elvis Presley, and the whole dirty culture that had invaded their households and corrupted their youth. With little staff or money, Wildmon started mobilizing fundamentalist church networks among others to generate thousands of letters protesting "unwholesome" shows.

When ABC, in 1977, scheduled *Soap*, a farcical send-up of sexually indulgent soap operas, it got 32,000 letters of protest, many of them mobilized by Wildmon. When ABC announced it was making a 1980 TV movie from Marilyn French's feminist novel *The Women's Room*, Wildmon denounced it, sight unseen, as antifamily, and letters flooded in again.* Wildmon wasn't interested in the ways in which the movie simplified the book, imposing an uplifting individualist ending in which the heroine harangues her rapt Harvard audience with a message about women's freedom of choice. Wildmon's campaign was sufficiently potent, though, to intimidate advertisers. According to ABC's Brandon Stoddard, ABC lost ten out of fourteen minutes of *Women's Room* spot ads before the air date; arguably bad business decisions, since the show drew a splendid 28.2 rating and a 45 share, but advertisers were nervous about being associated with controversy. Replacements came in at the last minute, but paid cut rates. Only a few letters of protest came in after the broadcast, but according to Stoddard ABC lost "a lot of money" on a high-rated show.

After Wildmon hooked up with the Rev. Jerry Falwell, and the right swept the 1980 elections, the press anointed him as newsworthy. Reporters saw Falwell as a kingmaker, and threats to the power of the media are customarily good fodder for headlines. Wildmon was able to attract Falwell and other leaders of the New Right to a founding meeting of a Coalition for Better Television (CBTV) in February 1981, just after the Reagan inauguration. The vehemently right-wing Sen. Jeremiah Denton of Alabama, who had joined Wildmon in an earlier crusade against network television permissiveness, told the gathering he was ready to die in this crusade to clean up television. CBTV's executive committee of four included Wildmon, Falwell deputy Ronald Godwin, and the prominent antifeminist Phyllis Schlafly. Falwell and Wildmon announced that monitoring groups would scrutinize the network prime-time schedule for signs of "obscenity"—broken down into "skin scenes," "sexual innuendo," "implied sexual intercourse"—"profanity," and "violence." By the end of June, they said, they would single out a sponsor whose commercials appeared in programs that the monitors found most offensive, and they would organize a boycott against that company.

With Falwell's drawing power, the founding of the Coalition and the threat of a boycott were instantly big news. For months reporters uncritically relayed Wildmon's claim that the Coalition included 200 groups—later boosted to 300, then to 401. Many were local letterhead organizations, but it took until June before a CBS News corre-

---

*To assuage criticism, ABC's Standards and Practices inserted an opening disclaimer, reminding viewers that the story—with its uniformly insensitive men and victimized, if eventually triumphant, women—belonged to an earlier and presumably outlived time.

spondent reported that, of a sample of some sixty organizations and individuals whom Wildmon counted in CBTV, about 30 percent denied membership. When I asked Wildmon about this, he said that he had signed cards from all 401 in his possession, and that he would not have given CBS News a misleading list. "I may be from Mississippi but I'm not stupid," he said. But having been burned, he refused to give out any more totals, let alone names.

Nor did the press get very far in probing the CBTV monitoring process, not at least until Hodding Carter, Jr.'s PBS series *Inside Story* ran a piece in the fall in which some of the monitors were actually interviewed. Evidently the monitoring process had been designed by Wildmon himself. During an earlier survey, Wildmon had been so incensed by a four-letter word uttered by *Saturday Night Live*'s Charles Rocket that he had threatened to double the offensiveness ratings for all NBC shows—not exactly sound survey technique, even as a warning.* For months Wildmon successfully stonewalled on the identities of his alleged 4,000 monitors, and on their training and representativeness as well. Television news regularly played along, seeming to substantiate Wildmon's scientific aura with shots of photogenic computer print-out machines chugging away at CBTV headquarters.

In virtual chorus, top network executives were quick to brandish their First Amendment rights. "We will not change or remove any of our programs," declared CBS senior vice-president Gene Mater. "Although TV is today's target, movies, books, magazines, and newspapers will not be far behind." At the May 1981 affiliates meeting, president Thomas Wyman of CBS, Inc., called the Moral Majority— the CBTV's largest constituent group—"a constitutionally immoral minority" that threatened "to disenfranchise the real majority of viewers from making their own decisions about what to watch." The Moral Majority and the CBTV, he said, "strike at the heart of the American ideal of a free marketplace. We must make it clear that what is at stake is not the propriety of the networks but the freedom of the airwaves."

Needless to say, the networks' "freedom of the airwaves" is their own particular freedom to decide what shows "the real majority of viewers" will get to choose among. But that freedom is far from absolute, and most pointedly advertisers in the aggregate possess a sort of veto power. The major advertising companies functionally set the outer limits of permissible television. "We have two markets," as NBC research vice-president Gerald M. Jaffe puts it. "With a movie,

---

*NBC fired Rocket for violating the FCC's obscenity rules, as it would have done, Wildmon or no.

there's one audience; whether people like it or not, they've still paid for the ticket. But with TV there are two audiences: advertisers and people at home. With the audience, you could get very high ratings with frontal nudity, penetration, torture, and people being cut up with chainsaws. But Congress would shriek, and so would advertisers. It would make a hard sell for Hamburger Helper."

"It is an advertiser-supported medium," as NBC chairman Grant Tinker says, "and to the extent that support falls out, then programming will change." The major producers of consumer goods are drawn to network television because it is, in the words of S. C. Johnson's August Priemer, an "intrusive" medium.* Television affords such good access to the broadest public, it "penetrates" so well, to use another advertising term, that it destroyed the glossy national weeklies, *Life, Look, Collier's,* and the *Saturday Evening Post,* as competing advertising vehicles.

That the bulk of major advertisers retain a veto power is important, but no less important is the fact that advertiser power ordinarily comes into play only after the networks make the essential decisions. The networks in turn vaguely take into account whether they think major advertisers in the aggregate (the qualification is important, as we shall see in a moment) are going to consider a show a hospitable setting for their commercials. I asked many network programming executives whether they took advertiser attitudes into account in deciding whether to put a show on the air, and most said no, pointing out that network television is a seller's market, with advertisers often standing in line to buy choice time. They argue, or would like to believe, that some advertisers will turn up to buy time on any show the networks put on the air. After all, the shows are concocted to be popular and inoffensive in the first place. But more revealing, I think, was CBS Entertainment president Bud Grant's answer. "We don't," he started to say, then interrupted himself and went on, "we try not to think of the world of advertisers out there. We know how important it is, and they give us our weekly check, but I think that in terms of just entertainment programming we take the merits of the show into account as to whether we'd do it or not." Knowledge of who pays the bills can't be dispelled, even when it doesn't always rise to consciousness. Network executives internalize the desires of advertisers as a whole. CBS's Herman Keld, who has taken part in CBS scheduling meetings for many years, didn't qualify his answer when I asked

---

*In a 1966 speech, Priemer, the director of marketing services for the company that makes Johnson's Wax, went on: "Products can be injected where they are not wanted —which doesn't sound very moral but which is a fact of life with television. . . . Television is the medium which depends least on consumer cooperation to develop a rich response to symbolic stimulation."

him whether ad agencies—and affiliates—are taken into account in programming decisions. "I would say they are always taken into account. Always taken into account."

To fathom both the power and limits of the Coalition for Better Television (and other pressure groups), we also have to understand the mechanics of advertiser time-buying. To advertisers, the programs amount to packaging for commercials. Accordingly, in the companies' behalf, what the advertising agencies are shopping for each year is "environments." More than 90 percent of the buying is done for an entire year, or a particular quarter. This is so-called up-front buying. Each spring, after the networks announce their new schedules, the agencies screen samples of the new season's shows. If the American Widget Company wants to spend, say, $10 million advertising its new models, its agency calls the network sales departments and says it wants to spend a certain proportion of the $10 million over the coming year to reach, say, eighteen- to thirty-four-year-old men during prime time. The network estimates the audience each of its shows can be expected to reach, along with the expected demographic breakdown. It takes into account the show's past history (if it is a renewal), its lead-in and competition, the characteristics of the time-slot, and in the case of a new show, the look of the pilot (if any) and its producer's track record. The network might offer American Widget ten spots in show A, twelve in B, seven in C, and so forth over the course of the coming year. The agency makes its own audience estimates and counterproposals: It wants only nine spots in B, but three in D. It plays one network's offer off against the other's. Negotiations ensue. Eventually the network and the agency agree on a price for the entire package. Whatever time the networks don't sell up front, they sell later on, usually for less.

The networks are fully aware, though, that even in an economic recession network time is a seller's market. Since a high proportion of television advertisers sell package goods, which hold up relatively well in a contracting economy, rather than durables, which don't, the networks weather recessions rather well. So time is a scarce and valuable commodity. Even at $155,000 per thirty seconds, the price of a M*A*S*H spot in 1981, advertisers are eager to line up early. That is why the network executives who develop shows, order pilots, and make up the schedules can safely assume that advertisers will buy time in virtually any show that promises to be very popular. In this sense, no single advertiser can truly wield a veto power over the network. Yet without even troubling to think about it, network executives are likely to rule out any show likely to offend a critical mass of advertisers. *The Adventures of Ralph Nader*, for instance, would be hard to sell to advertisers across the board, even if it might promise to be a popular series; that is where the ideological line, in effect, is drawn. In the present ideological climate, the executives won't think *The Adventures of Ralph Nader* promising in the first place, so the question of advertiser censorship never comes up.

Some advertisers and most network executives reproached the Reverends Wildmon and Falwell not only for threatening network power, but for crediting advertisers with a control, and therefore a responsibility, they had long since lost. But Falwell and Wildmon well knew that advertisers no longer exercised direct control over programs as they had in the early days of television. Their strategy, in effect, was to intimidate the advertisers into reasserting control— by holding them responsible. Like the blacklisters of the fifties, they understood that advertisers were the weak link in the system.

Old-time writers, directors, and producers often gaze back fondly on "the golden age" of the fifties, when the airwaves were full of live drama. However, nostalgia conveniently overlooks the way in which advertisers and their agencies not only blacklisted the actors, writers, and directors listed in the *Red Channels* registry, but regularly read scripts a day or two in advance of shooting. Many advertisers were sole sponsors: *The U.S. Steel Hour, Armstrong Circle Theater, The Lux Show Starring Rosemary Clooney.* Sponsors who bought whole shows, or major portions, didn't shrink from direct censorship. Proprietary concern for the image of the product was a major motive. At the behest of an ad agency for a gas company sponsor, CBS took out half a dozen instances of the word "gas" referring to gas chambers in a *Playhouse 90* drama on the Nuremberg trials; when a few uses of the offending word nevertheless slipped through, an eager engineer deleted them on the air. Less grotesque excisions were commonplace. "If you were doing a show that was sponsored by Kent cigarettes," Ethel Winant recalls about the fifties, "you couldn't say, 'American' "—Lucky Strikes were a competing brand, American Tobacco a competing company. "You couldn't say 'lucky guy'; you'd have to say, 'He was a fortunate fellow.' "

Industry economics changed the advertising system and built up network control at the expense of the advertisers. The number of homes with television sets doubled from 1954 to 1964, rising from 56 percent to 92 percent of all American homes. As the television set became an obligatory domestic appliance, the price of commercial time rose steeply. Advertisers could no longer afford to buy entire shows, except for occasional showcase specials that improved public-relations images for companies like Hallmark, IBM, and Xerox.* Moreover, the advertising agencies came to feel that scatter-buying was a more efficient way of reaching audiences for the money.

---

*In this sense the Public Broadcasting System is the last refuge of old-style television.

Meanwhile, the quiz-show-rigging scandal of 1958, which at first brought the industry a wave of bad publicity and congressional investigations, in the long run actually served the networks' drive to stabilize and rationalize production under their own command. Soon after the scandal broke, the networks cleaned house in a number of ways. They upgraded their broadcast standards divisions. At CBS, President Frank Stanton set down an explicit rule: Advertisers would no longer be permitted to read scripts in advance and intervene if they thought their corporate images at risk. Instead, they would be permitted to screen the filmed episodes, and, if they wanted to beg off a particular one, the network would excuse them. Many hands now paid the piper, and the piper, the network, would call the tune.

The quiz-show scandal also accelerated the ongoing shift to filmed shows, which were not only easier to police but potentially much more remunerative for networks and production companies alike, since they produced reusable commodities. The shift to film, for which Hollywood was better equipped than New York, had already been proceeding for several years. Moreover, the top sponsors now preferred to be associated with the standardized formats and continuing stars of episodic series. Dramatic anthologies were declining. In New York, the top writers of golden-age drama were wearying of censorship and vacating live TV drama for the greener, freer pastures of Broadway and the movies.

The quiz shows went off the air in the fall of 1958. The next fall, there were already thirty new Hollywood film series on the air. The new system was in place, and it left the networks perfectly poised to keep ad rates climbing at a pace faster than production costs and license fees. But it left them with one lingering nuisance—advertiser cancellations. True, prime-time spots are a seller's market, but advertisers still have the right to cancel. The agencies and larger individual advertisers started contracting with special screening agencies based in New York, to monitor forthcoming series episodes. If the screening agency flags an episode as potentially troublesome, it flags the ad agency, which looks at the show itself. Or an ad agency or advertiser might learn about a sexually charged episode from a network press release or a newspaper or *TV Guide* article. In that case, a CBS sales vice-president explains, "We have people waiting in line, people who may not be as sensitive. Maybe it's a show on toxic shock syndrome, and because they had a problem with Rely [tampons], maybe P&G [Procter & Gamble] says, 'Hey, I really don't want to be in that show tonight.' And so we say, 'Okay, we'll flip you to next week.' Or let's say we're running a movie and there are a lot of car crashes, and we got Ford automotive in there. But they want to run during this period of time. You might try to flip-flop, week for week. Instead of running on March 1, you run on March 8, and you get another advertiser to move back. You go to the other advertiser and he says, 'Well, how come Ford doesn't want to run in there?' And you say, 'Because there are nine car crashes.' The guy says, 'Sure, I'll move.' " But if no such exchange is possible, the network offers the spot to other clients, usually for a lower price than the original advertiser would have paid. "Depending on how well we do our job," this executive says, "we can lose a little money, a lot of money, or no money." Usually it is misleading hyperbole to say that the network loses money; almost always the network brings in considerably more than the license fee it pays out. It is simply making less money than it would have without the controversy.

Early in 1981, at CBS, such last-minute cancellations were taking place at a rate of only six or eight a month, usually for violent movies. But a few months later, as the press granted the Coalition for Better Television rising momentum, the networks began to notice and grow nervous about a rising rate of withdrawals. Producers and writers smelled incipient censorship. In May, the industry's elite held a summit conference in palmy Ojai, near Los Angeles. Although it had been called months earlier to address the threat of pressure groups across the ideological board, by May there was only one pressure group whose spirit stalked the manicured lawns of the Ojai Valley Inn. This was what Grant Tinker called the "galvanizing specter" of the fundamentalist right, "the first group to attack the entire medium." At Ojai, Alfred Schneider, the head of ABC's Standards and Practices department, rattled the assemblage of producers, writers, advertisers and top network executives when he told them that in recent weeks there had been an acceleration of advertisers "asking to be relieved of their obligations to a particular program." This involved less than 2 percent of all shows, but ABC had not publicly acknowledged any such trouble before.

The statements of television's major advertisers sounded defensive, even panicky. Bristol-Myers's Marvin Koslow summed up their view when he said, "I know they have female mud-wrestling in Evansville, Indiana, I've been there, but people don't want it in their homes." Tom Ryan of Gillette declared that his company had indeed accelerated its withdrawals in the previous year; although not, he insisted, under fundamentalist pressure. It was simply that Gillette didn't want to be associated with the networks' "gratuitous sex and violence." So, too, vice-president F. Kent Mitchel of General Foods (television's second-largest advertiser) told me that the number of shows from which his company was withdrawing had been on the rise, to an average of over a hundred episodes a year. Mitchel also expressed concern about sex and violence, and defended General Foods's pull-out from the rerun of a 1977 *Lou Grant* episode about a crooked nursing home, insisting, "It wasn't as balanced as we would have wished." General Foods was already being boycotted by a Church of Christ campaign headed by the Rev. John Hurt of Joelton, Tennessee, for buying spots on *Charlie's Angels* among other shows, but Mitchel did say that the boycott wasn't hurting sales. After all, it isn't so easy to discover just which brands on the supermarket shelf are General's. General Foods might, however, have feared that the Reverend Wildmon's cadres, with the visible help of the Reverend Falwell, would be better organized and more numerous than the Reverend Hurt's. But corporate timidity is not necessarily so rational. The companies are not in business to defend freedom of expression, and even a few letters can terrify them with the fear of loss, the only fear that counts.

The question of how a boycott may actually affect an advertiser was raised by CBS commentator Jeff Greenfield in an informal conversation with Gail Smith, the top advertising executive at General Motors (television's third-largest advertiser). Greenfield remarked that if, say, General Motors were boycotted, and if the company lost ten thousand sales to people who wouldn't be caught dead parking a Chevy in their church parking lot, the loss would add up to something like $75 million. Gail Smith nodded, jabbing his finger for emphasis: "And we've lost 'em for four years!" Later he added with indignation, "We're not in the business of antagonizing people. I don't think our company will be hit, but God help the companies that are!"

The advertisers' recoil at Ojai proved to be a preview of a more dramatic public event. In mid-June, two weeks before Wildmon was to hold a press conference announcing a boycott, Owen B. Butler, the board chairman of Procter & Gamble, which is far and away television's biggest spender, stunned a Hollywood audience when he announced that, despite concern about CBTV's methods, "We think the Coalition is expressing some very important and broadly held views about gratuitous sex, violence, and profanity." During the 1980–81 season, Butler said, P&G had "withdrawn sponsorship from over fifty programs, including movies, for reasons of taste."

In a way, not much was new. As the speech itself and several press reports failed to make clear, Butler was speaking of fifty discrete prime-time series episodes and movies, not entire series. Fifty programs added up to something like 3 percent of P&G's prime-time total. But the big news, which the press proceeded to inflate still bigger, was that Butler was saying this out loud. Why? Was business swinging right with Reagan in the White House? Was P&G trying to co-opt Wildmon, to avoid boycotts? Former CBS president Frank Stanton, referring to the bad publicity surrounding P&G's Rely tampon toxic-shock-syndrome disaster, surmised to me that "they must still be in shock over that, because that was a very costly and troublesome situation. It could be that that cast a shadow over a lot of their executive decison-making." It was also at least interesting that Butler himself came from Lynchburg, Virginia, the city that is Jerry Falwell's home base.

Butler did decry the boycott tactic and, trying to dispel any odor of blacklist, refused to name any of the vacated shows. One of them, ABC's Brandon Stoddard told me, was the *East of Eden* miniseries. According to Stoddard, a former advertising man himself, P&G objected to a scene in which the Jane Seymour character sleeps with her husband's brother, a segment that Stoddard thought central to her character. P&G objected not to "the way we *executed*" the scene, stressed Stoddard, but to its inclusion at all.

Reaction to Butler's speech was immediate. Some advertisers and agency executives were privately dismayed at the public cave-in. One top Madison Avenue executive said privately that Butler had single-handedly kept Wildmon's crusade alive. General Mills told CBTV that it would keep its own standards, thank you. But Butler's speech was welcomed by many. "It's going to awaken other companies to develop policies along these lines," said Joseph Block, PepsiCo vice-president of public relations. Representatives of at least two major companies—SmithKline and Miles Laboratories—met secretly with Wildmon, tendering assurances that they were on the side of clean TV. SmithKline even wrote to the networks to express "concern" about "the level of gratuitous sex and violence." The Reverend Wildmon was gratified and in a telephone interview took credit for Butler's action.

By going public, Butler helped legitimize Wildmon—and also handed him his out. Two weeks later, Wildmon held his long-ballyhooed press conference in Washington, and announced that the boycott was off, at least temporarily, because it was unnecessary. "Those advertisers that were not concerned," he said, "during our monitoring period, are now concerned." Network executives crowed that victory was theirs, insisting they had not budged, would not budge, and had succeeded in warding off a threat to free expression rivaling the burning of books. Some pointed out that the threat of boycott was more potent unused than used. If network-commissioned polls were accurate, the Coalition had more support among America's leading advertisers than among the population at large (as the failed law-and-order shows of the same year also seemed to demonstrate). Reverend Wildmon had to have been mindful of a poll commissioned by ABC, suggesting that as little as 1.3 percent of the population would support a product boycott. NBC produced a poll to like effect, showing that people who associated themselves with the Moral Majority watched about the same kinds of programs as

everybody else. With several major advertisers on the run, there was
no reason for Wildmon to press his luck.

At this point, one top Madison Avenue executive thought the Coalition was "melting away. I suspect we're dealing with ten people and
a mimeograph machine." But he granted that at the networks, "everybody is a little more careful." The Coalition's insinuating *bêtes
noires,* including *Dallas* and *Three's Company,* were safe as long as
their ratings remained irreproachable, but Wildmon might have
made the margin of difference in keeping new titillations off the air
and muting what was already on. Low necklines were raised, and
gays were dispatched to the closet again. The networks adjusted to
pressure as they customarily do, by finding reasons to trim whatever
might make vociferous enemies.

During these years, TV's treatment of homosexuals has been something of a bellwether. Network executives like to travel down the
middle of the road, as they construe it. In 1972, they were beginning
to think the road was veering leftward. That was the year ABC
commissioned the movie *That Certain Summer,* in which Hal Hol-
brook played a homosexual struggling to explain himself to his son.
ABC Standards and Practices assigned a consultant psychiatrist and
lawyer to "balance" the script. They wanted the writers Richard
Levinson and William Link to add a police officer or "an Archie
Bunker character" to condemn homosexuality, to defuse "latent
homosexual viewers." In the end, to placate opposition, Levinson
and Link agreed to write in new lines. Where the homosexual hero
said to his son at the end, "A lot of people—most people, I guess—
think it's wrong . . . they say it's a sickness . . . they say it's something
that has to be cured . . .," they added, "Maybe they're right. I don't
know. . . . I *do* know that it isn't easy. If I had a choice, it's not
something I'd pick for myself." Gay liberationists damned them, and
later they regretted the concession.

Subsequently, the networks tilted against the guardians of ortho-
dox morality. They began to send scripts to gay consultants routinely.
"Anything that crops up in a script that even is remotely gay," said
the writer Allan Burns, "they get it. And they really make themselves
heard." On a few occasions when *Lou Grant* dealt with gays, they
had to deal with "interminable phone calls," Burns said. Liberal
writers thought the well-organized gay lobby had somehow acquired
veto power, and resented it. Ernest Kinoy (who wrote *Roots, Roots
II, Skokie,* and many other politically sensitive TV movies) noted that
the black lobby could not keep *Beulah Land* off the screen, but, by
contrast, one of the things you'd have a hard time getting on "is a
program which involved a hero who is a homosexual and is distressed
about it and goes to an analyst and they decide that this is not a good
way to be, and so he works on it, because the analyst says yes, this

is a character disorder, and he becomes much improved. You can handle homosexuality—as long as you handle it in a lovely, tolerant fashion that will not upset the gay-liberation lobby."

Nigel McKeand, who produced *Family*, agrees that "no one can (whether you believe this or not) say that, for instance, homosexuality is infantile, and it is an absurd way to lead your life, and it's an arrested development. You can say two lesbians should be allowed to live in peace." At Ojai, the story circulated of a TV-movie script about a woman who left her husband, had a lesbian affair, and in the end went back to the husband. The story had been approved, but at the script stage Standards and Practices said, "We're deeply concerned about the last scene," in which the woman fell into her husband's arms and said, "It's good to be home again." Standards said, "Don't you realize that will offend every lesbian in America?" The line was cut. In the end the movie wasn't made anyway. In 1981, the gay lobby could still trim images, but it couldn't get movies made.

The political winds can be hard to track; producers learn to tack and veer. In 1976, *Family* ran an episode in which the teenage son discovered his best friend was a homosexual. The rating was high, whereupon ABC displayed what Nigel McKeand calls "an unseemly haste to get another homosexual show on." For the next season, *Family* prepared an episode in which the younger daughter, played by Kristy McNichol, found out her teacher was a lesbian, and the school tried to fire her. By the time the episode was ready, the backlash was beginning to gather. It was the autumn of the Briggs ballot initiative, which would have barred homosexuals from teaching in California. The news was full of Anita Bryant's crusade against gay rights. ABC now wanted to defer the episode until after the election, and to bury it opposite *The Godfather*. They didn't want to have to give equal time, they said. They were afraid viewers would think the McNichol character homosexual. McKeand kept insisting that the show was innocuous. "For Christ's sake," he told Standards and Practices chief Al Schneider, "Lillian Hellman wrote *The Children's Hour* fifty years ago. This doesn't even make the statement that *The Children's Hour* makes. It simply says, Don't dump on someone because of their problems or their proclivities." He mobilized Aaron Spelling and Leonard Goldberg, who owned the show, to exercise their clout. He reminded Schneider of ABC's own "unseemly haste" and argued that to present a simple case for tolerance was all the more important now that the climate had turned nasty. In the end, with Spelling and Goldberg's help, the episode was aired as scheduled.

In 1981, while Tony Randall's clout could get a "homosexual" on the air, his character in *Love, Sidney* was stripped of all sexuality. The way NBC read the political climate, the trick was to satisfy the

gay lobby that Sidney Shorr's image wasn't derogatory, while satisfying the "far righteous" that it wasn't laudatory either. In the pilot,
a TV movie called *Sidney Shorr,* a few brief references suggested
that Randall's Sidney had once had a male lover. The series Sidney
who followed, however, was a man without a sex life. His homosexuality was essentially a plot device to keep his relationship with the
young woman Laurie platonic. In the pilot, Sidney talked the pregnant and unmarried Laurie out of having an abortion and pledged
to care for both her and her child.

Sidney was an eighties version of *Father Knows Best.* The scripts
were contrived to legitimate unpracticing homosexuals and family
traditions at the same time. Oliver Hailey, who wrote the pilot, told
me that "if the Moral Majority could just see it, they'd love it. Sidney's
a throwback. He's profamily. He's almost a prude about sex." For all
that the show was "a timid groundbreaker," Hailey said after the
pilot, "I felt everyone beginning to panic." Randall denied that there
was network pressure to get him to trim his character, but Hailey said
that Sidney's homosexuality had been toned down in successive
drafts. Randall defended Sidney as an authentic middle-aged gay
type, and with his star's clout, fought to keep Sidney as gay (if inac-
tively so) as he was in the pilot.

Newt Deiter, the much consulted head of the Gay Media Task
Force, had been shown the pilot script, and the question he was paid
to answer was simply, Are there homosexuals like Sidney Shorr? He
advised NBC that Sidney did, in fact, correspond to a sexless, sub-
limating type of homosexual. Deiter said that in 1977 the networks
had had in development perhaps thirty different projects—movies,
pilots, and series episodes—involving gay characters. "At this point,"
he told me in the fall of 1981, "I know of five. Now something has
to be so superb that it can overcome the presumption against a gay
show." Richard Levinson said he doubted *That Certain Summer*
could get made in this atmosphere. That same fall, one major television star was committed to a TV movie in which her character,
having just lost her lover, was thrown together with a man who had
just lost his male lover. The homosexuality was "backstory" only, but
the network's top executive in charge of TV movies told the producer that homosexual characters could not be done now because
the network couldn't take a chance on estranging its southern affiliates.

In May 1981, however, affiliate managers from Salt Lake City,
Utah; Biloxi, Mississippi; Baton Rouge, Louisiana; and Columbia, Missouri, told me they were not experiencing any upsurge of fundamentalist mail. Nevertheless, the networks were convinced the popular
pendulum was swinging away not just on the matter of homosexuality, but from titillation shows featuring the female body. What the

industry called the "jiggle" genre had been distinctly overexposed. On top of this, the Coalition was beating the drums, mobilizing a public mood—not the only public mood, but never mind that—and intimidating frightened advertisers. Norman Lear organized People for the American Way, to fight the New Right, but he along with other Hollywood liberals shared the Reverend Wildmon's distaste for smarmy sex jokes, and what he called "reprehensible" jiggling. No prominent voice in the industry, except for the producers of shows like *Three's Company* (who warned against another wave of *Red Channels*–style blacklisting), was prepared to stand up for T&A. The upshot was that by the fall of 1981, jiggle was conspicuous by its absence from the new schedule, and the half-draped, alluring male body was more evident than that of the female.

The "far righteous" had succeeded in their limited objectives. Partly for that reason, and partly perhaps because of internal fissures over strategy and the attention worth paying to television compared to other New Right bugaboos, the Coalition dropped out of sight. The Reverend Falwell decided to concentrate on other New Right issues. When the Reverend Wildmon went public again, it was to call for a boycott of NBC's movie *Sister, Sister,* and then NBC itself—because of their alleged anti-Christian aspects. This time the press paid little attention, and Wildmon's media star set. But the Bible Belt had already sent the networks a message guaranteed to reverberate through network corridors for a long time to come.

CHAPTER 13

The Temple Stands

Just as network executives were misreading the conservative mood and recoiling from the fundamentalist right, another political attack broke upon them. Unlike the fundamentalist challenge, this one surged up from the bedrock of television politics—a steady politics that can't be fended off, that doesn't disappear from decade to decade. This is the politics of business, of the advertisers who underwrite living-room entertainment and who now, in the early eighties, were anxiously worrying about their look. The networks weren't panicked by the business offensive as they were by the fundamentalists, but coming at a time of shrinking market shares and severe economic pressures, the business attack underscored the essential power relations in what is, after all, show *business*. It opened a window into Hollywood's deepest politics.

As television became prey to all manner of criticisms from the right, none on the face of it seemed more intriguing and astounding than the charge, by neoconservative critics and business alike, that this glittering medium decked out with bulletins about the splendors of the capitalist way of life undermines the image of capitalism. Entertainment now joined the news on the big-business danger list. Polls showed that the reputation of big business fell during the late sixties, then recouped part of its loss, then dove again after the OPEC oil shock of 1973. The nightly news brought item after item about pollution, bribery, dangerous products, cartels, corporate tax write-offs. . . . Prominent businessmen began speechmaking against what they took to be cruel and unusual treatment in the media. Neoconservatives in *Commentary,* the *New Leader,* and the *Wall Street Journal*—later joined by the paleoconservatives of *National Review* —developed the theme that intellectuals were the core of a "new class" rooted in the nonprofit sector of the economy, lacking any direct experience of business and its problems, uncomprehending of the entrepreneurial ethic, mesmerized by the siren songs of self-expression, and effectively undermining confidence in American business. Daniel Patrick Moynihan and Nathan Glazer declared that intellectuals had accomplished a "surprising conquest of the mass media."

If the "new class" were as antibusiness and well entrenched in the mass media as neoconservatives said, and if the media were so effective as conditioners of public opinion, it was hard to imagine that Ronald Reagan could ever have been elected president of the United States, let alone that Jeane Kirkpatrick, Norman Podhoretz, and William Buckley could be regularly consulted in high places. Lacking a sense of irony, neoconservatism and some of the more articulate right-wing businessmen agreed that the right needed to mobilize, and the Reagan election did not dampen their enthusiasm. Already by the mid-seventies, many of the most powerful American businessmen were feeling that the general crisis of legitimacy had fallen with particularly crushing weight on them in particular, and that the universities and the news media were responsible for their bad image.

Feeling excluded from the media mainstream, many corporations took direct action to woo opinion-makers and criticize the news. Kaiser Aluminum ran full-page newspaper ads blasting the networks for refusing to let them air commercials on public policy. (Eventually, in 1981, ABC decided to permit a limited amount of general, "philosophical" advertising, but only during late-night hours.) An Illinois utility widely distributed a videotape juxtaposing a *60 Minutes* piece criticizing its nuclear plant cost overruns to its own tapes of the full interviews conducted by *60 Minutes;* the result was not flattering to *60 Minutes*'s fairness. Meanwhile, Mobil Oil and other major corporations began running direct political statements on the *New York Times* Op-Ed Page and in other prominent places. They also took to sponsoring so much depoliticized culture on public television that wags took to calling it the Petroleum Broadcasting System.

Meanwhile, foundations on the right set out to bolster the theoretical rationale of capitalism and spread the ideals of deregulated business throughout the university world and public discourse at large. Although business and the neoconservatives were most prone to spot ideology in news and in formal education, entertainment eventually found its way into their sights, too. The new conservative wave took over from Lionel Trilling the idea that Western culture is an "adversary culture," a cathedral to self-expression arrayed against capitalist rationality and public virtue. Moreover, they saw this cult of the self as a powerful disintegrative force.*

Previously, cultural conservatives had rarely paid enough attention to popular music, movies, television, or comic books to bother decoding them for ideology, although a suspicion of popular forms lived an underground life outside intellectual circles. (One recalls, for example, Vice-President Spiro T. Agnew singling out the lyrics of popular music for containing dangerous messages about the beneficence of drugs.) Only recently has the new, neoconservative critique found its way to the most popular entertainment. In the words of Philip Marcus, the executive director of the Institute for Educational Affairs (conceived in 1978 by Irving Kristol and William Simon to fight "adversary sentiments" and "utopian expectations" with corporate and right-wing foundation grants), "The impulses of our culture since the turbulences of the 1960s still reverberate in public portrayals: John Wayne gives way to Woody Allen, Herbert Hoover is transformed into J. R. Ewing, Sergeant York's replacement is *M*A*S*H*. The 'heroes' of comedy and derision replace the heroes of tradition and faith."

Neoconservative journalism began to argue that television is a trove of skewed images. Ben Stein, in particular, began publishing articles on popular TV entertainment in *The Wall Street Journal* and *The Public Interest,* and in 1979 published a book called *The View from Sunset Boulevard.* After an impressionistic scan of some popular shows, Stein concluded that television was populated by corrupt and murderous businessmen, an unprincipled and destructive military, the "evil or pompous" rich, and the "saintly but honest" poor. Small towns were "wicked, dangerous places." "In the thousands of hours I have spent watching adventure shows," Stein wrote, "I have never seen a major crime committed by a poor, teenage, black, Mexican, or Puerto Rican youth, even though they account for a high percentage of all violent crime." After some time on the job in Hollywood, and interviews with "about forty important TV writers and producers," Stein concluded that prime time was what it was because it bore the impress of the "creative community's" own val-

---

*In this they are joined by the left-wing antimodernism of Christopher Lasch in *The Culture of Narcissism.*

ues. They are sentimental about the poor (from which, Stein wrote mistakenly, they descend) and hostile to the powerful because they are "a class that once was powerless, dominated by other classes— businessmen, heirs, and so forth—held in political thrall by an America dominated politically by small towns and their remnants, and that had then emerged into a position of power and influence." Television "represents nothing more than the views of a few hundred people in the western section of Los Angeles. It is a highly parochial, idiosyncratic view of the world that comes out on TV screens, the world view of a group whose moment has come."

A vulgar Marxism has become the prevailing style of such neoconservative critics. All social complexity, industry structure, and market relations collapse into the self-serving strategies of elites, sometimes called classes. Stein succeeded in writing a book about television content and production without taking seriously the fact that the producers and writers work under contract to networks that accumulate large audiences whose attention they sell to advertisers. He failed to ask why major corporations would pay good money to other multibillion-dollar companies to order distortions from these sentimental liberals, let alone why anyone would watch these exercises in self-serving propaganda. In the view from Ben Stein, there is no social system, there are no organizations, there are no structural limits on what the writers and producers can pump into the pipeline. And this is not even to speak of Stein's flawed method, the scattershot quality of his examples, and the restricted circle of his interviews.

Like many exaggerations, however, Stein's idea was provocative, and left-wing critics of popular culture have for the most part sidestepped his charges. And although Stein was naïve to attribute television's values to writers and producers pure and simple, his impressions of prime-time television had the virtue of inspiring a more elaborate if not more persuasive study. A more sophisticated analysis, with more sophisticated flaws, was undertaken by the Media Institute, an organization whose board of trustees includes several corporate executives, including Herbert Schmertz of Mobil Oil. The Media Institute set out to test Stein's idea that businessmen in prime time are overwhelmingly, as they put it, "crooks, con-men, and clowns," and their findings were brought to the networks' attention.

Using standard content-analysis techniques, coders viewed 4 episodes of each of the fifty prime-time shows broadcast between December 1979 and April 1980. Of this total of two hundred episodes, eighty-eight from thirty-seven different series—contained businessmen with plot functions. A total of 118 businessmen appeared in these eighty-eight episodes. The Media Institute concluded that two-thirds of them were portrayed as foolish, greedy, or criminal; only one-quarter were shown in a positive light. Even these white-hats were good in their private lives, not in the normal pursuit of their economic activities. The biggest businesses showed up the worst. Over half the corporate leaders (fifteen out of a total of twenty-eight characters) broke the law.

Of all the businessmen portrayed, major continuing characters fared the best, but even this collection had more negative functions than positive. On the other hand, of those businessmen appearing in no more than a single episode, only 6 percent were presented in a favorable light. Hard work was normally labeled "workaholism" and blamed for stress and strained personal relations. In short, the Media Institute concluded, "The business world in general is portrayed in a rather curious light—as the embodiment of all that is wrong with American capitalism. Bosses reap major rewards at the expense of both their workers and the general public. The interests of business are unalterably opposed to those of working people and consumers. What is good for business is not likely to be in the interest of American society."

Again, there are methodological eyebrows to be raised. The Media Institute sample is small, the results statistically insignificant. Their coding is also somewhat problematic. What is gained, for example, by coding Archie Bunker as a businessman, although that is literally how he makes his living? But methodological quibbles aside, I think there is little doubt that businessmen's images, if not quite as grim as either Ben Stein or the Media Institute claim, are—to put it mildly—unflattering. In a much more comprehensive forthcoming study, George Gerbner, dean of the Annenberg School of Communications at the University of Pennsylvania, reports that "good" business characters in prime time outnumbered the "bad" two to one, whereas the ratio for police was twelve to one and for doctors, sixteen to one. The question is, Why might this be true, and what should we make of it?

The Media Institute itself has surprisingly little to say by way of explanation: only that television entertainment displays "ignorance, bigotry and lack of taste." But the question of what television makes of businessmen has been too narrowly posed. Consider it in the context of television's depiction of capitalism as an entire system. As Ben Stein recognizes, television's world is relentlessly upbeat, clean, and materialistic. Even more sweepingly, with few exceptions, prime time gives us people preoccupied with personal ambition. If not utterly consumed by ambition and the fear of ending up as losers, these characters take both the ambition and the fear for granted. If not surrounded by middle-class arrays of consumer goods, they themselves are glamorous incarnations of desire. The happiness they long for is private, not public; they make few demands on society as a whole, and even when troubled they seem content with the existing institutional order. Personal ambition and consumerism are the driving forces in their lives. The sumptuous and brightly lit settings of most series amount to advertisements for a consumption-centered version of the good life, and this doesn't even take into consideration the incessant commercials, which convey the idea that human aspirations for liberty, pleasure, accomplishment, and status can be fulfilled in the realm of consumption. The relentless background hum of prime time is this packaged good life.

Television did not, of course, invent these aspirations. The desire for comfort and convenience, the equation of freedom and individualism with the acquisitive style, have been core values in American life for a century and a half, all the more so with the coming of industrial society and an economy predicated on the mass production of consumer goods. In the world built on this foundation, one must never lose sight of the obvious: Television programs must attract an audience in order to be useful to advertisers. Audiences aren't disenchanted with these values, or they would flee television in disgust. True, consumerism on television doesn't usurp all cultural space any more than it does in real life. People care about love, friendship, safety, trust, adventure, the nurture of the weak, not just material wealth. Programs must cater to those cares, too, in order to be popular, but on television, these other motives and desires are lived out, for the most part, against the settings of a well-appointed good life.

This is television's fundamental politics. Whatever the shifts in program emphasis to left or right, Maude's living room and that of Farrah Fawcett's fictional Angel don't look all that different. In other words, if television is unkind to businessmen, it is scarcely unkind to the values of a business civilization. Capitalism and the consumer society come out largely uncontested. To understand, then, why the proprietors of that business civilization look bad in so many shows, we have to consider not just the attitudes of writers and producers but the nature of TV conventions and the industry's strategy for gathering audiences. Throughout popular culture, characters oversimplify traits. On cartoonlike television shows, characters are usually written, directed, and acted to represent an embodiment and caricature of some attribute. Moreover, by TV convention, white-hats fight black-hats. The obligatory villains are naturally going to be individuals who have the power to hurt their victims. Producers, writers, and network executives share the culture's individualist premises: People are what they make of themselves, and little guys deserve to succeed. The pathos of individualism, though, is that if everyone succeeds, the drama dissolves. Individualism is a powerful and in many ways attractive ideology, but not because it promises universal happiness. In fiction as in reality, there is not all that much room at the top. So to keep conflict fresh, and give victory its tang,

characters need to encounter obstacles in society; and by the convention that television takes over from standard American ideology,
obstacles have to be personified. Structures rarely exist; culprits do.
Moreover, if the culprits are social inferiors, the drama of striving for
upward mobility loses its edge. A small shopkeeper afflicted by muggers appeals to our anger, our sense of pathos, perhaps our conflict
of loyalties between two underdogs. The same shopkeeper afflicted
by crooked developers appeals more unequivocally to our sense of
identification with the little guy. The convincing culprits, then, will
be the big guys who have the power to hurt everyone else, who by
getting and staying big threaten to keep the little guys little.

Today's political economy, quite obviously, is dominated by giant
corporations and the state. At their peaks stand the owners and
managers of capital and the political elite of elected officials, top
bureaucrats, and fixers. Their freedom is constrained, too, for they
work within structures; but if anyone has the power to shape those
structures, to make the decisions that set the ground rules for everyone else, and to profit from them, this elite does. People with less
power and privilege who follow the culture's rules for getting their
just deserts bang up against the massive institutions of business and
government, as well as the fact that there have to be losers to remind
winners how far they've come. That is why none of the big institutions—neither business, nor government, nor unions—is popular
today. Businessmen do fare badly on television. It would be interesting to see how government bureaucrats and union leaders do—at
least as badly, I suspect.

It could be argued, then, that whatever the private views of writers
and producers, popular sentiment as registered by the networks
impels them to make a reasonably large percentage of their villains
big shots. None of which is to deny that many writers and producers
dislike big business, or that their hostility makes it easy for them to
resort to such business villains. However magnificently rewarded,
writers and producers have ample reason to resent the power of the
corporations they know best: television networks and major suppliers.

Ben Stein perceives accurately that writers are not abstracted
ideologues. They learn to detest businessmen by getting to know
them. "The Hollywood TV writer," he observes, "is actually in a
business, selling his labor to brutally callous businessmen. One actually has to go through the experience of writing for money in Hollywood or anywhere else to realize how unpleasant it is. Most of the
pain comes from dealings with business people. . . . The TV writer
. . . is actually down there in the pit with the clawing agents and
businessmen, and he often has reason to feel that he has been shortchanged, to say the least." But what Stein misses is that writers and

especially producers (who hire, fire, and constrain writers) measure the real world of business against an ideal standard of fair business practice. They don't wish to destroy business, but to regulate businessmen to improve their own position as businessmen in a business system. They themselves are small proprietors in a world dominated by big capital. Their attitude is the traditional *petit-bourgeois* mixture of admiration and fear, approach and envy, respect and resentment of the powerhouses on whom they depend for their considerable livelihood. This ambivalence is the typical American attitude toward authority.

Even if the image of businessmen were as bad as Stein and the Media Institute say, it couldn't be traced simply to the ambivalent feelings of writers and producers toward the major suppliers and networks. The fact is, though, that the images themselves are more complex than the neoconservative content analysis has allowed. Simply to count "positive" and "negative" behaviors, and to equate them automatically with "good" and "bad" images, will not do. If the gangster hero is, as Robert Warshow has written, what we want to be and what we are afraid we may become, then J. R. Ewing is the man we love to hate but (in a corner of our souls) hope we may become. In an age of rampant self-assertion, when *Winning Through Intimidation* can become a best-seller, it is too simple to say that this character, who all by himself accounts for a considerable percentage of the Media Institute's "crooks and con-men," places businessmen in disrepute. We covertly admire, too, the people we love to fear.

Most likely the explanation for J. R. Ewing and the incidental killer realtor alike is tangled. Writers and producers reach into their repertoires for popular stereotypes, and where their own feelings about big bad businessmen match their sense of what the traffic will bear, there they find their convincing villains. Even if it happened that TV writers in their private lives were crusading anticorporate liberals, or socialists for that matter—and very few are either—they wouldn't be free to propagandize as they see fit. If most Americans loved businessmen and were deeply offended at the sight of a murderous, fictional tycoon, the writers would have to change the occupations of their fictional killers—or the networks would find new writers.

What business chooses to forget, in short, is what the media never forget for a minute: that the media are businesses. As individuals, businessmen may crave recognition, but as advertisers they share with television an interest in the sure-fire audience. "You're asking for complexity," as George Gerbner of Pennsylvania's Annenberg School of Communications aptly told a conference of businessmen, "but you're paying for circulation."

Seen this way, television highlights one of the ironies of capitalism. By engorging the profit motive, business itself fails to offer capitalist society a unifying creed. "Free enterprise" liberty means rather more to those who own and control huge corporations than to the majority who work for them. The ladder of opportunity looks more solid from its top than its bottom. What we have instead of a unifying creed is—commercial television.

In its slapdash way, network television accomplishes exactly the task that American business pays for, government permits, and audiences have come to expect: to assemble maximum numbers of people in their living rooms and keep them minimally diverted. Advertisers want people to buy their products, the television industry wants them to tune in again, and people want to be amused, distracted, "entertained"; none has any deeper purpose. Industry hands say that everyone has two businesses, his own and show business. Just so, almost everyone lives two lives. Television is the background stream.

Just as American audiences learned to take commercials for granted, the industry takes for granted the prerogatives of advertisers as a whole. The networks obsess about marketability; writers write their scripts in standardized "acts" designed to be punctuated by commercials; producers deliver film or tape with blank stretches inserted for commercials; and audiences, indeed, often look forward to interruptions for visits to kitchen, bathroom, and the other sites of their set-aside life. The commercial financing first brought into radio in the twenties and automatically transferred to television is the very sea in which the entire industry swims. And like water, it is all but invisible to the creatures who inhabit it. As everyone in the industry knows so deeply it scarcely needs saying, the advertisers set the terms, the networks order up the shows, the producers produce to order, and audiences play their part by accepting the results.

C H A P T E R 1 4

Hill
Street Blues:
"Make It Look Messy"

In network television, even the exceptions reveal the rules. Everything emerges at the end of a chain of *ifs*. If a producer gets on the inside track; *if* he or she has strong ideas and fights for them intelligently; *if* they appear at least somewhat compatible with the networks' conventional wisdom about what a show ought to be at a particular moment; *if* the producer is willing to give ground here and there; *if* he or she is protected by a powerhouse production company that the network is loath to kick around; *if* the network has the right niche for the show; *if* the project catches the eye of the right executive at the right time, and doesn't get lost in the shuffle when the guardian executive changes jobs . . . then the system that cranks out mind candy occasionally proves hospitable to something else, while at the same time betraying its limits. As Universal Studios executive Jennings Lang once said about the work of the writer Howard Rodman, "Every department store needs a boutique." In the early eighties, *Hill Street Blues* was network television's most conspicuous boutique. This intelligent, literate ensemble police series with its rough texture and intertangled plots, its complex mix of crime melodrama and absurdist comedy, was commissioned by the same network executive who brought America *Real People, The Brady Brides,* and *Sheriff Lobo.* As the networks scrambled to cash

273

in on the presumed trend toward national discipline, Fred Silverman at NBC wanted a down-and-dirty cop show. But because he assigned the notion to two particular writer-producers at the right moment in their careers; because they were working for the right company; because they caught some of the richness of American life at that moment; because they made the right choices of director, line producer, and cast; and because they took some chances and fought for them, what Silverman got was *Hill Street Blues*, at its best a mature and even brilliant show that violated many conventions, pleased critics, caught the undertow of cultural change, and ran away with the Emmys. Then, in defiance of virtually all predictions, after puny first-season ratings *Hill Street* in its second and third seasons also became NBC's top series hit. But for all its singularity, *Hill Street* in the end was also commercial television banging up against its limitations, revealing at the moment of its triumph just how powerful are the pressures and formulas that keep prime time close to dead center. For when network television aspires to be extraordinary, the industry's everyday mentality doesn't dissolve. Breakthroughs in form soon become fossilized as formula. This season's odd characters become next season's stereotypes. The weekly assembly line is not kind to writing, acting, or risk-taking. Thus, the story of the extraordinary *Hill Street Blues*—the product of "a long series of flukes," as its cocreator Michael Kozoll puts it—underscores not only the possibilities of popular culture, but the industry's most ordinary boundaries.

Hill Street's achievement was first of all a matter of style. Thirteen principal characters and several other regulars careened through this show, making it, by conventional wisdom, overpopulated. To thicken the plot further, most of the episodes were written in four-show blocks, with at least four major stories running concurrently, each starting at a different moment and often not resolving at all. In *Hill Street* shop talk, the stories were "knitted." This intercutting, which is characteristic of soap opera, was joined to a density of look and sound that was decidedly un–soap operatic. Quick cuts, a furious pace, a nervous camera made for complexity and congestion, a sense of entanglement and continuous crisis that matched the actual density and convolution of city life, of life in a ghetto police precinct in particular. In one episode, for example, five major stories were set up in the first three minutes. In the course of that two-hour sequence, three more story lines were introduced and two others continued. By the end, at least eight major stories were still unresolved. No wonder many people who watched an episode or two found the series hard to follow. During the first season the producers actually wondered if ratings were bad not only because NBC had shuttled the show among five different time-slots, but because the episodes were simply too confusing.

The language of *Hill Street* was also uncommonly quick, smart, and, at least at first, rarely damaged by episodic television's occupational hazard, the sure-shot, trademark line. In bad television, every point is made twice. In mediocre television, an expository line is certain to come once, framed for effect. On *Hill Street Blues* at its best, the obvious line was uttered in passing, or not at all. In one core story line in the pilot, two teenagers were holding hostages during a robbery. No one burst into Hill Street Station to announce sonorously, "There's a holdup in progress; they're holding hostages!" Instead, in a rushed moment, Capt. Frank Furillo said over the phone, "It may or may not be a hostage situation in that liquor store. We haven't made contact yet," while his lines overlapped with Sgt. Phil Esterhaus's comically baroque dialogue over another phone: "We don't know that yet, Commander. We won't know that until we've interfaced with the perpetrators."

By television's standards, several of the characters were new departures. Veronica Hamel's Joyce Davenport, the liberal public defender, was the first woman television regular at once professional, tough, elegant, intelligent, and sexy. Bruce Weitz's Det. Mick Belker was a growler who, one time in a fit of rage, bit off the nose of a police-academy recruit; he was also the frequent object of lectures and matchmaking by his Jewish mother. James B. Sikking's Lt. Howard Hunter, head of the equipment-heavy Emergency Action Team, was the caricature of a right-winger, denouncing the ghetto's "genetic degenerates."

Gags aside, *Hill Street* was also a show that knew race and class tear this society apart, that behaving decently under these conditions is an everyday trial, and that there are no blindingly obvious solutions for the accumulated miseries of the ghetto. The show's racial byplay honored the everyday street sense of race without sliding into race baiting. And despite the occasional quick fix to move into or out of a segment, the growing number of action stunts to cover over writing problems in later seasons, the growing reliance on predictable character shtick, the payoff in *Hill Street* was usually not really a deed done, a criminal caught. Instead it was a provisional sort of knowledge, what Michael Kozoll called "a very Henry Jamesian finish."

Hill Street Blues wasn't the standard hybrid or mutant, although some of its features had precedents. MTM, which owned it, had done other shows in which quasi-families of co-workers played out their relations in the workplace: *The Mary Tyler Moore Show, Lou Grant, WKRP in Cincinnati.* Drama-comedy fusions and a certain social realism were also MTM specialties. Most to the point, MTM has a reputation for giving writer-producers their heads; and in Steven Bochco and Michael Kozoll it had acquired two writer-producers with heads. The tale of *Hill Street Blues* is first of all the tale of writers and their scripts. However watchful the industrial eyes gazing over the writers' shoulders, the medium still does bear the mark of its writers.

When the chance to do *Hill Street* came, Bochco and Kozoll were already in their late thirties. The lean, graying, effusive Bochco was the entrepreneur. He grew up on the Upper West Side of Manhattan, went to the High School of the Performing Arts, studied dramatic arts at Carnegie Tech, then moved west to Universal Studios as an assistant story editor. For a dozen years Bochco worked his way up in television's major factory. Universal was cranking out vast numbers of television shows, and a bright young writer could move from show to show with relative ease, rubbing elbows with some of the industry's steadiest practitioners of television craft, those masters of elementary formula whom aspirants to quality called hacks.

Bochco was bright, aggressive, and lucky. He had a wicked wit and an ear for sharp dialogue, just the combination that flourished in some of the cop shows of the early seventies. Hence he was able to move up to story-editing (which requires imposing consistency on scripts written by many hands): first, *The Name of the Game*, a late-sixties adventure series about a crusading publisher and his reporter sidekicks; then *McMillan and Wife* and *Columbo*. He did not excel at clear plot lines, according to a producer who worked with him then; but what was a weakness at the formula factory later stood him in good stead when he set out to concoct stories that didn't quite resolve about cops who never quite made the streets safe or got the criminals behind bars.

Bochco then moved up to the more satisfying and better-paying specialty trade of pilot-writing. He wrote and produced the pilot for *The Invisible Man*, a show that failed to last more than a season. No matter. The prestige of pilot-writers doesn't hang on the success of their products. The next step was not only to write a pilot but to produce the series, and so in 1976–77 Bochco wrote and produced an L.A. cop show called *Delvecchio*, which starred, alongside Judd Hirsch, a character actor named Michael Conrad and a younger one named Charles Haid. *Delvecchio*'s one-dimensional plots sported brash, staccato, sometimes mildly raunchy one-liners: "These days you walk down the street smoking a joint, they give you a moving violation." "Macavan'll have my bagels in a sling." Scattered among squealing tires and clear plot resolutions were Bochco's telltale bathroom jokes.

Hirsch was more tender and Haid more tough, but both were liberal cops on the side of the downtrodden. In one episode Bochco wrote, Hirsch and Haid came to an Arizona town to take an Indian youth (played by Erik Estrada, later of *CHiPs* fame) back to L.A., where he had escaped from prison. They had to fight off the bad-guy sheriff who wore an American flag insignia on his shoulder, chain-smoked big cigars, and kept calling the youth "Geronimo." They also had to remind the youth's grandfather, who had turned on him, that "you either love that kid or you don't." Liberal values and superior knowhow eventually prevailed against the small-minded racist town.

Delvecchio lasted a year, and in retrospect it is most noteworthy for having brought Steven Bochco together with Michael Kozoll. Kozoll was a droll, slow-speaking Milwaukeean in a town full of fast-talking coastal types. A few years older than Bochco, Kozoll had come into the business by accident. While still a student at the University of Wisconsin, he had published short stories in literary journals. Elizabeth Bowen thought highly of his writing. *Playboy* and *Esquire* courted him, but "it was all too much for me," he said later; he didn't think he had the patience and discipline for a writer's life. So he went off to Europe, did graduate work in linguistics at the Sorbonne and in Barcelona, and wrote nothing for ten years. When he returned to America in the late sixties, he took off for San Francisco, worked with friends in a pottery collective, hung around Golden Gate Park, joined antiwar demonstrations, and taught English at Bay Area community colleges until antiwar activity shortened that career. Kicking around San Francisco, lacking money, repelled by the thought of reentering academia in earnest, Kozoll started to watch television for the first time in his life, and there came to him the classic thought: "I can do that!"

If the story of his life were to have been screened in the Hollywood of the thirties, a big storybook marked SUCCESS would have unfurled its sumptuous vellum pages at this moment. Kozoll cooked up some episode scripts and sent them to six agents whose names he got out of a writer's almanac; all six wrote back to say they would handle him, but to be available for steady work he had to move to L.A. A few television writers manage to keep working while living in the San Francisco Bay area or around Carmel, but L.A. is almost obligatory for a young writer seeking the main chance. So Kozoll landed at Universal, where he deployed his irony to keep his distance from the flimsy enthusiasms of the television business. "When I read Thomas Mann," he says, "I know he's better than Ross Macdonald. I don't think there are a lot of people in the television business who understand the difference." But although Kozoll retained respect for a well-turned sentence, he had long since given up hopes of literary glory. There wasn't much he was burning to say, and he held few illusions about his work. "It doesn't take brilliance. Anyone who really has talent can make it in this business. There's so fucking much hunger for competent work."

Kozoll refined his craft as story editor for *Quincy, McCloud, Switch, Kojak,* and then *Delvecchio,* where he hooked up with

Steven Bochco under the mantle of executive producer William Sackheim. "Billy pushed us into the belief we could do good things," Kozoll says. "Commerciality and excellence were not diametrically opposed. But I swore I'd never do any episodic shows again." He hated the grind and was frustrated by endless formula, so he took off to Warner Brothers to write feature films.

Bochco, meanwhile, tried his hand at two more pilots—*Richie Brockelman, Private Eye,* a glib spinoff of *The Rockford Files,* and *Turnabout,* a sitcom he did not much admire. Through all this, Universal had let him advance, paid him handsomely, and gotten his shows on the air. However, he was wearying of frenetic production schedules and tight budgets. When his shows failed to get on the air, he wondered whether his pilots were nothing more than chips in big-league studio games. Yet in later years he still gave Universal credit for having schooled him. "They're not evil," he told a reporter. "They're just bigger—and there are certain inherent problems with being big. Because they deal in volume, they make volume decisions. It's the difference between factory-made goods and handmade goods. It doesn't mean the handmade good is always going to be better, but you're probably going to enjoy making it a lot more."

By now Bochco had mastered the producing trade and was well enough regarded as a skilled craftsman to get offers from other suppliers. He jumped at a chance to go to MTM, where Grant Tinker had the reputation for backing his producers without meddling unduly in their works; and there was plenty of money—"Mary's money," it was called around the company—to keep a show from looking impoverished. He collaborated with Kozoll on a TV movie called *Vampire,* but his first series attempt at MTM was a 1979 cop show called *Paris,* built around the fine Shakespearean actor James Earl Jones. Jones's character, though, was wooden and the stories simple and predictable. The show lasted only half a season on CBS before it got canceled for bad ratings.

Paris wasn't yet down the tubes when Bochco got his real break. On the strength of his previous pilots, NBC extended Bochco an "open" pilot commitment: a commitment to make a pilot on a mutually agreeable subject. In 1979 he produced a pilot called *Every Stray Dog and Kid,* an MTM-style drama with comic overtones about a woman just out of prison who sets up a halfway house for other recent inmates. It didn't sell. But NBC chief Fred Silverman and the president of the entertainment division, Brandon Tartikoff, liked Bochco's work, and a lengthy track record does not suffer from one or two failures. "They know who does what in this town," as Bochco says. "They know who can deliver." The arrangement was that Bochco would pitch an idea. If the network didn't like it, they would bounce back with their own. It didn't hurt that the aggressive young Texan

Michael Zinberg had become vice-president for comedy develop-ment at NBC. Zinberg had directed and produced at MTM, and when he got together with Silverman and Tartikoff to discuss what NBC should be looking for, and Silverman put forward the notion of a cop show set in a neighborhood with a "heavy ethnic mix," Zinberg suggested Bochco, Kozoll, and MTM.

As usual, the discussions at this point were quick, sketchy, and recombinant. "It was Fred's inspiration," Tartikoff says. Silverman mused out loud in classical shorthand style that if *Barney Miller* were done one-camera—i.e., on film and not tape, and not in front of a studio audience—and in the worst neighborhood, as in the forthcom-ing movie *Fort Apache, The Bronx*, something interesting would result. Caught in the incipient law-and-order network mood, Silver-man wanted a nervy, rough show from the viewpoint of police on the real-world frontier. Paddy Chayevsky's movie *Hospital* was cited for its ragged, frantic style, its absurdist ballooning of the horrors of medical life, its mockery of the conventions of medical shows. David Gerber's TV series *Police Story* was mentioned because its police had personal lives. "The shorthand came down to a cross between *Barney Miller* and *Police Story*," Zinberg remembers.

Whereupon Tartikoff and Zinberg met with Bochco, Kozoll, and MTM's Stu Erwin for a classically long lunch at Beverly Hills's La Scala Restaurant. Bochco and Kozoll came primed with a couple of their own ideas, of which their favorite was a sort of *Grand Hotel* set, Kozoll remembers, "someplace like the Hyatt Regency, which is a little city, where people can constantly walk in the door with prob-lems and situations." "*Love Boat* set in a San Francisco hotel," goes Tartikoff's shorthand recollection. But Silverman had spoken: NBC wanted a cop show. Cop shows were what they associated with Bochco's record. Cop shows were a premium genre, equipped with heroes, with villains, with a "franchise" to meddle in many other lives, with steady conflict and steady resolution. They were also, whether network executives thought this way or not—and usually they did not—rituals for the maintenance of social order.

Cop shows had not been doing well for a few years, but perhaps the great wheel of the genre cycle was about to turn again. Tartikoff said to Kozoll and Bochco, "You guys are good at cop shows, with *Delvecchio* and all. Fred Silverman would like to do a cop show that is not a standard cops-and-robbers show. A little bit of *M*A*S*H*, a little bit of *Barney Miller*. We'd like for you guys to develop a show that has more to do with cops' personal lives." But if Kozoll was cool toward cranking out episodic television of any kind, he was positively cold toward cop shows. "Because no matter how well intentioned you are when you go out to do a cop show, it's almost impossible not to end up with a bag of shit afterward. Because we've all done those

boring, heroic, tired, tired shows, and you're going to kill yourself and
the public doesn't even want to watch them anymore, and they
really don't address a very serious issue." Moreover, Bochco had
been drained by his season of producing *Paris:* "I was personally so
dismayed with the work. I wasn't happy with what I did at all. And
so I sure wasn't looking to do another cop show."

And then there would be all the network nonsense to put up with.
Kozoll, no lover of network meetings, was already bothered by the
recombinant talk. "They knew it was a dangerous choice of words
with us, saying we want a cross between . . . *Police Story* and *I
Remember Mama,* because we're not going to rip off somebody else's
television show. We don't think of ourselves as creative bank robbers.
I said, 'Someone's doing *Fort Apache.* Who wants to do *Fort Apache*?'
That's one of the reasons we said no right away." The meeting ended
with what Bochco calls a "qualified no."

But as they left the restaurant together, Bochco said, "Let's not be
hasty." Who could sneeze at a pilot commitment? Pilots are "serious
money," as Kozoll puts it, "so you go into it with a different attitude
than, 'Go write a script for me.' " Not only would the networks pay
the creators to write an hour-long pilot script, but if the show got on
the air there would be royalties in the tens of thousands of dollars for
every episode ever aired, whether the creators wrote it or disappeared into the jungles of the Amazon. The network's commitment
to shoot the pilot raised the odds of converting a pilot script to a series
on the air from thirty to one to perhaps three to one. A series lasting
long enough on the network to go into syndication could make the
creators rich.

Bochco also fastened on Tartikoff's intimation that NBC was inviting them to produce something out of the ordinary. As they talked,
characters the two men had been carrying around in their heads for
years, in search of slots, began to surface. (Belker, for example, came
out of an unproduced Kozoll movie script.) Actors they had liked
working with popped to mind. The notion of a division of labor began
to form. Bochco would handle the network flak, leaving Kozoll reasonably free to do his work. In the end, with the prospect of big
money glimmering in the background, the two men felt encouraged
by the lunch. "They were talking about giving us carte blanche to do
what we wanted to do within that genre, the likes of which I had
never heard from a network before," Bochco recalls. "And that was,
for me, real seductive. On the other hand, neither one of us is a
virgin. There's a big difference between sitting around a lunch table,
and then a network guy saying 'Fuck lunch, fellows'—having to deal
with the realities of, say Broadcast Standards, which can devastate a
show."

So Bochco and Kozoll decided they would produce the pilot under two conditions: "One," in Bochco's words, was "that the programming people would genuinely leave us alone to do what we wanted to do. And two, before we ever put a pen to paper, we demanded a meeting with Broadcast Standards, to see if we could somehow get a sense from them whether the things that we were talking about doing, in the broadest terms, were going to die there. Because if they were, our attitude was 'Fuck it, why bother?' " Broadcast Standards, NBC's name for its censorship department, was an independent entity that reported over the collective head of programming. "If NBC's primary concern was to protect its corporate image against pressures from minorities, the FCC, and special-interest groups, then we felt we couldn't do the series," Bochco said later. "This show had to be grim, gritty, and rude if it was going to accurately capture the police mentality. I said, only half-jokingly, that we were going to be equal-opportunity offenders."

As for the programming itself, Bochco recalls Tartikoff saying, " 'We will absolutely let you be.' And I might add parenthetically that that is a commitment that NBC has honored to this day. Astonishingly, I might add. It is not typical behavior on the part of the network. If you want to find out the reasons why, I suggest you ask somebody at NBC."

I did ask around, but could never get a clear answer. The show was strong and intelligent; it was produced under the auspices of the reliable MTM; Zinberg was a passionate in-house advocate; Silverman and Tartikoff were fond of the show; later, when ratings were abysmal to low, the critics were almost universally enthusiastic; so why should NBC, the network in the cellar, needlessly antagonize critics when it had no other critical success on the schedule, precious little commercial success either, and no compelling backup alternative? But the most convincing guess about Bochco and Kozoll's good fortune pointed back to Fred Silverman's mysterious imprimatur. "Steven's track record was very inauspicious and I'm pretty much of a nobody," Kozoll says. "It's a very superstitious business with irrational reasons. I think Fred had an instinct about the project and about us. Fred Silverman and Brandon Tartikoff really wanted this show."

Whatever the exact reasons, NBC interfered surprisingly little over the next months. The network's young Current Programming staff did hover about, conducting their normal work: monitoring scripts, attending the "dailies," and otherwise keeping the network hand in. But they were uncharacteristically restrained.

There remained the matter of Broadcast Standards. Tartikoff arranged for Bochco and Kozoll to meet with Jerome Stanley, the head of West Coast Broadcast Standards. (NBC divided its Broadcast Standards department, with the New York office dealing mostly with commercials and Burbank dealing with the bulk of the shows.) In principle, as the network's politic guardian of public morality, Standards could abort a series altogether, or reject any particular episode. Short of wielding its ax of last resort, Standards could certainly flatten a show by ordering changes in language or picture, changes it judged necessary to honor the taboos of some sufficiently powerful social group. At the very least, Standards could hector a show unmercifully. Standards cast a long, sometimes exaggerated shadow over writers who regarded themselves as tribunes of liberty.

And Jerry Stanley was Standards incarnate. Stanley was a polite fellow in his fifties who had worked himself up through production jobs in the NBC hierarchy, with a brief interlude at Universal Studios. He seemed genuinely to believe in the morality he had been hired to police. He detested blood-squirting movies. He was appalled at the broom-handle molestation that NBC had permitted to appear in a 1974 television movie called *Born Innocent*, a corporate lapse that had led to his promotion to the Standards job. He believed that the phrase "son of a bitch" was obscene because it didn't refer literally to a real-world phenomenon; the male offspring of a bitch is, after all, a pup. "Son of a bitch" therefore had no other use than as an insult, he maintained, and so NBC wouldn't permit it. But Stanley allowed "bastard" in *Shōgun*, since "bastard" had its own passable dictionary meaning. All scripts had to be submitted to Standards, even if only a few days before air time, and they were routinely sent back with notes: "Please eliminate references to the Deity." "Delete 'Oh, God' unless it is delivered reverentially." "Delete 'hell.'" "Delete 'damn.'" Writers played the game of automatically dropping in extra hells and damns as bargaining chips, and the Standards people knew it.

Rarely did Standards reject a show out of hand, but the threat was always there. Stanley once axed a television movie under development, about prostitution, because the script was rankly exploitive and the producer only went through the motions of making the called-for changes. Stanley's Standards were in his bones. They were not written down anywhere, he said, and not discussed—not in need of discussion—at the corporate level. But Stanley maintained he would lean over backward to give the benefit of the doubt to producers whose taste he respected. Clout also counted. Stanley rejected a 1979 *Quincy* script on father-daughter incest—the daughter jumped to her death; Quincy determined that she had been pregnant by her father—only to be overruled by Fred Silverman. Jack Klugman was, after all, the powerful star of one of NBC's few high-rated series.* Stanley maintained he didn't want to harass the creative people who respected what he considered *his* creativity—and therefore he didn't send his staff "editors," as the censors are called, to dailies. A screening of the rough cut almost always sufficed.

Stanley knew that Standards often worked at cross-purposes to programming. He had heard of programming executives saying, "Let's get a little more eye candy in there," and he knew full well they meant T&A, bouncing women with skirts in the air. But above all, like his ABC and CBS counterparts in the late sixties and seventies, Stanley had to be politically sensitive. In television's early days, Standards departments had done the bidding of elite groups like doctors, lawyers, police chiefs, the FBI, and most of all advertisers themselves. At all three networks the censors tried to anticipate the feelings of network affiliates and sales departments, and to protect the networks from any conceivable charges that position-taking, "imbalance," might be violating the FCC's Fairness Doctrine. But as mass movements and interest groups—blacks, Hispanics, feminists, gays, antiviolence parents, eventually white ethnics and even businessmen—began to press on the networks, commerce came to dictate morality. Accordingly, Standards evolved into a kind of political brokerage house.

By the late seventies, Standards' *modus operandi* was to co-opt potential hostility before the fact. "Where we see a property that deals with a special-interest group," Stanley says, "and if we feel that there is any potential problem, a derogation, or misrepresentation, we will then get in touch with them," with an organized group of representatives deemed legitimate, in other words, "and either send them the script, or we will oftentimes ask the production company to invite them in as technical consultants. Under no circumstances [though] do they have the right of approval."

Like the other Standards chiefs, Jerry Stanley sounded more than a bit jaded when he referred to the "seasonal" nature of public uproars. "The Reverend Wildmon is now raising the issue of morality of television as such," he said, referring to the Coalition for Better

---

*Like another hugely successful episode that gave Standards pause, about child pornography, this one was never rerun. These were the only *Quincy* episodes never rerun. (Rumor had it that onetime NBC chairman Jane Cahill Pfeiffer had found the child-porn show offensive.) Meanwhile, the actor who played the father in the incest show lost $250,000 in a contract to record the voice-over on a commercial. Although television had flirted with the more titillating although rare form of mother-son incest, this was the first network episode to address the far more common father-daughter kind. In another case, Standards wouldn't permit the vacationing Quincy to share a cruise-ship stateroom with his lady love.

Television, then in the full flood of publicity for its demands that the networks get rid of "obscenity, profanity, and violence." "And if it isn't Wildmon, it's the Parent Teachers Association complaining about what we are showing to the children [i.e., violence]. And if it isn't them, it's the Italian-Americans, and if it isn't them, it's somebody else. We always have some vocal group. It was the Gay Task Force a few years back. When I say it's seasonal, I suppose that I was being facetious, but those things become a major problem and then they kind of go away, and then something else comes up, and then maybe that will come back, or whatever. Depending on who is carrying the torch at the time, and how much publicity he or she or that organization may be getting. If we find that we are in danger of offending a substantial percentage of the majority, we have to step back and examine what it is we are doing."

Stanley and Bochco had overlapped in their days at Universal. The two men liked each other, but the roles clashed. "He's a very dear, sweet man, with a real sense of humor," Bochco says about Stanley. Stanley later remembered their *Hill Street* summit meeting as amicable. But Bochco remembers it differently: "I actually have been put on this earth for one primary reason, and that is to torment network Broadcast Standards people. That's my real mission in life. We went into this meeting with Broadcast Standards, and we yelled at them for an hour. We came in saying, 'You son of a bitches aren't going to let us make the show.' And Jerry's attitude was 'What show are we talking about?' And we said—it was Catch-22—'There's no show, because we haven't written it yet, and we ain't going to unless you let us write it.' I mean, it was bizarre. We yelled and screamed for an hour about a show that didn't exist. We set him up a little bit, I think. We gave them our calling card. We let them know that they were going to have war with us." Stanley, for his part, thought Bochco liked to play the bad boy, and relished the performance. Each side, in short, found a way to define the result as consonant with his image: Stanley the conciliator, Bochco the rebel. Broadcast Standards, though, was now on notice. "Given what Programming has asked of you guys," so goes Bochco's recollection of Stanley's summing up, "we'll try to be understanding, blah, blah, blah, that kind of thing." He thought he had finessed Standards to a standstill.

Bochco and Kozoll started writing, but old network habits die hard. They were a few days into their script when a program executive called and said, "When are we going to get together and talk about the story?" Bochco retorted, "We've already started writing the script." "What?" "We said, 'Hey, fellas, come on, you said you were going to leave us alone.'" "Well, but we want to know what the story is before you go to the screenplay." "We'll be more than happy to come in and tell you what we're doing. But we're just going to tell you what we've already started to do." "All right, mumble, grumble, mumble, grumble, okay." "We went over and we told them certain highlights of our story, and they said, 'Well, okay.' "

The script Bochco and Kozoll turned in covered a full day of narrative time, from early-morning roll-call to late night. One hundred twenty scenes wedged into each other in the course of fifty-nine pages, introducing thirteen principals and eighteen other speaking parts. Story lines overlapped, interwove, broke off only to resume later. In bare-bones summary, along with many short atmospheric scenes, the plot tracked through everyday crisis upon everyday crisis. The strikingly attractive public defender, Joyce Davenport, stalks into the chaotic, run-down Hill Street Station looking for a client who has disappeared into a bureaucratic pigeonhole. The cocky, handsome detective J. D. LaRue tries to insuinuate himself into her good embraces. Davenport tells off the low-key captain, Frank Furillo. Officers Bobby Hill (black, patient, intelligent) and Andy Renko (loudmouthed, racist urban cowboy) observe two Hispanic teenagers robbing a liquor store and taking hostages. Lt. Howard Hunter, the pipe-smoking, tough-talking, self-parodying head of the counterinsurgency squad, counsels an attack with heavy weaponry, while the liberal community-relations officer Henry Goldblume advises careful persuasion. Furillo agrees to let a swaggering Hispanic gang leader enter the negotiations. In the middle of everything, Furillo's ex-wife Fay storms into the station, shrieking because his child-support check has bounced. Meanwhile, Hill and Renko are called to cope with a family feud in a black household. The man of the house has slept with his lover's daughter, and she is threatening to kill him. Hill defuses the skirmish by laying down provisional law: The man has to stay away from the daughter, the daughter has to be less seductive, the woman has to be more available to her man. Leaving the apartment building, Hill and Renko discover that their car has been stolen. Looking for a functioning phone, they amble into an abandoned apartment building, where a group of junkies happen to be shooting up. One of the junkies pulls a gun and fires, leaving Hill and Renko for dead. Back at the liquor store, Furillo coaxes the thieves to give up, just before Hunter's squad blows up the store. Davenport, lured back to the station by LaRue's false claim that her missing client has turned up, charmingly pours coffee all over his pants. Back in her apartment that night, Davenport denounces the police as "reactionary, fascistic, high-handed, uncaring animals" to her unseen lover— who turns out to be Frank Furillo. They are about to make love when his beeper goes off. The lumbering, baroque Sgt. Phil Esterhaus tells him the two men have been found: "one DOA, one critical."

Broadcast Standards was not overjoyed. Could Bochco and Kozoll meet with Stanley again? So a second meeting took place, and as

Stanley ran through his notes, the writers listened, frowned, and by prior arrangement said nothing. Language . . . sexual innuendo . . . the black family scene . . . the violence of the shooting. Again, each side claims victory. Bochco recalls Stanley backing away from half his notes, in sheer embarrassment. And then, over the next few days, he says, "We negotiated their remaining notes down to almost nothing. I was amazed. We have done things in our script and put on the screen that I've never seen in a TV show before." "Failings that heroes have," Kozoll chimes in. "Cops who drink. Cops who smoke controlled substances. We don't show it but we allude to it."

Stanley thought he had won the important points. First off, he insisted that the show drop specific references to the Bronx and New York; the locale was now made indefinite, universal. Second, Stanley insisted that the show not offend people of color. Censorship is "liberal" as well as "conservative"; in fact, Standards policies in the seventies had the effect of systematically overrepresenting whites among television's criminals. "One of the major points of the discussion at the time was, as Steve very astutely pointed out, that the criminal element at this particular precinct was almost 100 percent black or Chicano. The only whites that live in that kind of neighborhood are people who are too poor or too old to move away, and consequently they were prisoners in their own environment. Our quarrel with them, if you want to call it that, was that they were simply going to have to fictionalize it to the extent of saying that all criminals weren't black. There are some white Anglo-Saxon Protestant thieves and killers and pimps." This is one point, he says, that Bochco and Kozoll did not resist. "What they did to accommodate us —and I don't know that they did it to accommodate us, they may have had it in mind already—was that they put a mixture of various ethnic types in the station, so that you had a counterbalance for the problems that we might be confronted with as broadcasters, [with protesting groups] saying that all the bad guys are Chicanos or blacks. And we were quickly pointing out that a lot of the [cops are] blacks and Chicanos as well, so it's saying that there is good and bad in every group."

Stanley was also unhappy with what he called the stereotyping of the family feud scene. "We went round and round on that for a long time," Stanley says.

"We were not trying to make a specific comment about blacks per se," Bochco says, "though there is a very high incidence of abandonment within the black community in ghettoes. There are certain sociological realities there."

"Ultimately," says Stanley, "we conceded that they could do it." With his faith in Bochco's honorable motives, he struck a custom-made bargain, comparable to the sort of swap that Standards people usually work out with their trigger-list of taboo words, letting the writers swap this "damn" for that "hell." The junkies encountered by Hill and Renko eventually were cast as one black, one white, one apparently Hispanic, and the fourth wholly unrecognizable; the one who pulls the trigger—seen only for a split second—is white. In the end, Bochco and Kozoll were men of liberal conscience. "We were concerned about that scene, too" Kozoll says. "We read dozens and dozens of black actors for the parts, and every single one of them we asked if they thought this scene was offensive. We asked other black people who were involved in the show in one way or another if they thought it was offensive. And you might argue that it's really a coercive question, given their situation and our power to hire." But, Bochco interjected, "We got some pretty straight answers. Some people were troubled, and they admitted it." Michael Warren, cast as Hill, was one of them.*

In the end, Stanley was persuaded the black household could have existed, and that was enough. Having a high-level L.A. police adviser helped. Shows written from the viewpoint of a profession always retain an adviser from that profession. Thus do producers avail themselves of the claim of realism when censors apply their moralism, when protesters write their letters, even when interviewers make nuisances of themselves. Yet this realist stratagem is necessarily selective, if sincere—for the most "realistic" show is never strictly so. Even in a vérité documentary, filmmakers make choices about where and when to plant cameras and microphones, which scenes will be juxtaposed, what will be edited in and out. And moreover, everyday life in a ghetto precinct is simply too dense, indeed at times too vile and violent, to be exactly "mirrored." When *Hill Street* came on the air, along with the many police who lauded it for realism were some who accused it of prettying up the ghetto "assholes" who Renko and Hunter called "animals."

By deploying the claim to realism, producers can beat back some of Broadcast Standards' demands, but only, in effect, by giving some of their autonomy back to authoritative advisers. *Hill Street*'s claim to realism makes selectively "real" police practice the touchstone of

---

*Stanley didn't register any feminist objection, however. The networks had taken much more heat from angry ethnics than organized feminists. I told Bochco and Kozoll I had heard a feminist object to the scene's suggestion that the family problem was caused by the woman not "giving" her man enough sex. "That wasn't what the scene was about," Kozoll replied. "The scene was about two police officers using anything at their disposal to cool out a situation, regardless of what impact it really may have. [It was a] con job. We talked with our police technical adviser Jess Brewer about that: 'Would you, Jess, have done it that way?' And he said to us he *has* done it that way." Hill was saying, in other words, "You cool this off or I'll turn you over to Renko."

creative choices: In a moral universe supervised by censors, fiction establishes its bona fides by borrowing selectively from fact. To protect themselves from censors and potential critics alike, producers make a fetish of fact; they rely not only on official advisers but on fact-checking agencies that specialize in verifying the details intended to guarantee the look of authenticity.

Yet in the end, when official morality is at stake, even the defense of realism may not prevail. Broadcast Standards sometimes intervenes as the strong right arm of ideology pure and simple. Jerry Stanley, for example, was disturbed by what he called the *Hill Street* pilot's "depiction of the police as being casually indifferent to the law." In one scene, the script had Officer J. D. LaRue smash open a Laundromat coinbox to find a dime for his call to Joyce. The point could be defended on realist grounds. It does happen that police cut the corners of the law. Besides, by the show's internal logic, LaRue's transgression was a character point. He was a notorious fuck-up who was caught, as we would learn in subsequent episodes, in a downward spiral of alcoholism. But in this case Bochco and Kozoll could not prevail.

"We said absolutely not," according to Stanley, "We would not permit that kind of wanton disregard for the law." After the revision, LaRue got his dime—and his laugh—from a grotesque old woman. It was permissible to show LaRue making a joke at the expense of a *zhlub,* but not to show a cop as a casual criminal.* No police uproar was needed to remind the network to go an extra mile to serve and protect that image. This time censorship was a matter of principle.

A different principle came up in the matter of the shooting of Hill and Renko, where again the claim of realism had to yield—this time to the claim of good taste. Years of organized protest against televised blood and gore had retooled network standards. Stanley was concerned that the shooting of Hill and Renko "not be exploited. The shooting should be done carefully. We didn't want blood squibs. The point was made that the two guys were shot down, and that's all that was needed." On this point the writers did not need convincing. What they wanted from that scene was the sting of sudden death, not the horror of smashed corpses.

At this point, Stanley was satisfied with the preliminaries. NBC's programming executives were satisfied, too. Now the show had to be

---

*At least not at the start of the series. In later episodes, when the show was established, and Standards placated, we would see cops screwing up, taking out their frustration in brutality and lies, covering up for buddies, keeping deceptive records in good causes; we would see a bad cop led to bribe-taking and then perjury by way of bigamy. LaRue even got demoted to the motor pool. But it's true that no regular cop was ever again shown as a casual crook.

cast, the director hired, the pilot shot. In a sort of recombinant fashion, Bochco and Kozoll had in mind some actors they had worked with before: Bruce Weitz, from *Every Stray Dog and Kid*, as Mick Belker, the snarling cop; Michael Warren, from *Paris*, as Hill; Michael Conrad and Charles Haid, from *Delvecchio*, as Esterhaus and Renko, respectively; Kiel Martin, from *Delvecchio* and *Paris*, as LaRue; Barbara Bosson, Mrs. Steven Bocho, as Fay Furillo. These, and the others eventually hired, had been around, working in little theater, commercials, improvisational comedy, bit parts here and there. Most of them were not conventionally pretty, and they weren't well known. "We had huge casting arguments with NBC," Bochco recalls, "and we just bolted through. We really played some hardball." NBC casting executives didn't want Kiel Martin, for example, but Grant Tinker was enlisted to support him, and Brandon Tartikoff went along. When casting still demurred, Bochco and Kozoll threatened to quit, and NBC caved in. Kozoll thought the lower-level executives were figuring they might as well let the show go down the tubes.

On one occasion, Grant Tinker himself had to be talked into going along with a casting decision. Bruce Weitz had never played a semi-comic leading part like Belker. Tinker was against him, but Bochco knew he could do it. Bochco thereupon set up a casting meeting at which Weitz growled his way down the corridors, stormed into the room snarling, and jumped on and off desks. Tinker smiled and said, "I'm not going to be the one to tell him he can't play this part."

The biggest fight was over the casting of the public defender, Joyce Davenport. NBC's casting people pushed for the voluptuous bomb-shell type. A casting executive at the network raved about one such candidate, "This is the one Freddie will like."

"And we're going: 'Just because she's got big tits and blue eyes?' " recalled Gregory Hoblit, the line producer. Eventually opposition dissolved when in walked Veronica Hamel, a slender former cover girl who had failed to make it in the movies and had never done regular television. Despite the push for realism, the *Hill Street* regulars as cast were (with the exception of Conrad's Esterhaus and René Enriquez's Ray Calletano) in their mid- to late thirties, roughly the ages of Bochco, Kozoll, and Hoblit, and probably older than their real counterparts in a city precinct.

Bochco and Kozoll wanted the show to look singular, and in Greg Hoblit they had an unusually adept and visually sophisticated line producer. Hoblit had gone to Berkeley in the early sixties, gotten involved in the Free Speech Movement and the Vietnam Day Committee, but not managed to balance his dawning politics with his family background (his father was second in charge of the Berkeley FBI office). So he had dropped out, shipped to China in the merchant marine, disabused himself of romantic ideas about the working class, and eventually graduated in film from UCLA. Bochco had seen and admired Hoblit's documentary, *A Difficult Man*, about the Northern California guru Bubba Free John, and later hired him to produce *Paris*, then *Vampire*. Hoblit knew his film lore, and he was quick to learn the nuts and bolts of producing: casting, coping with lost film and compensating for film botched in the lab, massaging the egos of actors, briefing the directors, keeping a sharp eye on the editing, supervising the sound mix. He had opinions but spoke softly, and mostly he worked his ten- to twelve-hour days with a steady humming energy. Entrusted with an unusual degree of authority for a line producer, he got along well with everyone. He was the native Californian in the inner circle. He was Bochco's age, middle thirties, and his hair, like Bochco's, was prematurely gray.

Hoblit was of the film-school generation, Francis Ford Coppola, Martin Scorsese, Paul Shrader, and company, who brought visual stylishness into the Hollywood movies of the seventies. "I read the script," Hoblit remembers, "and immediately a whole visual sense came to me about what it ought to be. Hand-held camera. Let's get the film as dirty as we can. What I said is, 'Let's go for the *Serpico* look.' " In television even complexity and dirtiness require their own lineage. What was unusual was to find Hoblit's film sensibility erupting in television, the province of the well-trimmed image.

High density, nervous energy, and a look of controlled chaos were alien to commercial television, so who would know how to direct such a show? The industry had cultivated a tame and uniform directorial style. Indeed, instead of style there were techniques. The dialogue would come out mechanical but oh so clear (two-shot, close-up, over-the-shoulder, close-up, cut); actors would be run through their paces with dispatch to meet tight schedules and budgets. The directorial innovations celebrated within the industry were techniques, like the invention of the standard, efficient three-camera method in sitcoms. There were directors who were more or less skilled in working with actors, but with no time to rehearse an episode, and rarely even time for a complete reading by the actors, directors were relatively interchangeable. If movies were a director's medium, television was the producer's.

"People were afraid of the material," Hoblit says. "And there were directors who wanted to do two-hour series or miniseries, and they considered one-hour pilots to be less than up to their status at this point." One of these veterans was Robert Butler, whose experience extended back to the days of live drama on *Playhouse 90*. Butler had directed episodes of *East Side, West Side*, of *N.Y.P.D.*, of *The Blue Knight*, and of *Columbo*, Bochco's first show. After twenty years of directing episodes, he had graduated to pilots and a feature film

(Night of the Juggler). Butler was much in demand for pilots, but had a reputation for being "unorthodox," in Greg Hoblit's words, for being a renegade, or delivering what other people would have thought was crappy film."

Butler had once done a project with Grant Tinker. "They both have eastern prep-school manners, and they do well together," according to Hoblit. A week before *Hill Street* preproduction began in earnest, Butler happened to call Tinker, who told him he had a new show looking for a director. MTM offered him "a hell of a lot of money," Butler says; he loved the script, the dialogue, the story, the "touches." Later, when the pilot was complete, Barbara Bosson suggested to her husband Steven Bocho that Butler be hired to shoot the next four episodes. Shooting four shows in a block would give him more than the usual time to achieve some extraordinary effects. Hour-long episodes usually had to be shot in seven days (compared to twelve for a pilot), and such pressures made for sloppiness and corner-cutting. Shooting the episodes together would make for valuable efficiencies. In one day he could shoot all the scenes on a particular location, for example, saving transportation and setup time that could be applied to run-throughs and lighting effects.

In days and weeks of meetings, Bochco, Kozoll, Butler, and Hoblit together thrashed out the details of look, sound, costumes, sets, locations. Bochco and Kozoll held final authority, but everyone agreed that Butler deserved much of the credit for the show's tone as he worked to match the show's look and sound to the "layered, laminated, potentially confusing complication" of its script. No slack time, no flab, momentum was all. The show should look messy because the problems police deal with are messy, solutions are fleeting, the police vulnerable, situations morally ambiguous.

There is much talk in Hollywood about "production values"—fancy sets and gorgeous costumes and crisp portrayals. But for most shows, the preoccupation is more vivid than the outcome is evident. Craft is hamstrung by the false presumption that only conventional lines of goods will sell. Butler, like the producers, was interested in exploring the boundaries. If this was an ensemble show, dense with principals, filled with short scenes, whose action was "knitted" from fragments, then the screen should look busy, the editing often abrupt. "The show is movement," as Butler put it, and if the characters were to keep moving, then so should the camera in the sort of long takes so splendidly done in movies by Max Ophuls, Orson Welles, and Kenzo Mizoguchi. Scenes should flow into each other with minimal editing, as in *Casablanca* or Michael Kozoll's original model, *Grand Hotel.* "Twelve people standing around looks like the Acropolis. It's the worst," says Butler.

The camera might open in Furillo's office as he talks to a frantic

Hill and Renko about their shooting, but without the usual master shot that shows all three of them together and slows down the action. Esterhaus opens the door, tells Furillo that LaRue has been arrested for taking a bribe, and exits. A phone call tells Furillo that Belker nabbed a rapist. Enter Fay Furillo shrieking about the latest catastrophe in her life. In the background, through the window, we see Goldblume lecturing a gang member. The camera might then follow Furillo out of his office to Goldblume—all this without a cut.

Each strand would be picked up later in the hour, or perhaps in the next episode or several episodes after that, and be taken its own distance, overlapping new ones. Other cops would walk through the background or foreground, filing papers, answering phone calls, typing reports, shuffling suspects in and out of the squad room. With plenty of tight shots, the station would feel cramped. The fragmentation and juxtaposition of shots and conversations would reproduce the fragmentation and simultaneity of society. Characters would brush past each other, reach over each other's shoulders, break into each other's conversations, suggesting that its people depend on each other, crisis is everyday, no man or woman is an island. The heroism of these cops would not be the swagger of loners lording it over society, or over the screen. "It wasn't new," Butler said, "but it had never been done that densely before."

The camera would avoid the conventional tableau-with-Ping-Pong effect of most television drama, in which each scene begins with the obligatory shot of the whole stiff group on display, followed by close-ups of A, then B, then A again. Butler wanted to break down what he called "all that heritage of visual cleanliness." As the script was spare of narrative exposition, so should the film be compact. "I hate establishing shots," Butler declares. "We can go from a close-up of Furillo in his office to a medium shot of Davenport at a restaurant, instead of seeing the cab pull up and the doorman opening the door: all that shoe leather that drives you crazy. If she's tamping a cigarette or having a glass of wine and there are two plates in front of her, you know what's going on. Your establishing shots are a big yawn." Television had followed Hollywood movies in flashing obvious signals whenever the action moved to a new site: the shot of the name of the building, followed by a pan up the side to the umpty-umpth floor; the shot of the plane landing to suggest a change of locale. Now, at long last, television would follow commercial film's movement into the territory of more economical, more tantalizing kinetic technique. "Less is more" was Hoblit's slogan for *Hill Street* style. He and Butler were looking for "lightning in a bottle," a character's truth in a moment of revelation.

Butler was also tempted by the producers' talk of shooting the whole show with hand-held cameras, in black and white, to heighten the grainy, documentary look. He even proposed shooting in the relatively primitive 16 mm. But 16 mm. proved impractical, since the labs were not equipped to handle it on a weekly television schedule; and no one thought the networks were ready for black and white. Accordingly, Butler began shooting the episodes in the normal 35 mm., but with everything hand-held and nervous. This stretched the conventions too far. The producers, Butler recalls, "got a little spooky with it and asked that I do only certain heightened sequences hand-held," like the roll-call sequence that opens every show, and certain moments of violence. Influenced by the PBS documentary *The Police Tapes,* he shot roll-call with two cameras running simultaneously. He let the camera operators watch rehearsals with their eyes only, not with their machines. "I told them, 'Don't worry if you have to find focus [in the middle of shooting].' When I saw the dailies they looked pretty raunchy, and I said, Hmm, I wonder, but you mustn't express doubts directorially. But when it strung together, it got smoothed a little bit, and still had the texture and the juice." Then he told the editors, "Don't use the stuff once the shot has settled down. Use the bad stuff. It's terrific."

The edgy look of roll-call was reinforced by sound. While the screen was still black, a background mutter started up. Instantly *Hill Street* looked and sounded ragged. The shaky hand-held frame reinforced the sense of irreverent, antic, raucous, sometimes hung-over cops at seven in the morning, playing against the robust, almost self-mocking orderliness of Sgt. Phil Esterhaus as he ticked off his list of items. In the pilot, for example: "Item fourteen: We've still got a gang of juveniles on 119th Street hitting old people cashing Social Security checks. Now, how about let's give that situation a little extra effort. . . . Item fifteen: At this point in time we've got the same purse-snatcher working Wolf from the projects on South. He is a male black, age approximately thirty, six feet six inches tall, medium build. He is further described as wearing a long blond wig and powder-blue cocktail-style dress, gathered in little tucks at the waste. [Snickers from the cops] . . ." And so on through Esterhaus's list to his cautionary trademark, the coda that revealed the precinct's jeopardy in a world it could barely police: "Let's roll, and hey—let's be careful out there."

Butler wanted the ragged look of reality in the makeup of individual shots as well. He tried to break camera operators of their training to get clear, neat, balanced shots. "'Make it look messy,' I'm saying to Billy [Cronjager, director of photography]. 'Don't make that pretty stuff we all know how to make. Make it look bad.' They kept coming to me, both on the pilot and on the episodes, saying, 'It's pretty ba-ad.' And I said, 'Make it worse. Make it worse. It makes it more real.' Soft light is unreal. Occasionally there'd be a place where a big shadow would come across somebody, and he wouldn't clean it up, and he'd say, 'It's pretty bad,' and I'd say 'Yeah, I know it is, and it's marvelous. Keep going.' " As for the twenty background characters, Butler remembers telling the assistant directors, "Get the people up, get 'em moving. Have 'em walk right through the scene." "Between the lens and the principals?" "Please." He wanted background characters "bumping into principals, reaching across their desks to pick up forms, nobody honoring anybody's privacy."

Butler dimmed the lighting, too, to make the print look down and dirty. He "ground the film down" in the lab to get away from "magazine-cover stuff." He played tricks with filters, and made sure the cops' wardrobe was irregular, all contributing to an urban tone people generally associate with the East and Midwest. (Actually, the title sequence and a smattering of other exteriors were shot in Chicago; almost all the other exteriors were done on location in the skid row section of Los Angeles.) The multiracial cast also worked against flashy upbeat color. So did the nighttime shooting, the alleys, the litter of dumpsters and dismantled cars dragged into the streets, the graffiti sprayed on walls.

And this messiness extended to sound. In the name of realism, Butler and Hoblit performed the television equivalent of Robert Altman's approach to simultaneous talk in the movies. Less extravagantly than Altman, but more radically than television had seen before, they ushered in overlapping dialogue. Indeed, parts of the script were already written that way, characters talking against each other in the crisis-ridden clutter of precinct life; but Butler pulled out the stops and fought to overcome the normal conventions of TV craft. "What we're all taught in the business is that one person speaks at a time," Butler says. "And you and I know it's nonsense." To Butler the awkward interference patterns of natural speech were gestures in the name of honesty. This he had to make his editor understand, even while acknowledging the technical fact that dialogue overlaps robbed the editor of some flexibility when it came time to assemble sequences of takes into a continuous dialogue. In the intricate division of labor that stands behind Hollywood performance, craft militates toward conservatism of method. Butler had to push: "I said to the editor, 'Look, let's just not discuss overlaps, because it's too boring. Let's not even get into it. I'm going to do it. I know you can cut. I know you give up freedom; we both give up freedom—let's just do it. It's more real—the hell with it.' "

Once the film was assembled, Hoblit laid on a separate background track of ambient sound. He hired an improvisational comedy troupe called Off the Wall to screen selected scenes in a sound studio and improvise everything from squad-room phone murmurs to dispatch calls and crowd noises. When the half dozen comics of Off the Wall recorded their murmurs, they ambled toward and away from their microphones, so the background noise sounded unusually authentic. Off the Wall's buzz set the show's feeling-tone: the sense that foreground action takes place amid the interference of a myriad of events, and that islands of order are, as Robert Frost said about poetry, "momentary stays against confusion."

This buzz was the bulk of the show's music. The rest, variations on the muted, downbeat theme by Mike Post, reverberated through odd moments in the show. Post himself was no stranger to blunt, blaring pop styles. He produced records for Dolly Parton, and (with his partner) composed the music for *The White Shadow, The Rockford Files, Magnum, P.I.,* and other TV shows. But the *Hill Street* producers wanted to avoid the clanging chords by which television melodrama signals strong emotion or imminent disclosure. Sometimes there was so little music on *Hill Street* that Post said to Hoblit, "I can't charge you for this." The producers had even toyed with the radical notion of dispensing with music altogether; but that, they concluded, would have been too gross a departure from audience expectations. Post's discreet, wistful theme was a far cry from the peremptory, martial bursts that had once blared forth from *Dragnet,* or the resounding Prokofiev march that had conveyed the strident certitudes of *The FBI.* Whenever *Hill Street* did indulge in musical excess, to plug the holes in a weak script, Hoblit felt abashed.

Butler himself was no theorist of modernist method. He thought he was a realist, period. He said he wanted "to get the texture and the reality, to bring reality to the people and thereby heighten the trip. I contend that all we're trying to do is transport them anyway. I don't have any philosophical beliefs about the purpose. All I think [TV's] for is to turn it on for an hour because it's been a hard day." But Butler did enjoy the chance to unfold his craft. For years that craft had crouched in the shadows of convention. How much Bob Butler—or Steven Bochco or Michael Kozoll—had felt, and suppressed, the desire to surpass the limits of paint-by-numbers television is something I couldn't judge; perhaps something they couldn't know either, since the pressure of everyday accommodation renders such desires a demoralizing nuisance. The streamlining of TV production pushes for assembly-line efficiency; too much daydreaming about grand aesthetic designs would prove distracting as well. Anyway, people who are burning to break through the conventional limits are not likely to be making careers in commercial television in the first place. Still, normal pride in craft sometimes flares into an interest in novel methods, and who knows when that interest may slide over into artistry. Enough touches of the relatively novel, in the company of peers who are willing to take a chance, within the right constellation of power relations, can crystallize into a striking piece of work. That is why network executives and admen are disingenuous when they throw up their hands in interviews and say they would love to be patrons of excellence but where is the talent. As *Hill Street* shows, much talent stays hidden right within the confines of television itself, because the system prizes reliability more than native talent. Indeed, a reputation for excessive talent can prove troublesome.

This particular maverick was protected, though, by MTM and—in its own fashion—NBC. The whole amounted to something new, and jarring. It was new to the network and new to the test audience that viewed it for NBC in the spring of 1980. Of all the pilots the network tested during pilot season, *Hill Street Blues* tested among the lowest. Like *All in the Family* and *The Mary Tyler Moore Show* at CBS ten years earlier, this freak defied expectations. "People didn't get involved with the characters," Brandon Tartikoff says. Greg Hoblit was told that the test viewers were "very disconcerted by the speed at which things went. It's an unsettling show. The pilot is very fast, and unresolved, and did not fit any notions that people who go to these tests have about what's a television show. And people were very unhinged by the shooting of Hill and Renko."

According to one NBC research executive, the test audience thought there were too many characters. They found Furillo a strange hero indeed, an authority who couldn't control his extremist subordinate Hunter, who was publicly embarrassed by his ex-wife, who didn't seem to react emotionally to the shooting of his men. They wanted their heroes to be take-charge men and not plodders, this executive thought. He was convinced the show was going to fail.

Meanwhile, NBC asked a consulting psychologist for a scientific opinion about the number of plots an audience could hold in its mind simultaneously. The general industry assumption was that no more than three subplots were manageable within a single episode. The consultant relayed empirical psychology's conclusion that the "magic number" was seven, plus or minus two; but added the qualification that as the characters became more familiar, their appearance could trigger associated memories and boost the viewers' capacity to handle subplots.

Despite the test, the top network executives who proceeded to screen the pilot were taken by it. "The majority of the people in the room," says Michael Zinberg, "said that it was as fine a pilot as they had ever seen, anywhere, at any network, at any time. We're talking about people like Fred Silverman and Irwin Segelstein [president of NBC Television], Robert Mulholland [president of the NBC Television Network], Herminio Traviesas [for many years the head of Broadcast Standards]—God knows how many pilots he's seen."

"We said, Jesus," Tartikoff recalls, "this is a small movie. We said we're gonna throw out the testing. We said, if we can't take a chance of getting this on the air, we're in the wrong business."

The skeptical inquirer grows hardened to the rhetoric of pioneering in network circles, when corporate public relations so regularly fuses with show-business hype. Since extravagance was the norm, I wondered how to evaluate these retrospective raves for the *Hill Street* pilot. When I interviewed Tartikoff in the spring of 1981, mightn't it have been simply good image-making for an executive in the lowest-prestige and—much worse—lowest-rated network, saddled with Fred Silverman's bad press, to tell an interloping professor how highly NBC's executives had thought of the only literate show the network had put on the air? Yet in the same interview Tartikoff was also boosting his pet series *The Gangster Chronicles* without claiming that the pilot had stunned the assembled executives.

What I did sense was that had Tartikoff simply judged *Hill Street* by standards other than commercial potential, its quality by itself would not have been decisive. However, every now and then a show was seen as "different," a catchall category that skirted the potentially subversive ground of aesthetic standards. The difference was a pile of leftovers that couldn't be categorized. So it was that Tartikoff counted *Hill Street Blues* not as something upscale, literate, and uncommercial, but as "unusual." "You can try one of them a year," he told me, indiscriminately ticking off Larry Gelbart's failed dark comedy, *United States,* a variety series called *The Big Show,* and the vulgar *Real People* as the comparable standout oddities of earlier years. So while there was good reason for programming executives to be impressed with the *Hill Street* pilot—enough so to override a low test result—to justify putting the show on the air they had to classify it as 1980's entry in the oddball category.

Although they overrode the test results, Silverman, Tartikoff, and Irwin Segelstein took them seriously for diagnostic purposes. The main problem was that the buddies Hill and Renko, this "salt and pepper team" of the earnest, responsible black and the self-doubting, wisecracking southern racist farmboy, tested as the pilot's most popular relationship. To kill off two winning characters in the opening hour would be too startling a departure from television convention. The ambush itself was extraordinarily jarring. One minute, Hill and Renko were joking their way across the street; the next, they were going down in a barrage of bullets.* This *Hill Street* trademark resembled the movie realism of the seventies more than its signposted television counterpart. True, Hill was supposed to have been

---

*When the pilot eventually aired in January 1981, audience viewing actually fell off by several rating points right after the shooting.

critically wounded and was intended to recover. But the cable test seemed to show that the audience was drawn by interplay *between* the two partners. So Tartikoff, for one, wanted to bring Hill and Renko back to life. He also thought that if the show succeeded, Hill and Renko might turn out to be spinoff material.

At first the issue of resurrection seemed moot. When he had signed up to make the pilot, the actor Charles Haid had declined to be a series regular, especially a character in danger—or so he thought— of lapsing into a walking cliché from the boondocks. Indeed, he had already signed on as the star of another proposed series, but then the other pilot failed to sell. "He came to the screening that we had of the pilot," Hoblit remembers, "and he walked out of the screening and he said, 'I think I made a big mistake.' And we said, 'Well, it's undoable.' " The conversion of Charlie Haid by witnessing the fruits of his own labor became a *Hill Street* legend.

So Tartikoff got what he wanted, the resuscitation of Hill and Renko, and the producers did not object. The shooting scene remained exactly as shot, with the ambushed Hill and Renko twisting in a fitful, agonized "step-frame" process that Hoblit had specially devised. (Technically it was not exactly slow motion, in which the entire film is projected at slow speed. In Hoblit's method, one frame was printed once, the second twice, the next three times, and so on.) Each shot echoed in the closed chamber of the hallway. Hill and Renko fell like deadweights. There was a look of finality to their inert bodies. The only thing reshot was Esterhaus's closing words to Furillo. No longer did he say, "One DOA, one critical." Now it was, "They're both in intensive care." When I first saw the pilot, I never doubted that Hill and Renko were quite dead, never mind the balm applied by the words "intensive care."

So executive enthusiasm for this strange and overpowering pilot carried the series onto the air. NBC agreed to buy thirteen episodes on top of the pilot: not a full year's worth, but enough to carry through the spring season. Now the skirmishes resumed. In normal operating procedure, Bochco and Kozoll's starting scripts went to one of Broadcast Standards' rank-and-file "editors." Standards was keenly interested in the way *Hill Street* handled "sex," which is everyone's term for sexual innuendo and female skin. The touchstone was a scene in which Furillo and Davenport were to end their day in her bathtub. Despite the concessions that Bochco and Kozoll thought they had won at the outset, the repercussions were predictable. "They start off by saying, 'You cannot have a bathtub scene,' " Bochco recalls. " 'We cannot have two nude people in a bathtub. Married or unmarried. We just cannot have it. Forget it. It's impossible.' So, we trooped over to NBC, and we quit. 'If we can't make this show with two naked people in a bathtub, fuck you, we don't want to do this show. . . .' And we left that meeting saying, 'We're going to make our bathtub scene.' "

"Steve assured us," in Stanley's more mannerly recollection, "that it would be done tastefully and sensitively. And we assured him that if it wasn't that, he would have to reshoot it."

"Boy," Hoblit recalls, "when we saw the dailies we thought we were in trouble. There was a lot of backside, and a lot of front side, and a lot of two bodies that looked awfully naked on top of each other, and I went, Jesus. But I went into the editing room"—part of Hoblit's function as line producer—"and did a lot of work on that stuff, and then took a version over to them [NBC] that I knew was unacceptable. You do that, then they go, 'This is unacceptable,' and I go, 'Well, what about this?' And they go, 'Oh, that's okay.' You always have a backup position ready, which if you went in with the backup position to begin with, they'd say no to."

Eventually they agreed on a version that maintained a sufficient altitude of bubble-bath suds. "It was done tastefully," Stanley says. But he is quick to add that he went to special lengths when he trusted Bochco to shoot the scene in the first place. "We don't accept that kind of commitment from anyone, not because we don't trust them, but invariably what they see in their mind's eye is never the same as what we see in our mind's eye."

Like many network executives, Stanley wanted not only authorized power but acknowledgment for his creativity, and he was offended by the way many producers scoffed at his function. Stanley thought he was creative because Standards did more than criticize: It proposed alternatives, and to come up with alternative ways to bring in the largest possible audience was also to bring something valuable into the world. Was not the packaging of the audience a creative act? No one said as much, but the unconscious mind of the network thought it. So while Bochco may have been blunt, the fact that Stanley felt respected by him helps explain why *Hill Street* got relatively permissive treatment. Moreover, this was a ten-o'clock show intended for an older audience, and a classy show to boot. "The one thing that we've been able to make abundantly clear to them," Hoblit declares, "is that we're not a tits and ass show." And therefore, as he puts it with satisfaction, "There's a whole set of rules just for *Hill Street,* as far as Standards and Practices go." One show used the word "clap," for gonorrhea: an NBC first. Cops might say "Jeez," which trod treacherously close to the forbidden expletive "Jesus"; they had to enunciate the single syllable carefully, or else Hoblit would have to edit around it. Howard Hunter often exclaimed, "Judas Priest!" or "Judas H. Priest!" or simply "Judas H!"—substituting of course for the taboo "Jesus Christ!" Hoblit says, "I keep waiting for them to lurch at that, but they don't." By the third season, a nasty character was getting away with the expletive "faggot."

The trickier issues came with some arguably kinky sexual innuendo, as in a LaRue line in one script: "Oh, she'd go out with a
German shepherd." The line passed muster in the script, but when
actor Kiel Martin spoke it, what he said was, "Oh, she'd make it with
a German shepherd." Bochco lost that one to Standards, and since
there was not time to reshoot the line he edited it out altogether. But
more obscure lines could get through, and more than once the writers would include lines which amounted, as Hoblit admitted, to "our
own private little adolescent jokes," usually scatological. The uptight,
ideologically constipated Hunter character was particularly devoted
to anal humor. In one script, Hunter ordered a Japanese tank for
special expeditions through the ghetto. The company that manufactured the tank was called Nishitsu, but Standards either didn't notice
or didn't care. By the second season, the producers were feeling their
oats. One show sent Hunter in pursuit of a pack of attack dogs, with
corny, predictable jokes about dogshit and a less predictable one
about farts. To my ears it was far wittier, astonishing actually, when
Furillo and Davenport lay lasciviously in bed and he told her she
"gives good succor." Hoblit says Standards had queried that one, but
the producers played dumb and got away with it.

As Hoblit's term "adolescent" indicates, these are the games of
parents and rebellious children locked in a system of paternalism.
The network lays down rules for what the "creatives" will be permitted to say; the creatives violate the taboos and construe their violations as freedom. The network acts *in loco parentis* for the audience,
and the creatives act like children inserting secret messages in a kind
of code to their confreres in televisionland. Many of television's feuds
over "creative freedom" are frittered away on this sort of issue,
neither party quite recognizing that as long as writers understand
defiance as the violation of taboo, they are bound to the taboo and
therefore unfree. True, too, the networks' belief that the audience
is childish, at least when it sits down to watch television, is partly a
projection of their own childishness. It happened, for example, that
just as the *Hill Street* pilot was about to air, Fred Silverman decided
that the original series title, *Hill Street Station*, was too bland. The
network helpfully spewed forth a list of possible titles. One proposal
was *The Blue Zoo*, to which Michael Kozoll replied, "Okay, we won't
call it *The Blue Zoo*, we'll call it *Jungle Bunnies*." The network still
liked *The Blue Zoo*. The producers demanded a brainstorming session at the network, whereupon someone in Business Affairs at NBC
came up with *Hill Street Blues*, with the double connotation of police
uniforms and lyrical melancholy.

Few of these network intrusions were more than nibbles, but they added up. Fending them off took time and energy. Privately, Bochco could acknowledge the point of some of the network's complaints, but he felt he still had to fight over every inch. "I get very combative, and maybe foolishly so," he says, "but I get very concerned about giving in on the little things, because fifteen little things suddenly make a huge difference in the overall look of your show." This is where MTM's sheltering auspices made a difference. At Universal, Bochco and Kozoll had always felt "under siege." "You had to please [the studio] before you could even send [the script] to the goddamn network," Bochco says. "It was impossible. When I think back to what we went through at Universal, the mind boggles. They had to justify that incredible bureaucracy they have." All those tiers of executives, Kozoll remembers, interested themselves in "everything from the script to the color of somebody's shoes. . . ." At MTM, things were simple. There were sometimes "differences of opinion" over a script or a film; but Bochco and Kozoll dealt directly with the network, and in any major dispute they could count on the potent support of Grant Tinker.

"We've had a couple of meetings," Tinker said while still at MTM, "and I don't want to overemphasize them because I can remember other shows [including *Lou Grant*] on which we had bigger, more important meetings, where networks were urging us to do, I don't know, whatever they wanted us to do." Although *Hill Street* was suffering from bad first-season ratings, NBC stayed low-key. "I can remember one [meeting] with Fred [Silverman], which was just a good long talk-out of what we were doing," Tinker said. "And a couple more where Fred hasn't been present but Tartikoff and a few of those lieutenants have been there. And I would go to those because, as an old, elder whatever-I-am, elder statesman in the business, just being present says something for Steven and Michael, obviously, or to them. But it also means that should it get to be a war, I'm one more soldier on our side. Some asshole at the drone level will find some fault that you haven't expected, and you have to beat him to his knees. If you feel strongly enough. And I do feel strongly that it would be hard to do this show much better than Michael and Steven are doing it. There are occasions when I've gone with creative people to networks and really wished I wasn't there, because I wasn't that crazy about what we were doing. Even in those cases obviously you have to be supportive, but in the case of *Hill Street* it's a pleasure." And so no big changes came of these meetings except, Tinker said, perhaps in the sense that Bochco and Kozoll, "in the give and take of it, might have learned things whether they knew it or not; maybe even made a better show as a result." Writers, he said, can get their noses so close to the typewriter that they lose some objectivity, or bang into dead-end streets: "I think to be exposed to people who are really objective is helpful." The once and future network executive was speaking.

Founts of objectivity network executives are not, but they do keep attention riveted to the problem of marketability, and in commercial television the ability to tend to the market is the only "objectivity" the system honors. What to do, then, when the voice of the sovereign market is slurred? In the continuing battle over how to interpret the low ratings, Tinker carried authority when he argued that the show needed time to find its audience. Indeed, since NBC was shifting the program from night to night and slot to slot, the audience needed time to find it. Tinker's confidence in the show helped keep morale up. As Greg Hoblit commented, "He'll be concerned that something is amiss, and he'll flag it, but he'll never steamroll it. Then we pay attention. We discuss. When somebody of his intelligence or perception flags something, you've got to pay attention. Now you say, 'That's alterable,' or 'There's a reason we've chosen to do it this way.' And either way he'll accept it." For example, Hoblit went on, "I think he was very concerned with the character of Belker. That this guy was too outrageous and too violent, and an asshole. We had a number of discussions about that, and certain decisions were made to alter that or quiet that. The thing we have to be very careful of is that, because Michael and Steven and I are urban and college-educated, we're almost by definition not mainstream in our thinking. We often need some guidance as to where that mainstream is. Grant, I think, knows what that mainline thinking is better than we do, because his job is selling." No matter how spunky and literate the creative people, they hold themselves fortunate to count on their side a partisan salesman like Grant Tinker, a top supplier who can successfully deploy counterarguments about public taste in the face of network preconceptions. After all, arguments about artistic integrity are simply beside the point.

Hill Street Blues went on the air on January 15, 1981, to less than resounding ratings. The pilot rated 15.2 (or 11,856,000 households), for a 26 share. The next week the show sank to an 11.5 rating (8,-947,000 households) and a 19 share. It hovered in the low-20 share range for the rest of the season. But the show was greeted by an almost universal chorus of critical accolades, which helped loosen the network's supervisory hand. Some network executives bantered that critical praise could kill a show, branding it as something too fancy for the hoi-polloi, but *Hill Street*'s partisans were too visible and vehement to be so easily ignored. Moreover, the third-place network offered the critics nothing else to cheer their hearts. This same season, Silverman was reeling from critical onslaught for having programmed such shows as *Speak Up, America* (a pseudo-populist

People magazine of the air stuffed full of man-in-the-street one-liners and unscientific polls, a show not only excoriated by NBC News but low-rated at that) and the tasteless musical-beds soap-opera series *Number 96.* The onetime golden boy, losing his touch, also felt insulted and injured. Inclined as he might be to wonder how many Nielsen households followed the critics, he could hardly afford to sneer at the only prestige coming his way.

Meanwhile, below the busy Silverman, other network executives went on complaining about the show. With my usual mixture of naïveté and inquisitiveness, I once asked Bochco where he thought these network moods originated. He startled me by asking back if I was Jewish. Yes, I said. "Ich weiss," said Bochco. The Yiddish means, with a shrug, "I should know?" "It just comes. It comes from the building." The show remained more ragged, the heroes less heroic, than the building wanted. Brandon Tartikoff, for one, had felt since the pilot that there were "not enough victories." Like all network executives, he thought the presumably unitary and unchanging mass audience craved closure, or at least the satisfaction of knowing that social institutions could get something done. "In Bochco's words," Tartikoff said, diplomatically, "*Hill Street* is a holding action. I support that, but you've got to have some small victories along the way. You have to settle a civil disturbance, or get some rapists behind bars."

"We raised unanswerable questions," Kozoll reflected. "They don't like that." In one early show, the recovering Renko, after his gaze at death, hit the skids when the junkie who had shot him was freed for lack of sufficient evidence. Renko began drinking on the job. In uniform, he was seen carrying on with a couple of whores in a restaurant. In Bochco's pungent words, "He was making an asshole of himself." Network executives, he recalled, "got really upset. This is a hero." How could he be permitted to carry on so recklessly? Then there was the episode in which, shortly after a minor character's death of a heart attack, the fifty-five-ish Sgt. Phil Esterhaus decides to marry a high-school girl. Delicately the network complained, "We are real concerned about what you have Esterhaus doing in this show." Bochco: "Why might that be?" Answer: "We feel that he's going to look foolish doing what he's doing." Bochco: "Someone going through a crisis, a midlife crisis, compounded by the death of a fellow officer from natural causes, fifteen years younger than himself—yeah, a guy can act rather foolish. And then they say, 'Well, but you're damaging your character.' And then you say, 'We disagree.' And then you're at an advantage. The bottom line is, We're going to do it the way we want it."

In a sense, the network was cowed. The rules of their own game undercut their power. In a system that paid lip service to the princi-

ple of "making a good show," the executives didn't know just how
to tinker with a show that not only critics but they themselves liked
to watch. Broadcast Standards could, of course, issue straightforward
notes like "Delete 'damn.' " It could even issue affirmative injunctions like "Maintain level of soap suds sufficiently high to cover Davenport's chest." In cases so clear-cut, the test of compliance was
precise. But it was not so easy to enforce vague injunctions like "Tie
up loose ends" or "Make your heroes more heroic"—at least against
determined resistance. And long TV experience had taught Bochco
and Kozoll the art of maneuver.

Sometimes, for example, someone in NBC's Current Programming
department might object to something in the rough cut, which is the
first stage of the assembled film. The producers could finesse such
objections by counting on the inefficiency of the organization. "It's
amazing how much they don't know about film," said Michael Kozoll.
"You say to them, you know, 'That's just the rough cut; it will be
smoothed and fixed.' By the time they see the [late-stage] answer
print, they don't remember anymore." There were simply too many
shows and not enough time to police them. The network's desire to
control the show was defeated by organizational overload, by inefficiency, and also by ignorance. "They didn't know what they
wanted," said a delighted and relieved Kozoll. "You'd go to meetings
and say, Yeah, yeah, yeah, and go off and do what you want. If you
did everything they wanted you'd end up in Cedars of Sinai—do they
have a psychiatric ward?"

Kozoll was convinced network executives were envious and vin-
dictive. "All the guys in programming want to be in production," he
said. "They all would want to do what we're doing if they could." To
creative people like Kozoll, the executives' seemingly rational arguments for changing a show were not only intrusive, annoying, and
insulting, but slapdash, ill-considered, and ephemeral. Even granting
the executives their market-maximizing purposes, they seemed un-
reasonable and inconsistent by their own lights. Even as censors they
were erratic. Perhaps, then, given network rhetoric about scientific
testing and rational decision-making, the worst thing of all about
network interference was not that it was ill-motivated, but that it
might actually be senseless. "We both of us have learned, I think,
over the years," said Bochco at the end of *Hill Street*'s first season,
"a very harsh fact of life from television. And that is, that if you bend
to their continual anxieties about the way things should be, you'll
wind up with a show very different than that which you started out
with. And if it then bombs, they blame you anyway. So we finally
came to the feeling that as long as we're going to take the heat, we
may as well at least really feel that we're taking the heat for our
show."

Again and again Bochco's feelings about the magnitude of that heat oscillated. In the back of his mind, he knew the autonomy *Hill Street* had won was always provisional. Each time he resisted a network intervention, he once told me, "I'm sure they must mark it on their chart, and wait for us to fall on our asses." Yet he also cautioned me not to exaggerate the discord. "I know it would make good copy, but if you were to take ten producers and ten shows, and ask for a rundown, in any given season, of the beefs, the conflicts, the problems that they had with the network over the content of their show, you could fill books and books. With us you couldn't fill one page in a scratch pad." I had, of course, filled dozens of pages in many scratch pads with tales of the network's actual and attempted interference. The point was that Bochco and Kozoll, all in all, considered all these obstacles relatively trivial.

In May 1981, *Hill Street* was renewed for a second half-season, thirteen new episodes of what was possibly, in Greg Hoblit's words, "the lowest-rated show renewed in the history of television." The Nielsen figures ranked the show eighty-third in a field of ninety-seven for the year. But disheveled NBC could take a chance or two, especially since the number-three network was not exactly brimming with sure-fire backup series. And *Hill Street* had found its devotees, people who had chased it over two different time-slots on four different nights, people who had stayed with it even Saturday nights at ten. Moreover, the show was drawing disproportionately high demographics, relatively younger, more male, more prosperous viewers whose attention was worth proportionately more to advertisers. By the end of the spring, all the second-season spots were already bought out in up-front buying, bringing in rates higher than numbers alone would have ordained. Looking at all the factors, it was a reasonable business judgment that word of mouth might finally prevail, and that the show, once it stayed put in a single time-slot, might take off. The precedents of other first-season flops like *All in the Family* and *M*A*S*H* did not go unnoticed.

But NBC exacted a price for renewal. In no uncertain terms, Brandon Tartikoff told Bochco and Kozoll to build each episode around a single story line, complete with beginning, middle, and end. All along, NBC believed that a large part of the audience was baffled by all the continuing threads. To make matters worse, the subplots started and trailed off at different moments, just as they pleased. "My wife is confused," one programming executive had grumbled, "and she is a smart broad." NBC had always wanted a modular story, one piece of resolved business in an unresolved world, one hook to catch the wriggling viewer who might well have missed the previous episode. They had brought up the issue before, and Bochco had said yes, and "forgotten," or finessed them. "There were times when they'd call us up and say, 'This is a great script, but where's that one story with a beginning and middle and end?' And we'd mumble something. They'd go, 'Oh, oh, oh, okay.' " Now the request had become an imperative.

"I see the validity of that, I gotta tell you," said Bochco just after renewal, putting on a brave face. "I hate having to do it, in a sense, because I loved the freedom we had last season with our stories. This makes it a little more difficult. But it can be done. I do see the wisdom of that. Beyond that I would be very reluctant to want to change anything else. Win, lose, or draw, our curse and our blessing is that format. I would rather see the show go down than to change it so drastically that it's no longer the show we created and produced this season."

With a second season guaranteed, Kozoll and Bochco—like their characters—were ready to reflect on the ways of the world. "I guess you'd say we're liberal," Kozoll said, "probably unfashionably liberal people politically. I guess we all feel that the government could be doing more to help ameliorate some terrible situations. I don't think we're cop-lovers at all.* At the same time we do have a kind of compassion for the hopeless situation that those people are in. And I really think that's the strongest point of view that comes through *Hill Street.* I sometimes wonder if we aren't a little out of fashion with the rest of the country."

"It's very probable," Bochco chimed in, "and that could be a source of some of our ratings problems. Because there's no other explanation for why people aren't watching us in droves. We're funny, we're dramatic, we have wonderful actors, we have good stories. There's got to be something, aside from NBC putting us all over their schedule, that people resist in what we're doing. We don't answer questions that people desperately want answered simplistically. The appeal of a Ronald Reagan—and I am absolutely prepared to give the guy the benefit of the doubt; I wish him the best—but his appeal to a great many people has always been solid, simple answers to very complex questions. I think what Michael means when he says that we are unfashionably liberal is in our perception that those simple, easy answers don't yield results. They never have. The bureaucracy is too cumbersome. The system is too complex. I think people sit at home, and they want to be entertained, they want to laugh, and when it's all done they want to feel that all is right with the world. Even though somewhere back there they know that's not really true. That's a very attractive notion that they would like to see

---

*The letters *Hill Street* gets, though, along with scattered interviews I conducted with police in Los Angeles, suggest that many cops do love the show.

reinforced. We don't do that. We don't solve problems, by and large. We're constantly dramatizing the frustrations and limits of power. I'm not sure that's the way to easy quick success.

"One of the problems of our show," Bochco continued, "is that there's not necessarily one character that you're going to fixate on and say, 'That's the star of that show.' Television audiences are creatures of comfort. They want something easy and recognizable. Maybe the biggest problem with *Hill Street*, in terms of popular success, is that it is a show that demands to be watched. And most people do not watch television. They simply are in its presence. They use television as a narcotic. And when television grabs you by the throat and says, 'Wait a second, pay attention to what's going on here,' you're gonna get remarkable resistance. And I think we do."

Although the ratings were dreadful by network standards, the show was gathering prestige. The critics were part of a larger groundswell. A large proportion of letters received at MTM headquarters were lengthy and literate—typed, in fact. Among people who ordinarily disdain television, including many industry people themselves, the show began to accumulate what the industry calls WOM, word of mouth. Savvy old hands knew that this wasn't nearly enough to affect the Nielsen ratings, but they thought a small audience, suitably fanatical, could foreshadow a big boost in the ratings. There were even advertisers who were sufficiently impressed with the show's quality to call the producers and congratulate them.

As craft, the first season of *Hill Street* was as good as series television has gotten. It goes without saying that American commercial television is hostile to the nuance and resonance of art, but *Hill Street* demonstrated that the instinct for craftsmanship does not automatically disqualify a show from noticeable, if not epoch-making, popularity. Intelligent writing, it seemed, had its appeals; so did some unusually good acting, the serial form, ensemble work, an interesting texture. Complexity of plot and atmosphere did not intimidate ten or fifteen million American households. But what then?

For those of us who like to speculate about the larger significance of popular culture, the frustrating thing is that whatever we say about a show's appeal, beneath the surface of ratings numbers, amounts to guesswork. But I proceed from the belief that people came to watch the show not only because of its casting and texture, its undoubted and much commented on "chemistry," but because it spoke to, and for, a particular cultural and political moment. *Hill Street* "worked" in part because it immersed itself in major popular cross-currents—far more than the law-and-order shows that hit the airwaves at the same moment. The energy swarming through in *Hill Street* was the energy of American liberal-middle-class ideology turned on itself, at a loss for direction. Bochco and Kozoll had floated into a maelstrom point of popular consciousness.

At its strongest, *Hill Street* was positively rhapsodic about the contradictions built into the liberal world view in the early eighties. It not only acknowledged uncertainties but embraced them. To put it another way, *Hill Street Blues* was the first postliberal cop show. I say postliberal and not conservative, because some of the hopes of the sixties did hang on fitfully, in the incarnation of Henry Goldblume. Joe Spano, who played Goldblume, even told Bochco he thought his character should be outfitted with a radical past, at least a radical upbringing. Bochco said that Goldblume was especially dear to him, "insofar as I think he's terribly, terribly troubled all the time, about being an essentially passive man in a violent world, and yet remaining in it because of his hope that he can be a pacifying force." Goldblume was forever trying to negotiate peace in the community where Howard Hunter wanted to send in the heavy artillery. James B. Sikking, with his perpetual grin and pretentious vocabulary, didn't so much inhabit Hunter's cartoon racist role as present it from the outside; Hunter's character therefore didn't give weight to his outlook, but rather filtered it through irony. By contrast, Goldblume embodied his arguments and made them tenderly. He was a loving father and struggling (if eventually separated) husband, while Hunter could barely muster a sexual life until the second season*— which made Goldblume's moments of comeuppance poignant where Hunter's were merely comically pathetic.

The pivotal moment in Goldblume's sentimental reeducation came in the fourth episode, when Furillo dispatched him to do something about a suicide threat. By the time he got to the scene, the twenty-year-old black man had jumped. The suicide's weary, broken sister said the boy had been unemployed, unable to get into vocational school, disconsolate. Goldblume seemed to take this stranger's death personally. Driving back to the precinct, he got a flat tire. A gang of black teenagers appeared, took his jack, menaced him. Goldblume demanded the jack, asked to be left alone, played the nice

---

*But not even Hunter was immune to the middle-class therapeutic ethos of this cultural moment. Late in the first season Hunter sampled the psychological calisthenics of a seminar program called SUM, for Scheinkopf Utilitarian Mode ("sort of like est without the toilet training," opined Detective Goldblume). Early in the second season the repressed Hunter briefly achieved a sexual liaison with Grace Gardner, Sergeant Esterhaus's previous "squeeze," only to lose her and his pose of invulnerability at the same time. Even as a hard-liner, Hunter was imperfect and often discredited: his Japanese tank was stolen, for example, and found at the bottom of the river. And despite his caricature of a colonial mentality, Hunter often in fact deferred to the moderate position. Whether he was referring to "genetic tidepools," or the good old counterinsurgent days in Vietnam, or selling bomb-shelter-equipped condominiums in First Strike Estates, Hunter remained a comical human being.

guy, until finally he could take no more. He pulled his gun to get away. Back at the station, he came uncorked. "In twelve years I never so much as unsnapped the holster," he confided to a black cop. "Until Frank found out, I never used to load it." "What's wrong with those people, Alf?" he asked. "Are we past fixing it up between us? I mean—if that's the way it is, what the hell's the sense?"

Nonetheless, in future episodes Goldblume remained the dogged negotiator, the principled understander of social conditions who was, for example, devoted to getting the goods on slum landlords. Goldblume believed in talking criminals into surrender whenever possible, but he always tested his beliefs in the crucible of the streets, unlike the pompous, puffy-faced liberal Chief Daniels, whose "concern" for the community, one gathered, was less a matter of principle than a response to political pressures. If a conservative was a liberal who'd been mugged, as the saying goes, then Goldblume after the flat-tire sequence was the absurd hero who holds to his values not because he expects them to accomplish anything but purely and simply because they are right and they are his. They are right but insufficient. A liberal cop who pulls his gun in a pinch doesn't give up caring how ghetto conditions grind people down, but neither does he flatter himself that his personal compassion can stop switchblades, let alone move mountains. By the third season, Goldblume was fed up enough to manhandle a prisoner, knowing no one would believe it of him. Joe Spano, who didn't look the part of the Jewish liberal, was cast against type anyway, which kept his character clear of the standard package of knee-jerk liberal expectations.

Goldblume, disillusioned yet hopeful, expressed the society's more widespread separation between political hopes and practical life. "As I get older," Bochco said, "I find that I have a tendency less and less to identify things in political terms. For instance, law and order used to be a political issue. As a kid I tended to be real antipolice. There are times when I still am. You were a liberal or a conservative. For me this no longer applies. It's not a relevant label pro or con. Law enforcement is failing, and I don't see conservatives necessarily having an answer, or liberals having an answer, nor do I believe necessarily that the answer lies in a philosophical position. I don't have the answer, but I have cut that one loose from my political leanings."

Kozoll agreed. "Like a lot of onetime liberals, I think we've gotten to a point where we just throw up our hands and say let's be honest. There's no visible way to change anything anymore. You want to try to live through it, survive, keep the lid on. Things changed from the sixties to the seventies where we wanted to cure the society, and we got to a point around 1971, 1972, where the focus changed, the emphasis shifted away from fixing the world to fixing ourselves. And we all ended up in hot tubs drinking carrot juice." The show carried

his own credo, he said, when it settled for coping. Active coping, I
called it, since I didn't see the show representing defeatism. "Although certainly," Kozoll replied, "there is very little illusion about
things ever getting better."

Resignation coiled within the daily struggle to cope with a violent
society, nobility coiled in the battle against resignation: The world of
Hill Street was a world of a Sisyphus periodically breaking into stand-
up comic routines. "A quiet sufferer and a stoic," Michael Kozoll
called Frank Furillo, who personified the show's point of view.
"Furillo is a pragmatist," said Bochco. "Furillo is very rooted in the
real world. One of the things I like about Furillo is that he understands that he's not going to solve crime. By and large that's not what
he's there for. He negotiates truces; he keeps the peace to some
extent. He negotiates survival on the hill. And I like that because it's
real." No one would have called Jack Webb's Sergeant Friday or
Telly Savalas's Kojak a quiet sufferer or a stoic; those earlier generations of authority were going to solve crime or, by God, their under-
lings were going to pay.

At lunch one day, I asked Bochco and Kozoll whether they knew
anyone who reminded them of Frank Furillo. Bochco pointed to
Kozoll. At exactly that moment Kozoll, who couldn't see Bochco's
gesture, answered, "Furillo's Steven." It may not, then, be coinciden-
tal that Furillo's jockeying to keep an easy balance between his
bureaucratic superiors and his men is analogous to Bochco and Kozoll's uneasy positions as producers, perched between the network
on one side and their actors, consciences, and writerly judgments on
the other. Bochco and Kozoll, like their creature Furillo, supervised
an unruly organization that had its own obstinate structure, its own
powers, desires, and limits. Up against relentless time, restricted by
budgets too small for their hopes, beholden to bureaucracies, obli-
gated to their publics, producers and police captains all had to produce results *today*. The world cared about outcomes, not
extenuating circumstances. And then, too, the politics of a police
precinct are not altogether alien to the politics of a television production, with its collectivity, its squabbles, its array of off-center personalities, its moods and morale problems and delicate balances of
ego and responsibility.

But if organizational realities as well as personal psychologies
helped shape the show and form its subtext, none of this could explain why Furillo "clicked." What the writers wrote into him—what
they recognized in each other or in some ideal image of each other
—were qualities abroad in the land in the psychologizing, post-Viet-
nam, postfeminist eighties. As a culture hero Furillo was inconceivable before the late seventies. He represents a new image of benign
authority cultivated in the middle class, especially those in their

thirties and forties, especially in California, but now diffused via management training seminars and therapeutic encounters, *Ms.* and *Kramer vs. Kramer,* to the far corners of American culture. As an image of sensitive male authority in contemporary American life, Travanti's Furillo stands as an alternative to Al Pacino's predatory, power-hungry, paranoid godfather. As a police captain, of course, he also stands apart from Hawkeye's brash, boyish acerbity in *M*A*S*H.* Furillo stands for commanding patience, wry humor, self-control under fire. He manages his men without judging them. He listens to everyone and understands everyone's frailties: the frantic ex-wife, the dangerous cops, the worn out, the self-destroyers. He plays his emotions with a soft pedal; his voice usually stays in the same muted register.

Travanti describes Furillo this way: "He's not a simp, not a sap, he's not naïve; he's bright, he's aware, he's sophisticated, but he's also vulnerable." His brightness, awareness, and sophistication operate not so much on crime, however, as on his men and his loved ones. He knows when to be stern and when to bend the rules. Disdaining political ambition, he is *Ms.* magazine's ideal male and the eighties' ideal manager of relationships: honorable ex-husband, caring and guilty part-time father, compassionate counselor to his men, egalitarian lover. He stands above, but not too far above, the neuroses of machismo: Belker the snarler, LaRue the alcoholic, Renko the blusterer.

Put it this way and Furillo is almost too good to believe. True, he did bounce a child-support check once, and he does lose his temper now and again, though always for good reason. He is a reformed alcoholic—so we learn at an Alcoholics Anonymous meeting the miserable LaRue stumbles into at the end of the first season. By the third season, pressures from Chief Daniels compel him to twist some rules to get a conviction. But Furillo's flaws—or rather, our knowledge of the price he has paid for his stability—make him all the more interesting as a hero. There is even the suggestion that his recovery from alcoholism is precisely what enables him to understand other people and exact the best from them. "People who defeat self-defeat are heroes, and that's a heroism that we find very, very moving," as Bochco puts it.

Furillo is the updated version of an old American hero, the self-remade man. What makes him right for his moment is that he unites the inner with the outer man. This pragmatist is no hot-tub liberal. He shows no sign of sharing Goldblume's social ideals. His realism even displays a social-Darwinist edge. He says, at one point, echoing Bochco's private credo, "It's a dog-eat-dog world, and no dog's going to eat me." In this dog's world, flawed, tense, willful, brutalized and sometimes brutal men and women at risk have to depend on each other for human connections. Furillo prevents them from flying apart. When his men take up baseball bats to go out to bash the "animals" outside, he stops them by reminding them they represent the law. When gang leaders violate a trust, he puts the lid on them, too. When his men's personal lives fall apart (even the saintly Goldblume has an affair and loses his marriage in the second season), he reminds them he's been there. In a crumbling society, all human bonds are provisional; a pragmatist's work is never done. Mediating between Goldblume's community-relations liberalism and Hunter's toughness, coping with Chief Daniels downtown and the goons and gangs all around, Furillo harnesses a powerful emotional charge that drives the show. Only his soft-pedaled embodiment of old-fashioned professional duty, combining self-discipline, service, and care, can stave off the utter, catastrophic dissolution of the social contract. In a world that has lost its rhyme and reason, Furillo's soft authority presides over his raw, needful, quasi-family of cops.

Furillo is always on call, and his private life suffers. Even so, he is rewarded by the companionship of the regal Joyce Davenport, herself as much the New Woman as Furillo is the New Man. Indeed, like the successful professional of the women's magazines, she dresses with enormous style on her public defender's salary. In proper feminist fashion, Davenport fends off Furillo's desire to get married—or at least go public with their "relationship"—with barbed reminders about the importance of her career. Where Esterhaus's Grace Gardner lives for sex and Fay Furillo for marriage and motherhood, Davenport lives for her work and takes offense when Furillo calls it her "job." Yet she is also a connoisseur of whatever pleasures of bed, table, and beach can be snatched from the rigors of Furillo's and her dutiful lives; she bristles with frustration when Furillo's beeper frequently summons him from their restaurant table or her bed.

Hill Street is indeed a series of holding actions. It occupies a time when the right actions don't lead to grand results. For whatever reasons—poverty, the rules of evidence, or the dissolution of social norms—the police cannot keep the peace. They are ordinary people asked to accomplish something extraordinary. One reason many police officers like the show, perhaps, is that it says, in Bochco's words, "We put cops in an untenable position. Cops have to deal with the fact that nobody likes them and everybody needs them, and most people are afraid of them. They're damned if they do and they're damned if they don't. We give them enormous power, we give them weapons. Assholes abuse them."

Hill Street speaks to a larger cultural sense, stretching across political positions, that the major government institutions—education, welfare, health—and the cities as a whole simply do not work. Like *M*A*S*H* and *Barney Miller*, it shows the state to be inept; the best that can be said for top authority is that, quaintly, it tries to keep order. People suffer, and the institutions authorized to redress that suffering fail in their stated purposes. What is left is a creative coping that honors both the suffering and the failure of a society now seemingly beyond remedy, one in which a change in the social structure seems out of the question.

In this acknowledgment, not just in style, lies *Hill Street*'s realism. Bochco recalls that when he produced *Paris*, "I used to get into really big arguments with James Earl [Jones] about that very issue. He had a very different sense of heroism. He very much wanted to be a much more traditional hero in, no pun intended, a black-and-white sense. He wanted to be a symbol of law and order. You go after those bad guys and you nail them. And I always found that what interested me about doing *Paris* was exploring the limits of the power and the realities of compromise, and how can you be effective under that constriction."

Indeed, Bochco's basic intuitions could be confirmed by the universal failure of the "you go after the crooks and you nail them" shows of the 1981–82 season. In fact, the last nail-them show to land in the top twenty had been *Baretta*, in 1976–77, and Baretta himself was a nonconformist rogue. Network cynics were ready to write the failures off to Standards and Practices, which in rolling back small-screen violence had kept the rough-tough cop shows from doing what they do best: rallying audiences with pools of blood. But clearly it was more that the nail-them mood failed to carry conviction, even TV-style conviction, for writers or, indeed, for audiences. As American culture struggled to remake its verities about legitimate authority, Hollywood writers couldn't convincingly create an updated John Wayne who could begin to rival the moral and political complexities of *Hill Street Blues*.

Race issues perfectly illustrated the show's approach to the real world. *Hill Street* conveyed the ambivalence of white middle-class feelings about the black and brown underclass, and if it sounds strange to speak of a show carrying conviction about ambivalence, this is because television is ordinarily designed to strip away such complexity and to leave pure feelings glaring in neon splendor. The show's split image of ethnics matches both a split in the mind of the white middle class and a real divide in the black community between respectable, upwardly mobile ethnics and the underclass. Inside the stationhouse stand the embattled cops who engage our sympathies, poised for trouble in the roiling menace of the ghetto. (In one episode, the blues even barricade themselves against an assault from "out there.") "Out there" are the killers, muggers, rapists, and thieves, the street criminals and gang members who make life miserable for everyone else. And it is these small-potato underclass criminals who fire the show's imagination. "We prefer to deal with street crime," says Anthony Yerkovich, the writer in his mid-twenties who first practiced his talent for pungent dialogue on *Starsky and Hutch* and became one of *Hill Street*'s regular writers. "When we deal with organized crime, it looks like *Kojak.*"

The producers long expected trouble from Third World audiences, not so much because of Howard Hunter (so much the caricature of a militarist that he isn't taken seriously enough to draw forth protest mail) as because of stereotyping in their own portrayals of those Third World types. *Hill Street* premiered just as *Fort Apache, The Bronx* opened to a storm of Third World protest against its nasty and unrepresentative stereotyping, a storm that actually got the film banned in Philadelphia. "We haven't even gotten the kinds of backlash that *Fort Apache* is getting," Hoblit told me during the first season, "and we fully expected it, on the grounds that we were portraying Puerto Ricans in a negative light. For instance, in the pilot, while Ray Calletano is obviously a bright, capable, and responsible Latin, everybody else who's Latin in that thing is a lunatic." Yet during the first season there was no protest at all. "I've got to assume," Hoblit said, that Third World groups "think that we are more favorable in our portrayal, or at least we're more balanced in our portrayal of blacks and Latins and others." Jerry Velasco, an actor who was head of Nosotros, the Hispanic show-business organization, confirmed Hoblit's assumption. As long as René Enriquez was a regular in the cast, however a minor one, Nosotros wouldn't make trouble for *Hill Street Blues.* With the possible exception of Erik Estrada's ambiguously ethnic happy-go-lucky motorcycle cop in *CHiPs*, Calletano was at that point the only Hispanic character on prime-time television.

Dealing regularly with Third World criminals whose grim life-situation got short shrift, the show was often trading in potentially derogatory material. The three black and Latin principals in the cast, especially Michael Warren, the black actor who played Hill, were alert to the problem. Twice during the first season frightened Hispanics broke into rapid-fire prayer in Spanish. Easy laughs, easy writing. The first time it happened in one of Warren's scenes, and he said later, "This caused me to think, Jesus Christ, the only Hispanics on this show are these stereotypes." True, the staunch Calletano was a regular, but Warren was bothered by the fact that when juxtaposed to other Hispanics Calletano became another kind of stereotype, the strong, silent tough guy. He was given virtually no private life and few lines. The gang leader Jesús Martínez was a semiregular and another kind of stereotype—which is not to say stereotypes do not draw on reality. Warren went to the producers and asked them if they couldn't give Calletano something more to do. He was concerned about viewers who never see minorities except on television, who get educated and miseducated by what he called "a sponge medium." The producers said they would find more for Enriquez, but by the end of the second season they hadn't found much. (Finally, in one stirring third-season episode, Calletano at an awards dinner denounced the department's prejudices—and then, good company man to the end, felt guilty for doing so. Later that season, the writers brilliantly transformed Enriquez's disgruntlement into Calletano's feeling that he was never going to get promoted: "Damn it, Frank, I don't get any respect from anyone. How can I? I spend the whole day saying, 'Phone call, Frank,' 'Your car is ready.' I feel useless. I feel like everyone is moving up except me.") Calletano and Washington remained the least developed of the principals, but at least the farcically prayerful Hispanics had disappeared.

Whenever lines drew on white stereotypes about blacks, Warren had some pull. Especially at first, the Hill-Renko dialogue often played on stereotypes. Once, for example, Renko made a crack about Hill enjoying barbecues. "I knew what the producers were trying to do," Warren told me. "They were trying to say that these guys are so easy with each other they can fool around. But I changed it. We didn't have to do the bit. I found out that Steven Bochco didn't like the change, because he thought these guys had reached the point where they could joke around." Another time the script had Renko calling Hill "Beulah." "We eighty-sixed the line," said Warren. "Charlie changed it. I said, 'There's no way you're gonna call me Beulah.' When social kinds of things like that come up, we talk them out together. It's to the producer's advantage to listen to the people he's working with, to try to open up channels. These are two Jewish guys from New York [actually one was from Milwaukee]; they can't know the black experience, and vice versa."

Warren readily granted that "the producers are real flexible." Hearing criticism that the staff of the stationhouse was too white for a mostly nonwhite district, in the second season, they hired more black and brown actors for background work and bit parts. There were times when they also played against stereotypes. Warren recalled the time Hill and Renko were called to break up a family fight. A woman named Louella, and known to be large, was running amok in her apartment. Neighbors clustered in the hallway were black. From inside came the sounds of objects being smashed. Hill and Renko burst in—to discover that Louella was white. "When I read the script," Warren said, "I thought she was black. I was going to say something. But I loved it that she was white. It shows a certain sensitivity you don't normally see."

It also showed the writers' playfulness in writing against type, which sometimes extended to other stereotypes. A wonderfully pow-

erful show at the end of the first season centered on a scuzzy white
narcotics cop named Weeks, who, during a stakeout one night, was
fired upon by black youths who were up to some unholy business.
Weeks fired back and killed one of the youths. Internal investigation
ensued. It turned out that this was the third time Weeks had shot a
person of color under suspicious circumstances. Weeks himself was
outspokenly racist, and in the early stages of the investigation he
could not convincingly explain what he was doing on that stakeout.
Community groups clamored for Weeks's indictment and conviction. Even so, the black officer Neal Washington worked to clear
Weeks, although Weeks sneered at him and called him "Sunburn."
Why? Washington's record had been suffering from the sloppiness of
his deteriorating partner LaRue. Washington, Bochco said, needed
to restore his self-image as a professional. The message was that
professionalism was more important than race-consciousness. If
Washington and Hill were the more reliable members of their respective salt-and-pepper teams, the producers argued, this wasn't
liberal guilt but reality: Black cops were always busy proving themselves.

The effect, though, was to deepen the rift in image between good
blacks, who are professional, and bad blacks, who are criminal or
radical or both. The community groups campaigning for Weeks's
hide were comprehensible, if insensitive, but they were off camera.
As in the standard cop show, it was the police alone who kept the
lawless ghetto from sinking into utter barbarism. The community
lacked its own forms of solidarity, however tenuous. And in the
second season, the rift between police and community deepened. In
the opening shows, the central continuing plot revolved around one
Jesse John Hudson, the once and future king of a community group
called the Black Arrow. Hudson had served time for murder, and was
now returning to the streets with a published book, a political program for community self-help, and a political manner that impressed
Henry Goldblume if not the warier Furillo. Actually Hudson was
hell-bent on constructing a criminal empire. It took the deaths of two
people, one an undercover cop, the other a pure innocent, both
black, to expose him. Against criticism that the show thereby discredited ghetto movements in general, the producers insisted that there
are indeed black gangsters who prey on the ghetto. Only a fool would
deny it. But Jesse John Hudson was not comprehended or given any
complexity; he was dropped into the story as an unambiguous given.
Bad ghetto blacks were not given the benefit of the complicated
motives of corrupt cops. The show was, after all, a cop show, the
producers argued, and the neighborhood, funny or poignant or poi-
sonous as it might be, remained a backdrop against which the heroes
could strut their stuff.

Especially in the second season, social movements had no place in *Hill Street*'s conception of heroism. Heroism was a lonely, private struggle to light up the darkness. In another important second-season story line, the Black Officers Coalition prevailed upon Bobby Hill to run for vice-president. Hill got time off from regular duties, leaving Renko abandoned by his buddy. An old-line member of the Black Officers Coalition made strong arguments for their political position, but the more powerful emotional force lay with Renko's hurt feelings. Renko was assigned an incompetent partner, and as a result got knife-slashed in the line of duty. Hill felt contrite, and eventually yielded to Renko's appeals and hurt feelings. In the end, loyalty to his partner mattered to him more than organizing for affirmative action. The private code prevailed.

Around the same time, Fay Furillo threw in with a feminist sit-in organized by a group saddled with the name Women Against Discrimination, or WAD. Functionally, her arrest amounted to another way of hectoring hapless Frank; it also reaffirmed that movements are frivolous and unnecessary. Officer Lucy Bates fought back when her fellow officers treated her as a sex object, but this was again the private code: Women should deal with sexism through personal acts of courage. Despite *Hill Street*'s claim to realism, Fay at one point referred to WAD's demand for "quota hiring," a term thrown against advocates of affirmative action and rarely if ever used by them. More profoundly, during the same sequence, Joyce Davenport was badly shaken by the killing of a devoted public defender colleague, a black woman—only to see her killer, a snarling black monster, released because of a technical violation in the way the police gathered evidence. Now, as in other episodes as well, she had to confront the real-life consequences of civil-liberties statutes and the rest of her liberal principles. By the end of the season, against Furillo's counsel, she had bought herself a gun.

Davenport's metamorphosis made good drama (and reflected the entry of a lawyer, Jeffrey Lewis, onto the *Hill Street* writing staff). Whatever its dramatic use, however, this sequence ratified the conservative drift of *Hill Street*'s second year. In a single episode, Davenport considered quitting her job in disgust with the springing of the killer; the Black Officers Coalition pulled Hill away from Renko; and Furillo denounced WAD as "radical activists." Yet amid this neoconservative surge, Henry Goldblume got the goods on a bully slumlord who beat up any tenants who got up the nerve to complain (including a Hispanic law student: a major change from the first season's images of street Hispanics). So *Hill Street* remained complex. But by season two the defense of liberal values was being left more and more to the liberal cop. A year later, the show dealt with an armored-car holdup-killing by a hard-bitten remnant of sixties radicals, obviously based on Weather Underground holdovers. The sloganeering terrorists were realistic sketches of a self-caricaturing reality, while Goldblume and Davenport wondered aloud whether their onetime idealism was still tenable. (Joe Spano and Veronica Hamel didn't sound as if they meant their lines, though, because they didn't ring true to character, and the director didn't grasp the point of the episode. What looks like poor acting on television can often be traced back to muddled writing.) But at the same time, the FBI was held up to scorn for shoddy police work. The local police, including former radicals slogging through the reality of the eighties, remained the best hope for humane values.

Obviously, *Hill Street* has hardly been a left-wing, even a politically motivated show. None of the writers carries didactic purposes uppermost in his mind, but they are mindful of criticisms that emerged in conversation and in mail; and it seems to me that they have often tried to accommodate. While the show drifted rightward, the liberal conscience stayed alive. "If we show those people out there as animals," Kozoll had said during the first season, "that would show we'd given up." The most successful struggle against this tendency came in a show late in the second season. Hill and Renko were called to stop a black man named (symbolically?) Carter from beating up his common-law wife. The man had been a housing-authority cop until the fiscally starved city laid him off. Now he can't find another job. "There's nothing out there," the woman says. "It got him down so bad he just finally stopped looking altogether. . . . Carter's unemployment insurance ran out last month and he's too proud to let me go to the welfare office. . . . It's turned him crazy." Hill wants to help. Later in the day Carter gets drunk and threatens to kill her and her little son. Goldblume tries to talk him into giving up. "Your commanding officer . . . was very sympathetic," Goldblume tells him. "He said he'd do everything in his power to get you your job back." "You're too late," the man replies. "I'm over the line, baby—I crossed it." He wounds the woman critically, kills himself, and leaves the child dumb with horror.

All Hill's and Goldblume's personal decency are too little and far too late. Good intentions fail and happy endings come very seldom. The story also makes a liberal-radical political statement about the profundity of the problem of unemployment, about its terrible personal consequences, about the fine line that divides the ghetto's mainstream working class from its down and out. With this tale *Hill Street* conveyed the deep trauma being inflicted upon the ghetto, wiped away any easy do-good hopes, and preserved the series' distinctive sense of the absurd disconnection between wishes and facts. All this without anyone seizing the occasion to trumpet forth a moral about The Menace of Unemployment. It was one of the rare occasions when network television lent itself, even for a while, to a view-point from the underclass. Even *Hill Street* customarily restricted itself to a world view according to decent, dogged local police.

At its best, and its best is very good, *Hill Street* honors something of the enormity of urban misery in the United States. At other times, *Hill Street* abjectly fails to measure up to the terrible and wonderful territory it claims. For the most part, though, the show wrestles plausibly with the vast burdens of race and class. It bears witness. For all the criticisms, including my own, I was often struck by the fact that the cast of *Hill Street Blues* was the most integrated social group I had seen in many years: more than the neighborhoods where I've lived in four cities, more than university classrooms, certainly more than the New Left circles, the newsrooms and academic departments I have glimpsed in the days since the civil-rights movement. And that, in the thick of the Reagan years, is itself no small achievement.

But while *Hill Street* broke a mold of racial uniformity, inevitably it hardened into a new mold: its own. Network kibbitzing was only a small part of the trouble. NBC's need for formula was well enough satisfied by the recombinant idea of the comic *Barney Miller* superimposed on *Fort Apache.* True, the network was queasy. Early in the first season, when ratings were low, Stu Sheslow, the young former toy-company executive brought over to inherit Michael Zinberg's position in charge of drama development, wanted the show more comic. Perry Lafferty, among others, wanted it simplified, with crime stories as the "central spine" of each episode now that the characters had been introduced. Nevertheless, with powerful network protection, Bochco and Kozoll had wrested the right of authorship and gotten the show on the air in approximately the form they wanted. What did they want now?

Released from the external pressure to conform to a standard genre, but required to turn out *something* week in, week out, Kozoll later said that he and Bochco felt they were floating weightless. For most of the first season, he thought they kept losing the show and scrambling to find it again. Sometimes—though not, they insisted, at NBC's behest—they veered toward farce. They indulged in Howard Hunter's self-caricature and Mick Belker's snarls. They built one particularly silly show around Hunter's search for alligators in the city sewers. "We lost the drive of the police work in that show," Kozoll said, "in our attempt to really hammer home some wild comedy." There was another gag involving a switch between a corpse and pirated beef. "We laughed for hours over that goddamn thing in the office," Bochco said, "and it never worked. We became so enamored of the joke that we kept steering all of our other actions to pay that goddamn joke off." Then came a group of episodes organized along the spine of a linear crime plot: A prostitute was brutally killed, and it turned out the killer was a self-righteous member of the city council. "Every time we get neat," Bochco concluded, "we make mistakes."

Careening from tone to tone, Bochco and Kozoll were constantly running the risk of undermining the absurd balance that had distinguished the pilot. But the more serious difficulty, Kozoll thought, was that the pressure of weekly television, more even than network panic about low ratings, cheapened the show and sometimes reduced it to self-imitation. The whole often added up to less than the sum of its parts. The show was still confined by convention. Kozoll would have liked new principal characters to replace old ones periodically, for example, but network television wanted the same actors returning week after week, star popularity being their main route to ratings. The actors prized stability, too, and so did their contracts. You could not kill off Hill or Renko once Michael Warren and Charles Haid were under contract; and moreover, you were paying so many salaries already you couldn't afford new regulars. Kozoll also wanted more of the regulars to reveal their dark sides the way LaRue had, but this idea made other people nervous. It was widely believed that actors who play unpleasant characters—except, perhaps, in soap opera—hurt their careers. Whether the networks used the "TVQ" familiarity and likability scores or not, actors thought that TVQ ratings shaped their fates; and it was plausible to think that the people who rated actors were actually rating the characters these actors had most recently played.

There were other *Hill Street* mannerisms that Kozoll didn't single out for criticism, but that also damaged the show. It was fresh when Belker first snarled, pounced, called unwholesome criminals "dog-breath" and "hairbag," and played the embarrassed Jewish son to his "ballbusting" (the script's word) mother on the phone while his regular arrestee, a tall bald black pickpocket, smirked. Likewise, when Fay Furillo made her first shrieking entrance, when Davenport first jauntily called Furillo "Pizza Man," when Hunter first sneered at the "genetically disenfranchised." But over the months, the show's own conventions became burdens piled upon fragile imagination. Like the conventions of all lines of work, these amounted to time-savers, routines to streamline assembly-line production, to get maximum amounts of minimally competent work from ordinary practitioners. Bochco also came to see these formulas as crowd-pleasers, and indeed people did write letters saying how much they liked, for example, the Belker-pickpocket routine. If such formulas were fated to stay, Greg Hoblit thought, the challenge was to refresh them. But the only major success along these lines was that Belker gradually shook off his snarling persona and took on a sheltering paternal role, first toward a self-appointed freelance crime-fighter, Captain Freedom, then toward a stereotypical gay male prostitute. Fay remained an automatic hysteric, her predictable shrillness justified by Bochco with the argument that a single mother in her late thirties with little money and few economic prospects was entitled to panic. In the macho atmosphere of *Hill Street* production headquarters, such stereotyping could pass.

At the end of the second season, Tony Yerkovich acknowledged, "We've been repeating ourselves. Some of our scripts were garbage." Bochco said, "We fall into formula not because we get lazy but because we get tired. I thought we were batting five hundred last year. This year it's three thirty-three." Of course three thirty-three these days may be good enough to win the batting crown; and against poor competition *Hill Street* won another twenty-one Emmy nominations and six more Emmys in 1982. Because of the 1982 writers' strike, the season started late, and with a smaller backlog of scripts. By the time shooting started, the writers were having to crank out one new script a week, putting out scripts that Bochco thought were really first drafts. As a result, the late-season shows grew more stereotypic; fatigue took a toll. Bochco also thought the writing had grown rusty during the strike. One of the advantages of episodic television is that the crew stays together continuously, as in the old movie-studio system, and as opposed to the new Hollywood, in which every crew is a pickup crew hired for the occasion and then disbanded forever. The strike undermined that continuity.

But the hardest blow to the show's second-season scripts was the departure of Michael Kozoll. Kozoll had long hated the pressures of writing weekly television, let alone the executive-producing tasks of casting, staffing, teaching, tinkering, and troubleshooting. When the first season ended he backed away from co-executive-producing and became, simply, creative consultant, meaning that he and Bochco were still composing the story lines but he was no longer writing and rewriting scripts. At last he was back to writing feature films; his work was in demand now, and he declared that only dire financial need would ever drive him back to the television grind. By the time filming began for the second season, Bochco, Hoblit, and the actors were feeling his loss. One actor thought the scripts were being invaded by blunt, dumb lines, more typical of *B.J. and the Bear* than *Hill Street*.

Even before I knew that Kozoll wasn't writing lines anymore, I thought an edge was missing. Some of the two-person dialogue in particular was stilted, redundant Ping-Pong. Zippy one-liners were much in evidence. Bochco was writing less as well. Two less experienced writers, the lawyer, Jeffrey Lewis, and the would-be novelist, Michael Wagner, were working with Yerkovich and Bochco on the scripts, and learning fast, but the occupational hazard of series television, the grind, was also working against coherence. Each of the four would write an act, and Bochco then would try to unify the script—at the same time he was busy reassuring actors and generally keeping up on everything. Anyway, Kozoll had been the most writerly of the crowd and his absence was unmistakable. By the third season, Hoblit was saying, "What we're up to now is a highly paid maintenance operation. Knowing the show's not creative anymore takes its toll."

When I saw Kozoll midway through the second season, he criticized both seasons roundly. What he had valued most in the show, he said, was its abiding sense of the absurd. His model was a scene in the first episode, in which the president of the United States was due to visit the Hill on a fact-finding mission, whereupon Furillo summoned the leaders of the neighborhood's warring gangs. In full regalia, these rough, surly, imperious blacks, Hispanics, Irish, and Hasidic Jews slouched and stalked their way through the stationhouse while Furillo restrained both his own men and his distaste. Wheedling and threatening, he negotiated a cease-fire for the duration of the president's visit. A police captain reduced to negotiating with goons, right there in his unruly citadel!

But in the second season he thought the show had sunk into soap opera; the gestures of absurdity, too often repeated, had degenerated into shtick, and Furillo had become too shrill and moralistic. By the time Kozoll had figured out what *Hill Street* was, toward the end of the first season, it had ceased to interest him. Now he saw the show using pyrotechnics—rapid cuts, abrupt violence—to cover for its loss of complexity. And it was true. Hoblit had counted the number of "stunts" in each episode: fights, shootouts, car wrecks, chases, and so on. During the first season, they had averaged fewer than 0.8 stunts per show; during the second, 2.4. Stunts were easier to write than dialogue, and the producers also thought they translated into higher ratings.*

And high the ratings became. Upward of thirty million people watched the September 13, 1981 Emmy ceremony, where *Hill Street*'s unprecedented twenty-one nominations and eight awards amounted to extraordinary promotion. "It was," says the agent Bill

---

*Ironically, though, the stunts also worsened the production time crunch, exhausted the actors and crew, and led to sloppiness. Most stunts were shot on location, which increased the amount of time required for transportation and setting up. And if stunts were easy to write, they were long to shoot. A shooting day heavy with stunts might get through only three and a half script pages a day, leaving some fifty-three pages to be shot in the remaining six days. The normal eight-plus pages a day was hard enough.

Haber, "and I don't mean the word derogatorily, one of the great hypes in the history of the TV industry." A huge number must have decided then to sample this much-decorated show; having sampled it, they must have decided to sample it again. Around the same time, Mike Post's theme song—oddly unrecognized by an Emmy—slipped onto the top-ten pop music charts.

What had been a cult hit now moved into the mainstream, confounding the conventional wisdom.* Finally ensconced in a steady time period, Thursday night at ten, the show began to get ratings of 18 and higher, and audience shares consistently around 33, 34, 35, 36. At least one-third of those who watch television at that hour were watching *Hill Street Blues.* The shares stayed in the middle thirties even when NBC began repeating old episodes, out of order, in the middle of the schedule.** They went up as high as 38 during the summer, when NBC resorted to reruns from the first season. For 1981–82 overall, the series was NBC's biggest hit, and by the time it was renewed for a third season it had become the mainstay of NBC's Thursday schedule. In the fall of 1982, it was prime time's top-ranked show among men eighteen to thirty-four years old, a group that advertisers normally found hard to reach.

I asked Bill Haber what conclusions the industry would draw from the second-season success of *Hill Street,* and he said, "I don't believe it'll lead to any conclusions. I think the people who believe, like Grant Tinker, that if you put a good show on the air, if you leave it on and give it a chance, still believe that, with or without *Hill Street Blues.* And the people who don't believe that, *Hill Street Blues* won't make any difference to them."

Were people staying tuned, then, because the show had been stripped down? Was NBC vindicated for its insistence on the single modular plot? No definitive answer was possible, and yet it seemed unlikely, as Sergeant Esterhaus would say, in the extremis. The single modular story line was often hard to detect. Greg Hoblit thought the story line was "barely" simplified. Sometimes I had to search hard to tease out the short thread that must have been embedded there to please the network. Each episode was still festooned with loose ends. The show was sometimes easier to watch now if one had missed the previous episode, but it defied good sense to believe that the same

---

*Months before the Emmys, a top network research executive said to me, "I would be willing to bet unlimited sums that it will never get a high rating. Even if they kept it in the same place. I'm not so sure I know precisely what's wrong with *Hill Street Blues,* but my feeling is that what's wrong with it is the things that the critics like about it. It's made too realistic. Too high-brow. It isn't mass media."

**Because the writers' strike delayed the start of the 1981–82 season, NBC ordered only eighteen new episodes, and held the last two back for the sweeps month of May.

audience who in the spring of 1981 had presumably been intolerant of complex and interweaving stories was now, in the fall of 1981, so keenly attentive as to be able to single out the modular story and to feel Aristotelian satisfaction because it did, in fact, resolve on schedule. No, *Hill Street* became a success story because the Emmys had persuaded people to take a look; they liked what they saw, and stayed tuned. For better and worse, *Hill Street* was now ritual. The ensemble was now part of the family. *Hill Street* itself became material for future imitation and recombination. In 1982 MTM produced a ragged hospital show, *St. Elsewhere*, that aped *Hill Street*'s texture if nothing else.

Inevitably *Hill Street* lost novelty. The stunning look that had leaped out of the screen in the pilot was no longer surprising. Several of the actors seemed to reach the limits of their competence. But *Hill Street* remained the liveliest, most open, richest series on the air. I found myself complaining about it, even missing one or two episodes the second season; then found myself turning back to it. Friends whom I had regaled with praise of the show reported to me that they were now addicted to it, just as I was showing them how it was becoming fossilized. Which truth to conclude with, the truth of ingenuity or the truth of fossilization? Let the last word go to Michael Kozoll, as responsible as anyone for the promise of *Hill Street Blues.* Halfway through the second season, Kozoll said he had finally found the metaphor for television he had long been seeking. Doing episodic television, he said, is like raising a retarded child. By which he meant that there are only so many things it will ever learn to do, no matter how much you love the child, no matter how much effort and care and intelligence you lavish upon it. It will never shine. One could add: Its little accomplishments are also miraculous.

E P I L O G U E

The networks' strongest argument for catering to a least common denominator has always rested on the insuperable fact that there were only three distributors rich enough to bankroll production. Every time critics charged that the networks were instrumental in shaping mediocre taste, or pointed out that they took the fewest possible chances in the course of grabbing for the largest possible audience, the networks and the advertisers who financed them could always respond that it was true. Their business, after all, was accumulating those huge and growing audiences, and this was the only game they were really interested in playing. The charge that the networks and their audiences were locked into a self-perpetuating loop, in which viewers came to expect nothing more than variations on the themes the networks had so long provided, simply failed to touch the economic bedrock of the industry. But, in principle at least, we might expect this style of network thinking to change, were the networks to begin to lose their grip on the collective American dial.

Television is teeming with new technologies for transmission and distribution, and the hype proclaims that this *deus ex machina* is already changing television in fundamental ways. At this writing, more than one-quarter of American homes are equipped with cable, which relays TV signals from a locality's central distribution point under the street and into the home; the customer usually pays a fee of about $10 a month.* The cable system operators, who acquire exclusive local franchises, choose from among broadcast signals available nationally via satellite (some fifty at this time), their choices being limited only by the capacity of the cable and the FCC's rule that the cable must carry all over-the-air channels broadcast in the vicinity. (If the cable can handle only twenty-seven channels, as in Berkeley, California, and nineteen must be reserved for all signals broadcast in San Francisco, San Jose, San Mateo, and Sacramento, obviously only eight channels are left for new services.) Moreover,

---

*Industry estimates of the number of households reached by cable in mid-1981 ranged between 22 and 27 percent, with about twice as many *passed* by cables and therefore easily hooked up upon subscription. No one has more precise figures, since the ratings services have not caught up to the new technologies. As the old, smaller (twelve-channel) systems are upgraded and new, more capacious systems are built, the proportion of cabled homes should grow, along with the percentage of homes reached by the new networks.

about half of all cable households also subscribe to pay-cable movie channels, specializing in recent Hollywood releases, for which they pay an additional monthly fee. Meanwhile, various corporations are seeking FCC permission to broadcast directly from satellites to home receiving dishes, bypassing local stations altogether. To swell the brave new cornucopian vision further, video cassettes, video discs, and video games are already multiplying the uses of the small screen. And public television, while down, is not out.

On the face of it, the multiplication of channels would seem to make for diversified content. No longer will we have to depend on the fare cooked up by the networks to satisfy twenty or twenty-five million households. In principle, it should become possible for the new cable suppliers to make money by distributing programs that might satisfy an audience of five million, or one million, through new *de facto* networks. Even the Big Three have hedged their bets and gotten in on the act. In October 1981, CBS Cable went on the air to over three million cable subscribers (within a year, five million) with an array of big-star drama, ballet, opera, movies, and interviews, thoughtfully produced with an eye to new forms for a high-spending, lengthily educated, mostly high-taste audience. ABC produced the more conventional performing-arts ARTS, with over seven million subscribers. RCA, NBC's parent company, started producing video discs and went into partnership with Rockefeller Center Television, a cable packager headed by former CBS Inc. president Arthur Taylor, to compete for the high-culture dollar with The Entertainment Channel. Not a month passed without the announcement of a new entry into the video-technology sweepstakes. In short, all the major concentrations of culture-industry capital—and many displaced former network executives, like Taylor—read the writing on the wall and decided to go for audiences who are willing to pay extra.

It isn't only with higher culture that cable is planning to "knock the corners off" the network audience, as Herbert S. Schlosser of RCA put it. There are pay cable services, of which Time Inc.'s Home Box Office controls more than half of the market with recent Hollywood films and a sprinkling of independently produced variety shows, and made-for-TV movies.* Aside from HBO and ARTS, the best-distributed satellite-relayed networks include Ted Turner's Atlanta WTBS "Superstation," with sports, old movies, and network reruns; the ESPN sports network; the Christian Broadcasting Network; Turner's Cable News Network; USA Cable Network, with sports, women's shows, and children's shows; C-SPAN, which covers

---

*In 1982, for example, David W. Rintels signed with Home Box Office to write a movie based on the life of the Soviet dissident scientist Andrei Sakharov.

the House of Representatives; Warner Amex's Nickelodeon, for children, and Music Channel, with inventive stagings of rock songs by the groups themselves; and another nationally relayed sports and old movie channel, WGN of Chicago. There are Spanish-language, black, Jewish, health-minded, and other specialized networks. As new cable franchises are granted, the older twelve- and fifteen-channel systems are replaced by Wurlitzer-style arrays. Routinely, the major cable operators win the competition for local franchises by promising to build eighty- or one hundred-channel arrays; and the more channels, the more suppliers have sprung up to beam programs to them.

What will come of all the glitter and gloss of this new technology? One hears the claim that greater consumer choice is already bringing a greater diversity of content and a closer fit between what particular publics might desire and what they can find in their living rooms. But claims of video revolution are best left to expire with last year's trade journals and stock prospectuses. It's already apparent that transformations in the video panoply will be less than meets the eye.

Growth industries go through rhythms of overexpansion and contraction; some of the more delicate little fish shrivel and die, others are eaten by big fish, and the industry resumes growing. Industry hype about the new cornucopia feeds on a collective longing for superior television; all the hopes that languished for decades get funneled into expectations that, at long last, cabled America can deliver cultural plenitude. But those expectations are already being disappointed by the same economic forces that have chained commercial broadcasting to the tyranny of the trivial and the self-imitative. Like most gold rushes, this boom was overadvertised as a source of both business and pleasure.

For one thing, competition doesn't necessarily generate substantive diversity when the competition is still, to a large extent, oligopolistic; and the cable TV system filters out variation at several levels. Closest to the viewer, the local cable operators are, like any television executive, looking for maximum audience. Under political pressure, many have agreed to open up public-access channels; nevertheless, these are underequipped, poorly advertised, often amateurish, and probably the first projects expendable when the operators run short of cash, which happens during the boom period of any growth industry. Meanwhile, the cost of laying cable is high at a time when cash is not yet flowing in; and some cable operators have overexpanded. To make things worse, the cost of borrowing has also been very high, placing the smaller-system operators at risk in the face of bigger corporations with sure supplies of cash, like the Warner Amex combine, which outfits Warner Communications with American Express's vast cash reserves. The bigger companies—Warner Amex, Times Mirror, Viacom, Cox, et al.—have been able to win local franchises by promising more channels; they have also been able to buy out many of the smaller operators. The result is that, by the end of 1981, the top ten operators of more than one local system accounted for 44 percent of all cable subscribers—a trend that is sure to accelerate in the years to come.

Still, city by city, there will be far more competition than the networks have hitherto known. But the bulk of the available programs will come from only a few suppliers, the new satellite-relayed networks, who are largely beholden to the mainstream conventions of Hollywood television and feature films. Moreover, most of the executives in charge of the new networks formed their idea of culture in the television-industrial complex. Network specifications have become well-nigh universal, while the cost of imitating network "production values," let alone surpassing them, is formidable and restrictive. Most important, capital demands of the new suppliers what it demands of the old networks: maximum achievable market shares. So, with few exceptions, and waning exceptions at that, the new networks don't contemplate running alternatives to the network conventions of personal affliction and women-in-jeopardy. They have quickly learned that the surest way to carve out a big national market is to take some existing segment of the network schedule and to stretch it throughout a longer broadcast day. Thus sports, old movies, news, and syndicated series are the staples of the new cable networks and are likely to remain so. What they offer is not so much different as more of the same. At the 1981 convention of the National Cable Television Association, Robert Wussler, a former CBS executive who moved through the revolving door to Ted Turner's cable enterprises, told his industry audience that there was "no reality" to any expectation that cable would transmit new types of programming "in the very near future." Innovation, he said, is not forthcoming "in the lifetime of most of the people in this room." As the pay movie channels run out of available Hollywood films, they have already begun to commission series, but then they reason as the networks do: How do they get maximum audience for maximum return?

To make the new-tech cornucopia still more a standard supermarket, advertising is already becoming the key to profitability. The new networks' share of monthly subscribers' fees doesn't make huge profits. In fact, competition for space on local systems is already so fierce that the cable networks have taken to paying the systems to carry them, rather than the other way around. Under pressure from local cable operators, feeling their own cash crunch, Warner Amex's Nickelodeon Children's Service, which made a brave attempt to run without commercials, moved toward taking ads. The most that can be hoped is that, as in European commercial television, commercials might be grouped at the beginnings and ends of shows, not disrupting their continuity. But the predictable entrepreneurial problem is that advertisers still want maximum audiences even at the upper demographic range. With high production costs, CBS Cable's five million subscribers were evidently insufficient; when the parent company discontinued this most ambitious of the higher-culture suppliers, the experiment in form was reputed to have lost $30 million in its first year. The RCA/Rockefeller Center Cable Entertainment Channel, which broadcast many BBC programs, also shut down after nine months with a $34 million before-tax loss.

As cable gets more popular and advertisers recover from the economic slump, cable may become still more tempting for advertisers, and they may land in a stronger position to interrupt shows and even produce their own, as in the Golden Years. In 1982, advertisers spent on cable networks only 4 percent of what they spent on the Big Three. As the number of subscribers continues to mushroom, advertising revenues may grow to a point where they can support eight or ten cable networks, but individually or collectively they will be able to exact control in return. Cable was once touted as the alternative to commercial interruption; the reversal of this assumption has been breathtaking, as much so as advertising's unanticipated takeover of radio financing in the 1920s.* Meanwhile, pay cable, dominated by Home Box Office, seems most interested in circulating Hollywood movies and their derivative forms; by 1982, in fact, pay-cable fees were the second largest source of movie revenue, 17.4 percent, amounting for the first time to more money than came in from foreign theater proceeds. Already, financing problems are shifting pay cable from a subscription to a pay-per-view system. Some subscribers today can pay to watch a boxing match or a Broadway play on a certain night. In that case, watching television will be less like subscribing to a periodical than going to a bookstore—but a chain bookstore with much shelf space devoted to bestsellers.

Alongside mass-market cable there will indeed be margins for so-called narrowcasting, the presentation of an array of fragmented speciality services. Cable promoters proclaim the era of "video publishing." But the analogy to the world of magazines, appealing at first, quickly disturbs. Inspect the standard drugstore, supermarket, airport, or bus station magazine rack, even the kiosk in most college

---

*As late as 1922, no less a guardian of *laissez-faire* than Secretary of Commerce Herbert Hoover opined about radio: "It is inconceivable that we should allow so great a possibility for service to be drowned in advertising chatter." David Sarnoff, one of the first entrepreneurs to see the commercial potential of radio, thought RCA would make its money by selling receivers, not ads. Advertisers seized the main chance in a way no one had anticipated.

towns, and one is not inspired by the relation between multiplicity and the prospect for enlivened culture. Coast to coast, the magazine rack belongs to flesh magazines of every sexual persuasion; tennis, golf, and running magazines; stereo magazines; car magazines; hairdo magazines; romance magazines; horoscope magazines; gun magazines; stamp and coin magazines; music magazines; upscale city magazines; gourmet magazines; finance magazines; celebrity magazines. All appeal to the buyer as hobbyist, a consumer who seeks satisfaction in the cultivation of personal style, competence, and a sense of linkage to otherwise anonymous others. In the corner, on the bigger racks, sit the money-losing opinion magazines. Whatever one thinks of their points of view, *The Nation, The New Republic, National Review, Harper's, The Atlantic, Mother Jones, The American Spectator*, et al., address their readers much of the time as citizens. They articulate, sharpen, question world views; they speak to, and for, a minority political counterculture. Arrayed against this political remnant is the dominant culture: antipolitical, valuing private goods over public expression. The common good is always being parceled out into the separate pursuits of private happiness, relief, and self-improvement.

So the magazine rack re-creates the long-lasting division of American culture into fragmented interest groups. As shoppers, people find satisfaction in the knowledge that they aren't alone in their enthusiasms. What they get from magazines is a kind of involvement, a feeling of participation in activities larger than themselves, built on standards independent of their lone egos. Organized consumption provides badges of identity: the result is a restricted pluralism of consumption. The market is formally open but can cater only to those interests that can be expressed as desires for commodities. By the *laissez-faire* logic that prevails in broadcasting today, the courts uphold the argument that, where there are so many channels, the free market will automatically end up serving minority tastes. If there are enough viewers who want unconventional movies, an entrepreneur will arise to serve them and succeed at it. By the same logic, however, if no such entrepreneur arises or if one tries and fails, the demand must not have existed. Demand knocks only after the fact.

Meanwhile, the networks whistle in an assumed twilight, although no one knows for sure how fast the light is fading. Their old domination is clearly sliding. In 1975, the three networks together averaged 91 percent of the audience in prime time; in 1981, 83 percent. The major inroads come from independent stations—playing one-time network hits in syndication—as much as from cable. But although the Ogilvy & Mather advertising agency predicts that the aggregate network share will drop to 59 percent by 1990, almost everyone in the networks as well as many advertisers project a less rapid slide. CBS, for example, anticipates an aggregate network share of 73 percent in 1990. For what it is worth, virtually everyone in the industry anticipates that the networks will continue to dominate American viewing time for at least a decade. They remain the advertiser's best buy for national reach. Although their shows are getting more expensive and less successful, aggregate ratings points are rising as shares fall, because the total number of sets and households continues to increase. Only NBC has lost ratings points since 1976.

Over a longer haul, who knows? Against growing competition, the networks may eventually become what former NBC programming chief Paul Klein—himself involved in cable now—calls "dinosaurs nibbled away by ants." "You don't have to cut off all a dinosaur's food," he says. "You have to cut off five percent of its food, and it starts to get thin and panicky, and starts getting a little more hungry . . . and that spiral down occurs. It panics into defense of its prior position." The networks accelerate into a cycle of self-imitation, audience boredom, the depletion of hits—as in the overdrilling of used-up oil fields—and a loss of still more viewers, especially in the upper demographic reaches. The economic logic has already driven the networks to expand the number of commercials per hour to make up for lost audience. Cost pressures will only grow.

Economic facts also threaten to rigidify the class structure of television. The new cable systems will be highly stratified. Warner Amex, for example, has already promised that its Dallas system will consist of eighty channels in three tiers. The lower tier of twenty-six channels—many of which will be the over-the-air stations—will sell for some $12 a month; but to buy all eighty, including the more diverse pay and "interactive" channels, and whatever "video publishing" materializes, will cost over $42 a month. So the bulk of whatever plurality is coming will be an upper-middle-class preserve. The unregulated market, as always, only serves those who can afford the cost of entry.

But even Paul Klein admits that the networks will keep their hold and remain vastly profitable for at least a decade more. "There is no organized competition," he says. It is as if the Big Three auto companies were losing a few share points a year, but without the Japanese offering serious alternatives. The networks will go on programming according to the conventions and criteria they have been accustomed to, and have helped accustom most of us to. The decision-making process will not change materially. The absolute market power of the ABC, CBS, and NBC networks will be undermined, but their conventions will still reign supreme, with minor variations. Marvin Mord, the head of ABC research, anticipates that the networks will need to "paint by the numbers," to "find a greater number of gratifications for multiple numbers of segments of the population." This search can only produce more synthetic shows offering something for everyone but nothing coherent for anyone. As the networks hasten to find magic solutions to audience slippage, they may go on shortening the runs of series that don't start off with good ratings. Current programming trends, in other words, will be likely to continue. Meanwhile, the networks are diversifying into pay cable and other new technologies so that, like the giant oil companies, they may end up controlling a considerable share of their competition. Even if not, in ten years we may have two networks garnering 25 shares, one with 20 and, say, six other networks gaining less than 5 percent—all competing, for the most part, for the same reliable mass audience, while the narrowcasters clamber to hold on to the remaining fringe.

To sum up, the brave new cornucopia is likely to create only minor, marginal chances for a diversity of substance—and fewer and fewer as time goes on. The workings of the market give Americans every incentive to remain conventionally entertainment-happy. Conglomeration proceeds apace. Homogeneity at the cultural center is complemented by consumer fragmentation on the margins. Technology opens doors, and oligopoly marches in just behind, slamming them. There can be no technological fix for what is, after all, a social problem.

The problem is the texture of American life. Americans rely on television's conventions because television suits the partitioned nature of everyday existence. Despite the lip service Americans pay to civic virtue, most of us believe that real life is private life, real ambition private ambition. The public world is a corrupt necessity, a jungle to be dropped into only when we have a direct—that is, private—interest at stake. As good democrats, we flatter ourselves that we live in the forum, but we can't wait to get home. As long as we understand the private and isolated to be the central sphere in which we define ourselves and live our real lives, we are primed for television, which is modern domesticity's eery umbilical connection with a larger world. Having dropped out of the public realm, because there are few institutions that might provide the arena for rich and informed public speech, we rely on television to stay "in touch." Instead of having the means for direct communication of what we might have in common—media in the literal sense—we get "the media."

That is why television has become a cultural force of such enormous proportions. Some scholars and industry representatives have argued that television's power is softened because viewers are free to take the screen or leave it. But it seems to me more apropos to say that, when a television set is switched on for almost seven hours a day in the average American household, the curious power of this electronic machinery begins with the fact that it requires so little of us. Turning a single set off seems almost beside the point. While we nod off, or get up to go to the refrigerator or the bathroom, the images go on living their strangely insubstantial yet ubiquitous lives. We hear about them at work, or from our children, or parents, or friends, or encounter them transfigured into the styles of people in the street.

Television symbolizes reality so strangely because the images are extraordinary at the same time that they appear in our most ordinary settings. They come from afar, but they loom up right there in our own living rooms and bedrooms. That is why journalistic and academic critics of particular shows or genres, or of specific features of television, like violence, miss the essential point about TV's force. The images register with us as symbols, as diversion and ideology at the same time, by virtue of the fact that our guard is down when we watch. It is certainly true, as many researchers remind us, that we screen these symbols differently according to who we are and how we already see the world. We notice and soak up and ignore selectively, although not always consciously. The presence of the medium is such that we don't so much reflect on the meanings or (most of the time) study them; we swim in them. Television inscribes images of the acceptable that go beyond its stereotypes of men and women, blacks and whites, history and domesticity, significant as these are. Television has become the collective, secondhand dream of American society, and we don't even need to tune in to be wired up, affected by the look and the values that TV radiates. "Ideology" to Americans usually smacks of a foreign disease: something that afflicts other people. But ideology means nothing more or less than a set of assumptions that becomes second nature; even rebels have to deal with it. Television can no more speak without ideology than we can speak without prose. We swim in its world even if we don't believe in it.

Shrugged off and imitated, ignored and dreamed about, television adds up to American culture's impoverished version of itself. Some of our collective fears it ratifies, others it suppresses, but in either case, and at virtually every choice-point in the production and scheduling process, the gatekeepers work up smoothed-out versions of public desire and feed them back to us. A host of stripped-down images returns to colonize our imagination in ways we cannot demonstrate conclusively but have good reason to suspect. *The Deer Hunter* is shown on television (not on the networks, though), and several people kill themselves playing Russian roulette. Fonzie takes out a library card on *Happy Days,* and thousands of teenagers take out library cards in the next few days. Over the longer haul, which is the haul most viewers undertake, the sum of studies on television violence seems persuasive: Television violence can kindle violence in the real world. And so it stands to reason that years of television, cumulatively, seep into the imagination in ways more sweeping than any simple influence on behavior. Television is as familiar to infants and illiterates as it is to the educated; television's images can shape childhood's cultural landscape more intensely than the literature of secular cultures. Television has probably rewired the collective nervous system, making discontinuity the norm of perception, shortening the collective attention span down toward the vanishing point.

One effect is indisputable. By its sheer inertia, network television convinces most Americans that the forms they see are the proper forms of entertainment, even of culture; and its styles, in turn, become the norm around much of the world. Many people are disgruntled with television, but American society tolerates it because, in the absence of compelling alternatives, it appears to help us "get by." But whatever television's uses as a domestic space-filler or a mild analgesic, its weightless images usurp the space of popular culture. The network product crowds out what could be more intelligent, complicated, true, beautiful, or public-spirited. Yet if we are serious about living in a democracy, the fundamental responsibility of the media should be to help people better pursue their rights and obligations as citizens, not to sell goods, or serve as an amplification system for politicians, or shore up the prestige of the privileged, or sprinkle flakes of celebrity and blips of disconnected fact upon the daily life of a society otherwise dedicated to private gain. Democracy requires an active, engaged citizenry committed to determining and seeking the public good. As it is, the bulk of commercial television (along with most of the other media) reminds us to think of ourselves as consumers first and foremost. In the daily barrage, much inventiveness is squandered, much intelligence dissipated, much pleasure dribbled away.

So the networks do just what they set out to do. They are not *trying* to stimulate us to thought, or inspire us to belief, or remind us of what it is to be human and live on the earth late in the twentieth century; what they are trying to do is to "hook" us. Meanwhile, the government regulatory agencies have been persuaded that "the marketplace" is its own regulator, which means that no interest that cannot be expressed as Nielsen numbers counts.

If there is ever to be an American television industry that aims to do something different, to challenge us rather than hook us and fawn on us and condescend to us, it would have to come because publics organize to insist on it, in part at least out of a felt need and desire to create a public domain where citizens can feel empowered to transact public affairs. By itself, the formal structure of a noncommercial television system along European lines wouldn't accomplish all that much; the mass-marketing mentality pervades much of non-commercial European television to almost the same degree as in America, though without the compulsion of the profit motive. In the end, if public life were sufficiently rich and engaging, people would already be communicating—literally, "making common"—rather than relying on the little electronic box to ease our days. Instead, our culture is soaked in prefabricated cant about "communication," and a president who does not know what his own government is doing gets dubbed "the Great Communicator." This is why the predicament of American television is the predicament of American culture and politics as a whole. Walt Whitman wrote: "To have great poets there must be great audiences, too."

ACKNOWLEDGMENTS

This book could not exist without the generous help of the following television-industry people—present and former network executives, producers, writers, actors, directors, advertisers, studio executives, consultants, lobbyists, journalists, and others—who graciously consented to interviews and conversation, and guided me through the labyrinth: Seymour Amlen, David Anspaugh, Danny Arnold, Edward Asner, Jonathan Axelrod, Deanne Barkley, Arnold Becker, Taurean Blacque, William Blinn, Steven Bochco, Robert Brilliant, Herbert Brodkin, James Brooks, Les Brown, Allan Burns, Bob Butler, Robert Butler, Ronald M. Cohen, Elizabeth Coleman, Barbara Corday, Karen Danaher, Ann Daniel, Newt Deiter, Richard Dysart, Candace Early, Sam Egan, Jane Egan, Michael Elias, Eric Engberg, René Enriquez, Rich Eustis, Mike Farrell, David Feldman, Jack Fields, Cassandra Foster, Ellen Franklin, Seth Freeman, Richard Friedenberg, William Froug, David Fuchs, Michele Gallery, Tony Ganz, Bret Garwood, Larry Gelbart, David Gerber, Richard Gilbert, Richard Gitter, Don Gold, Gary David Goldberg, Melvin Goldberg, Bob Gottlieb, Bud Grant, John Gray, Stanley Greenberg, Jeff Greenfield, Robert Greenwald, Larry Gross, William Haber, Charles Haid, Oliver Hailey, Aljean Harmetz, Barbara Hering, Len Hill, Gregory Hoblit, Gerald M. Jaffe, Randy Johnson, Oscar Katz, Jerry Katzman, Herman Keld, Linda Kelsey, Tom Kersey, Ernest Kinoy, Joseph T. Klapper, Paul Klein, Richard Kletter, Tom Koenig, Michael Kozoll, Perry Lafferty, Paul Leaf, Norman Lear, Richard Levinson, Richard H. Low, Philip Luttinger, Carol Evan McKeand, Nigel McKeand, Phil Mandelker, Stan Margulies, Garry Marshall, Gene P. Mater, John Matthes, Jack Michon, Arthur Miller, Steve Mills, Ronald Milavsky, F. Kent Mitchel, Marvin Mord, Joel Morwood, Simon Muntner, Mace Neufeld, Donn O'Brien, Diane Okrent, Al Ordover, John Steven Owen, Bruce Paltrow, Rod Parker, Brigit Potter, Richard Powell, Tony Randall, Richard M. Ravin, Richard Reisberg, Gayne Rescher, Gene Reynolds, Ted Rich, Jim Richardson, David W. Rintels, Howard Rodman, Sam Rolfe, Jane Rosenthal, Barney Rosenzweig, Michael Ross, Freyda Rothstein, William Rubens, David Rubin, Stu Samuels, Esther Shapiro, Harvey Shephard, Stuart Sheslow, Scott Siegler, James B. Sikking, April Smith, Joe Spano, Jerome H. Stanley, Frank Stanton, Dave Sterling, Brandon Stoddard, Percy Tannenbaum, Erik Tarloff, Brandon Tartikoff, Studs Terkel, Betty Thomas, Tony Thomopoulos, Chris Thompson, Grant Tinker, Daniel J. Travanti, Mitch Tuchman, Jerry Velasco, Michael Warren, Tom Werner, Mark Waxman, Bernie West, Donald Wildmon, Cindy Williams, Irv Wilson, Ethel Winant, Robert D. Wood, Bud Yorkin, Barbara Zheutlin, and Michael Zinberg.

I am very grateful to the Rockefeller Foundation for granting me a Humanities Fellowship, and to the National Endowment for the Humanities for its Basic Research Grant #RO-20114, without which I would not have been able to take the time away from teaching or to hire research assistants. The University of California, Berkeley, gave me leave and equipment, and covered some research expenses. The New York Institute for the Humanities kindly gave me an office in which to start writing in the summer of 1981. Troy Duster and the Institute for the Study of Social Change at the University of California, Berkeley, bailed me out with typing help when the going got rough. A. Lucia Torres, Norma Partridge-Wallace, and Jean Margolis in the sociology department were wonderfully helpful.

Bless my research assistants, Tom Andrae, Jon Cruz, Ron Lembo, Kathryn Oberdeck, Andrea Press, and Terry Strathman for spending a summer watching and analyzing more television shows than they had ever bargained for. For months thereafter, Kathy Oberdeck and Andrea Press also probed, typed, read, filed, fact-checked, and helped me far more than they know. Pamela Blair, and also Elisabeth S. Hasen and Kathy Pohl, transcribed hundreds of hours of interviews with extraordinary accuracy and persistence. Lisa Heilbronn, Karen Musalo, and Sharran Zeleke typed the manuscript.

Of the many people who gave me ideas, questions, tips, hospitality, encouragement, and solace along the way, I want especially to thank: Michael J. Arlen, Susan Bechaud, Robert N. Bellah, Marshall Berman, Silvia Bizio, Judith Coburn, Jean Cohen, Geoffrey Cowan, Gary Davis, Paul DiMaggio, Mary Douglas, Russell Ellis, Paul Espinosa, Robert Faulkner, Hamilton Fish III, Mickey Flacks, Richard Flacks, the late Erving Goffman, Stanhope Gould, Paul Hirsch, Arlie Hochschild, Doug Ireland, Jim Jasper, William Kornhauser, Leo Lowenthal, Rob Manoff, Annette Michelson, Marcia Millman, Victor Navasky, Aryeh Neier, Karen Paige, Marge Pearson, David Rieff, Howard A. Rodman, Michael Schudson, Clancy Sigal, Susan Sontag, Diane Tasoff, David Thomson, Gaye Tuchman, Luisa Valenzuela, Edmund White, Karen Wollaeger, and Mary Ann Worklan. Like every analyst of television, I am indebted to the writings of Erik Barnouw and Les Brown. My agent, Roberta Pryor, was a voice of encouragement when I needed one.

Many thanks, too, to the following for reading and criticizing parts of the manuscript: Tom Andrae, Victoria Bonnell, Ken Cloke, Melissa Doering, Michael Elias, Rich Eustis, Richard Friedenberg, Tony Ganz, Bob Gottlieb, Helena Hershel, Gregory Hoblit, Lorraine

Kahn, Lindsay King, Michael Kozoll, Ron Lembo, Ruth Rosen, Michael Schudson, Percy Tannenbaum, and Paul Thomas. My cup runneth over.

And not least, I was blessed by the extraordinary editing of Tom Engelhardt, who single-handedly preserves the waning craft ideal of the editor as ideal reader and tough, comprehending critic. There isn't a page in this book that hasn't been improved by his meticulous reading and close questioning (and there are many the reader is spared because Tom knew redundancy and excess in the manuscript when he saw it). Tom's ability to find my argument when I'd lost it restores my faith in artistry, logic, and mind reading all at the same time. No writer can expect more.

Earlier versions of some passages have previously appeared in articles I published in *American Film, The Nation,* the *Soho News, democracy,* and the *Los Angeles Times.*

NOTES

INDEX

N O T E S

Unless otherwise attributed, all quotations come from the author's interviews.

PROLOGUE

Page 4, last line.   Pat Aufderheide, "Spotlight on Politics in Hollywood," *In These Times*, March 10–16, 1982.

Page 10, line 17.   Gary Deeb, "CBS 'yellow' journalism humors Big Brother," *Chicago Sun-Times*, May 30, 1982, p. 13.

Page 10, line 23.   Daniel Schorr, *Clearing the Air* (Boston: Houghton Mifflin, 1977), p. 264.

Page 12, line 10.   There is a long line of such theorizing about movies. The key works, even where they exaggerate, are Max Horkheimer and T. W. Adorno, "The Culture Industry: Enlightenment as Mass Deception," in *Dialectic of Enlightenment* (New York: Seabury, 1972; first published 1944); Siegfried Kracauer, *From Caligari to Hitler* (Princeton: Princeton University Press, 1947); and Martha Wolfenstein and Nathan Leites, *Movies: A Psychological Study* (New York: Free Press, 1950). All such ideas eventually trace their origins to the idea of catharsis in Aristotle's *Poetics*, a mere offhand comment there, really, before Freud elaborated it. Today, pop sociological and psychological theorizing has become a staple of film criticism and the daily press.

Page 14, line 15.   Clifford Geertz, "Thick Description," *The Interpretation of Cultures* (New York: Basic Books, 1973), pp. 3–30.

Page 14, line 32.   See especially Paul M. Hirsch, "An Organizational Perspective on Television (Aided and Abetted by Models from Economics, Marketing, and the Humanities)," in Stephen B. Withey and Ronald P. Abeles, eds., *Television and Social Behavior: Beyond Violence and Children* (Hillsdale, N.J.: Lawrence Erlbaum Assoc., 1980), pp. 83–102. Other valuable theorizing bearing on organizational problems in the popular culture industry is to be found in Herbert A. Simon, *Administrative Behavior* (New York:

Macmillan, 1947); John Kenneth Galbraith, *The New Industrial State* (New York: Signet, 1967), pp. 37–38, 50; Paul M. Hirsch, "Processing Fads and Fashions: An Organization-Set Analysis of Cultural Industry Systems," *American Journal of Sociology* 77 (January 1972), pp. 639–59; Paul M. Hirsch, "Occupational, Organizational, and Institutional Models in Mass Media Research: Toward an Integrated Framework," in Paul M. Hirsch, P. V. Miller, and F. Gerald Kline, eds., *Strategies for Communication Research* (Beverly Hills: Sage, 1977); Paul DiMaggio and Paul M. Hirsch, "Production Organizations in the Arts," *American Behavioral Scientist* 19 (July–August 1976), pp. 735–52; R. A. Peterson, "The Production of Culture: A Prolegomenon," *American Behavioral Scientist* 19 (1976), pp. 669–85; Paul DiMaggio, "Market Structure, the Creative Process, and Popular Culture: Toward an Organizational Reinterpretation of Mass Culture Theory," *Journal of Popular Culture* 11 (1977), pp. 436–67; and Muriel G. Cantor, *Prime-Time Television: Content and Control* (Beverly Hills: Sage, 1980).

Page 15, line 26.   Joan Didion, *The White Album* (New York: Pocket Books, 1980), p. 161.

Chapter 1:   The Problem of Knowing

Page 15, line 42.   Frank Swertlow, "Hollywood's Cocaine Connection," *TV Guide*, February 28, 1981, pp. 6–12; " 'It's Snowing in Hollywood Every Day,' " *TV Guide*, March 7, 1981, pp. 35–40; Deborah Caulfield, "The Psychic Who Came in from the Cold," *Los Angeles Times*, Calendar Section, March 15, 1981, pp. 1, 96–98.

Page 21, line 7.   Many executives repeat comparable figures. Most of these come from NBC senior vice president for programs and talent (formerly in charge of prime time for CBS) Perry Lafferty, in "Dialogue on Film," *American Film*, April 1981, pp. 60–61.

Page 25, line 33.   Hans Magnus Enzensberger, *The Consciousness Industry* (New York: Seabury, 1974).

Page 27, line 21.   See Henry Nash Smith, *Virgin Land* (New York: Vintage, 1950), and Richard Slotkin, *Regeneration Through Violence* (Middletown, Conn.: Wesleyan University Press, 1973).

Page 27, line 28.   Alexis de Tocqueville, *Democracy in America*, revised by Francis Bowen, ed. by Phillips Bradley (New York: Vintage, 1945), vol. 2, pp. 50–89; David Thorburn, "Television

Melodrama," in Horace Newcomb, ed., *Television: The Critical View* (New York: Oxford University Press, 1979), second edition, pp. 536–53.

Page 27, line 31.   Tocqueville, *Democracy in America*, vol. 2, pp. 50, 52, 54, 62–63.

Page 28, line 6.   The American hold on world entertainment markets is convincingly described in Jeremy Tunstall, *The Media Are American* (New York: Columbia University Press, 1977).

Page 28, line 7.   Tocqueville, *Democracy in America*, vol. 2, p. 38.

Page 28, line 19.   See, for example, Richard Altick, *The Shows of London* (Cambridge, Mass.: Harvard University Press, 1978); Peter Burke, *Popular Culture in Early Modern Europe* (New York: New York University Press, 1978); Jacques Le Goff, *Time, Work, and Culture in the Middle Ages*, trans. by Arthur Goldhammer (Chicago: University of Chicago Press, 1980).

Page 28, line 28.   See Guy Debord, *The Society of the Spectacle* (Detroit: Black and Red, 1970); Jean Baudrillard, *For a Critique of the Political Economy of the Sign*, trans. by Charles Levin (St. Louis: Telos Press, 1981).

Page 28, line 36.   Hermann Broch, "Notes on the Problem of Kitsch," in Gillo Dorfles, ed., *Kitsch* (New York: Universe Books, 1969), p. 62.

Page 29, line 14.   In 1934, for example, the Wagner-Hatfield amendment to the proposed Communications Act would have reserved one-quarter of all radio frequencies to "educational, religious, agricultural, labor, cooperative, and similar non-profit-making associations." The commercial radio lobby killed this measure in Senate debate (Erik Barnouw, *The Golden Web* [New York: Oxford University Press, 1968], pp. 23–26). It took more than thirty years before Congress allocated funds for educational radio and TV, and even then, public broadcasting is perpetually embattled and impoverished.

Chapter 2:   Predicting the Unpredictable

Page 37, line 2.   Miles Beller, "How Networks Test for Audience Impact," *New York Times,* Arts and Leisure Section, June 3, 1979, pp. 1, 29; Richard M. Levine, "Testing: One, Two, Sixty Million," *New Times,* June 12, 1978, pp. 72–75.

Page 37, line 30.   Levine, "Testing."

Page 38, Fn.   Ibid.

Page 40, Fn. 1.   Ibid.

Page 42, line 20.   "TV's 'White-Bread' Movie Formula," *San Francisco Chronicle,* July 31, 1982, p. 1, from the *Los Angeles Times* News Service.

Page 44, line 28.   Harold Wilensky, *Organizational Intelligence: Knowledge and Policy in Government and Industry* (New York: Basic Books, 1967), p. 16.

Page 45, line 22.   *San Francisco Chronicle,* July 31, 1982.

Chapter 3:   By the Numbers

Page 49, line 11.   All Nielsen figures, unless otherwise attributed, come from materials kindly furnished by the A. C. Nielsen Co. and reprinted with their permission.

Page 49, line 37.   Martin Mayer, "How Good Are Television Ratings?" (New York: Committee on Nationwide Television Audience Measurements, 1966), p. 14.

Page 50, line 15.   See, for example, *Broadcast Ratings,* Parts 1–4, Hearings Before a Special Subcommittee on Investigations, Committee on Interstate and Foreign Commerce, 88th Congress, 1st and 2nd Sessions, 1963–64 (Washington, D.C.: Government Printing Office, 1964), pp. 1533, 1535, 1536, 1541, 1544, 1561, 1662, 1772, 1777, 1781, 1837, 1838, 1878, 1918ff.; Mayer, "How Good Are Television Ratings?" pp. 19–20.

Page 50, line 28.   Mayer, "How Good Are Television Ratings?" pp. 15–18.

Page 51, line 14.   In fact, ARB's diary cooperation rate was much lower than Nielsen's rate in placing its electronic meters. And therefore Nielsen's actual sample should more closely have approximated a true sample than did ARB's.

Page 51, line 24. *Broadcast Ratings,* p. 1131.

Page 51, line 31. Ibid., pp. 1278, 1530, 1781.

Page 51, line 34. Ibid., pp. 1154–55, 1533, 1535, 1536, 1541, 1544, 1561.

Page 52, line 3. "The Rating Game," *Newsweek,* November 21, 1977, p. 142.

Page 52, line 10. Mayer, "How Good Are Television Ratings?" pp. 20–23.

Page 52, line 17. Mayer, "How Good Are Television Ratings?" p. 27; and "Television Ratings Revisited . . ." (New York: Committee on Nationwide Television Audience Measurements, 1970), p. 37.

Page 52, line 29. René Anselmo, "Minority Undercount Remains Severe Research Problem," *Advertising Age,* April 16, 1979.

Page 52, line 43. "The Rating Game," *Newsweek,* November 21, 1977, p. 142.

Page 53, line 1. *Advertising Age,* October 20, 1980.

Chapter 4: Making Schedules

Page 57, Fn. A. C. Nielsen Co., *Television Audience 1979,* vol. 2, p. 30.

Page 58, line 6. Computed from figures supplied by the A. C. Nielsen Co.

Page 59, last line. Computed from figures in Nielsen, *Television Audience 1980,* p. 21.

Page 61, line 36. Paul Klein, "The Men Who Run TV Aren't Stupid . . . They Know Us Better Than You Think," *New York,* January 25, 1971, pp. 20–29.

Page 62, line 22. Robert E. Buchanan, executive vice-president and head of media at the J. Walter Thompson agency, has said: "We look at overall numbers and ratings first, of course, but within that, demographics are vital. No advertiser buys households. We're concerned with *who* is watching. CBS will only guarantee the number of households. But NBC, as the last-place runner, has had to guarantee demographics." Quoted in Bernice Kanner, "The Grant Tinker Show," *New York*, November 29, 1982, p. 18.

Chapter 5:   The Triumph of the Synthetic: Spinoffs, Copies, Recombinant Culture

Page 64, line 16.   William S. Paley, *As It Happened* (Garden City, N.Y.: Doubleday, 1979), p. 269.

Page 65, line 8.   Erik Barnouw, *A Tower in Babel* (New York: Oxford University Press, 1966), pp. 224–26.

Page 65, line 14.   Lary May, *Screening Out the Past* (New York: Oxford University Press, 1980), pp. 99–100, 196–97.

Page 66, line 16.   Federal Communications Commission, Network Inquiry Special Staff, *New Television Networks: Entry, Jurisdiction, Ownership and Regulation*, vol. 2, Background Reports (Washington, D.C.: Federal Communications Commission, 1980), p. 94.

Page 66, Fn. 3.   Les Brown, "The Cry of the Peacock," *Channels*, June–July 1982, p. 29.

Page 68, Fn.   See Leslie Wayne, "Hollywood Sequels Are Just the Ticket," *New York Times*, Business Section, July 18, 1982, pp. 1, 17. On the movie business's taste for movies "just like" but "completely different," see James Monaco, *American Film Now* (New York: Oxford University Press, 1979), pp. 14–16.

Page 69, line 28.   *Soho News*, September 1, 1981.

Page 69, line 39.   Quoted in Dave Kaufman, "H'wood Producers Take Shots at Webs, Actors, You Name It," *Variety*, May 26, 1982, p. 60.

Page 70, line 20.   Percy Tannenbaum, "Play It Again, Sam: Repeated Exposure to Television Programs," Working Paper No. 51, Survey Research Center, University of California, Berkeley, 1981.

Page 70, Fn.   Hermann Broch, "Notes on the Problem of Kitsch," in Gillo Dorfles, ed., *Kitsch* (New York: Universe Books, 1969), pp. 62, 72.

Page 70, Fn.   T. W. Adorno, "Television and the Patterns of Mass Culture," in Bernard Rosenberg and David Manning White, eds., *Mass Culture* (New York: Free Press, 1957), p. 474. First published 1954.

Page 71, line 41.   Sally Bedell, *Up the Tube: Prime-Time TV in the Silverman Years* (New York: Viking, 1981), p. 213.

Page 72, line 4.   Richard M. Levine, "The Jelling of Jiggle TV," *New Times,* November 3, 1978, pp. 66–72.

Page 72, line 32.   Walter Benjamin, "The Work of Art in the Age of Mechanical Reproduction," in *Illuminations,* trans. by Harry Zohn (New York: Harcourt, Brace, and World, 1968).

Page 73, Fn.   Quoted anonymously in David Lewin, "The Hidden Persuaders: The American Producers with the Powerful Punch," *San Francisco Sunday Examiner & Chronicle,* Datebook Section, April 20, 1980, p. 42.

Page 76, line 15.   Quoted in Richard Hack, "Televisions," *Hollywood Reporter,* July 28, 1981, p. 10.

Page 76, line 17.   Bedell, *Up the Tube,* p. 113.

Page 77, line 11.   Herbert A. Simon, *Administrative Behavior: A Study of Decision-Making Processes in Administrative Organizations* (New York: Macmillan, 1945).

Page 77, line 21.   Quoted in James K. Lyon, *Bertolt Brecht in America* (Princeton: Princeton University Press, 1980), pp. 51–52.

Page 77, line 42.   Fredric Jameson, "On Raymond Chandler," *Southern Review* 6:3 (Summer 1970), pp. 624–50.

Page 78, line 17.   See Marshall Berman, *All That Is Solid Melts into Air* (New York: Simon and Schuster, 1982).

Page 78, line 23.   Arthur Koestler, *The Act of Creation* (Danube Edition/London: Picador, 1975), p. 120.

Page 79, line 26.   Claude Lévi-Strauss has written of the "primitive" style of *bricolage,* the patching together of new entities from cultural odds and ends. But *bricolage* has returned full force in the modern recombinant principle, with its double sense of permutation and conservation. See *The Savage Mind* (Chicago: University of Chicago Press, 1962), pp. 16–22, 35–36.

Page 79, line 33.   Susan Sontag: in seminar on television, New York Institute for the Humanities, July 1981.

Page 80, line 32.   John Berger, "The Moment of Cubism," in *The Moment of Cubism and Other Essays* (New York: Pantheon, 1969).

Page 80, line 35.   Paul Fussell, *The Great War and Popular Memory* (New York: Oxford University Press, 1976).

Page 80, Fn.   Lyric by Daniel Miller, Mute/Sonet Publishing, London. Reprinted by permission.

Page 81, line 10.   Kennedy Fraser, *The Fashionable Mind* (New York: Knopf, 1981), pp. 237, 240, 241.

Chapter 6:   "Another American Dream Gone Astray"

Page 93, line 1.   Herbert Gold, *The Age of Happy Problems* (New York: Dial Press, 1962).

Chapter 7:   Inside Tracks in a Small World

Page 116, line 2.   On studio musicians, see Robert Faulkner, *Music on Demand: Composers and Careers in the Hollywood Film Industry* (New Brunswick, N.J.: Transaction Press, 1981). Thanks to Professor Faulkner for conversation on this point. On the airline industry, see John Newhouse, *The Sporty Game* (New York: Knopf, 1982).

Page 117, line 4.   *New York Times,* April 1, May 18, June 29, July 8, 1978; Teri Ritzer, "Begelman Out at MGM," *Hollywood Reporter,* July 13, 1982, p. 1; Aljean Harmetz, "Begelman Removed as Chief of United Artists," *New York Times,* July 13, 1982, p. 1; David McClintick, *Indecent Exposure* (New York: William Morrow, 1982), p. 450.

Page 125, line 24.   Tony Schwartz, "Carson Signs for Three Years on a Shorter Tonight Show," *New York Times,* May 7, 1980, p. 1.

Page 127, line 17.   Richard Levinson and William Link, *Stay Tuned* (New York: St. Martin's, 1981), p. 19.

Page 127, line 44.   On Bob Wood's back-end deal, see Bedell, *Up the Tube*, p. 188.

Page 135, line 4.   *Hollywood Reporter*, September 30, 1981, p. 1.

Page 137, line 8.   Tim Brooks and Earle Marsh, *The Complete Directory to Prime Time Network TV Shows 1946–Present*, rev. and enlarged edition (New York: Ballantine, 1981), p. 504; Bedell, *Up the Tube*, p. 135.

Page 138, line 42.   Bedell, *Up the Tube*, p. 132.

Page 139, line 1.   This tour of Spelling's *oeuvre* borrows heavily from Bob Schneider, "Spelling's Salvation Armies," *Cultural Correspondence*, no. 4 (Spring 1977), pp. 27–33, and from Brooks and Marsh, *Complete Directory*.

Page 140, Fn.   Kathryn Harris, "IRS Rules on Tax Credits Put TV-Land in a Tizzy," *Los Angeles Times*, August 2, 1982, Part IV, p. 1.

Chapter 8:   The Deal Is the Art Form

Page 144, line 33.   Among the rare journalistic accounts of agents and their work are Charles Shreger, "CAA: Packaging of an Agency," *Los Angeles Times*, April 23, 1979, Part IV, pp. 13, 16; Karen Stabiner, "Playing Hardball with a Hot Agent," *American Film*, July–August 1981, pp. 41–45, 67; Mark Singer, "Profiles (Sam Cohen)," *The New Yorker*, January 11, 1982, pp. 46–92.

Page 145, line 29.   On the decline of the studios, see John Gregory Dunne, *The Studio* (New York: Simon and Schuster Touchstone ed., 1979), pp. 10, 12; and Eric Rhode, *A History of the Cinema, From Its Origins to 1970* (New York: Hill & Wang, 1976), p. 438.

Page 145, line 41.   Bob Gottlieb, "How Lew Wasserman Foiled the Wicked Witches and Became the Wiz of MCA," *Los Angeles*, January 1979, pp. 120–25 and ff.

Page 153, line 6.   John Gregory Dunne, "Hollywood's Hessians," *New York Review of Books*, November 19, 1981, p. 34.

Chapter 9:   Movies of the Week

Page 158, line 7.   *Variety*, June 16, 1982, p. 3.

Page 162, line 23. " 'Holocaust' Audience Far Bigger Than West Germans Anticipated," *New York Times*, January 1, 1979, p. 15.

Page 168, Fn. See Lois Gibbs with Murray Levine, *Love Canal: My Story* (Albany, N.Y.: State University of New York Press, 1982).

Page 170, line 44. *Time*, September 22, 1980.

Page 176, Fn. Richard Severo, "Toxin Put in Feed Found in Humans 5 Years Later," *New York Times*, National Edition, April 16, 1982, p. 7.

Page 182, line 3. Howard Rosenberg, "NBC Delays Showing 2 Black Productions," *Los Angeles Times*, April 24, 1981, Part VI, p. 1.

Page 182, line 44. Erik Barnouw, *The Image Empire* (New York: Oxford University Press, 1970), pp. 35–36.

Page 183, line 7. David W. Rintels, "How Much Truth Does 'The F.B.I.' Tell About the F.B.I.?" *New York Times*, March 5, 1972, Arts and Leisure Section, p. 1.

Page 186, line 21. Sally Bedell, *Up the Tube: Prime-Time TV in the Silverman Years* (New York: Viking, 1981), p. 117.

Page 187, line 38. Henry Breitrose, "Up Close and Profitable: Football, Television, and the Manipulation of Social Integration," paper prepared for the Annenberg School of Communication-West Symposium on Communication Media and Social Integration, January 7–9, 1982.

Page 188, line 7. Quoted in John Vinocur, "The Third Reich According to Albert Speer," *New York Times*, May 9, 1982, Arts and Leisure Section, p. 27.

Page 189, line 36. Tony Schwartz, "CBS Plans Auschwitz Film for Sept. 30 Amid Protest," *New York Times*, August 30, 1980.

Page 190, line 28. Vinocur, "Third Reich," p. 25.

Page 190, Fn. T. W. Adorno, "Television and the Patterns of Mass Culture," in Bernard Rosenberg and David Manning White, eds., *Mass Culture* (New York: Free Press, 1957), p. 485.

Page 192, line 39.   Wayne Biddle, "Dramatic Improvement of TV Image in the Offing," *New York Times,* National Edition, January 4, 1983, p. 13.

Page 193, line 9.   Simon Frith, *Sound Effects* (New York: Pantheon, 1983), p. 113.

Page 194, line 26.   From *Variety,* September 30, 1981, pp. 88ff.

Page 195, line 32.   Studs Terkel, *American Dreams: Lost and Found* (New York: Pantheon, 1980), pp. 200–211.

Page 199, line 41.   On differences between the scenarios of *World War III* and the sixties movies *Fail-Safe* and *Dr. Strangelove,* see Gene Rochlin, "The Evolution of World War III," *New Political Science,* vol. 3, no. 4 (May 1983).

Page 200, line 20.   Federal Emergency Management Agency Public Affairs Director Jim Holton, quoted in Howard Kohn, "Nuclear War and TV: Are the Networks Playing Fair?" *TV Guide,* January 15, 1983, p. 10.

Chapter 10:   The Turn Toward "Relevance"

Page 204, line 25.   Ben Stein, *The View from Sunset Boulevard* (New York: Basic Books, 1979).

Page 204, line 40.   On assumptions that work their way into the news, see Gaye Tuchman, *Making News* (New York: Free Press, 1978); Herbert J. Gans, *Deciding What's News* (New York: Pantheon, 1979); and Todd Gitlin, *The Whole World Is Watching: Mass Media in the Making and Unmaking of the New Left* (Berkeley: University of California Press, 1980).

Page 205, Fn.   The classic essay is Robert K. Merton and Paul F. Lazarsfeld, "Mass Communication, Popular Taste and Organized Social Action," in Bernard Rosenberg and David Manning White, eds., *Mass Culture* (New York: Free Press, 1956), pp. 457–73.

Page 206, line 10.   Les Brown, *Television: The Business Behind the Box* (New York: Harcourt Brace Jovanovich, 1971), p. 239.

Page 206, line 30.   FCC figures as reported by Christopher H. Sterling and Timothy R. Haight, *The Mass Media: Aspen Institute*

Guide to Communication Industry Trends (New York: Praeger, 1978), p. 211. Subsequently, with the boom in network ad rates, the O&O share of profits slipped dramatically, sinking to 35 percent in 1976.

Page 209, line 39.   William S. Paley, *As It Happened* (Garden City, N.Y.: Doubleday, 1979), pp. 73–75.

Page 210, line 19.   Ibid., p. 264.

Page 212, line 32.   Tim Brooks and Earle Marsh, *The Complete Directory to Prime Time Network TV Shows, 1946–Present*, rev. and enlarged ed. (New York: Ballantine, 1981), p. 781.

Page 213, line 19.   On some of these fights, see Geoffrey Cowan, *See No Evil* (New York: Simon and Schuster, 1979), pp. 21, 25–27, 42, 109, 282.

Page 213, line 31.   See Michael J. Arlen, *The View from Highway 1* (New York: Farrar, Straus, and Giroux, 1976), pp. 53–66.

Page 213, line 38.   Neil Vidman and Milton Rokeach ("Archie Bunker's Bigotry: A Study in Selective Perception and Exposure," *Journal of Communication* 24 [Winter 1974], pp. 36–47) found that more than 60 percent of their American and Canadian samples liked and admired Archie more than Mike. In Holland, however, the overwhelming majority sided with Mike (Harold de Bock, " 'All in the Family' in Holland," *Journal of Communication*, Autumn 1976).

Page 215, line 9.   The often-cited evidence is in *Work in America*, Report of a Special Task Force to the Secretary of Health, Education and Welfare, prepared under the auspices of the W. E. Upjohn Institute for Employment Research (Cambridge, Mass.: MIT Press, 1973).

Page 215, Fn.   Brooks and Marsh, *Complete Directory*, p. 214.

Chapter 11:   Shifting Right: Yesterday's Vietnam, *Today's FBI*

Page 221, line 16.   Quoted in Howard Rosenberg, "Is the Nation Ready for a Series on the CIA?" *San Francisco Sunday Examiner & Chronicle*, Datebook Section, April 27, 1980.

Page 225, line 25.   Thanks to Luisa Valenzuela for making this point during a seminar on television at the New York Institute for the Humanities, August 1981.

Page 226, line 43.   Of course news's dissent was limited. See Edward Jay Epstein, *News from Nowhere: Television and the News* (New York: Random House, 1973); Herbert J. Gans, *Deciding What's News* (New York: Pantheon, 1979); David Halberstam, *The Powers That Be* (New York: Knopf, 1979); Todd Gitlin, *The Whole World Is Watching: Mass Media in the Making and Unmaking of the New Left* (Berkeley: University of California Press, 1980).

Page 227, line 9.   See Julian Smith, *Looking Away: Hollywood and Vietnam* (New York: Scribner, 1975).

Page 237, line 26.   William Shawcross, *Sideshow: Kissinger, Nixon, and the Destruction of Cambodia* (New York: Simon and Schuster, 1979), pp. 33–35.

Page 242, line 22.   Jane Mayer, "Television Plays Down Sex This Fall, Reacting to a New Public Mood," *Wall Street Journal*, November 5, 1981, p. 1.

Page 242, line 29.   Quoted by Richard Hack, "Televisions," *Hollywood Reporter*, June 16, 1981.

Page 244, line 33.   Stuart Taylor Jr., "Bureau to Polish Shield in a Prime Time Slot," *New York Times*, September 24, 1981.

Page 244, line 37.   Ibid.

Chapter 12:   The "Far Righteous" Shake the Temple of Commerce

Page 248, line 32.   See Daniel Boorstin, *The Image; or, What Happened to the American Dream* (New York: Atheneum, 1961); Roland Barthes, *Mythologies*, trans. by Annette Lavers (New York: Hill and Wang, 1972); Jean Baudrillard, *For a Critique of the Political Economy of the Sign*, trans. by Charles Levin (St. Louis: Telos Press, 1981).

Page 249, last line.   Herbert Marcuse, *Eros and Civilization: A Philosophical Inquiry into Freud* (New York: Vintage, 1962); Lionel

Trilling, *Beyond Culture* (New York: Harcourt Brace Jovanovich, 1965); Daniel Bell, *The Cultural Contradictions of Capitalism* (New York: Basic Books, 1976).

Page 250, line 6.   See Lary May, *Screening Out the Past* (New York: Oxford University Press, 1980), pp. 44–45.

Page 250, line 11.   Quoted in Eric Rhode, *A History of the Cinema, From Its Origins to 1970* (New York: Hill & Wang, 1976), pp. 335–36, 223.

Page 251, line 1.   Tim Brooks and Earle Marsh, *The Complete Directory to Prime Time Network TV Shows, 1946–Present*, rev. and enlarged ed. (New York: Ballantine, 1981), p. 695.

Page 251, line 10.   For an inventory of other differences between the movie and the novel, see Linda Blum, "Feminism and the Mass Media: A Case Study of *The Women's Room* as Novel and Television Film," *Berkeley Journal of Sociology* 27 (1982), pp. 1–26.

Page 253, Fn.   August Priemer in Stanley T. Donner, ed., *The Meaning of Commercial Television* (Austin, Texas: University of Texas Press, 1967), p. 27.

Page 255, line 19.   Erik Barnouw, *The Image Empire* (New York: Oxford University Press, 1970), pp. 10, 18, 38.

Page 255, line 23.   *Television Network Program Procurement*, Report of the House of Representatives Committee on Interstate and Foreign Commerce, May 8, 1963, pp. 370–71.

Page 255, line 33.   Christopher H. Sterling and Timothy R. Haight, *The Mass Media: Aspen Institute Guide to Communication Industry Trends* (New York: Praeger, 1978), p. 372.

Page 256, line 31.   Barnouw, *Image Empire*, pp. 36–37, 122–25, 128.

Page 260, line 21.   Richard Levinson and William Link, *Stay Tuned* (New York: St. Martin's, 1981), pp. 119–21.

Chapter 13:   The Temple Stands

Page 265, line 7.   B. Bruce-Biggs, ed., *The New Class?* (New Brunswick, N.J.: Transaction Books, 1979); Peter Steinfels, *The Neocon-*

servatives (New York: Simon and Schuster, 1979), ch. 8; Kevin Phillips, *Mediacracy* (New York: Doubleday, 1975).

Page 265, line 12.   Nathan Glazer and Daniel P. Moynihan, "Introduction to the Second Edition," *Beyond the Melting Pot* (Cambridge, Mass.: MIT Press, 1970), p. xvi.

Page 265, line 29.   Leonard Silk and David Vogel, *Ethics and Profits* (New York: Simon and Schuster, 1976), pp. 104–16.

Page 265, line 44.   See, for example, Peter H. Stone, "The I.E.A.—Teaching the 'Right' Stuff," *The Nation*, September 19, 1981, pp. 231–35.

Page 266, line 9.   Lionel Trilling, *Beyond Culture* (New York: Harcourt Brace Jovanovich, 1965); Daniel Bell, *The Cultural Contradictions of Capitalism* (New York: Basic Books, 1976). For a critique of Bell, see Michael Rogin, "Pa Bell," *Salmagundi* 57 (Summer 1982), pp. 145–58.

Page 266, line 20.   Quoted in Stone, "The I.E.A.," p. 234.

Page 266, line 29.   Ben Stein, *The View from Sunset Boulevard* (New York: Basic Books, 1979), pp. 65, 91, 99, 31, xiii, 136, 135, 137, 146. The chapter on TV images of businessmen was excerpted in the *New York Times*, Business Section, February 18, 1979.

Page 267, line 25.   For a critique of Stein's view, see Herbert J. Gans, "Televising Our Values," *The Nation*, March 10, 1979.

Page 267, line 36.   Leonard J. Theberge, ed., *Crooks, Conmen and Clowns* (Washington, D.C.: The Media Institute, 1981).

Page 268, line 17.   Ibid., pp. 9, 37, 38, 14, 15, 23, 20, 26, 32.

Page 268, line 33.   Ibid., p. vii.

Page 268, line 37.   Stein, *View from Sunset Boulevard*, pp. 105–16.

Page 270, line 27.   Gans, "Televising Our Values," makes the point that TV writers may simply be taking on the real or imputed attitudes of their audiences.

Page 271, line 18. Robert Warshow, *The Immediate Experience* (New York: Atheneum, 1971), p. 131.

Page 271, line 44. Amy Wilentz: personal communication.

Chapter 14: *Hill Street Blues:* "Make It Look Messy"

Page 278, line 20. Lee Margulies, "Can Universal Plug Its Talent Drain?" *Emmy*, Fall 1980, pp. 27–30, 46, 48.

Page 281, line 16. Tony Schwartz, "How 'Hill Street' Broke a TV Mold," *New York Times*, April 27, 1982.

Page 283, line 13. See Erik Barnouw, *The Image Empire* (New York: Oxford University Press, 1970), pp. 23, 33–36, 73; David W. Rintels, "How Much Truth Does 'The F.B.I.' Tell About the F.B.I.?" *New York Times*, March 5, 1972, Arts and Leisure Section, p. 1; David W. Rintels, "Will Marcus Welby Always Make You Well?" *New York Times*, March 12, 1972, Arts and Leisure Section, p. 1.

Page 300, line 33. Frithjof Bergmann's *On Being Free* (South Bend, Ind.: Notre Dame University Press, 1977) brilliantly explores the paradoxical bondage entailed in transgression.

Page 308, line 15. For this point about Howard Hunter, thanks to Ronald Lembo.

Page 313, line 39. See William Julius Wilson, *The Declining Significance of Race*, second edition (Chicago: University of Chicago Press, 1980).

Page 316, line 16. This point was made as criticism in the only serious attack on *Hill Street Blues:* Mark Crispin Miller, "Off the Prigs," *The New Republic*, July 18, 1981, pp. 27–29.

Page 321, line 26. This point was made to me by David Thomson.

Page 323, line 20. *Hollywood Reporter*, January 3, 1983, p. 8; Sally Bedell, *New York Times*, December 28, 1982. The average spread between women and men is computed from figures in *Television Audience 1980* (Northbrook, Ill.: A. C. Nielsen Co., 1981), p. 21.

Epilogue

Page 326, line 20.   Tony Schwartz, "Cable TV Programmers Find Problems Avoid Fast Growth," *New York Times*, September 28, 1982.

Page 326, line 32.   Schlosser, once president of NBC, was in charge of programming for RCA's videodiscs when he made this remark. "NAB seers forecast that new media will only 'knock corners' off TV's audience," *Broadcasting*, April 21, 1980, p. 53.

Page 329, line 8.   Schwartz, "Cable TV"; Sally Bedell, "Arts Cable Channel, 9 Months in Service, To Cease Operations," *New York Times*, February 23, 1983; Sandra Salmans, "How a Cable Channel Flopped," *New York Times*, Business Section, February 28, 1983.

Page 329, line 14.   Computed from figures in Schwartz, "Cable TV."

Page 329, line 22.   "How TV Is Revolutionizing Hollywood," *Business Week*, February 21, 1983, p. 78.

Page 329, Fn.   Sarnoff: see Erik Barnouw, *A Tower in Babel* (New York: Oxford University Press, 1966), pp. 78–80; Herbert Hoover, *Memoirs: The Cabinet and the Presidency, 1920–1933* (New York: Macmillan, 1952), p. 140, quoted in Barnouw, *Tower in Babel*, p. 96.

Page 330, last line.   "Ogilvy downbeat on network TV prospects by '90," *Broadcasting*, January 11, 1982.

Page 331, line 3.   "CBS at odds with O&M over future network audience," *Broadcasting*, February 15, 1982.

Page 331, line 37.   Paul Klein, "The Networks' Incredible Shrinking Pie," *Variety*, January 13, 1982, p. 158.

Page 333, line 19.   Joseph Klapper, "Mass Communication: Effects," in *International Encyclopedia of the Social Sciences* (New York: Macmillan and The Free Press, 1968), p. 85.

Page 333, line 41.   Peter Koper, "Can Movies Kill?" *American Film*, July–August 1982, pp. 46–51.

Page 334, line 2.   National Institute of Mental Health, *Television and Behavior: Ten Years of Scientific Progress and Implications for the Eighties,* vol. 1: Summary Report (Washington, D.C.: National Institute of Mental Health, 1982), pp. 36–44.

I N D E X

ABC audience, 57–9, 92; Circle
  Films, 160; and program
  testing, 36–45
ARTS, 326
Aaron Spelling Productions, 118,
  120, 137, 140
Act of Love, 171–2, 178n
actors and characters, appeal of,
  26, 67, 187
Adorno, T.W., 70n, 190n
advertisements, cancellation of, 6,
  256–7; cost of, 254–5
advertisers, boycotts of, 6, 11,
  158, 251
advertisers, role of, 3, 6, 10–11,
  53, 184, 186, 189, 197, 252–60,
  270, 329
advertising agencies, 146–7, 182,
  184, 186, 189, 254–6
affiliates, 57n, 65, 178, 178n,
  180n, 181n, 200, 210, 213, 247,
  254, 262
agents, 143–54
Alan Landsburg Productions, 120
Alda, Alan, 160, 216
Alice, 67, 74
All in the Family, 12, 35–6, 43,
  55, 67, 206, 211–17, 219, 230,
  235, 296, 305
All's Fair, 235
Aloha Paradise, 139
Alsberg, Clifford B., 92–4
American Civil Liberties Union, 10
American contemporary culture,
  307, 309–13, 330, 332–5
American Dream, 15, 84–112,
  115, 151, 180n, 205, 222,
  242–3, 245–6
American Family Corp., 5
American Film Institute, 24
American Girls, The, 72
American Research Bureau, 50–3

Amlen, Seymour, 64, 212
Amos, John, 5
Amos 'n' Andy, 65
Andrews, Peter, 181
Andy Griffith Show, 165
Angelou, Maya, 181
Animal House, 57, 240
Antonowsky, Marvin, 43
Apocalypse Now, 227
Archie Bunker's Place, 219
Arledge, Roone, 187
Armstrong Circle Theater, 255
Arness, James, 222–3
Arnold, Danny, 185–6
Asner, Ed, 3–7, 9–11, 123–4, 160,
  190, 215
Attica, 158, 188
audience composition, 57–60, 72;
  demographics, 34, 49, 57–61,
  72, 206, 208–11, 219, 254, 305;
  desires, 72–3, 203, 215, 217–18,
  248; and taste of, 2, 22, 29–30,
  38–9, 42, 67, 74, 84
Audience Studies Inc., 37, 39–40
authority, television images of,
  12, 211, 310, 313
Axelrod, Jonathan, 24, 93–8, 100,
  102–4, 107–8, 112, 241, 245–6

B. J. and the Bear, 67, 321
Babysitters, The, 195
back-end deals, 127–8, 131, 134
Balzac, Honoré de, 69, 79
Baretta, 313
Barkley, Deanne, 61–2, 159, 164
Barney Miller, 279, 312, 319
Barnouw, Erik, 182
Baryshnikov, Mikhail, 233
Basichis, Marcia, 107
Battlestar Galactica, 122
Beacon Hill, 219